MW00978768

THE LUSIADS

LUIS DE CAMOES

Copyright © 2015 Luis de Camoes

All rights reserved.

ISBN: 1517622174

ISBN-13: 978-1517622176

THE LUSIADS

OR,

THE DISCOVERY OF INDIA.

AN EPIC POEM.

TRANSLATED FROM THE PORTUGUESE OF LUIS DE CAMOËNS.

WITH A LIFE OF THE POET.

BY WILLIAM JULIUS MICKLE.

"As the mirror of a heart so full of love, courage, generosity, and patriotism as that of Camoëns, The Lusaid can never fail to please us, whatever place we may assign to it in the records of poetical genius."—Hallam.

THE LUSIADS

[ORIGINAL DEDICATION, 1776.]

TO THE

DUKE OF BUCCLEUGH.

My Lord,

The first idea of offering my Lusiad to some distinguished personage, inspired the earnest wish, that it might be accepted by the illustrious representative of that family under which my father, for many years, discharged the duties of a clergyman.

Both the late Duke of Buccleugh, and the Earl of Dalkeith, distinguished him by particular marks of their favour; and I must have forgotten him, if I could have wished to offer the first Dedication of my literary labours to any other than the Duke of Buccleugh.

I am, with the greatest respect,

My Lord,

Your Grace's most devoted

And most obedient humble servant,

WILLIAM JULIUS MICKLE.

THE LUSIADS

EDITOR'S PREFACE.

In undertaking, at the publishers' request, the function of editor of Mickle's Lusiad, I have compared the translation with the original, and, in some places, where another translation seemed preferable to, or more literal than, Mickle's, I have, in addition, given that rendering in a foot-note. Moreover, I have supplied the arguments to the several cantos, given a few more explanatory notes, and added a table of contents.

"The late ingenious translator of the Lusiad," says Lord Strangford, "has portrayed the character, and narrated the misfortunes of our poet, in a manner more honourable to his feelings as a man than to his accuracy in point of biographical detail. It is with diffidence that the present writer essays to correct his errors; but, as the real circumstances of the life of Camoëns are mostly to be found in his own minor compositions, with which Mr. Mickle was unacquainted, he trusts that certain information will atone for his presumption."

As Lord Strangford professes to have better and more recent sources of information regarding the illustrious, but unfortunate, bard of Portugal, I make no apology for presenting to the reader an abstract of his lordship's memoir. Much further information will be found, however, in an able article contained in No. 53 of the Quarterly Review for July, 1822, from the pen, I believe, of the poet Southey. "The family of Camoëns was illustrious," says Lord Strangford, "and originally Spanish. They were long settled at Cadmon, a castle in Galicia, from which they probably derived their patronymic appellation. However, there are some who maintain that their name alluded to a certain wonderful bird,[2] whose mischievous sagacity discovered and punished the smallest deviation from conjugal fidelity. A lady of the house of Cadmon, whose conduct had been rather indiscreet, demanded to be tried by this extraordinary judge. Her innocence was proved, and, in gratitude to the being who had restored him to matrimonial felicity, the contented husband adopted his name." It would appear that in a dispute between the families of Cadmon and De Castera, a cavalier of the latter family was slain. This happened in the fourteenth century. A long train of persecution followed, to escape which, Ruy de Camoëns, having embraced the cause of Ferdinand, removed with his family into Portugal, about A.D. 1370. His son, Vasco de Camoëns, was highly distinguished by royal favour, and had the honour of being the ancestor of our poet, who descended from him in the fourth generation. Luia de Camoëns, the author of the Lusiad, was born at Lisbon about A.D. 1524. His misfortunes began with his birth—he never saw a father's smile—for Simon Vasco de Camoëns perished by shipwreck in the very year which gave being to his illustrious son. The future poet was sent to the university of Coimbra—then at the height of its fame,—"and maintained there by the provident care of his surviving parent."

"Love," says Lord Strangford, "is very nearly allied to devotion, and it was in the exercise of the latter, that Camoëns was introduced to the knowledge of the former. In the Church of Christ's Wounds at Lisbon, on 11th April, 1542, Camoëns first beheld Doña Caterina de Atayde, the object of his purest and earliest attachment ... and it was not long before Camoëns enjoyed an opportunity of declaring his affection, with all the romantic ardour of eighteen and of a poet." The peculiar situation of the lady, as one of the maids of honour to the queen, imposed a restraint upon her admirer which soon became intolerable; and he, for having violated the sanctity of the royal precincts, was in consequence banished from the court. Whatever may have been the nature of his offence, "it furnished a pretext to the young lady's relations for terminating an intercourse which worldly considerations rendered highly imprudent."

But Love consoled his votary: his mistress, on the morning of his departure, confessed the secret of her long-concealed affection, and the sighs of grief were soon lost in those of mutual delight. The hour of parting was, perhaps, the sweetest of our poet's existence.

Camoëns removed to Santarem, but speedily returned to Lisbon, was a second time detected, and again driven into exile.[3]

The voice of Love inspired our poet "with the glorious resolution of conquering the obstacles which fortune had placed between him and felicity." He obtained permission, therefore, to accompany King John III. in an expedition then fitting out against the Moors in Africa. In one of the engagements with the enemy our hero had the misfortune to lose "his right eye, by some splinters from the deck of the vessel in which he was stationed. Many of his most pathetic compositions were written during this campaign, and the toils of a martial life were sweetened by the recollection of her for whose sake they were endured. His heroic conduct at length procured his recall to court," but to find, alas, that his mistress was no more.

Disappointed in his hope of obtaining any recognition of his valiant deeds, he now resolved, under the burning sun of India, to seek that independence which his own country denied. "The last words I uttered," says Camoëns, "on board the vessel before leaving, were those of Scipio: 'Ungrateful country! thou shalt not even possess my bones.'" "Some," says Lord Strangford, "attribute his departure to a very different cause, and assert that he quitted his native shores on account of an intrigue in which he was detected with the beautiful wife of a Portuguese gentleman. Perhaps," says Lord Strangford, "this story may not be wholly unfounded." On his arrival in India he contributed by his bravery to the success of an expedition carried on by the King of Cochin, and his allies, the Portuguese, against the Pimento Islands; and in the following year (1555) he accompanied Manuel de Vasconcelos in an expedition to the Red Sea. Here he explored the wild regions of East Africa, and stored his mind with ideas of scenery, which afterwards formed some of the most finished pictures of the Lusiad.

On his return to Goa, Camoëns devoted his whole attention to the completion of his poem; but an unfortunate satire which, under the title of Disparates na India, or Follies in India, he wrote against the vices and corruptions of the Portuguese authorities in Goa, so roused the indignation of the viceroy that the poet was banished to China.

Of his adventures in China, and the temporary prosperity he enjoyed there, while he held the somewhat uncongenial office of Provedor dos defuntos, i.e., Trustee for deceased persons, Mickle has given an ample account in the introduction to the Lusiad. During those years Camoëns completed his poem, about half of which was written before he left Europe. According to a tradition, not improbable in itself, he composed great part of it in a natural grotto which commands a splendid view of the city and harbour of Macao. An engraving of it may be seen in Onseley's Oriental Collections, and another will be found in Sir G. Staunton's Account of the Embassy to China.

A little temple, in the Chinese style, has been erected upon the rock, and the ground around it has been ornamented by Mr. Fitzhugh, one of our countrymen, from respect to the memory of the poet. The years that he passed in Macao were probably the happiest of his life. Of his departure for Europe, and his unfortunate shipwreck at the mouth of the river Meekhaun,[4] in Cochin China, Mickle has also given a sufficient account.

Lord Strangford has related, on the authority of Sousa, that while our poet was languishing in poverty at Lisbon, "a cavalier, named Ruy de Camera, called on him one day, asking him to finish for him a poetical version of the seven penitential psalms. Raising his head from his wretched pallet, and pointing to his faithful Javanese attendant, he exclaimed, 'Alas, when I was a poet, I was young, and happy, and blest with the love of ladies; but now I am a forlorn, deserted wretch. See—there stands my poor Antonio, vainly supplicating fourpence to purchase a little coals—I have them not to give him.' The cavalier, as Sousa relates, closed both his heart and his purse, and quitted the room. Such were the grandees of Portugal." Camoëns sank under the pressure of penury and disease, and died in an alms-house, early in 1579, and was buried in the church of Sta. Anna of the Franciscan Friars. Over his grave Gonzalo Coutinho placed the following inscription:—

"Here lies Luis de Camoëns.

He excelled all the poets of his time.

He lived poor and miserable, and he died so.

mdlxxix."

The translator of the Lusiad was born, in 1734, at Langholm, in Dumfriesshire, where his father, a good French scholar, was the Presbyterian minister. At the age of sixteen William Julius Mickle was removed, to his great dislike, from school, and sent into the counting-house of a relation of his mother's, a brewer, where, against his inclination, he remained five years. He subsequently, for family reasons, became the head of the firm, and carried on the business. It is not to be wondered at, however, that with his dislike to business in general and to this one in particular, he did not succeed; and it is quite reasonable to suppose that the cause of his failure, and subsequent pecuniary embarrassments, arose from his having devoted those hours to his poetical studies which should have been dedicated to business. Mickle obtained afterwards the appointment of corrector of the Clarendon Press in Oxford, and died at Wheatly, in Oxfordshire, in 1789.

Southey speaks of Mickle (Quarterly Review, liii. p. 29) as a man of genius who had ventured upon the chance of living by his literary labours, and says that he "did not over-rate the powers which he was conscious of possessing, knew that he could rely upon himself for their due exertion, and had sufficient worldly prudence to look out for a subject which was likely to obtain notice and patronage." His other poems, Pollio, Sir Martyn, etc., with the exception of his Cumnor Hall, are not held in high estimation.

Describing the several poetic versions of the Lusiad, Mr. Musgrave says,[5] of Fanshaw's version, that "its language is antiquated, and in many instances it travesties the original, and seldom long sustains the tone of epic gravity suited to the poem. It is, however," says he, "more faithful than the translation of Mickle, but it would be ungenerous," he adds, "to dwell on the paraphrastic licences which abound in Mickle's performance, and on its many interpolations and omissions. Mr. Mickle thought, no doubt," says Musgrave, "that by this process he should produce a poem which in its perusal might afford a higher gratification. Nor am I prepared to say that by all readers this would be deemed a miscalculation. Let it not be supposed, however, that I wish to detract from the intrinsic merit of his translation. It is but an act of justice to admit, that it contains many passages of exquisite beauty, and that it is a performance which discovers much genius, a cultivated taste, and a brilliant imagination. Many parts of the original are rendered with great facility, elegance, and fidelity. In poetical elegance I presume not to enter into competition with him."

For his own performance Musgrave claims the merit of greater fidelity to the original; but in respect of harmony, in true poetic grace, and sublimity of diction, his translation will bear no comparison with Mickle's version; for even Southey, in the article before quoted, though very hard upon his interpolations, admits that, "Mickle was a man of genius ... a man whom we admire and respect; whose memory is without a spot, and whose name will live among the English poets." (Quarterly Review, liii. p. 29.)

It only remains for me to say, that in order to place the reader in a position to judge of the merits of this sublime effort of genius, I have distinguished Mickle's longer interpolations by printing them in Bk. i. p. 24, in Italics, and in the first 300 lines of Bk. ix. by calling the attention of the reader to the interpolation by means of a foot-note. The notes are, in general, left as written by the translator, except in some cases where it seemed advisable to curtail them. Original notes are indicated by the abbreviation "Ed."

THE EDITOR.

London, 1877.

THE LUSIADS

THE LIFE OF CAMOËNS,

BY WILLIAM JULIUS MICKLE.

When the glory of the arms of Portugal had reached its meridian splendour, Nature, as if in pity of the literary rudeness of that nation, produced a great poet to record the numberless actions of high spirit performed by his countrymen. Except Osorius, the historians of Portugal are little better than dry journalists. But it is not their inelegance which rendered the poet necessary. It is the peculiar nature of poetry to give a colouring to heroic actions, and to express indignation against breaches of honour, in a spirit which at once seizes the heart of the man of feeling, and carries with it instantaneous conviction. The brilliant actions of the Portuguese form the great hinge which opened the door to the most important alterations in the civil history of mankind. And to place these actions in the light and enthusiasm of poetry—that enthusiasm which particularly assimilates the youthful breast to its own fires—was Luis de Camoëns the poet of Portugal, born.

Different cities have claimed the honour of his birth. But according to N. Antonio, and Manuel Correa, his intimate friend, this event happened at Lisbon in 1517.[6] His family was of considerable note, and originally Spanish. In 1370 Vasco Perez de Caamans, disgusted at the court of Castile, fled to that of Lisbon, where King Ferdinand immediately admitted him into his council, and gave him the lordships of Sardoal, Punnete, Marano, Amendo, and other considerable lands; a certain proof of the eminence of his rank and abilities. In the war for the succession, which broke out on the death of Ferdinand, Caamans sided with the King of Castile, and was killed in the battle of Aljabarota. But though John I., the victor, seized a great part of his estate, his widow, the daughter of Gonsalo Tereyro, grand master of the Order of Christ, and general of the Portuguese army, was not reduced beneath her rank. She had three sons, who took the name of Camoëns. The family of the eldest intermarried with the first nobility of Portugal, and even, according to Castera, with the blood royal. But the family of the second brother, whose fortune was slender, had the superior honour to produce the author of the Lusiad.

Early in life the misfortunes of the poet began. In his infancy, Simon Vaz de

Camoëns, his father, commander of a vessel, was shipwrecked at Goa, where, with his life, the greatest part of his fortune was lost. His mother, however, Anne de Macedo of Santarem, provided for the education of her son Luis, at the University of Coimbra. What he acquired there his works discover; an intimacy with the classics, equal to that of a Scaliger, but directed by the taste of a Milton or a Pope.

When he left the university he appeared at court. He was a polished scholar and very handsome,[7] possessing a most engaging mien and address, with the finest complexion, which, added to the natural ardour and gay vivacity of his deposition, rendered him an accomplished gentleman. Courts are the scenes of intrigue, and intrigue was fashionable at Lisbon. But the particulars of the amours of Camoëns rest unknown. This only appears: he had aspired above his rank, for he was banished from the court; and in several of his sonnets he ascribes this misfortune to love.

He now retired to his mother's friends at Santarem. Here he renewed his studies, and began his poem on the discovery of India. John III. at this time prepared an armament against Africa. Camoëns, tired of his inactive, obscure life, went to Ceuta in this expedition, and greatly distinguished his valour in several rencontres. In a naval engagement with the Moors in the Straits of Gibraltar, Camoëns, in the conflict of boarding, where he was among the foremost, lost his right eye. Yet neither the hurry of actual service, nor the dissipation of the camp, could stifle his genius. He continued his Lusiadas; and several of his most beautiful sonnets were written in Africa, while, as he expresses it,

"One hand the pen, and ant the sword employ'd."

The fame of his valour had now reached the Court, and he obtained permission to return to Lisbon. But while he solicited an establishment which he had merited in the ranks of battle, the malignity of evil tongues (as he calls it in one of his letters) was injuriously poured upon him. Though the bloom of his early youth was effaced by several years residence under the scorching sky of Africa, and though altered by the loss of an eye, his presence gave uneasiness to the gentlemen of some families of the first rank where he had formerly visited. Jealousy is the characteristic of the Spanish and Portuguese; its resentment knows no bounds, and Camoëns now found it prudent to banish himself from his native country. Accordingly, in 1553 he hailed for India, with a resolution never to return. As the ship left the Tagus he exclaimed, in the words of the sepulchral monument of Scipio Africanus, "Ingrata patria, non possidebis ossa mea!" (Ungrateful country, thou shalt not possess my bones!) But he knew not what evils in the East would awaken the remembrance of his native fields.

When Camoëns arrived in India, an expedition was ready to sail to revenge the King of Cochin on the King of Pimenta. Without any rest on shore after his long voyage, he joined this armament, and, in the conquest of the Alagada Islands, displayed his usual bravery. But his modesty, perhaps, is his greatest praise. In a sonnet he mentions this expedition: "We went to punish the King of Pimenta," says he, "e succedeones bem" (and we succeeded well). When it is considered that the poet bore no inconsiderable share in the victory, no ode can conclude more elegantly, more happily than this.

In the year following, he attended Manuel de Vasconcello in an expedition to the Red Sea. Here, says Faria, as Camoëns had no use for his sword, he employed his pen. Nor was his activity confined to the fleet or camp. He visited Mount Felix, and the adjacent inhospitable regions of Africa, which he so strongly pictures in the Lusiad, and in one of his little pieces, where he laments the absence of his mistress.

When he returned to Goa, he enjoyed a tranquility which enabled him to bestow his attention on his epic poem. But this serenity was interrupted, perhaps by his own imprudence. He wrote some satires which gave offence, and by order of the viceroy, Francisco Barreto, he was banished to China.

Men of poor abilities are more conscious of their embarrassment and errors than is commonly believed. When men of this kind are in power, they affect great solemnity; and every expression of the most distant tendency to lessen their dignity is held as the greatest of crimes. Conscious, also, how severely the man of genius can hurt their interest, they bear an instinctive antipathy against him, are uneasy even in his company, and, on the slightest pretence, are happy to drive him from them. Camoëns was thus situated at Goa; and never was there a fairer field for satire than the rulers of India at that time afforded. Yet, whatever esteem the prudence of Camoëns may lose in our idea, the nobleness of his disposition will doubly gain. And, so conscious was he of his real integrity and innocence, that in one of his sonnets he wishes no other revenge on Barreto than that the cruelty of his exile should ever be remembered.[8]

The accomplishments and manners of Camoëns soon found him friends, though under the disgrace of banishment. He was appointed Commissary of the estates of deceased persons, in the island of Macao, a Portuguese settlement on the coast of China. Here he continued his Lusiad; and here, also, after five years residence, he acquired a fortune, though small, yet equal to his wishes. Don Constantine de Braganza was now Viceroy of India; and Camoëns, desirous to return to Goa, resigned his charge. In a ship, freighted by himself, he set sail, but was shipwrecked in the gulf near the mouth of the river Meekhaun, in Cochin China. All he had acquired was lost in the waves: his poems, which he held in one hand, while he swam with the other, were all he found himself possessed of when he stood friendless on the unknown shore. But the natives gave him a most humane reception; this he has immortalized in the prophetic song in the tenth Lusiad;[9] and in the seventh he tells us that here he lost the wealth which satisfied his wishes.

Agora da esperança ja adquirida, etc.

"Now blest with all the wealth fond hope could crave,

Soon I beheld that wealth beneath the wave

For ever lost;——

My life like Judah's Heaven-doom'd king of yore

By miracle prolong'd."

On the banks of the Meekhaun, he wrote his beautiful paraphrase of the 137th Psalm, where the Jews, in the finest strain of poetry, are represented as hanging their harps on the willows by the rivers of Babylon, and weeping their exile from their native country. Here Camoëns continued some time, till an opportunity offered to carry him to Goa. When he arrived at that city, Don Constantine de Braganza, the viceroy, whose characteristic was politeness, admitted him into intimate friendship, and Camoëns was happy till Count Redondo assumed the government. Those who had formerly procured the banishment of the satirist were silent while Constantine was in power. But now they exerted all their arts against him. Redondo, when he entered on office, pretended to be the friend of Camoëns; yet, with the most unfeeling indifference, he suffered the innocent man to be thrown into the common prison. After all the delay of bringing witnesses, Camoëns, in a public trial, fully refuted every accusation against his conduct while commissary at Macao, and his enemies were loaded with ignominy and reproach. But Camoëns had some creditors; and these detained him in prison a considerable time, till the gentlemen of Goa began to be ashamed that a man of his singular merit should experience such treatment among them. He was set at liberty; and again he assumed the profession of arms, and received the allowance of a gentleman-volunteer, a character at that time common in Portuguese India. Soon after, Pedro Barreto (appointed governor of the fort of Sofála), by high promises, allured the poet to attend him thither. The governor of a distant fort, in a barbarous country, shares in some measure the fate of an exile. Yet, though the only motive of Barreto was, in this unpleasant situation, to retain the conversation of Camoëns at his table, it was his least care to render the life of his guest agreeable. Chagrined with his treatment, and a considerable time having elapsed in vain dependence upon Barreto, Camoëns resolved to return to his native country. A ship, on the homeward voyage, at this time touched at Sofála, and several gentlemen[10] who were on board were desirous that Camoëns should accompany them. But this the governor ungenerously endeavoured to prevent, and charged him with a debt for board. Anthony de Cabral, however, and Hector de Sylveyra, paid the demand, and Camoëns, says Faria, and the honour of Barreto were sold together.

After an absence of sixteen years, Camoëns, in 1569, returned to Lisbon, unhappy even in his arrival, for the pestilence then raged in that city, and prevented his publishing for three years. At last, in 1572, he printed his Lusiad, which, in the opening of the first book, in a most elegant turn of compliment, he addressed to his prince, King Sebastian, then in his eighteenth year. The king, says the French translator, was so pleased with his merit, that he gave the author a pension of 4000 reals, on condition that he should reside at court. But this salary, says the same writer, was withdrawn by Cardinal Henry, who succeeded to the crown of Portugal, lost by Sebastian at the battle of Alcazar.

But this story of the pension is very doubtful. Correa and other contemporary authors do not mention it, though some late writers have given credit to it. If Camoëns, however, had a pension, it is highly probable that Henry deprived him of it. While Sebastian was devoted to the chase, his grand-uncle, the cardinal, presided at the council board, and Camoëns, in his address to the king, which closes the Lusiad, advises him to exclude the clergy from State affairs. It was easy to see that the cardinal was here intended. And Henry, besides, was one of those statesmen who can perceive no benefit resulting to the public from elegant literature. But it ought also to be added in completion of his character, that under the narrow views and weak hands of this Henry, the kingdom of Portugal fell into utter ruin; and on his death, which closed a short inglorious reign, the crown of Lisbon, after a faint struggle, was annexed to that of Spain. Such was the degeneracy of the Portuguese, a degeneracy lamented in vain by Camoëns, whose observation of it was imputed to him as a crime.

Though the great[11] patron of theological literature—a species the reverse of that of Camoëns—certain it is, that the author of the Lusiad was utterly neglected by Henry, under whose inglorious reign he died in all the misery of poverty. By some, it is said, he died in an almshouse. It appears, however, that he had not even the certainty of subsistence which these houses provide. He had a black servant, who had grown old with him, and who had long experienced his master's humanity. This grateful dependant, a native of Java, who, according to some writers, saved his master's life in the unhappy shipwreck where he lost his effects, begged in the streets of Lisbon for the only man in Portugal on whom God had bestowed those talents which have a tendency to erect the spirit of a downward age. To the eye of a careful observer, the fate of Camoëns throws great light on that of his country, and will appear strictly connected with it. The same ignorance, the same degenerate spirit, which suffered Camoëns to depend on his share of the alms begged in the streets by his old hoary servant—the same spirit which caused this, sank the kingdom of Portugal into the most abject vassalage ever experienced by a conquered nation. While the grandees of Portugal were blind to the ruin which impended over them, Camoëns beheld it with a pungency of grief which hastened his end. In one of his letters he has these remarkable words, "Em fim accaberey à vida, e verràm todos que fuy afeiçoada a minho patria," etc.—"I am ending the course of my life, the world will witness how I have loved my country. I have returned, not only to die in her bosom, but to die with her." In another letter, written a little before his death, he thus, yet with dignity, complains, "Who has seen on so small a theatre as my poor bed, such a representation of the disappointments of Fortune. And I, as if she could not herself subdue me, I have yielded and become of her party; for it were wild audacity to hope to surmount such accumulated evils."

In this unhappy situation, in 1579, in his sixty-second year, the year after the fatal defeat of Don Sebastian, died Luis de Camoëns, the greatest literary genius ever produced by Portugal; in martial courage and spirit of honour nothing inferior to her greatest heroes. And in a manner suitable to the poverty in which he died was he buried. Soon after, however, many epitaphs honoured his memory; the greatness of his merit was universally confessed, and his Lusiad was translated into various languages.[12] Nor ought it to be omitted, that the man so miserably neglected by the weak king Henry, was earnestly enquired after by Philip of Spain when he assumed the crown of Lisbon. When Philip heard that Camoëns was dead, both his words and his countenance expressed his disappointment and grief.

From the whole tenor of his life, and from that spirit which glows throughout the Lusiad, it evidently appears that the courage and manners of Camoëns flowed from true greatness and dignity of soul. Though his polished conversation was often courted by the great, he appears so distant from servility that his imprudence in this respect is by some highly blamed. Yet the instances of it by no means deserve that severity of censure with which some writers have condemned him. Unconscious of the feelings of a Camoëns, they knew not that a carelessness in securing the smiles of fortune, and an open honesty of indignation, are almost inseparable from the enthusiasm of fine imagination. The truth is, the man possessed of true genius feels his greatest happiness in the pursuits and excursions of the mind, and therefore makes an estimate of things very different from that of him whose unremitting attention is devoted to his external interest. The profusion of Camoëns is also censured. Had he dissipated the wealth he acquired at

Macao, his profusion indeed had been criminal; but it does not appear that he ever enjoyed any other opportunity of acquiring independence. But Camoëns was unfortunate, and the unfortunate man is viewed—

"Through the dim shade his fate casts o'er him:

A shade that spreads its evening darkness o'er

His brightest virtues, while it shows his foibles

Crowding and obvious as the midnight stars,

Which, in the sunshine of prosperity

Never had been descried."

Yet, after the strictest discussion, when all the causes are weighed together, the misfortunes of Camoëns will appear the fault and disgrace of his age and country, and not of the man. His talents would have secured him an apartment in the palace of Augustus, but such talents are a curse to their possessor in an illiterate nation. In a beautiful, digressive exclamation at the end of the Lusiad, he affords us a striking view of the neglect which he experienced. Having mentioned how the greatest heroes of antiquity revered and cherished the muse, he thus characterizes the nobility of his own age and country.

"Alas! on Tago's hapless shore alone

The muse is slighted, and her charms unknown;

For this, no Virgil here attunes the lyre,

No Homer here awakes the hero's fire;

Unheard, in vain their native poet sings,

And cold neglect weighs dawn the muse's wings."

In such an age, and among such a barbarous nobility, what but wretched neglect could be the fate of a Camoëns! After all, however, if he was imprudent on his first appearance at the court of John III.; if the honesty of his indignation led him into great imprudence, as certainly it did, when at Goa he satirised the viceroy and the first persons in power; yet let it also be remembered, that "The gifts of imagination bring the heaviest task upon the vigilance of reason; and to bear those faculties with unerring rectitude, or invariable propriety, requires a degree of firmness and of cool attention, which doth not always attend the higher gifts of the mind. Yet, difficult as nature herself seems to have rendered the task of regularity to genius, it is the supreme consolation of dullness and of folly to point with Gothic triumph to those excesses which are the overflowings of faculties they never enjoyed. Perfectly unconscious that they are indebted to their stupidity for the consistency of their conduct, they plume themselves on an imaginary virtue which has its origin in what is really their disgrace.—Let such, if such dare approach the shrine of Camoëns, withdraw to a respectful distance; and should they behold the ruins of genius, or the weakness of an exalted mind, let them be taught to lament that nature has left the noblest of her works imperfect."[13]

DISSERTATION ON THE LUSIADS, AND ON EPIC POETRY, BY THE TRANSLATOR.

When Voltaire was in England, previous to his publication of his Henriade, he published in English an essay on the epic poetry of the European nations. In this he both highly praised, and severely attacked, the Lusiad. In his French editions of this essay, he has made various alterations, at different times, in the article on Camoëns. It is not, however, improper to premise, that some most amazing falsities will be here detected; the gross misrepresentation of every objection refuted; and demonstration brought, that when Voltaire wrote his English essay, his knowledge of the Lusiad was entirely borrowed from the bold, harsh, unpoetical version of Fanshaw.

"While Trissino," says Voltaire, "was clearing away the rubbish in Italy, which barbarity and ignorance had heaped up for ten centuries in the way of the arts and sciences, Camoëns, in Portugal, steered a new course, and acquired a reputation which lasts still among his countrymen who pay as much respect to his memory as the English to Milton."

Among other passages of the Lusiad which he criticises is that where "Adamastor, the giant of the Cape of Storms, appears to them, walking in the depth of the sea; his head reaches to the clouds; the storms, the winds, the thunders, and the lightnings hang about him; his arms are extended over the waves. It is the guardian of that foreign ocean, unploughed before by any ship. He complains of being obliged to submit to fate, and to the audacious undertaking of the Portuguese, and foretells them all the misfortunes they must undergo in the Indies. I believe that such a fiction would be thought noble and proper in all ages, and in all nations.

"There is another, which perhaps would have pleased the Italians as well as the Portuguese, but no other nation besides: it is the enchanted island, called the Island of Bliss, which the fleet finds in its way home, just rising from the sea, for their comfort, and for their reward. Camoëns describes that place, as Tasso some years after depicted his island of Armida. There a supernatural power brings in all the beauties, and presents all the pleasures which nature can afford, and the heart may wish for; a goddess, enamoured with Vasco de Gama, carries him to the top of a high mountain, from whence she shows him all the kingdoms of the earth, and foretells the fate of Portugal.

"After Camoëns hath given loose to his fancy, in the description of the pleasures which Gama and his crew enjoyed in the island, he takes care to inform the reader that he ought to understand by this fiction nothing but the satisfaction which the virtuous man feels, and the glory which accrues to him, by the practice of virtue; but the best excuse for such an invention is the charming style in which it is delivered (if we may believe the Portuguese), for the beauty of the elocution sometimes makes amends for the faults of the poet, as the colouring of Rubens makes some defects in his figures pass unregarded.

"There is another kind of machinery continued throughout all the poem, which nothing can excuse; that is, an injudicious mixture of the heathen gods with our religion. Gama in a storm addresses his prayers to Christ, but it is Venus who comes to his relief; the heroes are Christians, and the poet heathen. The main design which the Portuguese are supposed to have (next to promoting their trade) is to propagate Christianity; yet Jupiter, Bacchus, and Venus, have in their hands all the management of the voyage. So incongruous a machinery casts a blemish upon the whole poem; yet it shows at the same time how prevailing are its beauties since the Portuguese like it with all its faults."

The Lusiad, says Voltaire, contains "a sort of epic poetry unheard of before. No heroes are wounded a thousand different ways; no woman enticed away, and the world overturned for her cause." But the very want of these, in place of supporting the objection intended by Voltaire, points out the happy judgment and peculiar excellence of Camoëns. If Homer has given us all the fire and hurry of battles, he has also given us all the uninteresting, tiresome detail. What reader but must be tired with the deaths of a thousand heroes, who are never mentioned before, nor afterwards, in the poem. Yet, in every battle we are wearied out with such Gazette-returns of the slain and wounded as—

"Hector Priamides when Zeus him glory gave,

Assæus first, Autonoüs, he slew;

Ophites, Dolops, Klytis' son beside;

Opheltius also, Agelaüs too,

Æsymnus, and the battle-bide

Hippónoüs, chiefs on Danaian side,

And then, the multitude."

Homer's Iliad, bk. xi. 299, et seq.,

(W. G. T. Barter's translation.)

And corresponding to it is Virgil's Æneid, bk. x. line 747, et seq.:—

"By Cædicus Alcathoüs was slain;

Sacrator laid Hydaspes on the plain;

Orsès the strong to greater strength must yield,

He, with Parthenius, were by Rapo killed.

Then brave Messapus Ericetès slew,

Who from Lycaón's blood his lineage drew."

Dryden's version.

With, such catalogues is every battle extended; and what can be more tiresome than such uninteresting descriptions, and their imitations! If the idea of the battle be raised by such enumeration, still the copy and original are so near each other that they can never please in two separate poems. Nor are the greater part of the battles of the Æneid much more distant than those of the Iliad. Though Virgil with great art has introduced a Camilla, a Pallas, and a Lausus, still, in many particulars, and in the action upon the whole, there is such a sameness with the Iliad, that the learned reader of the Æneid is deprived of the pleasure inspired by originality. If the man of taste, however, will be pleased to mark how the genius of a Virgil has managed a war after Homer, he will certainly be tired with a dozen epic poems in the same style. Where the siege of a town and battles are the subject of an epic, there will, of necessity, in the characters and circumstances, be a resemblance to Homer; and such poem must therefore want originality. Happily for Tasso, the variation of manners, and his masterly superiority over Homer in describing his duels, has given to his Jerusalem an air of novelty. Yet, with all the difference between Christian and pagan heroes, we have a Priam, an Agamemnon, an Achilles, etc., armies slaughtered, and a city besieged. In a word, we have a handsome copy of the Iliad in the Jerusalem Delivered. If some imitations, however, have been successful, how many other epics of ancient and modern times have hurried down the stream of oblivion! Some of their authors had poetical merit, but the fault was in the choice of their subjects. So fully is the strife of war exhausted by Homer, that Virgil and Tasso could add to it but little novelty; no wonder, therefore, that so many epics on battles and sieges have been suffered to sink into utter neglect. Camoëns, perhaps, did not weigh these circumstances, but the strength of his poetical genius directed him. He could not but feel what it was to read Virgil after Homer; and the original turn and force of his mind led him from the beaten track of Helen's and Lavinia's, Achilles's and Hector's sieges and slaughters, where the hero hews down, and drives to flight, whole armies with his own sword. Camoëns was the first who wooed the modern Epic Muse, and she gave him the wreath of a first lover; a sort of epic poetry unheard of before; or, as Voltaire calls it, une nouvelle espèce d'epopée; and the grandest subject it is (of profane history) which the world has ever beheld.[14] A voyage esteemed too great for man to dare; the adventures of this voyage through unknown oceans deemed unnavigable; the eastern world happily discovered, and for ever indissolubly joined and given to the western; the grand Portuguese empire in the East founded; the humanization of mankind, and universal commerce the consequence! What are the adventures of an old, fabulous hero's arrival in Britain, what are Greece and Latium in arms for a woman compared to this! Troy is in ashes, and even the Roman empire is no more. But the effects of the voyage, adventures, and bravery of the hero of the Lusiad will be felt and beheld, and perhaps increase in importance, while the world shall remain.

Happy in his choice, happy also was the genius of Camoëns in the method of pursuing his subject. He has not, like Tasso, given it a total appearance of fiction; nor has he, like Lucan, excluded allegory and poetical machinery. Whether he intended it or not (for his genius was sufficient to suggest its propriety), the judicious precept of Petronius[15] is the model of the Lusiad. That elegant writer proposes a poem on the civil war, and no poem, ancient or modern, merits the character there sketched out in any degree comparative to the Lusiad. A truth of history is preserved; yet, what is improper for the historian, the ministry of Heaven is employed, and the free spirit of poetry throws itself into fictions which makes the whole appear as an effusion of prophetic fury, and not like a rigid detail of facts, given under the sanction of witnesses. Contrary to Lucan, who, in the above rules, drawn from the nature of poetry, is severely condemned by Petronius, Camoëns conducts his poem per ambages Deorumque ministeria. The apparition, which in the night hovers athwart the fleet near the Cape of Good Hope, is the grandest fiction in human composition; the invention his own! In the Island of Venus, the use of which fiction in an epic poem is also his own, he has given the completest assemblage of all the flowers which have ever adorned the bowers of love. And, never was the furentis animi vaticinatio more conspicuously displayed than in the prophetic song, the view of the spheres, and the globe of the earth. Tasso's imitation of the Island of Venus is not equal to the original; and, though "Virgil's myrtles[16] dropping blood are nothing to Tasso's enchanted forest," what are all Ismeno's enchantments to the grandeur and horror of the appearance, prophecy, and vanishment of the spectre of Camoëns![17] It has long been agreed among critics, that the solemnity of religious observances gives great dignity to the historical narrative of epic poetry. Camoëns, in the embarkation of the fleet, and in several other places, is peculiarly happy in the dignity of religious allusions. Manners and character are also required in the epic poem. But all the epics which have appeared are, except two, mere copies of the Iliad in these respects. Every one has its Agamemnon, Achilles, Ajax, and Ulysses; its calm, furious, gross, and intelligent hero. Camoëns and Milton happily left this beaten track, this exhausted field, and have given us pictures of manners unknown in the Iliad, the Æneid, and all those poems which may be classed with the Thebaid. The Lusiad abounds with pictures of manners, from those of the highest chivalry to those of the rudest, fiercest, and most innocent barbarism. In the fifth, sixth, and ninth books, Leonardo and Veloso are painted in stronger colours than any of the inferior characters in Virgil. But character, indeed, is not the excellence of the Æneid. That of Monzaida, the friend of Gama, is much superior to that of Achates. The base, selfish, perfidious and cruel character of the Zamorim and the Moors, are painted in the strongest colours; and the character of Gama himself is that of the finished hero. His cool command of his passions, his deep sagacity, his fixed intrepidity, his tenderness of heart, his manly piety, and his high enthusiasm in the love of his country are all displayed in the superlative degree. Let him who objects the want of character to the Lusiad, beware lest he stumble upon its praise; lest he only say, it wants an Achilles, a Hector, and a Priam. And, to the novelty of the manners of the Lusiad let the novelty of fire-arms also be added. It has been said that the buckler, the bow, and the spear, must continue the arms of poetry. Yet, however unsuccessful others may have been, Camoëns has proved that fire-arms may be introduced with the greatest dignity, and the finest effect in the epic poem.

As the grand interest of commerce and of mankind forms the subject of the Lusiad, so, with great propriety, as necessary accompaniments to the voyage of his hero, the author has given poetical pictures of the four parts of the world—in the third book a view of Europe; in the fifth, a view of Africa; and in the tenth, a picture of Asia and America. Homer and Virgil have been highly praised for their judgment in the choice of subjects which interested their countrymen, and Statius has been as severely condemned for his uninteresting choice. But, though the subject of Camoëns be particularly interesting to his own countrymen, it has also the peculiar happiness to be the poem of every trading nation. It is the epic poem of the birth of commerce, and, in a particular manner, the epic poem of whatever country has the control and possession of the commerce of India.[18]

An unexhausted fertility and variety of poetical description, an unexhausted elevation of sentiment, and a constant tenor of the grand simplicity of diction, complete the character of the Lusiad of Camoëns: a poem which, though it has hitherto received from the public most unmerited neglect, and from the critics most flagrant injustice, was yet better understood by the greatest poet of Italy. Tasso never did his judgment more credit than when he confessed that he dreaded Camoëns as a rival; or his generosity more honour than when he addressed the elegant sonnet to the hero of the Lusiad, commencing—

"Vasco, le cui felici, ardite antenne

In contro al sol, che ne riporta il giorno."

It only remains to give some account of the version of the Lusiad which is now offered to the public. Beside the translations mentioned in the life of Camoëns, M. Duperron De Castera, in 1735, gave, in French prose, a loose unpoetical paraphrase[19] of the Lusiad. Nor does Sir Richard Fanshaw's English version, published during the usurpation of Cromwell, merit a better character. Though stanza be rendered for stanza, though at first view it has the appearance of being exceedingly literal, this version is nevertheless exceedingly unfaithful. Uncountenanced by his original, Fanshaw—

"Teems with many a dead-born just."[20]

Nor had he the least idea of the dignity of the epic style,[21] or of the true spirit of poetical translation. For this, indeed, no definite rule can be given. The translator's feelings alone must direct him, for the spirit of poetry is sure to evaporate in literal translation.

Indeed, literal translation of poetry is a solecism. You may construe your author, indeed, but, if with some translators you boast that you have left your author to speak for himself, that you have neither added nor diminished, you have in reality grossly abused him, and deceived yourself. Your literal translation can have no claim to the original felicities of expression; the energy, elegance, and fire of the original poetry. It may bear, indeed, a resemblance; but such a one as a corpse in the sepulchre bears to the former man when he moved in the bloom and vigour of life.

Nec verbum verbo curabis reddere, fidus

Interpres,

was the taste of the Augustan age. None but a poet can translate a poet. The freedom which this precept gives, will, therefore, in a poet's hands, not only infuse the energy, elegance, and fire of his author's poetry into his own version, but will give it also the spirit of an original.

He who can construe may perform all that is claimed by the literal translator. He who attempts the manner of translation prescribed by Horace, ventures upon a task of genius. Yet, however daring the undertaking, and however he may have failed in it, the translator acknowledges, that in this spirit he has endeavoured to give the Lusiad in English. Even farther liberties, in one or two instances, seemed to him advantageous—— But a minuteness[22] in the mention of these will not appear with a good grace in this edition of his work; and besides, the original is in the hands of the world.

MICKLE'S INTRODUCTION TO THE LUSIADS.

If a concatenation of events centred in one great action—events which gave birth to the present commercial system of the world—if these be of the first importance in the civil history of mankind, then the Lusiad, of all other poems, challenges the attention of the philosopher, the politician, and the gentleman.

In contradistinction to the Iliad and the Æneid, the Paradise Lost has been called the Epic Poem of Religion. In the same manner may the Lusiad be named the Epic Poem of Commerce. The happy completion of the most important designs of Henry, Duke of Viseo, prince of Portugal, to whom Europe owes both Gama and Columbus, both the eastern and the western worlds, constitutes the subject of this celebrated epic poem. But before we proceed to the historical introduction necessary to elucidate a poem founded on such an important period of history, some attention is due to the opinion of those theorists in political philosophy who lament that India was ever discovered, and who assert that increase of trade is only the parent of degeneracy, and the nurse of every vice.

Much, indeed, may be urged on this side of the question; but much, also, may be urged against every institution relative to man. Imperfection, if not necessary to humanity, is at least the certain attendant on everything human. Though some part of the traffic with many countries resemble Solomon's importation of apes and peacocks; though the superfluities of life, the baubles of the opulent, and even the luxuries which enervate the irresolute and administer disease, are introduced by the intercourse of navigation, yet the extent of the benefits which attend it are also to be considered before the man of cool reason will venture to pronounce that the world is injured, and rendered less virtuous and happy by the increase of commerce.

If a view of the state of mankind, where commerce opens no intercourse between nation and nation be neglected, unjust conclusions will certainly follow. Where the state of barbarians, and of countries under different degrees of civilization are candidly weighed, we may reasonably expect a just decision. As evidently as the appointment of nature gives pasture to the herds, so evidently is man born for society. As every other animal is in its natural state when in the situation which its instinct requires, so man, when his reason is cultivated, is then, and only then, in the state proper to his nature. The life of the naked savage, who feeds on acorns and sleeps like a beast in his den, is commonly called the natural state of man; but, if there be any propriety in this assertion, his rational faculties compose no part of his nature, and were given not to be used. If the savage, therefore, live in a state contrary to the appointment of nature, it must follow that he is not so happy as nature intended him to be. And a view of his true character will confirm this conclusion. The reveries, the fairy dreams of a Rousseau, may figure the paradisaical life of a Hottentot, but it is only in such dreams that the superior happiness of the barbarian exists. The savage, it is true, is reluctant to leave his manner of life; but, unless we allow that he is a proper judge of the modes of living, his attachment to his own by no means proves that he is happier than he might otherwise have been. His attachment only exemplifies the amazing power of habit in reconciling the human breast to the most uncomfortable situations. If the intercourse of mankind in some instances be introductive of vice, the want of it as certainly excludes the exertion of the noblest virtues; and, if the seeds of virtue are indeed in the heart, they often lie dormant, and even unknown to the savage possessor. The most beautiful description of a tribe of savages (which we may be assured is from real life) occurs in these words:[23] And the five spies of Dan "came to Laish, and saw the people that were there, how they dwelt careless, after the manner of the Zidonians, quiet and secure; and there was no magistrate in the land, that might put them to shame in anything...." And the spies said to their brethren, "Arise, that we may go up against them; for we have seen the land, and, behold, it is very good.... And they came unto Laish, unto a people that were at quiet and secure: and they smote them with the edge of the sword, and burnt the city with fire. And there was no deliverer, because it was far from Zidon, and they had no business with any man." However the happy simplicity of this society may please the man of fine imagination, the true philosopher will view the men of Laish with other eyes. However virtuous he may suppose one generation, it requires an alteration of human nature to preserve the children of the next in the same generous estrangement from the selfish passions—from those passions which are the parents of the acts of injustice. When his wants are easily supplied, the manners of the savage will be simple, and often humane, for the human heart is not vicious without objects of temptation. But these will soon occur; he that gathers the greatest quantity of fruit will be envied by the less industrious. The uninformed mind seems insensible of the idea of the right of possession which the labour of acquirement gives. When want is pressing, and the supply at hand, the only consideration with such minds is the danger of seizing it; and where there is no magistrate to put to shame in anything, depredation will soon display all its horrors. Let it even be admitted that the innocence of the men of Laish could secure them from the consequences of their own unrestrained desires, could even this impossibility be surmounted, still are they a wretched prey to the first invaders, and because they have no business with any man, they will find no deliverer. While human nature is the same, the fate of Laish will always be the fate of the weak and defenceless; and thus the most amiable description of savage life raises in our minds the strongest imagery of the misery and impossible continuance of such a state. But if the view of these innocent people terminate in horror, with what contemplation shall we behold the wilds of Africa and America? The tribes of America, it is true, have degrees of policy greatly superior to anything understood by the men of Laish. Great masters of martial oratory, their popular assemblies are schools open to all their youth. In these they not only learn the history of their nation, and what they have to fear from the strength and designs of their enemies, but they also imbibe the most ardent spirit of war. The arts of stratagem are their study, and the most athletic exercises of the field their employment and delight; and, what is their greatest praise, they have magistrates "to put them to shame." They inflict no corporeal punishment on their countrymen, it is true; but a reprimand from an elder, delivered in the assembly, is esteemed by them a deeper degradation and severer punishment than any of those too often most impolitically adopted by civilized nations. Yet, though possessed of this advantage—an advantage impossible to exist in a large commercial empire— and though masters of great martial policy, their condition, upon the whole, is big with the most striking demonstration of the misery and unnatural state of such very imperfect civilization. "Multiply and replenish the earth" is an injunction of the best political philosophy ever given to man. Nature has appointed man to cultivate the earth, to increase in number by the food which its culture gives, and by this increase of brethren to remove some, and to mitigate all, the natural miseries of human life. But in direct opposition to this is the political state of the wild aborigines of America. Their lands, luxuriant in climate, are often desolate wastes, where thousands of miles hardly support a few hundreds of savage hunters. Attachment to their own tribe constitutes their highest idea of virtue; but this virtue includes the most brutal depravity, makes them esteem the man of every other tribe as an enemy, as one with whom nature had placed them in a state of war, and had commanded to destroy.[24] And to this principle their customs and ideas of honour serve as rituals and ministers. The cruelties practised by the American

25

savages on their prisoners of war (and war is their chief employment) convey every idea expressed by the word diabolical, and give a most shocking view of the degradation of human nature. But what peculiarly completes the character of the savage is his horrible superstition. In the most distant nations the savage is, in this respect, the same. The terror of evil spirits continually haunts him; his God is beheld as a relentless tyrant, and is worshipped often with cruel rites, always with a heart full of horror and fear. In all the numerous accounts of savage worship, one trace of filial dependence is not to be found. The very reverse of that happy idea is the hell of the ignorant mind. Nor is this barbarism confined alone to those ignorant tribes whom we call savages. The vulgar of every country possess it in certain degrees, proportionated to their opportunities of conversation with the more enlightened. Sordid disposition and base ferocity, together with the most unhappy superstition, are everywhere the proportionate attendants of ignorance and severe want. And ignorance and want are only removed by intercourse and the offices of society. So self-evident are these positions, that it requires an apology for insisting upon them; but the apology is at hand. He who has read knows how many eminent writers,[25] and he who has conversed knows how many respectable names, connect the idea of innocence and happiness with the life of the savage and the unimproved rustic. To fix the character of the savage is therefore necessary, ere we examine the assertion, that "it had been happy for both the old and the new worlds if the East and West Indies had never been discovered." The bloodshed and the attendant miseries which the unparalleled rapine and cruelties of the Spaniards spread over the new world, indeed disgrace human nature. The great and flourishing empires of Mexico and Peru, steeped in the blood of forty millions of their sons, present a melancholy prospect, which must excite the indignation of every good heart. Yet such desolation is not the certain consequence of discovery. And, even should we allow that the depravity of human nature is so great that the avarice of the merchant and rapacity of the soldier will overwhelm with misery every new-discovered country, still, are there other, more comprehensive views, to be taken, ere we decide against the intercourse introduced by navigation. When we weigh the happiness of Europe in the scale of political philosophy, we are not to confine our eye to the dreadful ravages of Attila the Hun, or of Alaric the Goth. If the waters of a stagnated lake are disturbed by the spade when led into new channels, we ought not to inveigh against the alteration because the waters are fouled at the first; we are to wait to see the streamlets refine and spread beauty and utility through a thousand vales which they never visited before. Such were the conquests of Alexander, temporary evils, but civilization and happiness followed in the bloody track. And, though disgraced with every barbarity, happiness has also followed the conquests of the Spaniards in the other hemisphere. Though the villainy of the Jesuits defeated their schemes of civilization in many countries, the labours of that society have been crowned with a success in Paraguay and in Canada, which reflects upon their industry the greatest honour. The customs and cruelties of many American tribes still disgrace human nature, but in Paraguay and Canada the natives have been brought to relish the blessings of society, and the arts of virtuous and civil life. If Mexico is not so populous as it once was, neither is it so barbarous;[26] the shrieks of the human victim do not now resound from temple to temple, nor does the human heart, held up reeking to the sun, imprecate the vengeance of Heaven on the guilty empire. And, however impolitically despotic the Spanish governments may be, still do these colonies enjoy the opportunities of improvement, which in every age arise from the knowledge of commerce and of letters—opportunities which were never enjoyed in South America under the reigns of Montezuma and Atabalipa. But if from Spanish, we turn our eyes to British America, what a glorious prospect! Here, formerly, on the wild lawn, perhaps twice in the year, a few savage hunters kindled their evening fire, kindled it more to protect them from evil spirits and beasts of prey, than from the cold, and with their feet pointed to it, slept on the ground. Here, now, population spreads her thousands, and society appears in all its blessings of mutual help, and the mutual lights of intellectual improvement. "What work of art, or power, or public utility, has ever equalled the glory of having peopled a continent, without guilt or bloodshed, with a multitude of free and happy commonwealths; to have given them the best arts of life and government!" To have given a savage continent an image of the British Constitution is, indeed, the greatest glory of the British crown, "a greater than any other nation ever acquired;" and from the consequences of the genius of Henry, Duke of Viseo, did the British American empire arise, an empire which, unless retarded by the illiberal and inhuman spirit of religious fanaticism, will in a few centuries, perhaps, be the glory of the world.

Stubborn indeed must be the theorist who will deny the improvement, virtue, and happiness which, in the result, the voyage of Columbus has spread over the western world. The happiness which Europe and Asia have received from the intercourse with each other, cannot hitherto, it must be owned, be compared either with the possession of it, or the source of its increase established in America. Yet, let the man of the most melancholy views estimate all the wars and depredations which are charged upon the Portuguese and other European nations, still will the eastern world appear considerably advantaged by the voyage of Gama. If seas of blood have been shed by the Portuguese, nothing new was introduced into India. War and depredation were no unheard-of strangers on the banks of the Ganges, nor could the nature of the civil establishments of the eastern nations secure a lasting peace. The ambition of their native princes was only diverted into new channels, into channels which, in the natural course of human affairs, will certainly lead to permanent governments, established on improved laws and just dominion. Yet, even ere such governments are formed, is Asia no loser by the arrival of Europeans. The horrid massacres and unbounded rapine which, according to their own annals, followed the victories of their Asian conquerors were never equalled by the worst of their European vanquishers. Nor is the establishment of improved governments in the East the dream of theory. The superiority of the civil and military arts of the British, notwithstanding the hateful character of some individuals, is at this day beheld in India with all the astonishment of admiration; and admiration is always followed, though often with retarded steps, by the strong desire of similar improvement. Long after the fall of the Roman empire the Roman laws were adopted by nations which ancient Rome esteemed as barbarous. And thus, in the course of ages, the British laws, according to every test of probability, will have a most important effect, will fulfil the prophecy of Camoëns, and transfer to the British the high compliment he pays to his countrymen—

"Beneath their sway majestic, wise, and mild,

Proud of her victor's laws thrice happier India smiled."

In former ages, and within these few years, the fertile empire of India has exhibited every scene of human misery, under the undistinguishing ravages of their Mohammedan and native princes; ravages only equalled in European history by those committed under Atilla, surnamed "the scourge of God," and "the destroyer of nations." The ideas of patriotism and of honour were seldom known in the cabinets of the eastern princes till the arrival of the Europeans. Every species of assassination was the policy of their courts, and every act of unrestrained rapine and massacre followed the path of victory. But some of the Portuguese governors, and many of the English officers, have taught them that humanity to the conquered is the best, the truest policy. The brutal ferocity of their own conquerors is now the object of their greatest dread; and the superiority of the British in war has convinced their princes,[27] that an alliance with the British is the surest guarantee of their national peace and prosperity. While the English East India Company are possessed of their present greatness, it is in their power to diffuse over the East every blessing which flows from the wisest and most humane policy. Long ere the Europeans arrived, a failure of the crop of rice, the principal food of India, had spread the devastations of famine over the populous plains of Bengal. And never, from the seven years' famine of ancient Egypt to the present day, was there a natural scarcity in any country which did not enrich the proprietors of the granaries. The Mohammedan princes, and Moorish traders have often added all the horrors of an artificial, to a natural, famine. But, however some Portuguese or other governors may stand accused, much was left for the humanity of the more exalted policy of an Albuquerque, or a Castro. And under such European governors as these, the distresses of the East have often been alleviated by a generosity of conduct, and a train of resources formerly unknown in Asia. Absurd and impracticable were that scheme which would introduce the British laws into India without the deepest regard to the manners and circumstances peculiar to the people. But that spirit of liberty upon which they are founded, and that security of property which is their leading principle, must in time have a wide and stupendous effect. The abject spirit of Asiatic submission will be taught to see, and to claim, those rights of nature, of which the dispirited and passive Hindus could, till lately, hardly form an idea. From this, as naturally as the noon succeeds the dawn, must the other blessings of civilization arise. For, though the four great castes of India are almost inaccessible to the introduction of other manners, and of other literature than their own, happily there is in human nature a propensity to change. Nor may the political philosopher be deemed an enthusiast who would boldly prophesy, that unless the British be driven from India the general superiority which they bear will, ere many generations shall have passed, induce the most intelligent of India to break the shackles of their absurd superstitions,[28] and lead them to partake of those advantages which arise from the free scope and due cultivation of the rational powers. In almost every instance the Indian institutions are contrary to the feelings and wishes of nature. And ignorance and bigotry, their two chief pillars, can never secure unalterable duration. We have certain proof that the horrid custom of burning the wives along with the body of the deceased husband has continued for upwards of fifteen hundred years; we are also certain that within these twenty years it has begun to fall into disuse. Together with the alteration of this most striking feature of Indian manners, other assimilations to European sentiments have already taken place. Nor can the obstinacy even of the conceited Chinese always resist the desire of imitating the Europeans, a people who in arts and arms are so greatly superior to themselves. The use of the twenty-four letters, by which we can express every language, appeared at first as miraculous to the Chinese. Prejudice cannot always deprive that people, who are not deficient in selfish cunning, of the ease and expedition of an alphabet; and it is easy to foresee that, in the course of a few centuries, some alphabet will certainly take the place of the 60,000 arbitrary marks which now render the cultivation of the Chinese literature not only a labour of the utmost difficulty, but even the attainment impossible beyond a very limited degree. And from the introduction of an alphabet, what improvements may not be expected from the laborious industry of the Chinese! Though most obstinately attached to their old customs, yet there is a tide in the manners of nations which is sudden and rapid, and which acts with a kind of instinctive fury against ancient prejudice and absurdity. It was that nation of merchants, the Phœnicians, which diffused the use of letters through the ancient, and commerce will undoubtedly diffuse the same blessings through the modern, world.

To this view of the political happiness which is sure to be introduced in proportion to civilization, let the divine add what may be reasonably expected from such opportunity of the increase of religion. A factory of merchants, indeed, has seldom been found to be a school of piety; yet, when the general manners of a people become assimilated to those of a more rational worship, something more than ever was produced by an infant mission, or the neighbourhood of an infant colony, may then be reasonably expected, and even foretold.

In estimating the political happiness of a people, nothing is of greater importance than their capacity of, and tendency to, improvement. As a dead lake, to continue our former illustration, will remain in the same state for ages and ages, so would the bigotry and superstitions of the East continue the same. But if the lake is begun to be opened into a thousand rivulets, who knows over what unnumbered fields, barren before, they may diffuse the blessings of fertility, and turn a dreary wilderness into a land of society and joy.

In contrast to this, let the Gold Coast and other immense regions of Africa be contemplated—

"Afric behold; alas, what altered view!

Her lands uncultured, and her sons untrue;

Ungraced with all that sweetens human life,

Savage and fierce they roam in brutal strife;

Eager they grasp the gifts which culture yields,

Yet naked roam their own neglected fields....

Unnumber'd tribes as bestial grazers stray,

By laws unform'd, unform'd by Reason's sway.

Far inward stretch the mournful sterile dales,

Where on the parch'd hill-side pale famine wails."

Lusiad X.

Let us consider how many millions of these unhappy savages are dragged from their native fields, and cut off for ever from all the hopes and all the rights to which human birth entitled them. And who would hesitate to pronounce that negro the greatest of patriots, who, by teaching his countrymen the arts of society, should teach them to defend themselves in the possession of their fields, their families, and their own personal liberties?

Evident, however, as it is, that the voyages of Gama and Columbus have already carried a superior degree of happiness, and the promise of infinitely more, to the eastern and western worlds; yet the advantages to Europe from the discovery of these regions may perhaps be denied. But let us view what Europe was, ere the genius of Don Henry gave birth to the spirit of modern discovery.

Several ages before this period the feudal system had degenerated into the most absolute tyranny. The barons exercised the most despotic authority over their vassals, and every scheme of public utility was rendered impracticable by their continual petty wars with each other; to which they led their dependents as dogs to the chase. Unable to read, or to write his own name, the chieftain was entirely possessed by the most romantic opinion of military glory, and the song of his domestic minstrel constituted his highest idea of fame. The classic authors slept on the shelves of the monasteries, their dark but happy asylum, while the life of the monks resembled that of the fattened beeves which loaded their tables. Real abilities were indeed possessed by a Duns Scotus and a few others; but these were lost in the most trifling subtleties of a sophistry which they dignified with the name of casuistical divinity. Whether Adam and Eve were created with navels? and How many thousand angels might at the same instant dance upon the point of the finest needle without one jostling another? were two of the several topics of like importance which excited the acumen and engaged the controversies of the learned. While every branch of philosophical, of rational investigation, was thus unpursued and unknown, commerce, which is incompatible with the feudal system, was equally neglected and unimproved. Where the mind is enlarged and enlightened by learning, plans of commerce will rise into action, and these, in return, will from every part of the world bring new acquirements to philosophy and science. The birth of learning and commerce may be different, but their growth is mutual and dependent upon each other. They not only assist each other, but the same enlargement of mind which is necessary for perfection in the one is also necessary for perfection in the other; and the same causes impede, and are alike destructive of, both. The INTERCOURSE of mankind is the parent of each. According to the confinement or extent of intercourse, barbarity or civilization proportionately prevail. In the dark, monkish ages, the intercourse of the learned was as much impeded and confined as that of the merchant. A few unwieldy vessels coasted the shores of Europe, and mendicant friars and ignorant pilgrims carried a miserable account of what was passing in the world from monastery to monastery. What doctor had last disputed on the peripatetic philosophy at some university, or what new heresy had last appeared, not only comprised the whole of their literary intelligence, but was delivered with little accuracy, and received with as little attention. While this thick cloud of mental darkness overspread the western world, was Don Henry, prince of Portugal, born; born to set mankind free from the feudal system, and to give to the whole world every advantage, every light that may possibly be diffused by the intercourse of unlimited commerce:—

"For then from ancient gloom emerg'd

The rising world of trade: the genius, then,

Of navigation, that in hopeless sloth

Had slumber'd on the vast Atlantic deep

For idle ages, starting heard at last

The Lusitanian prince, who, Heaven-inspir'd,

To love of useful glory rous'd mankind,

And in unbounded commerce mix'd the world."

Thomson.

In contrast to this melancholy view of human nature, sunk in barbarism and benighted with ignorance, let the present state of Europe be impartially estimated. Yet, though the great increase of opulence and learning cannot be denied, there are some who assert that virtue and happiness have as greatly declined. And the immense overflow of riches, from the East in particular, has been pronounced big with destruction to the British empire. Everything human, it is true, has its dark as well as its bright side; but let these popular complaints be examined, and it will be found that modern Europe, and the British empire in a very particular manner, have received the greatest and most solid advantages from the modern, enlarged system of commerce. The magic of the old romances, which could make the most withered, deformed hag, appear as the most beautiful virgin, is every day verified in popular declamation. Ancient days are there painted in the most amiable simplicity, and the modern in the most odious colours. Yet, what man of fortune in England lives in that stupendous gross luxury which every day was exhibited in the Gothic castles of the old chieftains! Four or five hundred knights and squires in the domestic retinue of a warlike earl was not uncommon, nor was the pomp of embroidery inferior to the profuse waste of their tables; in both instances unequalled by all the mad excesses of the present age.

While the baron thus lived in all the wild glare of Gothic luxury, agriculture was almost totally neglected, and his meaner vassals fared harder, infinitely less comfortably, than the meanest industrious labourers of England do now; where the lands are uncultivated, the peasants, ill-clothed, ill-lodged, and poorly fed, pass their miserable days in sloth and filth, totally ignorant of every advantage, of every comfort which nature lays at their feet. He who passes from the trading towns and cultured fields of England to those remote villages of Scotland or Ireland which claim this description, is astonished at the comparative wretchedness of their destitute inhabitants; but few consider that these villages only exhibit a view of what Europe was ere the spirit of commerce diffused the blessings which naturally flow from her improvements. In the Hebrides the failure of a harvest almost depopulates an island. Having little or no traffic to purchase grain, numbers of the young and hale betake themselves to the continent in quest of employment and food, leaving a few, less adventurous, behind, to beget a new race, the heir of the same fortune. Yet from the same cause, from the want of traffic, the kingdom of England has often felt more dreadful effects than these. Even in the days when her Henries and Edwards plumed themselves with the trophies of France, how often has famine spread all her horrors over city and village? Our modern histories neglect this characteristic feature of ancient days; but the rude chronicles of these ages inform us, that three or four times in almost every reign was England thus visited. The failure of the crop was then severely felt, and two bad harvests in succession were almost insupportable. But commerce has now opened another scene, has armed government with the happiest power that can be exerted by the rulers of a nation—the power to prevent every extremity[29] which may possibly arise from bad harvests; extremities, which, in former ages, were esteemed more dreadful visitations of the wrath of Heaven than the pestilence itself. Yet modern London is not so certainly defended against the latter, its ancient visitor, than the commonwealth by the means of commerce, under a just and humane government, is secured against the ravages of the former. If, from these great outlines of the happiness enjoyed by a commercial over an uncommercial nation, we turn our eyes to the manners, the advantages will be found no less in favour of the civilized.

Whoever is inclined to declaim at the vices of the present age, let him read, and be convinced, that the Gothic ages were less virtuous. If the spirit of chivalry prevented effeminacy, it was the foster-father of a ferocity of manners now happily unknown. Rapacity, avarice, and effeminacy are the vices ascribed to the increase of commerce; and in some degree, it must be confessed, they follow her steps. Yet infinitely more dreadful, as every palatinate in Europe often felt, were the effects of the two first under the feudal lords than can possibly be experienced under any system of trade. The virtues and vices of human nature are the same in every age: they only receive different modifications, and are dormant, or awakened into action, under different circumstances. The feudal lord had it infinitely more in his power to be rapacious than the merchant. And whatever avarice may attend the trader, his intercourse with the rest of mankind lifts him greatly above that brutish ferocity which actuates the savage, often the rustic, and in general characterizes the ignorant part of mankind. The abolition of the feudal system, a system of absolute slavery, and that equality of mankind which affords the protection of property, and every other incitement to industry, are the glorious gifts which the spirit of commerce, awakened by Prince Henry of Portugal, has bestowed upon Europe in general; and, as if directed by the manes of his mother, a daughter of England, upon the British empire in particular. In the vice of effeminacy alone, perhaps, do we exceed our ancestors; yet, even here we have infinitely the advantage over them. The brutal ferocity of former ages is now lost, and the general mind is humanized. The savage breast is the native soil of revenge; a vice, of all others, peculiarly stamped with the character of hell. But the mention of this was reserved for the character of the savages of Europe. The savage of every country is implacable when injured; but among some, revenge has its measure. When an American Indian is murdered his kindred pursue the murderer; and, as soon as blood has atoned for blood, the wilds of America hear the hostile parties join in their mutual lamentations over the dead, whom, as an oblivion of malice, they bury together. But the measure of revenge, never to be full, was left for the demi-savages of Europe. The vassals of the feudal lord entered into his quarrels with the most inexorable rage. Just or unjust was no consideration of theirs. It was a family feud; no farther inquiry was made; and from age to age, the parties, who never injured each other, breathed nothing but mutual rancour and revenge. And actions, suitable to this horrid spirit, everywhere confessed its virulent influence. Such were the late days of Europe, admired by the ignorant for the innocence of manners. Resentment of injury, indeed, is natural; and there is a degree which is honest, and though warm, far from inhuman. But if it is the hard task of humanized virtue to preserve the feeling of an injury unmixed with the slightest criminal wish of revenge, how impossible is it for the savage to attain the dignity of forgiveness, the greatest ornament of human nature. As in individuals, a virtue will rise into a vice, generosity into blind profusion, and even mercy into criminal lenity, so civilized manners will lead the opulent into effeminacy. But let it be considered, this consequence is by no means the certain result of civilization. Civilization, on the contrary, provides the most effectual preventive of this evil. Where classical literature prevails the manly spirit which it breathes must be diffused; whenever frivolousness predominates, when refinement degenerates into whatever enervates the mind, literary ignorance is sure to complete the effeminate character. A mediocrity of virtues and of talents is the lot of the great majority of mankind; and even this mediocrity, if cultivated by a liberal education, will infallibly secure its possessor against those excesses of effeminacy which are really culpable. To be of plain manners it is not necessary to be a clown, or to wear coarse clothes; nor is it necessary to lie on the ground and feed like the savage to be truly manly. The beggar who, behind the hedge, divides his offals with his dog has often more of the real sensualist than he who dines at an elegant table. Nor need we hesitate to assert, that he who, unable to preserve a manly elegance of manners, degenerates into the petit maître, would have been, in any age or condition, equally insignificant and worthless. Some, when they talk of the debauchery of the present age, seem to think that the former ages were all innocence. But this is ignorance of human nature. The debauchery of a barbarous age is gross and brutal; that of a gloomy, superstitious one, secret, excessive, and murderous; that of a more polished one, much happier for the fair sex,[30] and certainly in no sense so big with political unhappiness. If one disease has been imported from America,[31] the most valuable medicines have likewise been brought from those regions; and distempers, which were thought invincible by our forefathers, are now cured. If the luxuries of the Indies usher disease to our tables the consequence is not unknown; the wise and the temperate receive no injury, and intemperance has been the destroyer of mankind in every age. The opulence of ancient Rome produced a luxury of manners which proved fatal to that mighty empire. But the effeminate sensualists of those ages were not men of intellectual cultivation. The enlarged ideas, the generous and manly feelings inspired by a liberal education, were utterly unknown to them. Unformed by that wisdom which arises from science and true philosophy, they were gross barbarians, dressed in the mere outward tinsel of civilization.[32] Where the enthusiasm of military honour characterizes the rank of gentlemen that nation will rise into empire. But no sooner does conquest give a continued security than the mere soldier degenerates; and the old veterans are soon succeeded by a new generation, illiterate as their fathers, but destitute of their virtues and experience. Polite literature not only humanizes the heart, but also wonderfully strengthens and enlarges the mind. Moral and political philosophy are its peculiar provinces, and are never happily cultivated without its assistance. But, where ignorance characterizes the body of the nobility, the most insipid dissipation and the very idleness and effeminacy of luxury are sure to follow. Titles and family are then the only merit, and the few men of business who surround the throne have it then in their power to aggrandize themselves by riveting the chains of slavery. A stately grandeur is preserved, but it is only outward; all is decayed within, and on the first storm the weak fabric falls to the dust. Thus rose and thus fell the empire of Rome, and the much wider one of Portugal. Though the increase of wealth did, indeed, contribute to that corruption of manners which unnerved the Portuguese, certain it is the wisdom of legislature might certainly have prevented every evil which Spain and Portugal have experienced from their acquisitions in the two Indies.[33] Every evil which they have suffered from their acquirements arose, as shall be hereafter demonstrated, from their general ignorance, which rendered them unable to investigate or apprehend even the first principles of civil and commercial philosophy. And what other than the total eclipse of their glory could be expected from a nobility, rude and unlettered as those of Portugal are described by the author of the Lusiad—a court and nobility who sealed the truth of all his complaints against them by suffering that great man, the light of their age, to die in an almshouse! What but the fall of their state could be expected from barbarians like these! Nor can the annals of mankind produce one instance of the fall of empire where the character of the nobles was other than that ascribed to his countrymen by Camoëns.

MICKLE'S SKETCH OF THE HISTORY OF THE DISCOVERY OF INDIA.

No lesson can be of greater national importance than the history of the rise and the fall of a commercial empire. The view of what advantages were acquired, and of what might have been still added; the means by which such empire might have been continued, and the errors by which it was lost, are as particularly conspicuous in the naval and commercial history of Portugal as if Providence had intended to give a lasting example to mankind; a chart, where the course of the safe voyage is pointed out, and where the shelves and rocks, and the seasons of tempest are discovered and foretold.

The history of Portugal, as a naval and commercial power, begins with the designs of Prince Henry. But as the enterprises of this great man, and the completion of his designs are intimately connected with the state of Portugal, a short view of the progress of the power, and of the character of that kingdom, will be necessary to elucidate the history of the revival of commerce, and the subject of the Lusiad.

During the centuries when the effeminated Roman provinces of Europe were desolated by the irruptions of the northern barbarians, the Saracens spread the same horrors of brutal conquest over the finest countries of the eastern world. The northern conquerors of the finer provinces of Europe embraced the Christian religion as professed by the monks, and, contented with the luxuries of their new settlements, their military spirit soon declined. The Saracens, on the other hand, having embraced the religion of Mohammed, their rage for war received every addition which can possibly be inspired by religious enthusiasm. Not only the spoils of the vanquished, but Paradise itself was to be obtained by their sabres. Strengthened and inspired by a commission which they esteemed divine, the rapidity of their conquests far exceeded those of the Goths and Vandals. The majority of the inhabitants of every country they subdued embraced their religion and imbibed their principles; thus, the professors of Mohammedanism became the most formidable combination ever leagued together against the rest of mankind. Morocco and the adjacent countries had now received the doctrines of the Koran, and the arms of the Saracens spread slaughter and desolation from the south of Spain to Italy, and the islands of the Mediterranean. All the rapine and carnage committed by the Gothic conquerors were now amply returned on their less warlike posterity. In Spain, and the province now called Portugal, the Mohammedans erected powerful kingdoms, and their lust of conquest threatened destruction to every Christian power. But a romantic military spirit revived in Europe under the auspices of Charlemagne. The Mohammedans, during the reign of this sovereign, made a most formidable irruption into Europe; France in particular felt the weight of their fury. By the invention of new military honours that monarch drew the adventurous youth of every Christian power to his standards, which eventually resulted in the crusades, the beginning of which, in propriety, should be dated from his reign. Few indeed are the historians of this period, but enough remains to prove, that though the writers of the old romance seized upon it, and added the inexhaustible machinery of magic to the adventures of their heroes, yet the origin of their fictions was founded on historical facts.[34] Yet, however this period may thus resemble the fabulous ages of Greece, certain it is, that an Orlando, a Rinaldo, a Rugero, and other celebrated names in romance, acquired great honour in the wars which were waged against the Saracens, the invaders of Europe. In these romantic wars, by which the power of the Mohammedans was checked, several centuries elapsed, when Alonzo, King of Castile, apprehensive that the whole force of the Mohammedans of Spain and Morocco was ready to fall upon him, prudently imitated the conduct of Charlemagne. He availed himself of the spirit of chivalry, and demanded leave of Philip I. of France, and other princes, that volunteers from their dominions might be allowed to distinguish themselves, under his banners, against the Saracens. His desire was no sooner known than a brave army of volunteers thronged to his standard, and Alonzo was victorious. Honours and endowments were liberally distributed among the champions; and to Henry, a younger son of the Duke of Burgundy, he gave his daughter, Teresa, in marriage, with the sovereignty of the countries south of Galicia as a dowry, commissioning him to extend his dominions by the expulsion of the Moors. Henry, who reigned by the title of Count, improved every advantage which offered. The two rich provinces of Entro Minho e Douro, and Tras os Montes, yielded to his arms; great part of Beira also was subdued, and the Moorish King of Lamego became his tributary. Many thousands of Christians, who had lived in miserable subjection to the Moors, took shelter under the generous protection of Count Henry. Great numbers of the Moors also changed their religion, and chose rather to continue in the land where they were born than be exposed to the severities and injustice of their native governors. And thus, one of the most beautiful[35] and fertile spots of the world, with the finest climate, in consequence of a crusade[36] against the Mohammedans, became in the end the kingdom of Portugal, a sovereignty which in course of time spread its influence far over the world.

Count Henry, after a successful reign, was succeeded by his infant son, Don Alonzo-Henry, who, having surmounted the dangers which threatened his youth, became the founder of the Portuguese monarchy. In 1139 the Moors of Spain and Barbary united their forces to recover the dominions from which they had been driven by the Christians. According to the accounts of the Portuguese writers, the Moorish army amounted to near 400,000 men; nor is this number incredible when we consider what armies they at other times have brought into the field, and that at this time they came to take possession of lands from which they had been expelled. Don Alonzo, however, with a very small army, gave them battle on the plains of Ourique, and after a struggle of six hours, obtained a most glorious and complete victory, and one which was crowned with an event of the utmost importance. On the field of battle Don Alonzo was proclaimed King of Portugal by his victorious soldiers, and he in return conferred the rank of nobility on the whole army. The constitution of the monarchy, however, was not settled, nor was Alonzo invested with the regalia till six years after this memorable victory. The kind of government the Portuguese had submitted to under the Spaniards and Moors, and the advantages which they saw were derived from their own valour, had taught them the love of liberty, while Alonzo himself understood the spirit of his subjects too well to make the least attempt to set himself up as a despotic monarch. After six years spent in further victories, he called an assembly of the prelates, nobility, and commons, to meet at Lamego. When the assembly opened, Alonzo appeared seated on the throne, but without any other mark of regal dignity. Before he was crowned, the constitution of the state was settled, and eighteen statutes were solemnly confirmed by oath[37] as the charter of king and people; statutes diametrically opposite to the divine right and arbitrary power of kings, principles which inculcate and demand the unlimited passive obedience of the subject.

The founders of the Portuguese monarchy transmitted to their heirs those generous principles of liberty which complete and adorn the martial character. The ardour of the volunteer, an ardour unknown to the slave and the mercenary, added to the most romantic ideas of military glory, characterized the Portuguese under the reigns of their first monarchs. Engaged in almost continual war with the Moors, this spirit rose higher and higher; and the desire to extirpate Mohammedanism—the principle which animated the wish of victory in every battle—seemed to take deeper root in every age. Such were the manners, and such the principles of the people who were governed by the successors of Alonzo I.—a succession of great men who proved themselves worthy to reign over so military and enterprising a nation.

By a continued train of victories the Portuguese had the honour to drive the Moors from Europe. The invasions of European soil by these people were now requited by successful expeditions into Africa. Such was the manly spirit of these ages, that the statutes of Lamego received additional articles in favour of liberty, a convincing proof that the general heroism of a people depends upon the principles of freedom. Alonzo IV.,[38] though not an amiable character, was perhaps the greatest warrior, politician, and monarch of his age. After a reign of military splendour, he left his throne to his son Pedro, surnamed the Just. Ideas of equity and literature were now diffused by this great prince,[39] who was himself a polite scholar, and a most accomplished gentleman. Portugal began to perceive the advantages of cultivated talents, and to feel its superiority over the barbarous politics of the ignorant Moors. The great Pedro, however, was succeeded by a weak prince, and the heroic spirit of the Portuguese seemed to exist no more under his son Fernando, surnamed the Careless.

Under John I.[40] all the virtues of the Portuguese again shone forth with redoubled lustre. Happily for Portugal, his father had bestowed an excellent education upon this prince, which, added to his great natural talents, rendered him one of the greatest of monarchs. Conscious of the superiority which his own liberal education gave him, he was assiduous to bestow the same advantages upon his children, and he himself often became their preceptor in science and useful knowledge. Fortunate in all his affairs, he was most of all fortunate in his family. He had many sons, and he lived to see them become men of parts and of action, whose only emulation was to show affection to his person and to support his administration by their great abilities.

All the sons of John excelled in military exercises, and in the literature of their age; Don Edward and Don Pedro[41] were particularly educated for the cabinet, and the mathematical genius of Don Henry received every encouragement which a king and a father could give to ripen it into perfection and public utility.

History was well known to Prince Henry, and his turn of mind peculiarly enabled him to make political observations upon it. The history of ancient Tyre and Carthage showed him what a maritime nation might hope to become; and the flourishing colonies of the Greeks were the frequent topic of his conversation. Where Grecian commerce extended its influence the deserts became cultivated fields, cities rose, and men were drawn from the woods and caverns to unite in society. The Romans, on the other hand, when they destroyed Carthage, buried in her ruins the fountain of civilization, improvement and opulence. They extinguished the spirit of commerce, and the agriculture of the conquered nations. And thus, while the luxury of Rome consumed the wealth of her provinces, her uncommercial policy dried up the sources of its continuance. Nor were the inestimable advantages of commerce the sole motives of Henry. All the ardour that the love of his country could awaken conspired to stimulate the natural turn of his genius for the improvement of navigation.

As the kingdom of Portugal had been wrested from the Moors, and established by conquest, so its existence still depended on the superiority of force of arms; and even before the birth of Henry, the superiority of the Portuguese navies had been of the utmost consequence to the protection of the state. Whatever, therefore, might curb the power of the Moors, was of the utmost importance to the existence of Portugal. Such were the views and circumstances which united to inspire the designs of Henry, designs which were powerfully enforced by the religion of that prince. Desire to extirpate Mohammedanism was synonymous with patriotism in Portugal. It was the principle which gave birth to, and supported their monarchy. Their kings avowed it; and Prince Henry always professed, that to propagate the Gospel and extirpate Mohammedanism, was the great purpose of all his enterprises. The same principles, it is certain, inspired King Emmanuel, under whom the eastern world was discovered by Gama.[42]

The crusades, which had rendered the greatest political service to Spain and Portugal, had begun now to have some effect upon the commerce of Europe. The Hanse Towns had received charters of liberty, and had united together for the protection of their trade against the pirates of the Baltic. The Lombards had opened a lucrative traffic with the ports of Egypt, from whence they imported into Europe the riches of India; and Bruges, the mart between them and the Hanse Towns, was, in consequence, surrounded with the best agriculture of these ages,[43] a certain proof of the dependence of agriculture upon the extent of commerce. The Hanse Towns were liable, however, to be buried in the victories of a tyrant, and the trade with Egypt was exceedingly insecure and precarious. Europe was still enveloped in the dark mists of ignorance; commerce still crept, in an infant state, along the coasts, nor were the ships adapted for long voyages. A successful tyrant might have overwhelmed the system of commerce entirely, for it stood on a much narrower basis than in the days of Phœnician and Greek colonization. A broader and more permanent foundation of commerce than the world had yet seen was wanting to bless mankind, and Henry, Duke of Viseo, was born to give it.

In order to promote his designs, Prince Henry was appointed Commander-in-chief of the Portuguese forces in Africa. He had already, in 1412, three years before the reduction of Ceuta,[44] sent a ship to make discoveries on the Barbary coast. Cape Nam[45] (as its name implies) was then the ne plus ultra of European navigation; the ship sent by Henry, however, passed it sixty leagues, and reached Cape Bojador. About a league and a half from Cape St. Vincent (supposed to be the Promontorium Sacrum of the Romans), Prince Henry built his town of Sagrez, the best planned and fortified town in Portugal. Here, where the view of the ocean inspired his hopes, he erected his arsenals, and built and harboured his ships. And here, leaving the temporary bustle and cares of the State to his father and brothers, he retired like a philosopher from the world in order to promote its happiness. Having received all the information he could obtain in Africa, he continued unwearied in his mathematical and geographical studies; the art of ship-building received amazing improvement under his direction, and the correctness of his ideas of the structure of the globe is now confirmed. He it was who first suggested the use of the mariner's compass, and of longitude and latitude in navigation, and demonstrated how these might be ascertained by astronomical observations. Naval adventurers were now invited from all parts to the town of Sagrez, and in 1418 Juan Gonsalez Zarco and Tristran Vaz set sail on an expedition of discovery, the circumstances of which give us a striking picture of the state of navigation ere it was remodelled by the genius of Henry.

Cape Bojador, so named from its extent,[46] runs about forty leagues to the westward, and for about six leagues off land there is a most violent current, which, dashing upon the shallows, makes a tempestuous sea. This was deemed impassable, for it had not occurred to any one that by standing out to sea the current might be avoided. To pass this formidable Cape was the commission of Zarco and Vaz, who were also ordered to survey the African coast, which, according to the information given to Henry by the Moors, extended to the Equator. Zarco and Vaz, however, lost their course in a storm, and were driven to a small island, which, in the joy of their deliverance, they named Puerto Santo, or the Holy Haven. Nor was Prince Henry less joyful of their discovery than they had been of their escape: sufficient proof of the miserable state of navigation in those days; for this island is only a few days' voyage from Sagrez.

The discoverers of Puerto Santo, accompanied by Bartholomew Perestrello, were, with three ships, sent out on farther trial. Perestrello, having sown some seeds and left some cattle at Puerto Santo, returned to Portugal.[47] Zarco and Vaz directing their course southward, in 1419, perceived something like a cloud on the water, and sailing towards it, discovered an island covered with woods, which from this circumstance they named Madeira.[48] And this rich and beautiful island was the first reward of the enterprises of Prince Henry.

Nature calls upon Portugal to be a maritime power, and her naval superiority over the Moors, was, in the time of Henry, the surest defence of her existence as a kingdom. Yet, though all his labours tended to establish that naval superiority on the surest basis, though even the religion of the age added its authority to the clearest political principles in favour of Henry, yet were his enterprises and his expected discoveries derided with all the insolence of ignorance, and the bitterness of popular clamour. Barren deserts like Lybia, it was said, were all that could be found, and a thousand disadvantages, drawn from these data, were foreseen and foretold. The great mind and better knowledge of Henry, however, were not thus to be shaken. Twelve years had elapsed since the discovery of Madeira in unsuccessful endeavours to carry navigation farther. At length, one of his captains, named Galianez, in 1434 passed the Cape of Bojador, till then invincible; an action, says Faria, not inferior to the labours of Hercules.

Galianez, the next year, accompanied by Gonsalez Baldaya, carried his discoveries many leagues farther. Having put two horsemen on shore to discover the face of the country, the adventurers, after riding several hours, saw nineteen men armed with javelins. The natives fled, and the two horsemen pursued, till one of the Portuguese, being wounded, lost the first blood that was sacrificed to the new system of commerce. A small beginning, it soon swelled into oceans, and deluged the eastern and western worlds. The cruelties of Hernando Cortez, and that more horrid barbarian, Pizarro,[49] are no more to be charged upon Don Henry and Columbus, than the villainies of the Jesuits and the horrors of the Inquisition are to be ascribed to Him who commands us to do to our neighbour as we would wish our neighbour to do to us. But, if it be maintained that he who plans a discovery ought to foresee the miseries which the vicious will engraft upon his enterprise, let the objector be told that the miseries are uncertain, while the advantages are real and sure.

In 1440 Anthony Gonsalez brought some Moors prisoners to Lisbon. These he took two and forty leagues beyond Cape Bojador, and in 1442 he returned with his captives. One Moor escaped, but ten blacks of Guinea and a considerable quantity of gold dust were given in ransom for two others. A rivulet at the place of landing was named by Gonsalez, Rio del Oro, or the River of Gold. And the islands of Adeget, Arguim, and De las Garças were now discovered.

The negroes of Guinea, the first ever seen in Portugal, and the gold dust, excited other passions beside admiration. A company was formed at Lagos, under the auspices of Prince Henry, to carry on a traffic with the newly discovered countries; and, as the Portuguese considered themselves in a state of continual hostility with the Moors, about two hundred of these people, inhabitants of the Islands of Nar and Tider, in 1444, were brought prisoners to Portugal. Next year Gonzalo de Cintra was attacked by the Moors, fourteen leagues beyond Rio del Oro, where, with seven of his men, he was killed.

This hostile proceeding displeased Prince Henry, and in 1446 Anthony Gonsalez and two other captains were sent to enter into a treaty of peace and traffic with the natives of Rio del Oro, and also to attempt their conversion. But these proposals were rejected by the barbarians, one of whom, however, came voluntarily to Portugal, and Juan Fernandez remained with the natives, to observe their manners and the products of the country.

In 1447 upwards of thirty ships followed the route of traffic which was now opened; and John de Castilla obtained the infamy to stand the first on the list of those names whose villainies have disgraced the spirit of commerce, and afforded the loudest complaints against the progress of navigation. Dissatisfied with the value of his cargo, he seized twenty of the natives of Gomera (one of the Canaries), who had assisted him, and with whom he was in friendly alliance, and brought them as slaves to Portugal. But Prince Henry resented this outrage, and having given them some valuable presents of clothes, restored the captives to freedom and their native country.

The reduction of the Canaries was also this year attempted; but Spain having challenged the discovery of these islands, the expedition was discontinued. In the Canary Islands a singular feudal custom existed; giving to the chief man, or governor, a temporary right to the person of every bride in his district.

In 1448 Fernando Alonzo was sent ambassador to the king of Cape Verde with a treaty of trade and conversion, which was defeated at that time by the treachery of the natives. In 1449 the Azores were discovered by Gonsalo Vello; and the coast sixty leagues beyond Cape Verde was visited by the fleets of Henry. It is also certain that some of his commanders passed the equinoctial line.

Prince Henry had now, with inflexible perseverance, prosecuted his discoveries for upwards of forty years. His father, John I., concurred with him in his views, and gave him every assistance; his brother, King Edward, during his short reign, took the same interest in his expeditions as his father had done; nor was the eleven years' regency of his brother Don Pedro less auspicious to him.[50] But the misunderstanding between Pedro and his nephew Alonzo V., who took upon him the reins of government in his seventeenth year, retarded the designs of Henry, and gave him much unhappiness.[51] At his town of Sagrez, from whence he had not moved for many years, Don Henry, now in his sixty-seventh year, yielded to the stroke of fate, in the year of our Lord 1463, gratified with the certain prospect that the route to the eastern world would one day crown the enterprises to which he had given birth. He saw with pleasure the naval superiority of his country over the Moors established on the must solid basis, its trade greatly upon the increase, and flattered himself that he had given a mortal wound to

Mohammedanism. To him, as to their primary author, are due all the inestimable advantages which ever have flowed, or ever will flow from the discovery of the greatest part of Africa, and of the East and West Indies. Every improvement in the state and manners of these countries, or whatever country may be yet discovered, is strictly due to him. What is an Alexander, crowned with trophies at the head of his army, compared with a Henry contemplating the ocean from his window on the rock of Sagrez! The one suggests the idea of a destroying demon, the other of a benevolent Deity.

From 1448, when Alonzo V. assumed the power of government, till the end of his reign in 1471, little progress was made in maritime affairs. Cape Catherine alone was added to the former discoveries. But under his son, John II., the designs of Prince Henry were prosecuted with renewed vigour. In 1481 the Portuguese built a fort on the Gold Coast, and the King of Portugal took the title of Lord of Guinea. Bartholomew Diaz, in 1486, reached the river which he named dell'Infante on the eastern side of Africa, but deterred by the storms of that coast from proceeding farther, on his return he had the happiness to be the discoverer of the promontory, unknown for many ages, which bounds the south of Africa. From the storms he there encountered he named it Cape of Storms; but John, elated with the promise of India, which this discovery, as he justly deemed, included, gave it the name of the Cape of Good Hope. The arts and valour of the Portuguese had now made a great impression on the minds of the Africans. The King of Congo sent the sons of some of his principal officers to Lisbon, to be instructed in arts and religion; and ambassadors from the King of Benin requested teachers to be sent to his kingdom. On the return of his subjects, the King and Queen of Congo, with 100,000 of their people, were baptized. An ambassador also arrived from the Christian Emperor of Abyssinia, and Pedro de Covillam and Alonzo de Payva were sent by land to penetrate into the East, that they might acquire whatever intelligence might facilitate the desired navigation to India. Covillam and Payva parted at Toro in Arabia, and took different routes. The former having visited Conanor, Calicut, and Goa in India, returned to Cairo, where he heard of the death of his companion. Here also he met the Rabbi Abraham of Beja, who was employed for the same purpose by King John. Covillam sent the Rabbi home with an account of what countries he had seen, and he himself proceeded to Ormuz and Ethiopia, but, as Camoëns expresses it—

"To his native shore,

Enrich'd with knowledge, he return'd no more."

Men, whose genius led them to maritime affairs began now to be possessed by an ardent ambition to distinguish themselves; and the famous Columbus offered his service to King John, and was rejected. Every one knows the discoveries of this great adventurer, but his history is generally misunderstood.[52] The simple truth is, Columbus, who acquired his skill in navigation among the Portuguese, could be no stranger to the design, long meditated in that kingdom, of discovering a naval route to India, which, according to ancient geographers and the opinion of that age, was supposed to be the next land to the west of Spain. And that India and the adjacent islands were the regions sought by Columbus is also certain. John, who esteemed the route to India as almost discovered, and in the power of his own subjects, rejected the proposals of the foreigner. But Columbus met a more favourable reception from Ferdinand and Isabella, the king and queen of Castile. Columbus, therefore, proposed, as Magalhaens afterwards did, for the same reason, to steer a westward course, and having in 1492 discovered some western islands, in 1493, on his return to Spain, he put into the Tagus with great tokens of the riches of his discovery. Some of the Portuguese courtiers (the same ungenerous minds, perhaps, who advised the rejection of Columbus because he was a foreigner) proposed the assassination of that great man, thereby to conceal from Spain the advantages of his navigation. But John, though Columbus rather roughly upbraided him, looked upon him now with a generous regret, and dismissed him with honour. The King of Portugal, however, alarmed lest the discoveries of Columbus should interfere with those of his crown, gave orders to equip a war-fleet to protect his rights. But matters were adjusted by embassies, and that celebrated treaty was drawn up by which Spain and Portugal divided the western and eastern worlds between them. The eastern half of the world was allotted for the Portuguese, and the western for the Spanish navigation. A Papal Bull also, which, for obvious reasons, prohibited the propagation of the gospel in these bounds by the subjects of any other state, confirmed this amicable and extraordinary treaty.

Soon after this, however, while the thoughts of King John were intent on the discovery of India, his preparations were interrupted by his death. But his earnest desires and great designs were inherited, together with his crown, by his cousin Emmanuel; and in 1497 (the year before Columbus made the voyage in which he discovered the mouth of the river Oronoko), Vasco de Gama sailed from the Tagus for the discovery of India.

Of this voyage, the subject of the Lusiad, many particulars are necessarily mentioned in the notes; we shall therefore only allude to these, but be more explicit on the others, which are omitted by Camoëns in obedience to the rules of epic poetry.

Notwithstanding the popular clamour against the undertaking, Emmanuel was determined to prosecute the views of Prince Henry and John II. Three sloops of war and a store ship, manned with only 160 men, were fitted out; for hostility was not the purpose of this expedition. Vasco de Gama, a gentleman of good family, who, in a war with the French, had given signal proofs of his naval skill, was commissioned admiral and general, and his brother Paul, with his friend Nicholas Coello, were appointed to command under him. It is the greatest honour of kings to distinguish the characters of their officers, and to employ them accordingly. Emmanuel in many instances was happy in this talent, particularly in the choice of his admiral for the discovery of India. All the enthusiasm of desire to accomplish his end, joined with the greatest heroism, the quickest penetration, and coolest prudence, united to form the character of Gama. On his appointment he confessed to the king that his mind had long aspired to this expedition. The king expressed great confidence in his prudence and honour, and gave him, with his own hand, the colours which he was to carry. On this banner, which bore the cross of the military Order of Christ, Gama, with great enthusiasm, took the oath of fidelity.

About four miles from Lisbon is a chapel on the sea side. To this, the day before their departure, Gama conducted the companions of his expedition. He was to encounter an ocean untried, and dreaded as unnavigable, and he knew the power of religion on minds which are not inclined to dispute its authority. The whole night was spent in the chapel in prayers for success, and in the rites of their devotion. The next day, when the adventurers marched to the fleet, the shore of Belem[53] presented one of the most solemn and affecting scenes perhaps recorded in history. The beach was covered with the inhabitants of Lisbon. A procession of priests, in their robes, sang anthems and offered up invocations to heaven. Every one looked on the adventurers as brave men going to a dreadful execution; as rushing upon certain death; and the vast multitude caught the fire of devotion, and joined aloud in prayers for their success. The relations, friends, and acquaintances of the voyagers wept; all were affected; the sight was general; Gama himself shed manly tears on parting with his friends, but he hurried over the tender scene, and hastened on board with all the alacrity of hope. He set sail immediately, and so much affected were the thousands who beheld his departure, that they remained immovable on the shore, till the fleet, under full sail, vanished from their sight.

It was on the 8th of July when Gama left the Tagus. The flag ship was commanded by himself, the second by his brother, the third by Coello, and the store ship by Gonsalo Nunio. Several interpreters, skilled in Arabic, and other oriental languages, went along with them. Ten malefactors (men of abilities, whose sentences of death were reversed, on condition of their obedience to Gama in whatever embassies or dangers among the barbarians he might think proper to employ them), were also on board. The fleet, favoured by the weather, passed the Canary and Cape de Verde islands, but had now to encounter other fortune. Sometimes stopped by dead calms, but for the most part tossed by tempests, which increased in violence as they proceeded to the south. Thus driven far to sea they laboured through that wide ocean which surrounds St. Helena, in seas, says Faria, unknown to the Portuguese discoverers, none of whom had sailed so far to the west. From the 28th of July, the day they passed the isle of St. James, they had seen no shore, and now on November the 4th they were happily relieved by the sight of land. The fleet anchored in the large bay,[54] and Coello was sent in search of a river where they might take in wood and fresh water. Having found one, the fleet made towards it, and Gama, whose orders were to acquaint himself with the manners of the people wherever he touched, ordered a party of his men to bring him some of the natives by force, or stratagem. One they caught as he was gathering honey on the side of a mountain, and brought him to the fleet. He expressed the greatest indifference about the gold and fine clothes which they showed him, but was greatly delighted with some glasses and little brass bells. These with great joy he accepted, and was set on shore; and soon after many of the blacks came for, and were gratified with, the like trifles; in return for which they gave plenty of their best provisions. None of Gama's interpreters, however, could understand a word of their language, or obtain any information of India. The friendly intercourse between the fleet and the natives was, however, soon interrupted by the imprudence of Veloso, a young Portuguese, which occasioned a skirmish wherein Gama's life was endangered. Gama and some others were on shore taking the altitude of the sun, when in consequence of Veloso's rashness they were attacked by the blacks with great fury. Gama defended himself with an oar, and received a dart in his foot. Several others were likewise wounded, and they found safety in retreat. A discharge of cannon from the ships facilitated their escape, and Gama, esteeming it imprudent to waste his strength in attempts entirely foreign to the design of his voyage, weighed anchor, and steered in search of the extremity of Africa.

In this part of the voyage, says Osorius, "The heroism of Gama was greatly displayed." The waves swelled up like mountains, the ships seemed at one time heaved up to the clouds, and at another precipitated to the bed of the ocean. The winds were piercing cold, and so boisterous that the pilot's voice could seldom be heard, and a dismal darkness, which at that tempestuous season involves these seas, added all its horrors. Sometimes the storm drove them southward, at other times they were obliged to stand on the tack and yield to its fury, preserving what they had gained with the greatest difficulty.

"With such mad seas the daring Gama fought

For many a day, and many a dreadful night,

Incessant labouring round the stormy Cape,

By bold ambition led."

Thomson.

During any interval of the storm, the sailors, wearied out with fatigue, and abandoned to despair, surrounded Gama, and implored him not to suffer himself, and those committed to his care, to perish by so dreadful a death. The impossibility that men so weakened could endure much longer, and the opinion that this ocean was torn by eternal tempest, and therefore had hitherto been, and was impassable, were urged. But Gama's resolution to proceed was unalterable.[55] A conspiracy was then formed against his life. But his brother discovered it, and the courage and prudence of Gama defeated its design. He put the chief conspirators and all the pilots in irons, and he himself, his brother, Coello, and some others, stood night and day at the helm and directed the course. At last, after having many days, with unconquered mind, withstood the tempest and mutiny (molem perfidiæ) the storm suddenly ceased, and they beheld the Cape of Good Hope.

On November the 20th all the fleet doubled that promontory, and steering northward, coasted along a rich and beautiful shore, adorned with large forests and numberless herds of cattle. All was now alacrity; the hope that they had surmounted every danger revived their spirits, and the admiral was beloved and admired. Here, and at the bay, which they named St. Blas, they took in provisions, and beheld these beautiful rural scenes, described by Camoëns. And here the store sloop was burnt by order of the admiral. On December the 8th a violent tempest drove the fleet out of sight of land, and carried them to that dreadful current which made the Moors deem it impossible to double the Cape. Gama, however, though unlucky in the time of navigating these seas, was safely carried over the current by the violence of a tempest; and having recovered the sight of land, as his safest course he steered northward along the coast. On the 10th of January they discovered, about 230 miles from their last watering place, some beautiful islands, with herds of cattle frisking in the meadows. It was a profound calm, and Gama stood near to land. The natives were better dressed and more civilized than those they had hitherto seen. An exchange of presents was made, and the black king was so pleased with the politeness of Gama, that he came aboard his ship to see him. At this place, which he named Terra de Natal, Gama left two of the malefactors before mentioned to procure what information they could against his return. On the 15th of January, in the dusk of the evening, they came to the mouth of a large river, whose banks were shaded with trees laden with fruit. On the return of day they saw several little boats with palm-tree leaves making towards them, and the natives came aboard without hesitation or fear. Gama received them kindly, gave them an entertainment, and some silken garments, which they received with visible joy. Only one of them, however, could speak a little broken Arabic. From him Fernan

Martinho learned that not far distant was a country where ships, in shape and size like Gama's, frequently resorted. This gave the fleet great encouragement, and the admiral named this place "The River of Good Signs."

Here, while Gama refitted his ships, the crews were attacked with a violent scurvy, which carried off several of his men. Having taken in fresh provisions, on the 24th of February he set sail, and on the 1st of March they descried four islands on the coast of Mozambique. From one of these they perceived seven vessels in full sail bearing to the fleet. The Râis, or captain, knew Gama's ship by the admiral's ensign, and made up to her, saluting her with loud huzzas and instruments of music. Gama received them aboard, and entertained them with great kindness. The interpreters talked with them in Arabic. The island, in which was the principal harbour and trading town, they said, was governed by a deputy of the King of Quiloa; and many Arab merchants, they added, were settled here, who traded with Arabia, India, and other parts of the world. Gama was overjoyed, and the crew, with uplifted hands, returned thanks to Heaven.

Pleased with the presents which Gama sent him, and imagining that the Portuguese were Mohammedans from Morocco, the governor, dressed in rich embroidery, came to congratulate the admiral on his arrival in the east. As he approached the fleet in great pomp, Gama removed the sick out of sight, and ordered all those in health to attend above deck, armed in the Portuguese manner; for he foresaw what would happen when the Mohammedans should discover it was a Christian fleet. During the entertainment provided for him Zacocia seemed highly pleased, and asked several questions about the arms and religion of the strangers. Gama showed him his arms, and explained the force of his cannon, but he did not affect to know much about religion; however he frankly promised to show him his books of devotion whenever a few days refreshment should give him a more convenient time. In the meanwhile he entreated Zacocia to send him some pilots who might conduct him to India. Two pilots were next day brought by the governor, a treaty of peace was solemnly concluded, and every office of mutual friendship seemed to promise a lasting harmony. But it was soon interrupted. Zacocia, as soon as he found the Portuguese were Christians, used every endeavour to destroy the fleet. The life of Gama was attempted. One of the Moorish pilots deserted, and some of the Portuguese who were on shore to get fresh water were attacked by the natives, but were rescued by a timely assistance from the ships.

Besides the hatred of the Christian name, inspired by their religion, the Arabs had other reasons to wish the destruction of Gama. Before this period, they were almost the only merchants of the East; they had colonies in every place convenient for trade, and were the sole masters of the Ethiopian, Arabian, and Indian seas. They clearly foresaw the consequences of the arrival of

Europeans, and every art was soon exerted to prevent such formidable rivals from effecting any footing in the East. To these Mohammedan traders the Portuguese gave the name of Moors.

Immediately after the skirmish at the watering-place, Gama, having one Moorish pilot, set sail, but was soon driven back by tempestuous weather. He now resolved to take in fresh water by force. The Moors perceiving his intention, about two thousand of them rising from ambush, attacked the Portuguese detachment. But the prudence of Gama had not been asleep. His ships were stationed with art, and his artillery not only dispersed the hostile Moors, but reduced their town, which was built of wood, into a heap of ashes. Among some prisoners taken by Paulus de Gama was a pilot, and Zacocia begging forgiveness for his treachery, sent another, whose skill in navigation he greatly commended.

A war with the Moors was now begun. Gama perceived that their jealousy of European rivals gave him nothing to expect but open hostility and secret treachery; and he knew what numerous colonies they had on every trading coast of the East. To impress them, therefore, with the terror of his arms on their first act of treachery, was worthy of a great commander. Nor was he remiss in his attention to the chief pilot who had been last sent. He perceived in him a kind of anxious endeavour to bear near some little islands, and suspecting there were unseen rocks in that course, he confidently charged the pilot with guilt, and ordered him to be severely whipped. The punishment produced a confession and promises of fidelity. And he now advised Gama to stand for Quiloa, which he assured him was inhabited by Christians. Three Ethiopian Christians had come aboard the fleet while at Zacocia's island, and the opinions then current about Prester John's country inclined Gama to try if he could find a port where he might obtain the assistance of a people of his own religion. A violent storm, however, drove the fleet from Quiloa, and being now near Mombas, the pilot advised him to enter that harbour, where, he said, there were also many Christians.

The city of Mombas is agreeably situated on an island, formed by a river which empties itself into the sea by two mouths. The buildings are lofty and of solid stone, and the country abounds with fruit-trees and cattle. Gama, happy to find a harbour where everything wore the appearance of civilization, ordered the fleet to cast anchor, which was scarcely done, when a galley, in which were 100 men in oriental costume, armed with bucklers and sabres, rowed up to the flag ship. All of these seemed desirous to come on board, but only four, who by their dress seemed officers, were admitted; nor were these allowed, till stripped of their arms. When on board they extolled the prudence of Gama in refusing admittance to armed strangers; and by their behaviour, seemed desirous to gain the good opinion of the fleet. Their country, they boasted, contained all the riches of India; and their king, they

50

professed, was ambitious of entering into a friendly treaty with the Portuguese, with whose renown he was well acquainted. And, that a conference with his majesty and the offices of friendship might be rendered more convenient, Gama was requested to enter the harbour. As no place could be more commodious for the recovery of the sick, Gama resolved to enter the port; and in the meanwhile sent two of the pardoned criminals as an embassy to the king. These the king treated with the greatest kindness, ordered his officers to show them the strength and opulence of his city; and, on their return to the navy, he sent a present to Gama of the most valuable spices, of which he boasted such abundance, that the Portuguese, he said, if they regarded their own interest, would seek for no other India.

To make treaties of commerce was the business of Gama; and one so advantageous was not to be refused. Fully satisfied by the report of his spies, he ordered to weigh anchor and enter the harbour. His own ship led the way, when a sudden violence of the tide made Gama apprehensive of running aground. He therefore ordered the sails to be furled, and the anchors to be dropped, and gave a signal for the rest of the fleet to follow his example. This manœuvre, and the cries of the sailors in executing it, alarmed the Mozambique pilots. Conscious of their treachery, they thought their design was discovered, and leaped into the sea. Some boats of Mombas took them up, and refusing to put them on board, set them safely on shore, though the admiral repeatedly demanded the restoration of the pilots. These proofs of treachery were farther confirmed by the behaviour of the King of Mombas. In the middle of the night Gama thought he heard some noise, and on examination, found his fleet surrounded by a great number of Moors, who, with the utmost secrecy, endeavoured to cut his cables. But their scheme was defeated; and some Arabs, who remained on board, confessed that no Christians were resident either at Quiloa or Mombas. The storm which drove them from the one place, and their late escape at the other, were now beheld as manifestations of the Divine favour, and Gama, holding up his hands to heaven, ascribed his safety to the care of Providence.[56] Two days, however, elapsed before they could get clear of the rocky bay of Mombas. Having now ventured to hoist their sails, they steered for Melinda, a port, they had been told, where many merchants from India resorted. In their way thither they took a Moorish vessel, out of which Gama selected fourteen prisoners, one of whom he perceived by his mien to be a person of distinction. By this Saracen, Gama was informed that he was near Melinda, that the king was hospitable, and celebrated for his faith, and that four ships from India, commanded by Christian masters, were in that harbour. The Saracen also offered to go as Gama's messenger to the king, and promised to procure him an able pilot to conduct him to Calicut, the chief port of India.

As the coast of Melinda appeared to be dangerous, Gama anchored at some distance from the city, and, unwilling to risk the safety of any of his men, he landed the Saracen on an island opposite to Melinda. This was observed, and the stranger was brought before the king, to whom he gave so favourable an account of the politeness and humanity of Gama, that a present of several sheep, and fruits of all sorts, was sent by his majesty to the admiral, who had the happiness to find the truth of what his prisoner had told him confirmed by the masters of the four ships from India. These were Christians from Cambaya. They were transported with joy on the arrival of the Portuguese, and gave several useful instructions to the admiral.

The city of Melinda was situated in a fertile plain, surrounded with gardens and groves of orange-trees, whose flowers diffused a most grateful odour. The pastures were covered with herds; and the houses, built of square stones, were both elegant and magnificent. Desirous to make an alliance with such a state, Gama requited the civility of the king with great generosity. He drew nearer the shore, and urged his instructions as apology for not landing to wait upon his majesty in person. The apology was accepted, and the king, whose age and infirmity prevented him going on board, sent his son to congratulate Gama, and enter into a treaty of friendship. The prince, who had some time governed under the direction of his father, came in great pomp. His dress was royally magnificent, the nobles who attended him displayed all the riches of silk and embroidery, and the music of Melinda resounded all over the bay. Gama, to express his regard, met him in the admiral's barge. The prince, as soon as he came up, leaped into it, and distinguishing the admiral by his habit, embraced him with all the intimacy of old friendship. In their conversation, which was long and sprightly, he discovered nothing of the barbarian, says Osorius, but in everything showed an intelligence and politeness worthy of his high rank. He accepted the fourteen Moors, whom Gama gave to him, with great pleasure. He seemed to view Gama with enthusiasm, and confessed that the build of the Portuguese ships, so much superior to what he had seen, convinced him of the greatness of that people. He gave Gama an able pilot, named Melemo Cana, to conduct him to Calicut; and requested, that on his return to Europe, he would carry an ambassador with him to the court of Lisbon. During the few days the fleet stayed at Melinda, the mutual friendship increased, and a treaty of alliance was concluded. And now, on April 22, resigning the helm to his skilful and honest pilot, Gama hoisted sail and steered to the north. In a few days they passed the line, and the Portuguese with ecstasy beheld the appearance of their native sky. Orion, Ursa Major and Minor, and the other stars about the north pole, were now a more joyful discovery than the south pole had formerly been to them.[57] The pilot now stood out to the east, through the Indian ocean; and after sailing about three weeks, he had the happiness to congratulate Gama on the view of the mountains of Calicut, who, transported with ecstasy, returned thanks to Heaven, and ordered all his prisoners to be set at liberty.

About two leagues from Calicut, Gama ordered the fleet to anchor, and was soon surrounded by a number of boats. By one of these he sent one of the pardoned criminals to the city. The appearance of an unknown fleet on their coast brought immense crowds around the stranger, who no sooner entered Calicut, than he was lifted from his feet and carried hither and thither by the concourse. Though the populace and the stranger were alike earnest to be understood, their language was unintelligible to each other, till, happily for Gama, a Moorish merchant accosted his messenger in the Spanish tongue. The next day this Moor, who was named Monzaida, waited upon Gama on board his ship. He was a native of Tunis, and the chief person, he said, with whom John II. had at that port contracted for military stores. He was a man of abilities and great intelligence of the world, and an admirer of the Portuguese valour and honour. The engaging behaviour of Gama heightened his esteem into the sincerest attachment. Monzaida offered to be interpreter for the admiral, and to serve him in whatever besides he might possibly befriend him. And thus, by one of those unforeseen circumstances which often decide the greatest events, Gama obtained a friend who soon rendered him the most important services.

At the first interview, Monzaida gave Gama the fullest information of the climate, extent, customs, religion, and riches of India, the commerce of the Arabs, and the character of the sovereign. Calicut was not only the imperial city, but the greatest port. The king, or zamorim,[58] who resided here, was acknowledged as emperor by the neighbouring princes; and, as his revenue consisted chiefly of duties on merchandise, he had always encouraged the resort of foreigners to his ports.

Pleased with this promising prospect, Gama sent two of his officers with Monzaida to wait upon the zamorim at his palace, at Pandarene, a few miles from the city. They were admitted to the royal apartment, and delivered their embassy; to which the zamorim replied, that the arrival of the admiral of so great a prince as Emmanuel, gave him inexpressible pleasure, and that he would willingly embrace the offered alliance. In the meanwhile, as their present station was extremely dangerous, he advised them to bring the ships nearer to Pandarene, and for this purpose he sent a pilot to the fleet.

A few days after this, the zamorim sent his first minister, or catual,[59] attended by several of the nayres, or nobility, to conduct Gama to the royal palace. As an interview with the zamorim was absolutely necessary to complete the purpose of his voyage, Gama immediately agreed to it, though the treachery he had already experienced since his arrival in the eastern seas showed him the personal danger which he thus hazarded. He gave his brother, Paulus, and Coello the command of the fleet in his absence.

The revenue of the zamorim arose chiefly from the traffic of the Moors; the various colonies of these people were combined in one interest, and the jealousy and consternation which his arrival in the eastern seas had spread among them, were circumstances well known to Gama: and he knew, also, what he had to expect, both from their force and their fraud. But duty and honour required him to complete the purpose of his voyage. He left peremptory command, that if he was detained a prisoner, or any attempt made upon his life, they should take no step to save him or to reverse his fate; to give ear to no message which might come in his name for such purpose, and to enter into no negotiation on his behalf. They were to keep some boats near the shore, to favour his escape if he perceived treachery before being detained by force; yet the moment that force rendered his escape impracticable they were to set sail, and carry the tidings to the king. As this was his only concern, he would suffer no risk that might lose a man, or endanger the homeward voyage. Having left these orders, he went ashore with the catual, attended only by twelve of his own men, for he would not weaken his fleet, though he knew the pomp of attendance would in one respect have been greatly in his favour at the first court of India.

As soon as landed, he and the catual were carried in great pomp, in palanquins, upon men's shoulders, to the chief temple, and thence, amid immense crowds, to the royal palace. The apartment and dress of the zamorim were such as might be expected from the luxury and wealth of India. The emperor reclined on a magnificent couch, surrounded with his nobility and officers of state. Gama was introduced to him by a venerable old man, the chief brahmin. His majesty, by a gentle nod, appointed the admiral to sit on one of the steps of his sofa, and then demanded his embassy. It was against the custom of his country, Gama replied, to deliver his instructions in a public assembly; he therefore desired that the king and a few of his ministers would grant him a private audience. This was complied with, and Gama, in a manly speech, set forth the greatness of his sovereign Emmanuel, the fame he had heard of the zamorim, and the desire he had to enter into an alliance with so great a prince; nor were the mutual advantages of such a treaty omitted by the admiral. The zamorim, in reply, professed great esteem for the friendship of the King of Portugal, and declared his readiness to enter into a friendly alliance. He then ordered the catual to provide proper apartments for Gama in his own house; and having promised another conference, he dismissed the admiral with all the appearance of sincerity.

The character of this monarch is strongly marked in the history of Portuguese Asia. Avarice was his ruling passion; he was haughty or mean, bold or timorous, as his interest rose or fell in the balance of his judgment; wavering and irresolute whenever the scales seemed doubtful which to preponderate. He was pleased with the prospect of bringing the commerce of Europe to his harbours, but he was also influenced by the threats of the Moors.

Three days elapsed ere Gama was again permitted to see the zamorim. At this second audience he presented the letter and presents of Emmanuel. The letter was received with politeness, but the presents were viewed with an eye of contempt. Gama noticed it, and said he only came to discover the route to India, and therefore was not charged with valuable gifts, before the friendship of the state, where they might choose to traffic, was known. Yet, indeed, he brought the most valuable of all gifts, the offer of the friendship of his sovereign, and the commerce of his country. He then entreated the king not to reveal the contents of Emmanuel's letter to the Moors; and the king, with great apparent friendship, desired Gama to guard against the perfidy of that people. At this time, it is highly probable, the zamorim was sincere.

Every hour since the arrival of the fleet the Moors had held secret conferences. That one man of it might not return was their purpose; and every method to accomplish this was meditated. To influence the king against the Portuguese, to assassinate Gama, to raise a general insurrection to destroy the foreign navy, and to bribe the catual, were determined. And the catual (the master of the house where Gama was lodged) accepted the bribe, and entered into their interest. Of all these circumstances, however, Gama was apprised by his faithful interpreter, Monzaida, whose affection to the foreign admiral the Moors hitherto had not suspected. Thus informed, and having obtained the faith of an alliance from the sovereign of the first port of India, Gama resolved to elude the plots of the Moors; and accordingly, before the dawn, he set out for Pandarene, in hope to get aboard his fleet by some of the boats which he had ordered to hover about the shore.

But the Moors were vigilant. His escape was immediately known, and the catual, by the king's order, pursued and brought him back by force. The catual, however (for it was necessary for their schemes to have the ships in their power), behaved with politeness to the admiral, and promised to use all his interest in his behalf.

The eagerness of the Moors now contributed to the safety of Gama. Their principal merchants were admitted to a formal audience, when one of their orators accused the Portuguese as a nation of faithless plunderers: Gama, he said, was an exiled pirate, who had marked his course with blood and depredation. If he were not a pirate, still there was no excuse for giving such warlike foreigners any footing in a country already supplied with all that nature and commerce could give. He expatiated on the great services which the Moorish traders had rendered to Calicut; and ended with a threat, that all the Moors would leave the zamorim's ports and find some other settlement, if he permitted these foreigners any share in the commerce of his dominions.

However staggered with these arguments and threats, the zamorim was not blind to the self-interest and malice of the Moors. He therefore ordered, that

55

the admiral should once more be brought before him. In the meanwhile the catual tried many stratagems to get the fleet into the harbour; and at last, in the name of his master, made an absolute demand that the sails and rudders should be delivered up, as the pledge of Gama's honesty. But these demands were as absolutely refused by Gama, who sent a letter to his brother by Monzaida, enforcing his former orders in the strongest manner, declaring that his fate gave him no concern, that he was only unhappy lest the fruits of all their fatigue and dangers should be lost. After two days spent in vain altercation with the catual, Gama was brought as a prisoner before the king. The king repeated his accusation; upbraided him with non-compliance to the requests of his minister; urged him, if he were an exile or a pirate, to confess freely, in which case he promised to take him into his service, and highly promote him on account of his abilities. But Gama, who with great spirit had baffled all the stratagems of the catual, behaved with the same undaunted bravery before the king. He asserted his innocence, pointed out the malice of the Moors, and the improbability of his piracy; boasted of the safety of his fleet, offered his life rather than his sails and rudders, and concluded with threats in the name of his sovereign. The zamorim, during the whole conference, eyed Gama with the keenest attention, and clearly perceived in his unfaltering mien the dignity of truth, and the consciousness that he was the admiral of a great monarch. In their late address, the Moors had treated the zamorim as somewhat dependent upon them, and he saw that a commerce with other nations would certainly lessen their dangerous importance. His avarice strongly desired the commerce of Portugal; and his pride was flattered in humbling the Moors. After many proposals, it was at last agreed, that of his twelve attendants he should leave seven as hostages; that what goods were aboard his fleet should be landed; and that Gama should be safely conducted to his ship, after which the treaty of commerce and alliance was to be finally settled. And thus, when the assassination of Gama seemed inevitable, the zamorim suddenly dropped his demand for the sails and rudders, rescued him from his determined enemies, and restored him to liberty and the command of his navy.

As soon as he was aboard[60] the goods were landed, accompanied by a letter from Gama to the zamorim, wherein he boldly complained of the treachery of the catual. The zamorim, in answer, promised to make inquiry, and punish him, if guilty; but did nothing in the affair. Gama, who had now anchored nearer to the city, every day sent two or three different persons on some business to Calicut, that as many of his men as possible might be able to give some account of India. The Moors, meanwhile, every day assaulted the ears of the king, who now began to waver; when Gama, who had given every proof of his desire of peace and friendship, sent another letter, in which he requested the zamorim to permit him to leave a consul at Calicut to manage the affairs of King Emmanuel. But to this request—the most reasonable result of a commercial treaty—the zamorim returned a refusal full of rage and indignation. Gama, now fully master of the character of the zamorim, resolved to treat a man of such an inconstant, dishonourable disposition with a contemptuous silence. This contempt was felt by the king, who, yielding to the advice of the catual and the entreaties of the Moors, seized the Portuguese goods, and ordered two of the seven hostages—the two who had the charge of the cargo—to be put in irons. The admiral remonstrated by means of Monzaida, but the king still persisted in his treacherous breach of faith. Repeated solicitations made him more haughty, and it was now the duty and interest of Gama to use force. He took a vessel, in which were six nayres, or noblemen, and nineteen of their servants. The servants he set ashore to relate the tidings, the noblemen he detained. As soon as the news had time to spread through the city, he hoisted his sails, and, though with a slow motion, seemed to proceed on his homeward voyage. The city was now in an uproar; the friends of the captive noblemen surrounded the palace, and loudly accused the policy of the Moors. The king, in all the perplexed distress of a haughty, avaricious, weak prince, sent after Gama, delivered up all the hostages, and submitted to his proposals; nay, even solicited that an agent should be left, and even descended to the meanness of a palpable lie. The two factors, he said, he had put in irons, only to detain them till he might write letters to his brother Emmanuel, and the goods he had kept on shore that an agent might be sent to dispose of them. Gama, however, perceived a mysterious trifling, and, previous to any treaty, insisted upon the restoration of the goods.

The day after this altercation Monzaida came aboard the fleet in great perturbation. The Moors, he said, had raised great commotions, and had enraged the king against the Portuguese. The king's ships were getting ready, and a numerous Moorish fleet from Mecca was daily expected. To delay Gama till this force arrived was the purpose of the Court and of the Moors, who were now confident of success. To this information Monzaida added, that the Moors, suspecting his attachment to Gama, had determined to assassinate him; that he had narrowly escaped from them; that it was impossible for him to recover his effects, and that his only hope was in the protection of Gama. Gama rewarded him with the friendship he merited, took him with him, as he desired, to Lisbon, and procured him a recompense for his services.

Almost immediately seven boats arrived loaded with the goods, and demanded the restoration of the captive noblemen. Gama took the goods on board, but refused to examine if they were entire, and also refused to deliver the prisoners. He had been promised an ambassador to his sovereign, he said, but had been so often deluded he could trust such a faithless people no longer, and would therefore carry away the captives to convince the King of

Portugal what insults and injustice his ambassador and admiral had suffered from the Zamorim of Calicut. Having thus dismissed the Indians, he fired his cannon and hoisted his sails. A calm, however, detained him on the coast some days; and the zamorim, seizing the opportunity, sent what vessels he could fit out (sixty in all), full of armed men, to attack him. Though Gama's cannon were well handled, confident of their numbers, they pressed on to board him, when a sudden tempest arose, which Gama's ships rode out in safety, miserably dispersed the Indian fleet, and completed their ruin.

After this victory the admiral made a halt at a little island near the shore, where he erected a cross,[61] bearing the name and arms of his Portuguese majesty. From this place, by the hand of Monzaida, he wrote a letter to the zamorim, wherein he gave a full and circumstantial account of all the plots of the catual and the Moors. Still, however, he professed his desire of a commercial treaty, and promised to represent the zamorim in the best light to Emmanuel. The prisoners, he said, should be kindly used, were only kept as ambassadors to his sovereign, and should be returned to India when they were enabled from experience to give an account of Portugal. The letter he sent by one of the captives, who by this means obtained his liberty.

The fame of Gama had now spread over the Indian seas, and the Moors were everywhere intent on his destruction. As he was near the shore of Anchediva, he beheld the appearance of a floating isle, covered with trees, advance towards him. But his prudence was not to be thus deceived. A bold pirate, named Timoja, by linking together eight vessels full of men and covered with green boughs, thought to board him by surprise. But Gama's cannon made seven of them fly; the eighth, loaded with fruits and provision, he took. The beautiful island of Anchediva now offered a convenient place to careen his ships and refresh his men. While he stayed here, the first minister of Zabajo, king of Goa, one of the most powerful princes of India, came on board, and, in the name of his master, congratulated the admiral in the Italian tongue. Provisions, arms, and money were offered to Gama, and he was entreated to accept the friendship of Zabajo. The admiral was struck with admiration; the address and abilities of the minister appeared so conspicuous. He said he was an Italian by birth, but in sailing to Greece, had been taken by pirates, and after various misfortunes, had been necessitated to enter into the service of a Mohammedan prince, the nobleness of whose disposition he commended in the highest terms. Yet, with all his abilities, Gama perceived an artful inquisitiveness—that nameless something which does not accompany simple honesty. After a long conference, Gama abruptly upbraided him as a spy, and ordered him to be put to the torture. And this soon brought a confession, that he was a Polish Jew by birth, and was sent to examine the strength of the fleet by Zabajo, who was mustering all his power to attack the Portuguese. Gama, on this, immediately set sail, and took the spy along with him, who soon after was baptized, and named Jasper de Gama, the admiral being his godfather. He afterwards became of great service to Emmanuel.

Gama now stood westward through the Indian Ocean, and after being long delayed by calms, arrived off Magadoxa, on the coast of Africa. This place was a principal port of the Moors; he therefore levelled the walls of the city with his cannon, and burned and destroyed all the ships in the harbour. Soon after this he descried eight Moorish vessels bearing down upon him; his artillery, however, soon made them use their oars in flight, nor could Gama overtake any of them for want of wind. The hospitable harbour of Melinda was the next place he reached. His men, almost worn out with fatigue and sickness, here received a second time every assistance which an accomplished and generous prince could bestow. And having taken an ambassador on board, he again set sail, in hope that he might pass the Cape of Good Hope while the favourable weather continued; for his acquaintance with the eastern seas now suggested to him that the tempestuous season was periodical. Soon after he set sail his brother's ship struck on a sand bank, and was burnt by order of the admiral. His brother and part of the crew he took into his own ship, the rest he sent on board of Coello's; nor were more hands now alive than were necessary to man the two vessels which remained. Having taken in provisions at the island of Zanzibar (where they were kindly entertained by a Mohammedan prince of the same sect with the King of Melinda), they safely doubled the Cape of Good Hope on April 26, 1499, and continued till they reached the island of St. Iago, in favourable weather. But a tempest here separated the two ships, and gave Gama and Coello an opportunity to show the goodness of their hearts in a manner which does honour to human nature.

The admiral was now near the Azores, when Paulus de Gama, long worn with fatigue and sickness, was unable to endure the motion of the ship. Vasco, therefore, put into the island of Tercera, in hope of his brother's recovery. And such was his affection, that rather than leave him he gave the command of his ship to one of his officers. But the hope of recovery was vain. John de Sa proceeded to Lisbon with the flag ship, while the admiral remained behind to soothe the deathbed of his brother, and perform his funeral rites. Coello, meanwhile, landed at Lisbon, and hearing that Gama had not arrived, imagined he might either be shipwrecked or beating about in distress. Without seeing one of his family he immediately set sail again, on purpose to bring relief to his friend and admiral. But this generous design was prevented by an order from the king, ere he got out of the Tagus.

The particulars of the voyage were now diffused by Coello, and the joy of the king was only equalled by the admiration of the people. Yet, while all the nation was fired with zeal to express their esteem of the happy admiral, he himself, the man who was such an enthusiast to the success of his voyage that he would willingly have sacrificed his life in India to secure that success, was now in the completion of it a dejected mourner. The compliments of the Court, and the shouts of the street, were irksome to him; for his brother, the companion of his toils and dangers, was not there to share the joy. As soon as he had waited on the king, he shut himself up in a lonely house near the seaside at Belem, from whence it was some time ere he was drawn to mingle in public life.

During this important expedition, two years and almost two months elapsed. Of 160 men who went out, only 55 returned. These were all rewarded by the king. Coello was pensioned with 100 ducats a year, and made a fidalgo, or gentleman of the king's household, a degree of nobility in Portugal. The title of Don was annexed to the family of Vasco de Gama. He was appointed admiral of the eastern seas, with an annual salary of 3000 ducats, and a part of the king's arms was added to his. Public thanksgivings to Heaven were celebrated throughout the churches of the kingdom; while feasts, dramatic performances, and chivalrous entertainments (or tournaments), according to the taste of that age, demonstrated the joy of Portugal.

Pedro Alvarez Cabral was the second Portuguese admiral who sailed for India. He entered into alliance with Trimumpara, king of Cochin, and high priest of Malabar. (See Bk. x. p. 302.)

Gama, having left six ships for the protection of Cochin and Cananor, had sailed for Portugal with twelve ships, laden with the riches of the East. As soon as his departure was made known, the zamorim made great preparations to attack Cochin—a city situated on an island, divided by an arm of the sea from the main-land. At one part, however, this creek was fordable at low water. The zamorim having renewed the war, at length, by force of numbers and bribery, took the city; and the King of Cochin, stripped of his dominions, but still faithful to the Portuguese, fled to the island of Viopia. Francisco Albuquerque, with other commanders, having heard of the fate of Cochin, set sail for its relief; the garrison of the zamorim fled, and Trimumpara was restored to his throne. Every precaution by which the passage to the island of Cochin might be secured was now taken by Pacheco. The Portuguese took the sacrament, and devoted themselves to death. The King of Cochin's troops amounted only to 5000 men, while the army of the zamorim numbered 57,000, provided with brass cannon, and assisted by two Italian engineers. Yet this immense army, laying siege to Cochin, was defeated. Seven times the zamorim raised new armies; yet they were all vanquished at the fords of Cochin, by the intrepidity and stratagems of Pacheco. In the later battles the zamorim exposed himself to the greatest danger, and was sometimes sprinkled with the blood of his slain attendants—a circumstance mentioned in the Lusiad, bk. x. p. 304. He then had recourse to fraud and poison; but all his attempts were baffled. At last, in despair, he resigned his throne, and shut himself up for the rest of his days in one of the temples.

Soon after the kingdom of Cochin was restored to prosperity Pacheco was recalled. The King of Portugal paid the highest compliments to his valour, and gave him the government of a possession of the crown in Africa. But merit always has enemies: Pacheco was accused and brought to Lisbon in irons, where he remained for a considerable time chained in a dungeon. He was at length tried, and after a full investigation of the charges made against him, was honourably acquitted. His services to his country were soon forgotten, his merits were no longer thought of, and the unfortunate Pacheco ended his days in an alms-house—a circumstance referred to in the Lusiad, bk. x. p. 305.

CONTENTS.

She pauses to reflect on the ill-requited bravery of Pacheco

The siren resumes her prophetic song

Foretells the needless cruelty of Albuquerque, who puts to death a soldier for a venial offence

Soarez, Sequeyra, Menez, Mascarene, Nunio, Noronha, Souza, and other heroes

The nymph Tethys leads them to the summit of a rugged hill, where the globe in miniature is displayed before them

The Ptolemean system described

Sketch of the geography of the world

History of St. Thomas, the Apostle of India

Geographical description continued

Tethys bids the Portuguese farewell

Their return home and reception at Lisbon

The poet's conclusion, and patriotic exhortation to his sovereign

Dissertation on The Fiction of The Island of Venus.

Footnotes.

THE LUSIADS

BOOK I.

ARGUMENT.[62]

Statement of the subject. Invocation to the muses of the Tagus. Herald calls an assembly of the gods. Jupiter foretells the future conquests of the Portuguese. Bacchus, apprehensive that the Portuguese may eclipse the glory acquired by himself in the conquest of India, declares against them. Venus, who sees in the Portuguese her ancient Romans, promises to aid their enterprise. Mars induces Jupiter to support them, and Mercury is sent to direct their course. Gama, commander of the expedition, lands at Mozambique and Mombas. Opposition of the Moors, instigated by Bacchus. They grant Gama a pilot who designs treacherously to take them to Quiloa to ensure the destruction of the whole expedition.

ARMS and the Heroes, who from Lisbon's shore,

Thro' seas[63] where sail was never spread before,

Beyond where Ceylon lifts her spicy breast,

And waves her woods above the wat'ry waste,

With prowess more than human forc'd their way

To the fair kingdoms of the rising day:

What wars they wag'd, what seas, what dangers pass'd,

What glorious empire crown'd their toils at last,

Vent'rous I sing, on soaring pinions borne,

And all my country's wars[64] the song adorn;

What kings, what heroes of my native land

Thunder'd on Asia's and on Afric's strand:

Illustrious shades, who levell'd in the dust

The idol-temples and the shrines of lust:

And where, erewhile, foul demons were rever'd,

To Holy Faith unnumber'd altars rear'd:[65]

Illustrious names, with deathless laurels crown'd,

While time rolls on in every clime renown'd!

Let Fame with wonder name the Greek[66] no more,

What lands he saw, what toils at sea he bore;

Nor more the Trojan's wand'ring[67] voyage boast,

What storms he brav'd on many a perilous coast:

No more let Rome exult in Trajan's name,

Nor Eastern conquests Ammon's[68] pride proclaim;

A nobler hero's deeds demand my lays

Than e'er adorn'd the song of ancient days,

Illustrious Gama,[69] whom the waves obey'd,

And whose dread sword the fate of empire sway'd.

And you, fair nymphs of Tagus, parent stream,

If e'er your meadows were my pastoral theme,

While you have listen'd, and by moonshine seen

My footsteps wander o'er your banks of green,

O come auspicious, and the song inspire

With all the boldness of your hero's fire:

Deep and majestic let the numbers flow,

And, rapt to heaven, with ardent fury glow,

Unlike the verse that speaks the lover's grief,

When heaving sighs afford their soft relief,

And humble reeds bewail the shepherd's pain;

But like the warlike trumpet be the strain

To rouse the hero's ire, and far around,

With equal rage, your warriors' deeds resound.

And thou,[70] O born the pledge of happier days,

To guard our freedom and our glories raise,

Given to the world to spread Religion's sway,

And pour o'er many a land the mental day,

Thy future honours on thy shield behold,

The cross and victor's wreath emboss'd in gold:

At thy commanding frown we trust to see,

The Turk and Arab bend the suppliant knee:

Beneath the morn,[71] dread king, thine empire lies,

When midnight veils thy Lusitanian[72] skies;

And when, descending in the western main,

The sun[73] still rises on thy length'ning reign:

Thou blooming scion of the noblest stem,

Our nation's safety, and our age's gem,

O young Sebastian, hasten to the prime

Of manly youth, to Fame's high temple climb:

Yet now attentive hear the Muse's lay

While thy green years to manhood speed away:

The youthful terrors of thy brow suspend,

And, oh, propitious to the song attend—

The num'rous song, by patriot-passion fir'd,

And by the glories of thy race inspir'd:

To be the herald of my country's fame

My first ambition and my dearest aim:

Nor conquests fabulous nor actions vain,

The Muse's pastime, here adorn the strain:

Orlando's fury, and Rugero's rage,

And all the heroes of th' Aonian page,[74]

The dreams of bards surpass'd the world shall view,

And own their boldest fictions may be true;

Surpass'd and dimm'd by the superior blaze

Of Gama's mighty deeds, which here bright Truth displays.

Nor more let History boast her heroes old,

Their glorious rivals here, dread prince, behold:

Here shine the valiant Nunio's deeds unfeign'd,

Whose single arm the falling state sustain'd;

Here fearless Egas' wars, and, Fuas, thine,

To give full ardour to the song combine;

But ardour equal to your martial ire

Demands the thund'ring sounds of Homer's lyre.

To match the Twelve so long by bards renown'd,[75]

Here brave Magricio and his peers are crown'd

(A glorious Twelve!) with deathless laurels, won

In gallant arms before the English throne.

Unmatch'd no more the Gallic Charles shall stand,

Nor Cæsar's name the first of praise command:

Of nobler acts the crown'd Alonzo[76] see,

Thy valiant sires, to whom the bended knee

Of vanquish'd Afric bow'd. Nor less in fame,

He who confin'd the rage of civil flame,

The godlike John, beneath whose awful sword

Rebellion crouch'd, and trembling own'd him lord

Those heroes, too, who thy bold flag unfurl'd,

And spread thy banners o'er the Eastern world,

Whose spears subdu'd the kingdoms of the morn,

Their names and glorious wars the song adorn:

The daring Gama, whose unequall'd name

(Proud monarch) shines o'er all of naval fame:

Castro the bold, in arms a peerless knight,
And stern Pacheco, dreadful in the fight:
The two Almeydas, names for ever dear,
By Tago's nymphs embalm'd with many a tear;
Ah, still their early fate the nymphs shall mourn,
And bathe with many a tear their hapless urn:
Nor shall the godlike Albuquerque restrain
The Muse's fury; o'er the purpled plain
The Muse shall lead him in his thund'ring car
Amidst his glorious brothers of the war,
Whose fame in arms resounds from sky to sky,
And bids their deeds the power of death defy.
And while, to thee, I tune the duteous lay,
Assume, O potent king, thine empire's sway;
With thy brave host through Afric march along,
And give new triumphs to immortal song:
On thee with earnest eyes the nations wait,
And, cold with dread, the Moor expects his fate;
The barb'rous mountaineer on Taurus' brows
To thy expected yoke his shoulder bows;
Fair Thetis woos thee with her blue domain,
Her nuptial son, and fondly yields her reign,
And from the bow'rs of heav'n thy grandsires[77] see
Their various virtues bloom afresh in thee;
One for the joyful days of peace renown'd,
And one with war's triumphant laurels crown'd:
With joyful hands, to deck thy manly brow,
They twine the laurel and the olive-bough;
With joyful eyes a glorious throne they see,

In Fame's eternal dome, reserv'd for thee.
Yet, while thy youthful hand delays to wield
The sceptre'd power, or thunder of the field,
Here view thine Argonauts, in seas unknown,
And all the terrors of the burning zone,
Till their proud standards, rear'd in other skies,
And all their conquests meet thy wond'ring[78] eyes.

Now, far from land, o'er Neptune's dread abode
The Lusitanian fleet triumphant rode;
Onward they traced the wide and lonesome main,
Where changeful Proteus leads his scaly train;
The dancing vanes before the zephyrs flow'd,
And their bold keels the trackless ocean plough'd;
Unplough'd before, the green-ting'd billows rose,
And curl'd and whiten'd round the nodding prows.
When Jove, the god who with a thought controls
The raging seas, and balances the poles,
From heav'n beheld, and will'd, in sov'reign state,
To fix the Eastern World's depending fate,
Swift at his nod th' Olympian herald flies,
And calls th' immortal senate of the skies;
Where, from the sov'reign throne of earth and heav'n,
Th' immutable decrees of fate are given.
Instant the regents of the spheres of light,
And those who rule the paler orbs of night,
With those, the gods whose delegated sway
The burning South and frozen North obey;
And they whose empires see the day-star rise,

And evening Phœbus leave the western skies,
All instant pour'd along the milky road,
Heaven's crystal pavements glitt'ring as they trod:
And now, obedient to the dread command,
Before their awful lord in order stand.

Sublime and dreadful on his regal throne,
That glow'd with stars, and bright as lightning shone,
Th' immortal Sire, who darts the thunder, sat,
The crown and sceptre added solemn state;
The crown, of heaven's own pearls, whose ardent rays,
Flam'd round his brows, outshone the diamond's blaze:
His breath such gales of vital fragrance shed,
As might, with sudden life, inspire the dead:
Supreme Control thron'd in his awful eyes
Appear'd, and mark'd the monarch of the skies.
On seats that burn'd with pearl and ruddy gold,
The subject gods their sov'reign lord enfold,
Each in his rank, when with a voice that shook
The tow'rs of heav'n, the world's dread ruler spoke:

"Immortal heirs of light, my purpose hear,
My counsels ponder, and the Fates revere:
Unless Oblivion o'er your minds has thrown
Her dark blank shades, to you, ye gods, are known
The Fate's decree, and ancient warlike fame
Of that bold race which boasts of Lusus' name;
That bold advent'rous race, the Fates declare,
A potent empire in the East shall rear,

Surpassing Babel's or the Persian fame,

Proud Grecia's boast, or Rome's illustrious name.

Oft from these brilliant seats have you beheld

The sons of Lusus on the dusty field,

Though few, triumphant o'er the num'rous Moors,

Till, from the beauteous lawns on Tagus' shores

They drove the cruel foe. And oft has heav'n

Before their troops the proud Castilians driv'n;

While Victory her eagle-wings display'd

Where'er their warriors wav'd the shining blade,

Nor rests unknown how Lusus' heroes stood

When Rome's ambition dyed the world with blood;

What glorious laurels Viriatus[79] gain'd,

How oft his sword with Roman gore was stain'd;

And what fair palms their martial ardour crown'd,

When led to battle by the chief renown'd,

Who[80] feign'd a dæmon, in a deer conceal'd,

To him the counsels of the gods reveal'd.

And now, ambitious to extend their sway

Beyond their conquests on the southmost bay

Of Afric's swarthy coast, on floating wood

They brave the terrors of the dreary flood,

Where only black-wing'd mists have hover'd o'er,

Or driving clouds have sail'd the wave before;

Beneath new skies they hold their dreadful way

To reach the cradle of the new-born day:

And Fate, whose mandates unrevok'd remain,

Has will'd that long shall Lusus' offspring reign

The lords of that wide sea, whose waves behold

The sun come forth enthron'd in burning gold.
But now, the tedious length of winter past,
Distress'd and weak, the heroes faint at last.
What gulfs they dar'd, you saw, what storms they brav'd,
Beneath what various heav'ns their banners wav'd!
Now Mercy pleads, and soon the rising land
To their glad eyes shall o'er the waves expand;
As welcome friends the natives shall receive,
With bounty feast them, and with joy relieve.
And, when refreshment shall their strength renew,
Thence shall they turn, and their bold route pursue."

So spoke high Jove: the gods in silence heard,
Then rising, each by turns his thoughts preferr'd:
But chief was Bacchus of the adverse train;
Fearful he was, nor fear'd his pride in vain,
Should Lusus' race arrive on India's shore,
His ancient honours would be known no more;
No more in Nysa[81] should the native tell
What kings, what mighty hosts before him fell.
The fertile vales beneath the rising sun
He view'd as his, by right of victory won,
And deem'd that ever in immortal song
The Conqueror's title should to him belong.
Yet Fate, he knew, had will'd, that loos'd from Spain
Boldly advent'rous thro' the polar main,
A warlike race should come, renown'd in arms,
And shake the eastern world with war's alarms,
Whose glorious conquests and eternal fame

In black Oblivion's waves should whelm his name.

Urania-Venus,[82] queen of sacred love,

Arose and fixed her asking eyes on Jove;

Her eyes, well pleas'd, in Lusus' sons could trace

A kindred likeness to the Roman race,

For whom of old such kind regard she bore;[83]

The same their triumphs on Barbaria's shore,

The same the ardour of their warlike flame,

The manly music of their tongue the same:[84]

Affection thus the lovely goddess sway'd,

Nor less what Fate's unblotted page display'd,

Where'er this people should their empire raise,

She knew her altars would unnumber'd blaze,

And barb'rous nations at her holy shrine

Be humaniz'd and taught her lore divine.

Her spreading honours thus the one inspir'd,

And one the dread to lose his worship fir'd.

Their struggling factions shook th' Olympian state

With all the clam'rous tempest of debate.

Thus, when the storm with sudden gust invades

The ancient forest's deep and lofty shades,

The bursting whirlwinds tear their rapid course,

The shatter'd oaks crash, and with echoes hoarse

The mountains groan, while whirling on the blast

The thick'ning leaves a gloomy darkness cast;

Such was the tumult in the blest abodes,

When Mars, high tow'ring o'er the rival gods,

Stepp'd forth: stern sparkles from his eye-balls glanc'd,

And now, before the throne of Jove advanc'd,

O'er his left shoulder his broad shield he throws,

And lifts his helm[85] above his dreadful brows:

Bold and enrag'd he stands, and, frowning round,

Strikes his tall spear-staff on the sounding ground;

Heav'n trembled, and the light turn'd pale[86]—such dread

His fierce demeanour o'er Olympus spread—

When thus the warrior: "O Eternal Sire,

Thine is the sceptre, thine the thunder's fire,

Supreme dominion thine; then, Father, hear,

Shall that bold race which once to thee was dear,

Who, now fulfilling thy decrees of old,

Through these wild waves their fearless journey hold,

Shall that bold race no more thy care engage,

But sink the victims of unhallow'd rage!

Did Bacchus yield to Reason's voice divine,

Bacchus the cause of Lusus' sons would join,

Lusus, the lov'd companion of his cares,

His earthly toils, his dangers, and his wars:

But envy still a foe to worth will prove,

To worth, though guarded by the arm of Jove.

"Then thou, dread Lord of Fate, unmov'd remain,

Nor let weak change thine awful counsels stain,

For Lusus' race thy promis'd favour show;

Swift as the arrow from Apollo's bow

Let Maia's[87] son explore the wat'ry way,

Where, spent with toil, with weary hopes, they stray;

And safe to harbour, through the deep untried,

Let him, empower'd, their wand'ring vessels guide;

There let them hear of India's wish'd-for shore,

And balmy rest their fainting strength restore."

He spoke: high Jove assenting bow'd the head,

And floating clouds of nectar'd fragrance shed:

Then, lowly bending to th' Eternal Sire,

Each in his duteous rank, the gods retire.

Whilst thus in heaven's bright palace fate was weigh'd

Right onward still the brave Armada strayed:

Right on they steer by Ethiopia's strand

And pastoral Madagascar's[88] verdant land.

Before the balmy gales of cheerful spring,

With heav'n their friend, they spread the canvas wing,

The sky cerulean, and the breathing air,

The lasting promise of a calm declare.

Behind them now the Cape of Praso[89] bends,

Another ocean to their view extends,

Where black-topp'd islands, to their longing eyes,

Lav'd by the gentle waves,[90] in prospect rise.

But Gama (captain of the vent'rous band,

Of bold emprize, and born for high command,

Whose martial fires, with prudence close allied,

Ensur'd the smiles of fortune on his side)

Bears off those shores which waste and wild appear'd,

And eastward still for happier climates steer'd:

When gath'ring round, and black'ning o'er the tide,

A fleet of small canoes the pilot spied;

Hoisting their sails of palm-tree leaves, inwove
With curious art, a swarming crowd they move:
Long were their boats, and sharp to bound along
Through the dash'd waters, broad their oars and strong:
The bending rowers on their features bore
The swarthy marks of Phaeton's[91] fall of yore:
When flaming lightnings scorch'd the banks of Po,
And nations blacken'd in the dread o'erthrow.
Their garb, discover'd as approaching nigh,
Was cotton strip'd with many a gaudy dye:
'Twas one whole piece beneath one arm confin'd,
The rest hung loose and flutter'd on the wind;
All, but one breast, above the loins was bare,
And swelling turbans bound their jetty hair:
Their arms were bearded darts and faulchions broad,
And warlike music sounded as they row'd.
With joy the sailors saw the boats draw near,
With joy beheld the human face appear:
What nations these, their wond'ring thoughts explore,
What rites they follow, and what God adore!
And now with hands and 'kerchiefs wav'd in air
The barb'rous race their friendly mind declare.
Glad were the crew, and ween'd that happy day
Should end their dangers and their toils repay.
The lofty masts the nimble youths ascend,
The ropes they haul, and o'er the yard-arms bend;
And now their bowsprits pointing to the shore,
(A safe moon'd bay), with slacken'd sails they bore:
With cheerful shouts they furl the gather'd sail

That less and less flaps quiv'ring on the gale;

The prows, their speed stopp'd, o'er the surges nod,

The falling anchors dash the foaming flood;

When, sudden as they stopp'd, the swarthy race,

With smiles of friendly welcome on each face,

The ship's high sides swift by the cordage climb:

Illustrious Gama, with an air sublime,

Soften'd by mild humanity, receives,

And to their chief the hand of friendship gives,

Bids spread the board, and, instant as he said,

Along the deck the festive board is spread:

The sparkling wine in crystal goblets glows,

And round and round with cheerful welcome flows.

While thus the vine its sprightly glee inspires,

From whence the fleet, the swarthy chief enquires,

What seas they past, what 'vantage would attain,

And what the shore their purpose hop'd to gain?

"From farthest west," the Lusian race reply,

"To reach the golden Eastern shores we try.

Through that unbounded sea whose billows roll

From the cold northern to the southern pole;

And by the wide extent, the dreary vast

Of Afric's bays, already have we past;

And many a sky have seen, and many a shore,

Where but sea monsters cut the waves before.

To spread the glories of our monarch's reign,

For India's shore we brave the trackless main,

Our glorious toil, and at his nod would brave

The dismal gulfs of Acheron's[92] black wave.

And now, in turn, your race, your country tell,
If on your lips fair truth delights to dwell
To us, unconscious of the falsehood, show
What of these seas and India's site you know."

"Rude are the natives here," the Moor replied;
"Dark are their minds, and brute-desire their guide:
But we, of alien blood, and strangers here,
Nor hold their customs nor their laws revere.
From Abram's race our holy prophet sprung,[93]
An angel taught, and heaven inspir'd his tongue;
His sacred rites and mandates we obey,
And distant empires own his holy sway.
From isle to isle our trading vessels roam,
Mozambique's harbour our commodious home.
If then your sails for India's shore expand,
For sultry Ganges or Hydaspes'[94] strand,
Here shall you find a pilot skill'd to guide
Through all the dangers of the perilous tide,
Though wide-spread shelves, and cruel rocks unseen,
Lurk in the way, and whirlpools rage between.
Accept, meanwhile, what fruits these islands hold,
And to the regent let your wish be told.
Then may your mates the needful stores provide,
And all your various wants be here supplied."

So spake the Moor, and bearing smiles untrue
And signs of friendship, with his bands withdrew.
O'erpower'd with joy unhop'd the sailors stood,

To find such kindness on a shore so rude.

Now shooting o'er the flood his fervid blaze,

The red-brow'd sun withdraws his beamy rays;

Safe in the bay the crew forget their cares,

And peaceful rest their wearied strength repairs.

Calm twilight now[95] his drowsy mantle spreads,

And shade on shade, the gloom still deep'ning, sheds.

The moon, full orb'd, forsakes her wat'ry cave,

And lifts her lovely head above the wave.

The snowy splendours of her modest ray

Stream o'er the glist'ning waves, and quiv'ring play:

Around her, glitt'ring on the heaven's arch'd brow,

Unnumber'd stars, enclos'd in azure, glow,

Thick as the dew-drops of the April dawn,

Or May-flowers crowding o'er the daisy-lawn:

The canvas whitens in the silvery beam,

And with a mild pale red the pendants gleam:

The masts' tall shadows tremble o'er the deep;

The peaceful winds a holy silence keep;

The watchman's carol, echo'd from the prows,

Alone, at times, awakes the still repose.

Aurora now, with dewy lustre bright,

Appears, ascending on the rear of night.

With gentle hand, as seeming oft to pause,

The purple curtains of the morn she draws;

The sun comes forth, and soon the joyful crew,

Each aiding each, their joyful tasks pursue.

84

Wide o'er the decks the spreading sails they throw;

From each tall mast the waving streamers flow;

All seems a festive holiday on board

To welcome to the fleet the island's lord.

With equal joy the regent sails to meet,

And brings fresh cates, his off'rings, to the fleet:

For of his kindred race their line he deems,

That savage race[96] who rush'd from Caspia's streams,

And triumph'd o'er the East, and, Asia won,

In proud Byzantium[97] fix'd their haughty throne.

Brave Vasco hails the chief with honest smiles,

And gift for gift with liberal hand he piles.

His gifts, the boast of Europe's heart disclose,

And sparkling red the wine of Tagus flows.

High on the shrouds the wond'ring sailors hung,

To note the Moorish garb, and barb'rous tongue:

Nor less the subtle Moor, with wonder fir'd,

Their mien, their dress, and lordly ships admir'd:

Much he enquires their king's, their country's name,

And, if from Turkey's fertile shores they came?

What God they worshipp'd, what their sacred lore,

What arms they wielded, and what armour wore?

To whom brave Gama: "Nor of Hagar's blood

Am I, nor plough from Ismael's shores the flood;

From Europe's strand I trace the foamy way,

To find the regions of the infant day.

The God we worship stretch'd yon heaven's high bow,

And gave these swelling waves to roll below;

The hemispheres of night and day He spread,

He scoop'd each vale, and rear'd each mountain's head;

His Word produc'd the nations of the earth,

And gave the spirits of the sky their birth;

On earth, by Him, his holy lore was given,

On earth He came to raise mankind to heaven.

And now behold, what most your eyes desire,

Our shining armour, and our arms of fire;

For who has once in friendly peace beheld,

Will dread to meet them on the battle field."

Straight as he spoke[98] the warlike stores display'd

Their glorious show, where, tire on tire inlaid,

Appear'd of glitt'ring steel the carabines,

There the plum'd helms,[99] and pond'rous brigandines;[100]

O'er the broad bucklers sculptur'd orbs emboss'd

The crooked faulchions, dreadful blades were cross'd:

Here clasping greaves, and plated mail-quilts strong;

The long-bows here, and rattling quivers hung,

And like a grove the burnish'd spears were seen,

With darts and halberts double-edged between;

Here dread grenadoes and tremendous bombs,

With deaths ten thousand lurking in their wombs,

And far around, of brown and dusky red,

The pointed piles of iron balls were spread.

The bombardiers, now to the regent's view

The thund'ring mortars and the cannon drew;

Yet, at their leader's nod, the sons of flame

(For brave and gen'rous ever are the same)

Withheld their hands, nor gave the seeds of fire

To rouse the thunders of the dreadful tire.
For Gama's soul disdain'd the pride of show
Which acts the lion o'er the trembling roe.

His joy and wonder oft the Moor express'd,
But rankling hate lay brooding in his breast;
With smiles obedient to his will's control,
He veils the purpose of his treach'rous soul:
For pilots, conscious of the Indian strand,
Brave Vasco sues, and bids the Moor command
What bounteous gifts shall recompense their toils;
The Moor prevents him with assenting smiles,
Resolved that deeds of death, not words of air,
Shall first the hatred of his soul declare;
Such sudden rage his rankling mind possess'd,
When Gama's lips Messiah's name confess'd.[101]
Oh depth of Heaven's dread will, that ranc'rous hate
On Heaven's best lov'd in ev'ry clime should wait!
Now, smiling round on all the wond'ring crew
The Moor, attended by his bands, withdrew;
His nimble barges soon approach'd the land,
And shouts of joy receiv'd him on the strand.

From heaven's high dome the vintage-god[102] beheld
(Whom nine long months his father's thigh conceal'd);[103]
Well pleas'd he mark'd the Moor's determin'd hate
And thus his mind revolv'd in self-debate:—

"Has Heaven, indeed, such glorious lot ordain'd,

By Lusus' race such conquests to be gain'd

O'er warlike nations, and on India's shore,

Where I, unrivall'd, claim'd the palm before?

I, sprung from Jove! And shall these wand'ring few,

What Ammon's son[104] unconquer'd left, subdue

Ammon's brave son who led the god of war

His slave auxiliar at his thund'ring car?

Must these possess what Jove to him denied,

Possess what never sooth'd the Roman pride?

Must these the victor's lordly flag display

With hateful blaze beneath the rising day,

My name dishonour'd, and my victories stain'd,

O'erturn'd my altars, and my shrines profan'd?

No; be it mine to fan the Regent's hate;

Occasion seiz'd commands the action's fate.

'Tis mine—this captain, now my dread no more,

Shall never shake his spear on India's shore."

So spake the Power,[105] and with the lightning's flight

For Afric darted thro' the fields of light.

His form divine he cloth'd in human shape,[106]

And rush'd impetuous o'er the rocky cape:

In the dark semblance of a Moor he came

For art and old experience known to fame:

Him all his peers with humble deference heard,

And all Mozambique and its prince rever'd:

The prince in haste he sought, and thus express'd

His guileful hate in friendly counsel dress'd:

"And to the regent of this isle alone
Are these adventurers and their fraud unknown?
Has Fame conceal'd their rapine from his ear?
Nor brought the groans of plunder'd nations here?
Yet still their hands the peaceful olive bore
Whene'er they anchor'd on a foreign shore:
But nor their seeming nor their oaths I trust,
For Afric knows them bloody and unjust.
The nations sink beneath their lawless force,
And fire and blood have mark'd their deadly course.
We too, unless kind Heav'n and thou prevent,
Must fall the victims of their dire intent,
And, gasping in the pangs of death, behold
Our wives led captive, and our daughters sold.
By stealth they come, ere morrow dawn, to bring
The healthful bev'rage from the living spring:
Arm'd with his troops the captain will appear;
For conscious fraud is ever prone to fear.
To meet them there select a trusty band,
And, in close ambush, take thy silent stand;
There wait, and sudden on the heedless foe
Rush, and destroy them ere they dread the blow.
Or say, should some escape the secret snare,
Saved by their fate, their valour, or their care,
Yet their dread fall shall celebrate our isle,
If Fate consent, and thou approve the guile.
Give then a pilot to their wand'ring fleet,
Bold in his art, and tutor'd in deceit;
Whose hand advent'rous shall their helms misguide,

To hostile shores, or whelm them in the tide."

So spoke the god, in semblance of a sage
Renown'd for counsel and the craft of age.
The prince with transport glowing in his face
Approv'd, and caught him in a kind embrace:
And instant at the word his bands prepare
Their bearded darts and implements of war,
That Lusus' sons might purple with their gore
The crystal fountain which they sought on shore:
And, still regardful of his dire intent,
A skilful pilot to the bay he sent,
Of honest mien, yet practised in deceit,
Who far at distance on the beach should wait,
And to the 'scaped, if some should 'scape the snare
Should offer friendship and the pilot's care,
But when at sea, on rocks should dash their pride,
And whelm their lofty vanes beneath the tide.

Apollo[107] now had left his wat'ry bed,
And o'er the mountains of Arabia spread
His rays that glow'd with gold; when Gama rose,
And from his bands a trusty squadron chose:
Three speedy barges brought their casks to fill
From gurgling fountain, or the crystal rill:
Full arm'd they came, for brave defence prepar'd,
For martial care is ever on the guard:
And secret warnings ever are imprest
On wisdom such as wak'd in Gama's breast.

And now, as swiftly springing o'er the tide

Advanc'd the boats, a troop of Moors they spied;

O'er the pale sands the sable warriors crowd,

And toss their threat'ning darts, and shout aloud.

Yet seeming artless, though they dar'd the fight,

Their eager hope they plac'd in artful flight,

To lead brave Gama where, unseen by day,

In dark-brow'd shades their silent ambush lay.

With scornful gestures o'er the beach they stride,

And push their levell'd spears with barb'rous pride,

Then fix the arrow to the bended bow,

And strike their sounding shields, and dare the foe.

With gen'rous rage the Lusian race beheld,

And each brave breast with indignation swell'd,

To view such foes, like snarling dogs, display

Their threat'ning tusks, and brave the sanguine fray:

Together with a bound they spring to land,

Unknown whose step first trod the hostile strand.

Thus, when to gain his beauteous charmer's smile,

The youthful lover dares the bloody toil,[108]

Before the nodding bull's stern front he stands,

He leaps, he wheels, he shouts, and waves his hands:

The lordly brute disdains the stripling's rage,

His nostrils smoke, and, eager to engage,

His hornèd brows he levels with the ground,

And shuts his flaming eyes, and wheeling round

With dreadful bellowing rushes on the foe,

And lays the boastful gaudy champion low.

Thus to the sight the sons of Lusus sprung,

Nor slow to fall their ample vengeance hung:

With sudden roar the carabines resound,

And bursting echoes from the hills rebound;

The lead flies hissing through the trembling air,

And death's fell dæmons through the flashes glare.

Where, up the land, a grove of palms enclose,

And cast their shadows where the fountain flows,

The lurking ambush from their treach'rous stand

Beheld the combat burning on the strand:

They see the flash with sudden lightnings flare,

And the blue smoke slow rolling on the air:

They see their warriors drop, and starting hear

The ling'ring thunders bursting on their ear.

Amaz'd, appall'd, the treach'rous ambush fled,

And rag'd,[109] and curs'd their birth, and quak'd with dread.

The bands that vaunting show'd their threaten'd might,

With slaughter gor'd, precipitate in flight;

Yet oft, though trembling, on the foe they turn

Their eyes that red with lust of vengeance burn:

Aghast with fear, and stern with desperate rage

The flying war with dreadful howls they wage,

Flints, clods, and javelins hurling as they fly,

As rage[110] and wild despair their hands supply:

And, soon dispers'd, their bands attempt no more

To guard the fountain or defend the shore:

O'er the wide lawns no more their troops appear:

Nor sleeps the vengeance of the victor here;

To teach the nations what tremendous fate
From his right arm on perjur'd vows should wait,
He seized the time to awe the Eastern world,
And on the breach of faith his thunders hurl'd.
From his black ships the sudden lightnings blaze,
And o'er old Ocean flash their dreadful rays:
White clouds on clouds inroll'd the smoke ascends,
The bursting tumult heaven's wide concave rends:
The bays and caverns of the winding shore
Repeat the cannon's and the mortar's roar:
The bombs, far-flaming, hiss along the sky,
And, whirring through the air, the bullets fly;
The wounded air, with hollow deafen'd sound,
Groans to the direful strife, and trembles round.

Now from the Moorish town the sheets of fire,
Wide blaze succeeding blaze, to heaven aspire.
Black rise the clouds of smoke, and by the gales
Borne down, in streams hang hov'ring o'er the vales;
And slowly floating round the mountain's head
Their pitchy mantle o'er the landscape spread.
Unnumber'd sea-fowl rising from the shore,
Beat round in whirls at every cannon's roar;
Where o'er the smoke the masts' tall heads appear,
Hov'ring they scream, then dart with sudden fear;
On trembling wings far round and round they fly,
And fill with dismal clang their native sky.
Thus fled in rout confus'd the treach'rous Moors
From field to field,[111] then, hast'ning to the shores,

Some trust in boats their wealth and lives to save,
And, wild with dread, they plunge into the wave;
Some spread their arms to swim, and some beneath
The whelming billows, struggling, pant for breath,
Then whirl'd aloft their nostrils spout the brine;
While show'ring still from many a carabine
The leaden hail their sails and vessels tore,
Till, struggling hard, they reach'd the neighb'ring shore:
Due vengeance thus their perfidy repaid,
And Gama's terrors to the East display'd.

Imbrown'd with dust a beaten pathway shows
Where 'midst umbrageous palms the fountain flows;
From thence, at will, they bear the liquid health;
And now, sole masters of the island's wealth,
With costly spoils and eastern robes adorn'd,
The joyful victors to the fleet return'd.

With hell's keen fires still for revenge athirst
The regent burns, and weens, by fraud accurst,
To strike a surer yet a secret blow,
And in one general death to whelm the foe.
The promis'd pilot to the fleet he sends
And deep repentance for his crime pretends.
Sincere the herald seems, and while he speaks,
The winning tears steal down his hoary cheeks.
Brave Gama, touch'd with gen'rous woe, believes,
And from his hand the pilot's hand receives:
A dreadful gift! instructed to decoy,

In gulfs to whelm them, or on rocks destroy.

The valiant chief, impatient of delay,
For India now resumes the wat'ry way;
Bids weigh the anchor and unfurl the sail,
Spread full the canvas to the rising gale.
He spoke: and proudly o'er the foaming tide,
Borne on the wind, the full-wing'd vessels ride;
While as they rode before the bounding prows
The lovely forms of sea-born nymphs arose.
The while brave Vasco's unsuspecting mind
Yet fear'd not ought the crafty Moor design'd:
Much of the coast he asks, and much demands
Of Afric's shores and India's spicy lands.
The crafty Moor by vengeful Bacchus taught
Employ'd on deadly guile his baneful thought;
In his dark mind he plann'd, on Gama's head
Full to revenge Mozambique and the dead.
Yet all the chief demanded he reveal'd,
Nor aught of truth, that truth he knew, conceal'
For thus he ween'd to gain his easy faith,
And gain'd, betray to slavery or death.
And now, securely trusting to destroy,
As erst false Sinon[112] snar'd the sons of Troy,
"Behold, disclosing from the sky," he cries,
"Far to the north, yon cloud-like isle arise:
From ancient times the natives of the shore
The blood-stain'd image on the cross adore."
Swift at the word, the joyful Gama cried:

"For that fair island turn the helm aside;

O bring my vessels where the Christians dwell,

And thy glad lips my gratitude shall tell."

With sullen joy the treach'rous Moor complied,

And for that island turn'd the helm aside.

For well Quiloa's[113] swarthy race he knew,

Their laws and faith to Hagar's offspring true;

Their strength in war, through all the nations round,

Above Mozambique and her powers renown'd;

He knew what hate the Christian name they bore,

And hop'd that hate on Vasco's bands to pour.

Right to the land the faithless pilot steers,

Right to the land the glad Armada bears;

But heavenly Love's fair queen,[114] whose watchful care

Had ever been their guide, beheld the snare.

A sudden storm she rais'd: loud howl'd the blast,

The yard-arms rattled, and each groaning mast

Bended beneath the weight. Deep sunk the prows,

And creaking ropes the creaking ropes oppose;

In vain the pilot would the speed restrain,

The captain shouts, the sailors toil in vain;

Aslope and gliding on the leeward side,

The bounding vessels cut the roaring tide:

Soon far they pass'd; and now the slacken'd sail

Trembles and bellies to the gentle gale:

Now many a league before the tempest toss'd

The treach'rous pilot sees his purpose cross'd:

Yet vengeful still, and still intent on guile,

Behold, he cries, yon dim emerging isle:
There live the votaries of Messiah's lore
In faithful peace, and friendship with the Moor.
Yet all was false, for there Messiah's name,
Reviled and scorn'd, was only known by fame.
The grovelling natives there, a brutal herd,
The sensual lore of Hagar's son[115] preferr'd.
With joy brave Gama hears the artful tale,
Bears to the harbour, and bids furl the sail.
Yet, watchful still, fair Love's celestial queen
Prevents the danger with a hand unseen;
Now past the bar his vent'rous vessel guides,
And safe at anchor in the road he rides.

Between the isle and Ethiopia's land
A narrow current laves each adverse strand;
Close by the margin where the green tide flows,
Full to the bay a lordly city rose;
With fervid blaze the glowing evening pours
Its purple splendours o'er the lofty towers;
The lofty towers with milder lustre gleam,
And gently tremble in the glassy stream.
Here reign'd a hoary king of ancient fame;
Mombas the town, Mombas the island's name.

As when the pilgrim, who with weary pace
Thro' lonely wastes untrod by human race,
For many a day disconsolate has stray'd,
The turf his bed, the wild-wood boughs his shade,

97

O'erjoy'd beholds the cheerful seats of men
In grateful prospect rising on his ken:
So Gama joy'd, who many a dreary day
Had traced the vast, the lonesome, wat'ry way,
Had seen new stars, unknown to Europe, rise,
And brav'd the horrors of the polar skies:
So joy'd his bounding heart when, proudly rear'd,
The splendid city o'er the wave appear'd,
Where Heaven's own lore, he trusted, was obey'd,
And Holy Faith her sacred rites display'd.
And now, swift crowding through the hornèd bay,
The Moorish barges wing'd their foamy way,
To Gama's fleet with friendly smiles they bore
The choicest products of their cultur'd shore.
But there fell rancour veil'd its serpent-head,
Though festive roses o'er the gifts were spread.
For Bacchus, veil'd in human shape, was here,
And pour'd his counsel in the sov'reign's ear.

O piteous lot of man's uncertain state!
What woes on Life's unhappy journey wait!
When joyful Hope would grasp its fond desire,
The long-sought transports in the grasp expire.
By sea what treach'rous calms, what rushing storms,
And death attendant in a thousand forms!
By land what strife, what plots of secret guile,
How many a wound from many a treach'rous smile!
Oh where shall man escape his num'rous foes,
And rest his weary head in safe repose!

BOOK II.

THE ARGUMENT.

Arrival of the expedition at Mombas. Bacchus plots their destruction by new artifices. They are deceived into the belief that the natives are, like themselves, Christians: Bacchus assumes the character of a priest, and worships the god of the Christians. At the invitation of the king of Mombas, Gama enters the port, and reaches the place intended for his destruction. Venus, aided by the Nereids, effects their deliverance; and Gama sails away, fearing treachery. Venus hastens to Olympus to seek Jove's aid. Jupiter assures her of the future glory of the Portuguese, and commands Mercury to conduct the expedition to Melinda. The King of Melinda asks from Gama an historical account of his nation.

THE fervent lustre of the evening ray

Behind the western hills now died away,

And night, ascending from the dim-brow'd east,

The twilight gloom with deeper shades increas'd,

When Gama heard the creaking of the oar,

And mark'd the white waves length'ning from the shore.

In many a skiff the eager natives came,

Their semblance friendship, but deceit their aim.

And now by Gama's anchor'd ships they ride,

And "Hail, illustrious chief!" their leader cried,

"Your fame already these our regions own,

How your bold prows from worlds to us unknown

Have brav'd the horrors of the southern main,

Where storms and darkness hold their endless reign,

Whose whelmy waves our westward prows have barr'd

From oldest times, and ne'er before were dar'd

By boldest leader: earnest to behold

The wondrous hero of a toil so bold,

To you the sov'reign of these islands sends

The holy vows of peace, and hails you friends.

If friendship you accept, whate'er kind Heaven

In various bounty to these shores has given,

Whate'er your wants, your wants shall here supply,

And safe in port your gallant fleet shall lie;

Safe from the dangers of the faithless tide,

And sudden bursting storms, by you untried;

Yours every bounty of the fertile shore,

Till balmy rest your wearied strength restore.

Or, if your toils and ardent hopes demand

The various treasures of the Indian strand,

The fragrant cinnamon, the glowing clove,

And all the riches of the spicy grove;

Or drugs of power the fever's rage to bound,

And give soft languor to the smarting wound;

Or, if the splendour of the diamond's rays,

The sapphire's azure, or the ruby's blaze,

Invite your sails to search the Eastern world,

Here may these sails in happy hour be furl'd:

For here the splendid treasures of the mine,

And richest offspring of the field combine

To give each boon that human want requires,

And every gem that lofty pride desires;

Then here, a potent king your gen'rous friend,

Here let your perilous toils and wandering searches[116] end."

He said: brave Gama smiles with heart sincere,

And prays the herald to the king to bear
The thanks of grateful joy: "But now," he cries,
"The black'ning evening veils the coast and skies,
And thro' these rocks unknown forbids to steer;
Yet, when the streaks of milky dawn appear,
Edging the eastern wave with silver hoar,
My ready prows shall gladly point to shore;
Assur'd of friendship, and a kind retreat,
Assur'd and proffer'd by a king so great."
Yet, mindful still of what his hopes had cheer'd,
That here his nation's holy shrines were rear'd,
He asks, if certain, as the pilot told,
Messiah's lore had flourish'd there of old,
And flourish'd still. The herald mark'd with joy
The pious wish, and, watchful to decoy,
"Messiah here," he cries, "has altars more
Than all the various shrines of other lore."
O'erjoy'd, brave Vasco heard the pleasing tale,
Yet fear'd that fraud its viper-sting might veil
Beneath the glitter of a show so fair.
He half believes the tale, and arms against the snare.

With Gama sail'd a bold advent'rous band,[117]
Whose headlong rage had urg'd the guilty hand:
Stern Justice for their crimes had ask'd their blood,
And pale, in chains condemn'd to death, they stood;
But, sav'd by Gama from the shameful death,
The bread of peace had seal'd their plighted faith[117]
The desolate coast, when order'd, to explore,

And dare each danger of the hostile shore:

From this bold band he chose the subtlest two,

The port, the city, and its strength to view,

To mark if fraud its secret head betray'd,

Or if the rites of Heaven were there display'd.

With costly gifts, as of their truth secure,

The pledge that Gama deem'd their faith was pure.

These two, his heralds, to the king he sends:

The faithless Moors depart as smiling friends.

Now, thro' the wave they cut their foamy way,

Their cheerful songs resounding through the bay:

And now, on shore the wond'ring natives greet,

And fondly hail the strangers from the fleet.

The prince their gifts with friendly vows receives,

And joyful welcome to the Lusians gives;

Where'er they pass, the joyful tumult bends,

And through the town the glad applause attends.

But he whose cheeks with youth immortal shone,

The god whose wondrous birth two mothers[118] own,

Whose rage had still the wand'ring fleet annoy'd,

Now in the town his guileful rage employ'd.

A Christian priest he seem'd; a sumptuous[119] shrine

He rear'd, and tended with the rites divine:

O'er the fair altar wav'd the cross on high,

Upheld by angels leaning from the sky;

Descending o'er the Virgin's sacred head

So white, so pure, the Holy Spirit spread

The dove-like pictur'd wings, so pure, so white;

And, hov'ring o'er the chosen twelve, alight

The tongues of hallow'd fire. Amaz'd, oppress'd,

With sacred awe their troubled looks confess'd

The inspiring godhead, and the prophet's glow,

Which gave each language from their lips to flow

Where[120] thus the guileful Power his magic wrought

De Gama's heralds by the guides are brought:

On bended knees low to the earth they fall,

And to the Lord of heaven in transport call,

While the feign'd priest awakes the censer's fire,

And clouds of incense round the shrine aspire.

With cheerful welcome, here caress'd, they stay

Till bright Aurora, messenger of day,

Walk'd forth; and now the sun's resplendent rays,

Yet half emerging o'er the waters, blaze,

When to the fleet the Moorish oars again

Dash the curl'd waves, and waft the guileful train:

The lofty decks they mount. With joy elate,

Their friendly welcome at the palace-gate,

The king's sincerity, the people's care,

And treasures of the coast the spies declare:

Nor pass'd untold what most their joys inspir'd,

What most to hear the valiant chief desir'd,

That their glad eyes had seen the rites divine,

Their[121] country's worship, and the sacred shrine.

The pleasing tale the joyful Gama hears;

Dark fraud no more his gen'rous bosom fears:

As friends sincere, himself sincere, he gives

The hand of welcome, and the Moor's receives.

And now, as conscious of the destin'd prey,

The faithless race, with smiles and gestures gay,

Their skiffs forsaking, Gama's ships ascend,

And deep to strike the treach'rous blow attend.

On shore the truthless monarch arms his bands,

And for the fleet's approach impatient stands;

That, soon as anchor'd in the port they rode

Brave Gama's decks might reek with Lusian blood:

Thus weening to revenge Mozambique's fate,

And give full surfeit to the Moorish hate;

And now their bowsprits bending to the bay

The joyful crew the pond'rous anchors weigh,

Their shouts the while resounding. To the gale

With eager hands they spread the foremast sail.

But Love's fair queen[122] the secret fraud beheld:

Swift as an arrow o'er the battle-field,

From heav'n she darted to the wat'ry plain,

And call'd the sea-born nymphs, a lovely train,

From Nereus sprung; the ready nymphs obey,

Proud of her kindred birth,[123] and own her sway.

She tells what ruin threats her fav'rite race;

Unwonted ardour glows on every face;

With keen rapidity they bound away;

Dash'd by their silver limbs, the billows grey

Foam round: Fair Doto, fir'd with rage divine,

Darts through the wave; and onward o'er the brine

The lovely Nyse and Nerine[124] spring

With all the vehemence and speed of wing.

The curving billows to their breasts divide

And give a yielding passage through the tide.

With furious speed the goddess rush'd before,

Her beauteous form a joyful Triton bore,

Whose eager face with glowing rapture fir'd,

Betray'd the pride which such a task inspir'd.

And now arriv'd, where to the whistling wind

The warlike navy's bending masts reclin'd,

As through the billows rush'd the speedy prows,

The nymphs dividing, each her station chose.

Against the leader's prow, her lovely breast

With more than mortal force the goddess press'd;

The ship recoiling trembles on the tide,

The nymphs, in help, pour round on every side,

From the dread bar the threaten'd keels to save;

The ship bounds up, half lifted from the wave,

And, trembling, hovers o'er the wat'ry grave.

As when alarm'd, to save the hoarded grain,

The care-earn'd store for winter's dreary reign,

So toil, so tug, so pant, the lab'ring emmet train,[125]

So toil'd the nymphs, and strain'd their panting force

To turn[126] the navy from its fatal course:

Back, back the ship recedes; in vain the crew

With shouts on shouts their various toils renew;

In vain each nerve, each nautic art they strain,

And the rough wind distends the sail in vain:

Enraged, the sailors see their labours cross'd;

From side to side the reeling helm is toss'd:

High on the poop the skilful master stands;

Sudden he shrieks aloud, and spreads his hands.

A lurking rock its dreadful rifts betrays,

And right before the prow its ridge displays;

Loud shrieks of horror from the yard-arms rise,

And a dire general yell invades the skies.

The Moors start, fear-struck, at the horrid sound,

As if the rage of combat roar'd around.

Pale are their lips, each look in wild amaze

The horror of detected guilt betrays.

Pierc'd by the glance of Gama's awful eyes

The conscious pilot quits the helm and flies,

From the high deck he plunges in the brine;

His mates their safety to the waves consign;

Dash'd by their plunging falls on every side

Foams and boils up around the rolling tide.

Thus[127] the hoarse tenants of the sylvan lake,

A Lycian race of old, to flight betake,

At ev'ry sound they dread Latona's hate,

And doubled vengeance of their former fate;

All sudden plunging leave the margin green,

And but their heads above the pool are seen.

So plung'd the Moors, when, horrid to behold!

From the bar'd rock's dread jaws the billows roll'd,

Opening in instant fate the fleet to whelm,

When ready Vasco caught the stagg'ring helm:

Swift as his lofty voice resounds aloud,

The pond'rous anchors dash the whit'ning flood,

And round his vessel, nodding o'er the tide,

His other ships, bound by their anchors, ride.

And now revolving in his piercing thought

These various scenes with hidden import fraught:

The boastful pilot's self-accusing flight,
The former treason of the Moorish spite;
How headlong to the rock the furious wind,
The boiling current, and their art combin'd;
Yet, though the groaning blast the canvas swell'd,
Some wondrous cause, unknown, their speed withheld:
Amaz'd, with hands high rais'd, and sparkling eyes,
"A[128] miracle!" the raptur'd Gama cries,
"A miracle! O hail, thou sacred sign,
Thou pledge illustrious of the care divine!
Ah! fraudful malice! how shall wisdom's care
Escape the poison of thy gilded snare?
The front of honesty, the saintly show,
The smile of friendship, and the holy vow
All, all conjoin'd our easy faith to gain,
To whelm us, shipwreck'd, in the ruthless main;
But where our prudence no deceit could spy,
There, heavenly Guardian, there thy watchful eye
Beheld our danger: still, oh still prevent,
Where human foresight fails, the dire intent,
The lurking treason of the smiling foe;
And let our toils, our days of length'ning woe,
Our weary wand'rings end. If still for thee,
To spread thy rites, our toils and vows agree,
On India's strand thy sacred shrines to rear,
Oh let some friendly land of rest appear:
If for thine honour we these toils have dar'd,
These toils let India's long-sought shore reward."

So spoke the chief: the pious accents move

The gentle bosom of celestial Love:

The beauteous Queen[129] to heaven now darts away;

In vain the weeping nymphs implore her stay:

Behind her now the morning star she leaves,

And the[130] sixth heaven her lovely form receives.

Her radiant eyes such living splendours cast,

The sparkling stars were brighten'd as she pass'd;

The frozen pole with sudden streamlets flow'd,

And, as the burning zone, with fervour glow'd.

And now confess'd before the throne of Jove,

In all her charms appears the Queen of Love:

Flush'd by the ardour of her rapid flight

Through fields of æther and the realms of light,

Bright as the blushes of the roseate morn,

New blooming tints her glowing cheeks adorn;

And all that pride of beauteous grace she wore,

As[131] when in Ida's bower she stood of yore,

When every charm and every hope of joy

Enraptur'd and allur'd the Trojan boy.

Ah![132] had that hunter, whose unhappy fate

The human visage lost by Dian's hate,

Had he beheld this fairer goddess move

Not hounds had slain him, but the fires of love.

Adown her neck, more white than virgin snow,

Of softest hue the golden tresses flow;

Her heaving breasts of purer, softer white

Than snow hills glist'ning in the moon's pale light,

Except where cover'd by the sash, were bare,

And[133] Love, unseen, smil'd soft, and panted there:

Nor less the zone the god's fond zeal employs,

The zone awakes the flames of secret joys.

As ivy-tendrils round her limbs divine

Their spreading arms the young desires entwine:

Below her waist, and quiv'ring on the gale,

Of thinnest texture flows the silken veil:

(Ah! where the lucid curtain dimly shows,

With doubled fires the roving fancy glows!)

The hand of modesty the foldings threw,

Nor all conceal'd, nor all was given to view;

Yet her deep grief her lovely face betrays,

Though on her cheek the soft smile falt'ring plays.

All heaven was mov'd—as when some damsel coy,

Hurt by the rudeness of the am'rous boy,

Offended chides and smiles; with angry mien

Thus mixt with smiles, advanc'd the plaintive queen;

And[134] thus: "O Thunderer! O potent Sire!

Shall I in vain thy kind regard require?

Alas! and cherish still the fond deceit,

That yet on me thy kindest smiles await.

Ah heaven! and must that valour which I love

Awake the vengeance and the rage of Jove?

Yet mov'd with pity for my fav'rite race

I speak, though frowning on thine awful face,

I mark the tenor of the dread decree,

That to thy wrath consigns my sons and me.

Yes! let stern Bacchus bless thy partial care,

His be the triumph, and be mine despair.

The bold advent'rous sons of Tago's clime

I loved—alas! that love is now their crime:

O happy they, and prosp'rous gales their fate,

Had I pursued them with relentless hate!

Yes! let my woeful sighs in vain implore,

Yes! let them perish on some barb'rous shore,

For I have lov'd them." Here the swelling sigh

And pearly tear-drop rushing in her eye,

As morning dew hangs trembling on the rose,

Though fond to speak, her further speech oppose—

Her lips, then moving, as the pause of woe

Were now to give the voice of grief to flow;

When kindled by those charms, whose woes might move

And melt the prowling tiger's rage to love.

The thundering-god her weeping sorrows eyed,

And sudden threw his awful state aside:

With[135] that mild look which stills the driving storm,

When black roll'd clouds the face of heaven deform;

With that mild visage and benignant mien

Which to the sky restores the blue serene,

Her snowy neck and glowing cheek he press'd,

And wip'd her tears, and clasp'd her to his breast;

Yet she, still sighing, dropp'd the trickling tear,

As the chid nursling, mov'd with pride and fear,

Still sighs and moans, though fondled and caress'd;

Till thus great Jove the Fates' decrees confess'd:

"O thou, my daughter, still belov'd as fair,

Vain are thy fears, thy heroes claim my care:

No power of gods could e'er my heart incline,

110

Like one fond smile, one powerful tear of thine.

Wide o'er the eastern shores shalt thou behold

Thy flags far streaming, and thy thunders roll'd;

Where nobler triumphs shall thy nation crown,

Than those of Roman or of Greek renown.

"If by mine aid the sapient Greek[136] could brave

Th' Ogygian seas, nor sink a deathless slave;[137]

If through th' Illyrian shelves Antenor bore,

Till safe he landed on Timavus' shore;

If, by his fate, the pious Trojan[138] led,

Safe through Charybdis'[139] barking whirlpools sped:

Shall thy bold heroes, by my care disclaim'd,

Be left to perish, who, to worlds unnam'd

By vaunting Rome, pursue their dauntless way?

No—soon shalt thou with ravish'd eyes survey,

From stream to stream their lofty cities spread,

And their proud turrets rear the warlike head:

The stern-brow'd Turk shall bend the suppliant knee,

And Indian monarchs, now secure and free,

Beneath thy potent monarch's yoke shall bend,

And thy just laws wide o'er the East extend.

Thy chief, who now in error's circling maze,

For India's shore through shelves and tempests strays;

That chief shalt thou behold, with lordly pride,

O'er Neptune's trembling realm triumphant ride.

O wondrous fate! when not a breathing[140] gale

Shall curl the billows, or distend the sail,

The waves shall boil and tremble, aw'd with dread,

And own the terror o'er their empire spread.
That hostile coast, with various streams supplied,
Whose treach'rous sons the fountain's gifts denied;
That coast shalt thou behold his port supply,
Where oft thy weary fleets in rest shall lie.
Each shore which weav'd for him the snares of death,
To him these shores shall pledge their offer'd faith;
To him their haughty lords shall lowly bend,
And yield him tribute for the name of friend.
The Red-sea wave shall darken in the shade
Of thy broad sails, in frequent pomp display'd;
Thine eyes shall see the golden Ormuz'[141] shore,
Twice thine, twice conquer'd, while the furious Moor,
Amaz'd, shall view his arrows backward[142] driven,
Shower'd on his legions by the hand of Heaven.
Though twice assail'd by many a vengeful band,
Unconquer'd still shall Dio's ramparts stand,
Such prowess there shall raise the Lusian name
That Mars shall tremble for his blighted fame;
There shall the Moors, blaspheming, sink in death,
And curse their Prophet with their parting breath.

"Where Goa's warlike ramparts frown on high,
Pleas'd shalt thou see thy Lusian banners fly;
The pagan tribes in chains shall crowd her gate,
While the sublime shall tower in regal state,
The fatal scourge, the dread of all who dare
Against thy sons to plan the future war.
Though few thy troops who Conanour sustain,

The foe, though num'rous, shall assault in vain.

Great Calicut,[143] for potent hosts renown'd,

By Lisbon's sons assail'd shall strew the ground:

What floods on floods of vengeful hosts shall wage

On Cochin's walls their swift-repeated rage;

In vain: a Lusian hero shall oppose

His dauntless bosom and disperse the foes,

As high-swelled waves, that thunder'd to the shock,

Disperse in feeble streamlets from the rock.

When[144] black'ning broad and far o'er Actium's tide

Augustus' fleets the slave of love[145] defied,

When that fallen warrior to the combat led

The bravest troops in Bactrian Scythia bred,

With Asian legions, and, his shameful bane,

The Egyptian queen, attendant in the train;

Though Mars rag'd high, and all his fury pour'd,

Till with the storm the boiling surges roar'd,

Yet shall thine eyes more dreadful scenes behold,

On burning surges burning surges roll'd,

The sheets of fire far billowing o'er the brine,

While I my thunder to thy sons resign.

Thus many a sea shall blaze, and many a shore

Resound the horror of the combat's roar,

While thy bold prows triumphant ride along

By trembling China to the isles unsung

By ancient bard, by ancient chief unknown,

Till Ocean's utmost shore thy bondage own.

"Thus from the Ganges to the Gadian[146] strand,

From the most northern wave to southmost land:

That land decreed to bear the injur'd name

Of Magalhaens, the Lusian pride and shame;[147]

From all that vast, though crown'd with heroes old,

Who with the gods were demi-gods enroll'd:

From all that vast no equal heroes shine

To match in arms, O lovely daughter, thine."

So spake the awful ruler of the skies,

And Maia's[148] son swift at his mandate flies:

His charge, from treason and Mombassa's[149] king

The weary fleet in friendly port to bring,

And, while in sleep the brave De Gama lay,

To warn, and fair the shore of rest display.

Fleet through the yielding air Cyllenius[150] glides,

As to the light the nimble air divides.

The mystic helmet[151] on his head he wore,

And in his hand the fatal rod[152] he bore;

That rod of power[153] to wake the silent dead,

Or o'er the lids of care soft slumbers shed.

And now, attended by the herald Fame,

To fair Melinda's gate, conceal'd, he came;

And soon loud rumour echo'd through the town,

How from the western world, from waves unknown,

A noble band had reach'd the Æthiop shore,

Through seas and dangers never dar'd before:

The godlike, dread attempt their wonder fires,

Their gen'rous wonder fond regard inspires,

And all the city glows their aid to give,

To view the heroes, and their wants relieve.

'Twas now the solemn hour when midnight reigns,
And dimly twinkling o'er the ethereal plains,
The starry host, by gloomy silence led,
O'er earth and sea a glimm'ring paleness shed;
When to the fleet, which hemm'd with dangers lay,
The silver-wing'd Cyllenius[154] darts away.
Each care was now in soft oblivion steep'd,
The watch alone accustom'd vigils kept;
E'en Gama, wearied by the day's alarms,
Forgets his cares, reclin'd in slumber's arms.
Scarce had he clos'd his careful eyes in rest,
When Maia's son[154] in vision stood confess'd:
And "Fly," he cried, "O Lusitanian, fly;
Here guile and treason every nerve apply:
An impious king for thee the toil prepares,
An impious people weaves a thousand snares:
Oh fly these shores, unfurl the gather'd sail,
Lo, Heaven, thy guide, commands the rising gale.
Hark, loud it rustles; see, the gentle tide
Invites thy prows; the winds thy ling'ring chide.
Here such dire welcome is for thee prepar'd
As[155] Diomed's unhappy strangers shar'd;
His hapless guests at silent midnight bled,
On their torn limbs his snorting coursers fed.
Oh fly, or here with strangers' blood imbru'd
Busiris' altars thou shalt find renew'd:
Amidst his slaughter'd guests his altars stood

Obscene with gore, and bark'd with human blood:

Then thou, belov'd of Heaven, my counsel hear;

Right by the coast thine onward journey steer,

Till where the sun of noon no shade begets,

But day with night in equal tenor sets.[156]

A sov'reign there, of gen'rous faith unstain'd,

With ancient bounty, and with joy unfeign'd

Your glad arrival on his shore shall greet,

And soothe with every care your weary fleet.

And when again for India's golden strand

Before the prosp'rous gale your sails expand,

A skilful pilot oft in danger tried,

Of heart sincere, shall prove your faithful guide."

Thus Hermes[157] spoke; and as his flight he takes

Melting in ambient air, De Gama wakes.

Chill'd with amaze he stood, when through the night

With sudden ray appear'd the bursting light;

The winds loud whizzing through the cordage sigh'd,

"Spread, spread the sail!" the raptur'd Vasco cried;

"Aloft, aloft, this, this the gale of heaven,

By Heaven our guide, th' auspicious sign is given;

Mine eyes beheld the messenger divine,

'O fly,' he cried, 'and give the fav'ring sign.

Here treason lurks.'"——Swift as the captain spake

The mariners spring bounding to the deck,

And now, with shouts far-echoing o'er the sea,

Proud of their strength the pond'rous anchors weigh.

When[158] Heaven again its guardian care display'd;

Above the wave rose many a Moorish head,
Conceal'd by night they gently swam along,
And with their weapons saw'd the cables strong,
That by the swelling currents whirl'd and toss'd,
The navy's wrecks might strew the rocky coast.
But now discover'd, every nerve they ply,
And dive, and swift as frighten'd vermin fly.

Now through the silver waves that curling rose,
And gently murmur'd round the sloping prows,
The gallant fleet before the steady wind
Sweeps on, and leaves long foamy tracts behind;
While as they sail the joyful crew relate
Their wondrous safety from impending fate;
And every bosom feels how sweet the joy
When, dangers past, the grateful tongue employ.

The sun had now his annual journey run,
And blazing forth another course begun,
When smoothly gliding o'er the hoary tide
Two sloops afar the watchful master spied;
Their Moorish make the seaman's art display'd;
Here Gama weens to force the pilot's aid:
One, base with fear, to certain shipwreck flew;
The keel dash'd on the shore, escap'd the crew.
The other bravely trusts the gen'rous foe,
And yields, ere slaughter struck the lifted blow,
Ere Vulcan's thunders bellow'd. Yet again
The captain's prudence and his wish were vain;

No pilot here his wand'ring course to guide,

No lip to tell where rolls the Indian tide;

The voyage calm, or perilous, or afar,

Beneath what heaven, or which the guiding star:

Yet this they told, that by the neighb'ring bay

A potent monarch reign'd, whose pious sway

For truth and noblest bounty far renown'd,

Still with the stranger's grateful praise was crown'd.

O'erjoyed, brave Gama heard the tale, which seal'd

The sacred truth that Maia's[159] son reveal'd;

And bids the pilot, warn'd by Heaven his guide,

For fair Melinda[160] turn the helm aside.

'Twas now the jovial season, when the morn

From Taurus flames, when Amalthea's horn

O'er hill and dale the rose-crown'd Flora pours,

And scatters corn and wine, and fruits and flowers.

Right to the port their course the fleet pursu'd,

And the glad dawn that sacred day[161] renew'd,

When, with the spoils of vanquish'd death adorn'd,

To heaven the Victor[162] of the tomb return'd.

And soon Melinda's shore the sailors spy;

From every mast the purple streamers fly;

Rich-figur'd tap'stry now supplies the sail.

The gold and scarlet tremble in the gale;

The standard broad its brilliant hues bewrays,

And floating on the wind wide-billowing plays;

Shrill through the air the quiv'ring trumpet sounds,

And the rough drum the rousing march rebounds.

As thus, regardful of the sacred day,

The festive navy cut the wat'ry way,

Melinda's sons the shore in thousands crowd,

And, offering joyful welcome, shout aloud:

And truth the voice inspir'd. Unaw'd by fear,

With warlike pomp adorn'd, himself sincere,

Now in the port the gen'rous Gama rides;

His stately vessels range their pitchy sides

Around their chief; the bowsprits nod the head,

And the barb'd anchors gripe the harbour's bed.

Straight to the king, as friends to gen'rous friends,

A captive Moor the valiant Gama sends.

The Lusian fame, the king already knew,

What gulfs unknown the fleet had labour'd through,

What shelves, what tempests dar'd. His liberal mind

Exults the captain's manly trust to find;

With that ennobling worth, whose fond employ

Befriends the brave, the monarch owns his joy,

Entreats the leader and his weary band

To taste the dews of sweet repose on land,

And all the riches of his cultur'd fields

Obedient to the nod of Gama yields.

His care, meanwhile, their present want attends,

And various fowl, and various fruits he sends;

The oxen low, the fleecy lambkins bleat,

And rural sounds are echo'd through the fleet.

His gifts with joy the valiant chief receives,

And gifts in turn, confirming friendship, gives.

Here the proud scarlet darts its ardent rays,

And here the purple and the orange blaze;

O'er these profuse the branching coral spread,

The coral[163] wondrous in its wat'ry bed;

Soft there it creeps, in curving branches thrown,

In air it hardens to a precious stone.

With these a herald, on whose melting tongue

The copious rhetoric[164] of Arabia hung,

He sends, his wants and purpose to reveal,

And holy vows of lasting peace to seal.

The monarch sits amid his splendid bands,

Before the regal throne the herald stands,

And thus, as eloquence his lips inspir'd,

"O king," he cries, "for sacred truth admir'd,

Ordain'd by heaven to bend the stubborn knees

Of haughtiest nations to thy just decrees;

Fear'd as thou art, yet sent by Heaven to prove

That empire's strength results from public love:

To thee, O king, for friendly aid we come;

Nor lawless robbers o'er the deep we roam:

No lust of gold could e'er our breasts inflame

To scatter fire and slaughter where we came;

Nor sword, nor spear our harmless hands employ

To seize the careless, or the weak destroy.

At our most potent monarch's dread command

We spread the sail from lordly Europe's strand;

Through seas unknown, through gulfs untried before,

We force our journey to the Indian shore.

"Alas, what rancour fires the human breast!

By what stern tribes are Afric's shores possess'd!

How many a wile they tried, how many a snare!

Not wisdom sav'd us, 'twas the Heaven's own care:

Not harbours only, e'en the barren sands

A place of rest denied our weary bands:

From us, alas, what harm could prudence fear!

From us so few, their num'rous friends so near!

While thus, from shore to cruel shore long driven,

To thee conducted by a guide from heaven,

We come, O monarch, of thy truth assur'd,

Of hospitable rites by Heaven secur'd;

Such rites[165] as old Alcinous' palace grac'd,

When 'lorn Ulysses sat his favour'd guest.

Nor deem, O king, that cold Suspicion taints

Our valiant leader, or his wish prevents;

Great is our monarch, and his dread command

To our brave captain interdicts the land

Till Indian earth he tread. What nobler cause

Than loyal faith can wake thy fond applause,

O thou, who knowest the ever-pressing weight

Of kingly office,[166] and the cares of state!

And hear, ye conscious heavens, if Gama's heart

Forget thy kindness, or from truth depart,

The sacred light shall perish from the sun,

And rivers to the sea shall cease to run."[167]

He spoke; a murmur of applause succeeds,

And each with wonder own'd the val'rous deeds

Of that bold race, whose flowing vanes had wav'd

Beneath so many a sky, so many an ocean brav'd.

Nor less the king their loyal faith reveres,

And Lisboa's lord in awful state appears,

Whose least command on farthest shores obey'd,

His sovereign grandeur to the world display'd.

Elate with joy, uprose the royal Moor,

And smiling thus,—"O welcome to my shore!

If yet in you the fear of treason dwell,

Far from your thoughts th' ungen'rous fear expel:

Still with the brave, the brave will honour find,

And equal ardour will their friendship bind.

But those who spurn'd you, men alone in show,

Rude as the bestial herd, no worth they know;

Such dwell not here: and since your laws require

Obedience strict, I yield my fond desire.

Though much I wish'd your chief to grace my board,

Fair be his duty to his sov'reign Lord:

Yet when the morn walks forth with dewy feet

My barge shall waft me to the warlike fleet;

There shall my longing eyes the heroes view,

And holy vows the mutual peace renew.

What from the blust'ring winds and length'ning tide

Your ships have suffer'd, shall be here supplied.

Arms and provisions I myself will send,

And, great of skill, a pilot shall attend."

So spoke the king: and now, with purpled ray,

Beneath the shining wave the god of day

Retiring, left the evening shades to spread;

And to the fleet the joyful herald sped:

To find such friends each breast with rapture glows,

The feast is kindled, and the goblet flows;

The trembling comet's imitated rays[168]

Bound to the skies, and trail a sparkling blaze:

The vaulting bombs awake their sleeping fire,

And, like the Cyclops' bolts, to heaven aspire:

The bombardiers their roaring engines ply,

And earth and ocean thunder to the sky.

The trump and fife's shrill clarion far around

The glorious music of the fight resound;

Nor less the joy Melinda's sons display,

The sulphur bursts in many an ardent ray,

And to the heaven ascends, in whizzing gyres,

And ocean flames with artificial fires.

In festive war the sea and land engage,

And echoing shouts confess the joyful rage.

So pass'd the night: and now, with silv'ry ray,

The star of morning ushers in the day.

The shadows fly before the roseate hours,

And the chill dew hangs glitt'ring on the flowers.

The pruning-hook or humble spade to wield,

The cheerful lab'rer hastens to the field;

When to the fleet, with many a sounding oar,

The monarch sails; the natives crowd the shore;

Their various robes in one bright splendour join,

The purple blazes, and the gold stripes shine;

Nor as stern warriors with the quiv'ring lance,

Or moon-arch'd bow, Melinda's sons advance;

Green boughs of palm with joyful hands they wave,

An omen of the meed that crowns the brave:
Fair was the show the royal barge display'd,
With many a flag of glist'ning silk array'd,
Whose various hues, as waving thro' the bay,
Return'd the lustre of the rising day:
And, onward as they came, in sov'reign state
The mighty king amid his princes sat:
His robes the pomp of Eastern splendour show,
A proud tiara decks his lordly brow:
The various tissue shines in every fold,
The silken lustre and the rays of gold.
His purple mantle boasts the dye of Tyre,[169]
And in the sunbeam glows with living fire.
A golden chain, the skilful artist's pride,
Hung from his neck; and glitt'ring by his side
The dagger's hilt of star-bright diamond shone,
The girding baldric[170] burns with precious stone;
And precious stone in studs of gold enchas'd,
The shaggy velvet of his buskins grac'd:
Wide o'er his head, of various silks inlaid,
A fair umbrella cast a grateful shade.
A band of menials, bending o'er the prow,
Of horn wreath'd round the crooked trumpets blow;
And each attendant barge aloud rebounds
A barb'rous discord of rejoicing sounds.
With equal pomp the captain leaves the fleet,
Melinda's monarch on the tide to greet:
His barge nods on amidst a splendid train,
Himself adorn'd in[171] all the pride of Spain:

124

With fair embroidery shone his armèd breast,
For polish'd steel supplied the warrior's vest;
His sleeves, beneath, were silk of paly blue,
Above, more loose, the purple's brightest hue
Hung as a scarf in equal gath'rings roll'd,
With golden buttons and with loops of gold:
Bright in the sun the polish'd radiance burns,
And the dimm'd eyeball from the lustre turns.
Of crimson satin, dazzling to behold,
His cassock swell'd in many a curving fold;
The make was Gallic, but the lively bloom
Confess'd the labour of Venetia's loom.
Gold was his sword, and warlike trousers lac'd
With thongs of gold his manly legs embrac'd.
With graceful mien his cap aslant was turn'd.
The velvet cap a nodding plume adorn'd.
His noble aspect, and the purple's ray,
Amidst his train the gallant chief bewray.
The various vestments of the warrior train,
Like flowers of various colours on the plain,
Attract the pleas'd beholder's wond'ring eye,
And with the splendour of the rainbow vie.
Now Gama's bands the quiv'ring trumpet blow,
Thick o'er the wave the crowding barges row,
The Moorish flags the curling waters sweep,
The Lusian mortars thunder o'er the deep;
Again the fiery roar heaven's concave tears,
The Moors astonished stop their wounded ears;
Again loud thunders rattle o'er the bay,

And clouds of smoke wide-rolling blot the day;

The captain's barge the gen'rous king ascends,

His arms the chief enfold, the captain bends,

(A rev'rence to the scepter'd grandeur due):

In silent awe the monarch's wond'ring view

Is fix'd on Vasco's noble mien;[172] the while

His thoughts with wonder weigh the hero's toil.

Esteem and friendship with his wonder rise,

And free to Gama all his kingdom lies.

Though never son of Lusus' race before

Had met his eye, or trod Melinda's shore

To him familiar was the mighty name,

And much his talk extols the Lusian fame;

How through the vast of Afric's wildest bound

Their deathless feats in gallant arms resound;

When that fair land where Hesper's offspring reign'd,

Their valour's prize the Lusian youth obtain'd.

Much still he talk'd, enraptur'd of the theme,

Though but the faint vibrations of their fame

To him had echo'd. Pleas'd his warmth to view,

Convinc'd his promise and his heart were true,

The illustrious Gama thus his soul express'd

And own'd the joy that labour'd in his breast:

"Oh thou, benign, of all the tribes alone,

Who feel the rigour of the burning zone,

Whose piety, with Mercy's gentle eye

Beholds our wants, and gives the wish'd supply,

Our navy driven from many a barb'rous coast,

On many a tempest-harrow'd ocean toss'd,

At last with thee a kindly refuge finds,
Safe from the fury of the howling winds.
O gen'rous king, may He whose mandate rolls
The circling heavens, and human pride controls,
May the Great Spirit to thy breast return
That needful aid, bestow'd on us forlorn!
And while yon sun emits his rays divine,
And while the stars in midnight azure shine,
Where'er my sails are stretch'd the world around,
Thy praise shall brighten, and thy name resound."

He spoke; the painted barges swept the flood,
Where, proudly gay, the anchor'd navy rode;
Earnest the king the lordly fleet surveys;
The mortars thunder, and the trumpets raise
Their martial sounds Melinda's sons to greet,
Melinda's sons with timbrels hail the fleet.
And now, no more the sulphury tempest roars,
The boatmen leaning on the rested oars
Breathe short; the barges now at anchor moor'd,
The king, while silence listen'd round, implor'd
The glories of the Lusian wars to hear,
Whose faintest echoes long had pleas'd his ear:
Their various triumphs on the Afric shore
O'er those who hold the son of Hagar's[173] lore.
Fond he demands, and now demands again
Their various triumphs on the western main
Again, ere readiest answer found a place,
He asks the story of the Lusian race;

What god was founder of the mighty line,

Beneath what heaven their land, what shores adjoin;

And what their climate, where the sinking day

Gives the last glimpse of twilight's silv'ry ray.

"But most, O chief," the zealous monarch cries,

"What raging seas you brav'd, what low'ring skies;

What tribes, what rites you saw; what savage hate

On our rude Afric prov'd your hapless fate:

Oh tell, for lo, the chilly dawning star

Yet rides before the morning's purple car;

And o'er the wave the sun's bold coursers raise

Their flaming fronts, and give the opening blaze;

Soft on the glassy wave the zephyrs sleep,

And the still billows holy silence keep.

Nor less are we, undaunted chief, prepar'd

To hear thy nation's gallant deeds declar'd;

Nor think, tho' scorch'd beneath the car of day,

Our minds too dull the debt of praise to pay;

Melinda's sons the test of greatness know,

And on the Lusian race the palm bestow.

"If Titan's giant brood with impious arms

Shook high Olympus' brow with rude alarms;

If Theseus and Pirithoüs dar'd invade

The dismal horrors of the Stygian shade,

Nor less your glory, nor your boldness less

That thus exploring Neptune's last recess

Contemns his waves and tempests. If the thirst

To live in fame, though famed for deeds accurs'd,

Could urge the caitiff, who to win a name

Gave Dian's temple to the wasting flame:[174]

If such the ardour to attain renown,

How bright the lustre of the hero's crown,

Whose deeds of fair emprize his honours raise,

And bind his brows, like thine, with deathless bays!"

END OF THE SECOND BOOK.

BOOK III.

THE ARGUMENT.

Gama, in reply to the King of Melinda, describes the various countries of Europe; narrates the rise of the Portuguese nation. History of Portugal. Battle of Guimaraens. Egas offers himself with his wife and family for the honour of his country. Alonzo pardons him. Battle of Ourique against the Moors; great slaughter of the Moors. Alonzo proclaimed King of Portugal on the battle-field of Ourique. At Badajoz he is wounded and taken prisoner: resigns the kingdom to his son, Don Sancho. Hearing that thirteen Moorish kings, headed by the Emperor of Morocco, were besieging Sancho in Santarem, he hastens to deliver his son: gains a great battle, in which the Moorish Emperor is slain. Victories of Sancho; capture of Sylves from the Moors, and of Tui from the King of Leon. Conquest of Alcazar de Sul by Alfonso II. Deposition of Sancho II. Is succeeded by Alphonso III., the conqueror of Algarve; succeeded by Dionysius, founder of the University of Coimbra. His son, Alfonso the Brave. Affecting story of the fair Inez, who is crowned Queen of Portugal after her assassination. Don Pedro, her husband, rendered desperate by the loss of his mistress, is succeeded by the weak and effeminate Ferdinand. His wife Eleonora, torn from the arms of her lawful husband, dishonours his reign.

OH now, Calliope, thy potent aid!

What to the king th' illustrious Gama said

Clothe in immortal verse. With sacred fire

My breast, If e'er it loved thy lore, inspire:

So may the patron[175] of the healing art,

The god of day to thee consign his heart;

129

From thee, the mother of his darling son,[176]

May never wand'ring thought to Daphne run:

May never Clytia, nor Leucothoë's pride

Henceforth with thee his changeful love divide.

Then aid, O fairest nymph, my fond desire,

And give my verse the Lusian warlike fire:

Fir'd by the song, the list'ning world shall know

That Aganippe's streams from Tagus flow.

Oh, let no more the flowers of Pindus shine

On thy fair breast, or round thy temples twine:

On Tago's banks a richer chaplet blows,

And with the tuneful god my bosom glows:

I feel, I feel the mighty power infuse,

And bathe my spirit in Aonian[177] dews!

Now silence woo'd the illustrious chief's reply,

And keen attention watch'd on every eye;

When slowly turning with a modest grace,

The noble Vasco rais'd his manly face;

O mighty king (he cries), at thy[178] command

The martial story of my native land

I tell; but more my doubtful heart had joy'd

Had other wars my praiseful lips employ'd.

When men the honours of their race commend,

The doubts of strangers on the tale attend:

Yet, though reluctance falter on my tongue,

Though day would fail a narrative so long,

Yet, well assur'd no fiction's glare can raise,

Or give my country's fame a brighter praise;

Though less, far less, whate'er my lips can say,
Than truth must give it, I thy will obey.

Between that zone where endless winter reigns
And that where flaming heat consumes the plains;
Array'd in green, beneath indulgent skies,
The queen of arts and arms, fair Europe lies.
Around her northern and her western shores,
Throng'd with the finny race old ocean roars;
The midland sea,[179] where tide ne'er swell'd the waves,
Her richest lawns, the southern border, laves.
Against the rising morn, the northmost bound
The whirling Tanais[180] parts from Asian ground,
As tumbling from the Scythian mountains cold
Their crooked way the rapid waters hold
To dull Mæotis'[181] lake. Her eastern line
More to the south, the Phrygian waves confine:
Those waves, which, black with many a navy, bore
The Grecian heroes to the Dardan shore;
Where now the seaman, rapt in mournful joy,
Explores in vain the sad remains of Troy.
Wide to the north beneath the pole she spreads;
Here piles of mountains rear their rugged heads,
Here winds on winds in endless tempests roll,
The valleys sigh, the length'ning echoes howl.
On the rude cliffs, with frosty spangles grey,
Weak as the twilight, gleams the solar ray;
Each mountain's breast with snows eternal shines,
The streams and seas eternal frost confines.

131

Here dwelt the num'rous Scythian tribes of old,
A dreadful race! by victor ne'er controll'd,
Whose pride maintain'd that theirs the sacred earth,
Not that of Nile, which first gave man his birth.
Here dismal Lapland spreads a dreary wild,
Here Norway's wastes, where harvest never smil'd,
Whose groves of fir in gloomy horror frown,
Nod o'er the rocks, and to the tempest groan.
Here Scandia's clime her rugged shores extends,
And, far projected, through the ocean bends;
Whose sons' dread footsteps yet Ausonia[182] wears,
And yet proud Rome in mournful ruin bears.
When summer bursts stern winter's icy chain,
Here the bold Swede, the Prussian, and the Dane
Hoist the white sail and plough the foamy way,
Cheer'd by whole months of one continual day:
Between these shores and Tanais'[183] rushing tide
Livonia's sons and Russia's hordes reside.
Stern as their clime the tribes, whose sires of yore
The name, far dreaded, of Sarmatians bore.
Where, fam'd of old, th' Hercynian[184] forest lower'd,
Oft seen in arms the Polish troops are pour'd
Wide foraging the downs. The Saxon race,
The Hungar dext'rous in the wild-boar chase,
The various nations whom the Rhine's cold wave
The Elbe, Amasis, and the Danube lave,
Of various tongues, for various princes known,
Their mighty lord the German emperor own.
Between the Danube and the lucid tide

Where hapless Helle left her name,[185] and died:

The dreadful god of battles' kindred race,

Degenerate now, possess the hills of Thrace.

Mount Hæmus[186] here, and Rhodope renown'd,

And proud Byzantium,[187] long with empire crown'd;

Their ancient pride, their ancient virtue fled,

Low to the Turk now bend the servile head.

Here spread the fields of warlike Macedon,

And here those happy lands where genius shone

In all the arts, in all the Muses' charms,

In all the pride of elegance and arms,

Which to the heavens resounded Grecia's name,

And left in every age a deathless fame.

The stern Dalmatians till the neighb'ring ground;

And where Antenor anchor'd in the sound

Proud Venice, as a queen, majestic towers,

And o'er the trembling waves her thunder pours.

For learning glorious, glorious for the sword,

While Rome's proud monarch reign'd the world's dread lord,

Here Italy her beauteous landscapes shows;

Around her sides his arms old ocean throws;

The dashing waves the ramparts aid supply;

The hoary Alps high tow'ring to the sky,

From shore to shore a rugged barrier spread,

And lower destruction on the hostile tread.

But now no more her hostile spirit burns,

There now the saint, in humble vespers mourns

To Heaven more grateful than the pride of war,

And all the triumphs of the victor's car.

Onward fair Gallia opens to the view

Her groves of olive, and her vineyards blue:

Wide spread her harvests o'er the scenes renown'd,

Where Julius[188] proudly strode with laurel crown'd.

Here Seine, how fair when glist'ning to the moon!

Rolls his white wave, and here the cold Garoon;

Here the deep Rhine the flow'ry margin laves,

And here the rapid Rhone impervious raves.

Here the gruff mountains, faithless to the vows

Of lost Pyrene[189] rear their cloudy brows;

Whence, when of old the flames their woods devour'd,

Streams of red gold and melted silver pour'd.

And now, as head of all the lordly train

Of Europe's realms, appears illustrious Spain.

Alas, what various fortunes has she known!

Yet ever did her sons her wrongs atone;

Short was the triumph of her haughty foes,

And still with fairer bloom her honours rose.

Where, lock'd with land, the struggling currents boil

Fam'd for the godlike Theban's latest toil,[190]

Against one coast the Punic strand extends,

Around her breast the midland ocean bends,

Around her shores two various oceans swell,

And various nations in her bosom dwell.

Such deeds of valour dignify their names,

Each the imperial right of honour claims.

Proud Aragon, who twice her standard rear'd

In conquer'd Naples; and for art rever'd,

Galicia's prudent sons; the fierce Navarre,

And he far dreaded in the Moorish war,

The bold Asturian; nor Sevilia's race,

Nor thine, Granada, claim the second place.

Here too the heroes who command the plain

By Betis[191] water'd; here the pride of Spain,

The brave Castilian pauses o'er his sword,

His country's dread deliverer and lord.

Proud o'er the rest, with splendid wealth array'd,

As crown to this wide empire, Europe's head,

Fair Lusitania smiles, the western bound,

Whose verdant breast the rolling waves surround,

Where gentle evening pours her lambent ray,

The last pale gleaming of departing day;

This, this, O mighty king, the sacred earth,

This the loved parent-soil that gave me birth.

And oh, would bounteous Heaven my prayer regard,

And fair success my perilous toils reward,

May that dear land my latest breath receive,

And give my weary bones a peaceful grave.

Sublime the honours of my native land,

And high in Heaven's regard her heroes stand;

By Heaven's decree 'twas theirs the first to quell

The Moorish tyrants, and from Spain expel;

Nor could their burning wilds conceal their flight,

Their burning wilds confess'd the Lusian might.

From Lusus famed, whose honour'd name we bear,

(The son of Bacchus or the bold compeer),

The glorious name of Lusitania rose,

A name tremendous to the Roman foes,

When her bold troops the valiant shepherd[192] led,

And foul with rout the Roman eagles fled;

When haughty Rome achiev'd the treach'rous blow,

That own'd her terror of the matchless foe.[193]

But, when no more her Viriatus fought,

Age after age her deeper thraldom brought;

Her broken sons by ruthless tyrants spurn'd,

Her vineyards languish'd, and her pastures mourn'd;

Till time revolving rais'd her drooping head,

And o'er the wond'ring world her conquests spread.

Thus rose her power: the lands of lordly Spain

Were now the brave Alonzo's wide domain;

Great were his honours in the bloody fight,

And Fame proclaim'd him champion of the right.

And oft the groaning Saracen's[194] proud crest

And shatter'd mail his awful force confess'd.

From Calpe's summits to the Caspian shore

Loud-tongued renown his godlike actions bore.

And many a chief from distant regions[195] came

To share the laurels of Alonzo's fame;

Yet, more for holy Faith's unspotted cause

Their spears they wielded, than for Fame's applause.

Great were the deeds their thund'ring arms display'd,

And still their foremost swords the battle sway'd.

And now to honour with distinguish'd meed

Each hero's worth the gen'rous king decreed.

The first and bravest of the foreign bands

Hungaria's younger son, brave Henry[196] stands.

To him are given the fields where Tagus flows,

And the glad king his daughter's hand bestows;

The fair Teresa shines his blooming bride,

And owns her father's love, and Henry's pride.

With her, besides, the sire confirms in dower

Whate'er his sword might rescue from the Moor;

And soon on Hagar's race[197] the hero pours

His warlike fury—soon the vanquish'd Moors

To him far round the neighb'ring lands resign,

And Heaven rewards him with a glorious line.

To him is born, Heaven's gift, a gallant son,

The glorious founder of the Lusian throne.

Nor Spain's wide lands alone his deeds attest,

Deliver'd Judah Henry's might[198] confess'd

On Jordan's bank the victor-hero strode,

Whose hallow'd waters bath'd the Saviour-God;

And Salem's[199] gate her open folds display'd,

When Godfrey[200] conquer'd by the hero's aid.

But now no more in tented fields oppos'd,

By Tagus' stream his honour'd age he clos'd;

Yet still his dauntless worth, his virtue lived,

And all the father in the son survived.

And soon his worth was prov'd, the parent dame

Avow'd a second hymeneal flame.[201]

The low-born spouse assumes the monarch's place,

And from the throne expels the orphan race.

But young Alphonso, like his sires of yore

(His grandsire's virtues, as his name, he bore),

Arms for the fight, his ravish'd throne to win,
And the lac'd helmet grasps his beardless chin.
Her fiercest firebrands Civil Discord wav'd,
Before her troops the lustful mother rav'd;
Lost to maternal love, and lost to shame,
Unaw'd she saw Heaven's awful vengeance flame;
The brother's sword the brother's bosom tore,
And sad Guimaria's[202] meadows blush'd with gore;
With Lusian gore the peasant's cot was stain'd,
And kindred blood the sacred shrine profan'd.

Here, cruel Progne, here, O Jason's wife,
Yet reeking with your children's purple life,
Here glut your eyes with deeper guilt than yours;
Here fiercer rage her fiercer rancour pours.
Your crime was vengeance on the faithless sires,
But here ambition with foul lust conspires.
'Twas rage of love, O Scylla, urged the knife[203]
That robb'd thy father of his fated life;
Here grosser rage the mother's breast inflames,
And at her guiltless son the vengeance aims,
But aims in vain; her slaughter'd forces yield,
And the brave youth rides victor o'er the field.
No more his subjects lift the thirsty sword,
And the glad realm proclaims the youthful lord.
But ah, how wild the noblest tempers run!
His filial duty now forsakes the son;
Secluded from the day, in clanking chains
His rage the parent's agèd limbs constrains.

Heaven frown'd—Dark vengeance lowering on his brows,
And sheath'd in brass, the proud Castilian rose,
Resolv'd the rigour to his daughter shown
The battle should avenge, and blood atone.
A numerous host against the prince he sped,
The valiant prince his little army led:
Dire was the shock; the deep-riven helms resound,
And foes with foes lie grappling on the ground.
Yet, though around the stripling's sacred head
By angel hands etherial shields were spread;
Though glorious triumph on his valour smiled,
Soon on his van the baffled foe recoil'd:
With bands more num'rous to the field he came,
His proud heart burning with the rage of shame.
And now in turn Guimaria's[204] lofty wall,
That saw his triumph, saw the hero fall;
Within the town immured, distress'd he lay,
To stern Castilia's sword a certain prey.
When now the guardian of his infant years,
The valiant Egas, as a god appears;
To proud Castile the suppliant noble bows,
And faithful homage for his prince he vows.
The proud Castile accepts his honour'd faith,
And peace succeeds the dreadful scenes of death.
Yet well, alas, the generous Egas knew
His high-soul'd prince to man would never sue:
Would never stoop to brook the servile stain,
To hold a borrow'd, a dependent reign.
And now with gloomy aspect rose the day,

Decreed the plighted servile rights to pay;

When Egas, to redeem his faith's disgrace,

Devotes himself, his spouse, and infant race.

In gowns of white, as sentenced felons clad,

When to the stake the sons of guilt are led,

With feet unshod they slowly moved along,

And from their necks the knotted halters hung.

"And now, O king," the kneeling Egas cries,

"Behold my perjured honour's sacrifice:

If such mean victims can atone thine ire,

Here let my wife, my babes, myself expire.

If gen'rous bosoms such revenge can take,

Here let them perish for the father's sake:

The guilty tongue, the guilty hands are these,

Nor let a common death thy wrath appease;

For us let all the rage of torture burn,

But to my prince, thy son, in friendship turn."

He spoke, and bow'd his prostrate body low,

As one who waits the lifted sabre's blow;

When o'er the block his languid arms are spread,

And death, foretasted, whelms the heart with dread:

So great a leader thus in humbled state,

So firm his loyalty, his zeal so great,

The brave Alonzo's kindled ire subdu'd,

And, lost in silent joy, the monarch stood;

Then gave the hand, and sheath'd the hostile sword,

And, to such honour honour'd peace[205] restor'd.

Oh Lusian faith! oh zeal beyond compare!

What greater danger could the Persian dare,

Whose prince in tears, to view his mangled woe,

Forgot the joy for Babylon's[206] o'erthrow.

And now the youthful hero shines in arms,

The banks of Tagus echo war's alarms:

O'er Ourique's wide campaign his ensigns wave,

And the proud Saracen to combat brave.

Though prudence might arraign his fiery rage

That dar'd with one, each hundred spears engage,

In Heaven's protecting care his courage lies,

And Heaven, his friend, superior force supplies.

Five Moorish kings against him march along,

Ismar the noblest of the armèd throng;

Yet each brave monarch claim'd the soldier's name,

And far o'er many a land was known to fame.

In all the beauteous glow of blooming years[207]

Beside each king a warrior nymph appears;

Each with her sword her valiant lover guards,

With smiles inspires him, and with smiles rewards.

Such was the valour of the beauteous maid,[208]

Whose warlike arm proud Ilion's[209] fate delay'd.

Such in the field the virgin warriors[210] shone,

Who drank the limpid wave of Thermodon.[211]

'Twas morn's still hour, before the dawning grey

The stars' bright twinkling radiance died away,

When lo, resplendent in the heaven serene,

High o'er the prince the sacred cross was seen;

The godlike prince with Faith's warm glow inflam'd,
"Oh, not to me, my bounteous God!" exclaim'd,
"Oh, not to me, who well thy grandeur know,
But to the pagan herd thy wonders show."

The Lusian host, enraptur'd, mark'd the sign
That witness'd to their chief the aid divine:
Right on the foe they shake the beamy lance,
And with firm strides, and heaving breasts, advance;
Then burst the silence, "Hail, O king!" they cry;
"Our king, our king!" the echoing dales reply:
Fir'd at the sound, with fiercer ardour glows
The Heaven-made monarch; on the wareless foes
Rushing, he speeds his ardent bands along:
So, when the chase excites the rustic throng,
Rous'd to fierce madness by their mingled cries,
On the wild bull the red-eyed mastiff flies.
The stern-brow'd tyrant roars and tears the ground
His watchful horns portend the deathful wound.
The nimble mastiff springing on the foe,
Avoids the furious sharpness of the blow;
Now by the neck, now by the gory sides
Hangs fierce, and all his bellowing rage derides:
In vain his eye-balls burn with living fire,
In vain his nostrils clouds of smoke respire,
His gorge torn down, down falls the furious prize
With hollow thund'ring sound, and raging dies:[212]
Thus, on the Moors the hero rush'd along,
Th' astonish'd Moors in wild confusion throng;

They snatch their arms, the hasty trumpet sounds,
With horrid yell the dread alarm rebounds;
The warlike tumult maddens o'er the plain,
As when the flame devours the bearded grain:
The nightly flames the whistling winds inspire,
Fierce through the braky thicket pours the fire:
Rous'd by the crackling of the mounting blaze
From sleep the shepherds start in wild amaze;
They snatch their clothes with many a woeful cry,
And, scatter'd, devious to the mountains fly:
Such sudden dread the trembling Moors alarms,
Wild and confused, they snatch the nearest arms;
Yet flight they scorn, and, eager to engage,
They spur their foamy steeds, and trust their furious rage:
Amidst the horror of the headlong shock,
With foot unshaken as the living rock
Stands the bold Lusian firm; the purple wounds
Gush horrible; deep, groaning rage resounds;
Reeking behind the Moorish backs appear
The shining point of many a Lusian spear;
The mailcoats, hauberks,[213] and the harness steel'd,
Bruis'd, hack'd, and torn, lie scatter'd o'er the field;
Beneath the Lusian sweepy force o'erthrown,
Crush'd by their batter'd mails the wounded groan;
Burning with thirst they draw their panting breath,
And curse their prophet[214] as they writhe in death.
Arms sever'd from the trunks still grasp the steel,[215]
Heads gasping roll; the fighting squadrons reel;
Fainty and weak with languid arms they close,

And stagg'ring, grapple with the stagg'ring foes.

So, when an oak falls headlong on the lake,

The troubled waters slowly settling shake:

So faints the languid combat on the plain,

And settling, staggers o'er the heaps of slain.

Again the Lusian fury wakes its fires,

The terror of the Moors new strength inspires:

The scatter'd few in wild confusion fly,

And total rout resounds the yelling cry.

Defil'd with one wide sheet of reeking gore,

The verdure of the lawn appears no more:

In bubbling streams the lazy currents run,

And shoot red flames beneath the evening sun.

With spoils enrich'd, with glorious trophies[216] crown'd,

The Heaven-made sov'reign on the battle ground

Three days encamp'd, to rest his weary train,

Whose dauntless valour drove the Moors from Spain.

And now, in honour of the glorious day,

When five proud monarchs fell, his vanquish'd prey,

On his broad buckler, unadorn'd before,

Placed as a cross, five azure shields he wore,

In grateful memory of the heav'nly sign,

The pledge of conquest by the aid divine.

Nor long his falchion in the scabbard slept,

His warlike arm increasing laurels reap'd:

From Leyra's walls the baffled Ismar flies,

And strong Arroncha falls his conquer'd prize;

That hononr'd town, through whose Elysian groves

Thy smooth and limpid wave, O Tagus, roves.

Th' illustrious Santarene confess'd his power,

And vanquish'd Mafra yields her proudest tower.

The Lunar mountains saw his troops display

Their marching banners and their brave array:

To him submits fair Cintra's cold domain,

The soothing refuge of the Naiad train.

When Love's sweet snares the pining nymphs would shun:

Alas, in vain, from warmer climes they run:

The cooling shades awake the young desires,

And the cold fountains cherish love's soft fires.

And thou, famed Lisbon, whose embattled wall

Rose by the hand that wrought proud Ilion's[217] fall;[218]

Thou queen of cities, whom the seas obey,

Thy dreaded ramparts own'd the hero's sway.

Far from the north a warlike navy bore

From Elbe, from Rhine, and Albion's misty[219] shore;

To rescue Salem's[220] long-polluted shrine

Their force to great Alonzo's force they join:

Before Ulysses' walls the navy rides,

The joyful Tagus laves their pitchy sides.

Five times the moon her empty horns conceal'd,

Five times her broad effulgence shone reveal'd,

When, wrapt in clouds of dust, her mural pride

Falls thund'ring,—black the smoking breach yawns wide.

As, when th' imprison'd waters burst the mounds,

And roar, wide sweeping, o'er the cultur'd grounds;

Nor cot nor fold withstand their furious course;

So, headlong rush'd along the hero's force.

The thirst of vengeance the assailants fires,

The madness of despair the Moors inspires;

Each lane, each street resounds the conflict's roar,

And every threshold reeks with tepid gore.

Thus fell the city, whose unconquer'd[221] towers

Defied of old the banded Gothic powers,

Whose harden'd nerves in rig'rous climates train'd

The savage courage of their souls sustain'd:

Before whose sword the sons of Ebro fled,

And Tagus trembled in his oozy bed;

Aw'd by whose arms the lawns of Betis' shore

The name Vandalia from the Vandals bore.

When Lisbon's towers before the Lusian fell,

What fort, what rampart might his arms repel!

Estremadura's region owns him lord,

And Torres-vedras bends beneath his sword;

Obidos humbles, and Alamquer yields,

Alamquer famous for her verdant fields,

Whose murm'ring riv'lets cheer the traveller's way,

As the chill waters o'er the pebbles stray.

Elva the green, and Moura's fertile dales,

Fair Serpa's tillage, and Alcazar's vales

Not for himself the Moorish peasant sows;

For Lusian hands the yellow harvest glows:

And you, fair lawns, beyond the Tagus' wave,

Your golden burdens for Alonzo save;

Soon shall his thund'ring might your wealth reclaim,

146

And your glad valleys hail their monarch's name.

Nor sleep his captains while the sov'reign wars;
The brave Giraldo's sword in conquest shares,
Evora's frowning walls, the castled hold
Of that proud Roman chief, and rebel bold,
Sertorious dread, whose labours still remain;[222]
Two hundred arches, stretch'd in length, sustain
The marble duct, where, glist'ning to the sun,
Of silver hue the shining waters run.
Evora's frowning walls now shake with fear,
And yield, obedient to Giraldo's spear.
Nor rests the monarch while his servants toil,
Around him still increasing trophies smile,
And deathless fame repays the hapless fate
That gives to human life so short a date.
Proud Beja's castled walls his fury storms,
And one red slaughter every lane deforms.
The ghosts, whose mangled limbs, yet scarcely cold,
Heap'd, sad Trancoso's streets in carnage roll'd,
Appeas'd, the vengeance of their slaughter see,
And hail th' indignant king's severe decree.
Palmela trembles on her mountain's height,
And sea-laved Zambra owns the hero's might.
Nor these alone confess'd his happy star,
Their fated doom produc'd a nobler war.
Badaja's[223] king, a haughty Moor, beheld
His towns besieg'd, and hasted to the field.
Four thousand coursers in his army neigh'd,

147

Unnumber'd spears his infantry display'd;

Proudly they march'd, and glorious to behold,

In silver belts they shone, and plates of gold.

Along a mountain's side secure they trod,

Steep on each hand, and rugged was the road;

When, as a bull, whose lustful veins betray

The madd'ning tumult of inspiring May;

If, when his rage with fiercest ardour glows,

When in the shade the fragrant heifer lows,

If then, perchance, his jealous burning eye

Behold a careless traveller wander by,

With dreadful bellowing on the wretch he flies,

The wretch defenceless, torn and trampled dies.

So rush'd Alonzo on the gaudy train,

And pour'd victorious o'er the mangled slain;

The royal Moor precipitates in flight,

The mountain echoes with the wild affright

Of flying squadrons; down their arms they throw,

And dash from rock to rock to shun the foe.

The foe! what wonders may not virtue dare!

But sixty horsemen wag'd the conqu'ring war.[224]

The warlike monarch still his toil renews,

New conquest still each victory pursues.

To him Badaja's lofty gates expand,

And the wide region owns his dread command.

When, now enraged, proud Leon's king beheld

Those walls subdued, which saw his troops expell'd;

Enrag'd he saw them own the victor's sway,

And hems them round with battailous array.

With gen'rous ire the brave Alonzo glows;
By Heaven unguarded, on the num'rous foes
He rushes, glorying in his wonted force,
And spurs, with headlong rage, his furious horse;
The combat burns, the snorting courser bounds,
And paws impetuous by the iron mounds:
O'er gasping foes and sounding bucklers trod
The raging steed, and headlong as he rode
Dash'd the fierce monarch on a rampire bar—
Low grovelling in the dust, the pride of war,
The great Alonzo lies. The captive's fate
Succeeds, alas, the pomp of regal state.
"Let iron dash his limbs," his mother cried,
"And steel revenge my chains:" she spoke, and died;
And Heaven assented—Now the hour was come,
And the dire curse was fallen Alonzo's doom.[225]

No more, O Pompey, of thy fate complain,
No more with sorrow view thy glory's stain;
Though thy tall standards tower'd with lordly pride
Where northern Phasis[226] rolls his icy tide;
Though hot Syene,[227] where the sun's fierce ray
Begets no shadow, own'd thy conqu'ring sway;
Though from the tribes that shiver in the gleam
Of cold Boötes' wat'ry glist'ning team;
To those who parch'd beneath the burning line,
In fragrant shades their feeble limbs recline,
The various languages proclaim'd thy fame,
And trembling, own'd the terrors of thy name;

149

Though rich Arabia, and Sarmatia bold,

And Colchis,[228] famous for the fleece of gold;

Though Judah's land, whose sacred rites implor'd

The One true God, and, as he taught, ador'd;

Though Cappadocia's realm thy mandate sway'd,

And base Sophenia's sons thy nod obey'd;

Though vex'd Cilicia's pirates wore thy bands,

And those who cultur'd fair Armenia's lands,

Where from the sacred mount two rivers flow,

And what was Eden to the pilgrim show;

Though from the vast Atlantic's bounding wave

To where the northern tempests howl and rave

Round Taurus' lofty brows: though vast and wide

The various climes that bended to thy pride;

No more with pining anguish of regret

Bewail the horrors of Pharsalia's fate:

For great Alonzo, whose superior name

Unequall'd victories consign to fame,

The great Alonzo fell—like thine his woe;

From nuptial kindred came the fatal blow.

When now the hero, humbled in the dust,

His crime aton'd, confess'd that Heaven was just,

Again in splendour he the throne ascends:

Again his bow the Moorish chieftain bends.

Wide round th' embattl'd gates of Santareen

Their shining spears and banner'd moons are seen.

But holy rites the pious king preferr'd;

The martyr's bones on Vincent's Cape interr'd

(His sainted name the Cape shall ever bear),[229]

To Lisbon's walls he brought with votive care.

And now the monarch, old and feeble grown,

Resigns the falchion to his valiant son.

O'er Tagus' waves the youthful hero pass'd,

And bleeding hosts before him shrunk aghast.

Chok'd with the slain, with Moorish carnage dy'd,

Sevilia's river roll'd the purple tide.

Burning for victory, the warlike boy

Spares not a day to thoughtless rest or joy.

Nor long his wish unsatisfied remains:

With the besiegers' gore he dyes the plains

That circle Beja's wall: yet still untam'd,

With all the fierceness of despair inflam'd,

The raging Moor collects his distant might;

Wide from the shores of Atlas' starry height,

From Amphelusia's cape, and Tingia's[230] bay,

Where stern Antæus held his brutal sway,

The Mauritanian trumpet sounds to arms;

And Juba's realm returns the hoarse alarms;

The swarthy tribes in burnish'd armour shine,

Their warlike march Abyla's shepherds join.

The great Miramolin[231] on Tagus' shores

Far o'er the coast his banner'd thousands pours;

Twelve kings and one beneath his ensigns stand,

And wield their sabres at his dread command.

The plund'ring bands far round the region haste,

The mournful region lies a naked waste.

And now, enclos'd in Santareen's high towers,

The brave Don Sancho shuns th' unequal powers;

A thousand arts the furious Moor pursues,

And ceaseless, still the fierce assault renews.

Huge clefts of rock, from horrid engines whirl'd,

In smould'ring volleys on the town are hurl'd;

The brazen rams the lofty turrets shake,

And, mined beneath, the deep foundations quake;

But brave Alonzo's son, as danger grows,

His pride inflam'd, with rising courage glows;

Each coming storm of missile darts he wards,

Each nodding turret, and each port he guards.

In that fair city, round whose verdant meads

The branching river of Mondego[232] spreads,

Long worn with warlike toils, and bent with years,

The king reposed, when Sancho's fate he hears.

His limbs forget the feeble steps of age,

And the hoar warrior burns with youthful rage.

His daring vet'rans, long to conquest train'd,

He leads—the ground with Moorish blood is stain'd;

Turbans, and robes of various colours wrought,

And shiver'd spears in streaming carnage float.

In harness gay lies many a welt'ring steed,

And, low in dust, the groaning masters bleed.

As proud Miramolin[233] in horror fled,

Don Sancho's javelin stretch'd him with the dead.

In wild dismay, and torn with gushing wounds,

The rout, wide scatter'd, fly the Lusian bounds.

Their hands to heaven the joyful victors raise,

And every voice resounds the song of praise;
"Nor was it stumbling chance, nor human might;
"'Twas guardian Heaven," they sung, "that ruled the fight."

This blissful day Alonzo's glories crown'd;
But pale disease now gave the secret wound;
Her icy hand his feeble limbs invades,
And pining languor through his vitals spreads.
The glorious monarch to the tomb descends,
A nation's grief the funeral torch attends.
Each winding shore for thee, Alonzo,[234] mourns,
Alonzo's name each woeful bay returns;
For thee the rivers sigh their groves among,
And funeral murmurs wailing, roll along;
Their swelling tears o'erflow the wide campaign;
With floating heads, for thee, the yellow grain,
For thee the willow-bowers and copses weep,
As their tall boughs lie trembling on the deep;
Adown the streams the tangled vine-leaves flow,
And all the landscape wears the look of woe.
Thus, o'er the wond'ring world thy glories spread,
And thus thy mournful people bow the head;
While still, at eve, each dale Alonzo sighs,
And, oh, Alonzo! every hill replies;
And still the mountain-echoes trill the lay,
Till blushing morn brings on the noiseful day.

The youthful Sancho to the throne succeeds,
Already far renown'd for val'rous deeds;

Let Betis',[235] ting'd with blood, his prowess tell,

And Beja's lawns, where boastful Afric fell.

Nor less when king his martial ardour glows,

Proud Sylves' royal walls his troops enclose!

Fair Sylves' lawns the Moorish peasant plough'd,

Her vineyards cultur'd, and her valleys sow'd;

But Lisbon's monarch reap'd. The winds of heaven[236]

Roar'd high—and headlong by the tempest driven,

In Tagus' breast a gallant navy sought

The shelt'ring port, and glad assistance brought.

The warlike crew, by Frederic the Red,[237]

To rescue Judah's prostrate land were led;

When Guido's troops, by burning thirst subdu'd,

To Saladin, the foe, for mercy su'd.

Their vows were holy, and the cause the same,

To blot from Europe's shores the Moorish name.

In Sancho's cause the gallant navy joins,

And royal Sylves to their force resigns.

Thus, sent by Heaven, a foreign naval band

Gave Lisbon's ramparts to the sire's command.

Nor Moorish trophies did alone adorn

The hero's name; in warlike camps though born,

Though fenc'd with mountains, Leon's martial race.

Smile at the battle-sign, yet foul disgrace

To Leon's haughty sons his sword achiev'd:

Proud Tui's neck his servile yoke receiv'd;

And, far around, falls many a wealthy town,

O valiant Sancho, humbled to thy frown.

While thus his laurels flourish'd wide and fair

He dies: Alonzo reigns, his much-lov'd heir.

Alcazar lately conquer'd from the Moor,

Reconquer'd, streams with the defenders' gore.

Alonzo dead, another Sancho reigns:

Alas, with many a sigh the land complains!

Unlike his sire, a vain unthinking boy,

His servants now a jarring sway enjoy.

As his the power, his were the crimes of those

Whom to dispense that sacred power he chose.

By various counsels waver'd, and confus'd

By seeming friends, by various arts, abus'd;

Long undetermin'd, blindly rash at last,

Enrag'd, unmann'd, untutor'd by the past.

Yet, not like Nero, cruel and unjust,

The slave capricious of unnatural lust.

Nor had he smil'd had flames consum'd his Troy;

Nor could his people's groans afford him joy;

Nor did his woes from female manners spring,

Unlike the Syrian,[238] or Sicilia's king.

No hundred cooks his costly meal prepar'd,

As heap'd the board when Rome's proud tyrant far'd.[239]

Nor dar'd the artist hope his ear to[240] gain,

By new-form'd arts to point the stings of pain.

But, proud and high the Lusian spirit soar'd,

And ask'd a godlike hero for their lord.

To none accustom'd but a hero's sway,

Great must he be whom that bold race obey.

Complaint, loud murmur'd, every city fills,
Complaint, loud echo'd, murmurs through the hills.
Alarm'd, Bolonia's warlike Earl[241] awakes,
And from his listless brother's minions takes
The awful sceptre.—Soon was joy restor'd,
And soon, by just succession, Lisbon's lord
Beloved, Alonzo, nam'd the Bold, he reigns;
Nor may the limits of his sire's domains
Confine his mounting spirit. When he led
His smiling consort to the bridal bed,
"Algarbia's realm," he said, "shall prove thy dower,"
And, soon Algarbia, conquer'd, own'd his power.
The vanquish'd Moor with total rout expell'd,
All Lusus' shores his might unrivall'd held.
And now brave Diniz reigns, whose noble fire
Bespoke the genuine lineage of his sire.
Now, heavenly peace wide wav'd her olive bough,
Each vale display'd the labours of the plough,
And smil'd with joy: the rocks on every shore
Resound the dashing of the merchant-oar.
Wise laws are form'd, and constitutions weigh'd,
And the deep-rooted base of Empire laid.
Not Ammon's son[242] with larger heart bestow'd,
Nor such the grace to him the Muses owed.
From Helicon the Muses wing their way,
Mondego's[243] flow'ry banks invite their stay.
Now Coimbra shines Minerva's proud abode;

And fir'd with joy, Parnassus' bloomy god

Beholds another dear-lov'd Athens rise,

And spread her laurels in indulgent skies;

Her wreath of laurels, ever green, he twines

With threads of gold, and baccaris[244] adjoins.

Here castle walls in warlike grandeur lower,

Here cities swell, and lofty temples tower:

In wealth and grandeur each with other vies:

When old and lov'd the parent-monarch dies.

His son, alas, remiss in filial deeds,

But wise in peace, and bold in fight, succeeds,

The fourth Alonzo: Ever arm'd for war

He views the stern Castile with watchful care.

Yet, when the Libyan nations cross'd the main,

And spread their thousands o'er the fields of Spain,

The brave Alonzo drew his awful steel,

And sprung to battle for the proud Castile.

When Babel's haughty queen[245] unsheath'd the sword,

And o'er Hydaspes' lawns her legions pour'd;

When dreadful Attila,[246] to whom was given

That fearful name, "the Scourge of angry Heaven,"

The fields of trembling Italy o'erran

With many a Gothic tribe, and northern clan;

Not such unnumber'd banners then were seen,

As now in fair Tartesia's dales convene;

Numidia's bow, and Mauritania's spear,

And all the might of Hagar's race was here;

Granada's mongrels join their num'rous host,

To those who dar'd the seas from Libya's coast.

Aw'd by the fury of such pond'rous force

The proud Castilian tries each hop'd resource;

Yet, not by terror for himself inspir'd,

For Spain he trembl'd, and for Spain was fir'd.

His much-lov'd bride,[247] his messenger, he sends,

And, to the hostile Lusian lowly bends.

The much-lov'd daughter of the king implor'd,

Now sues her father for her wedded lord.

The beauteous dame approach'd the palace gate,

Where her great sire was thron'd in regal state:

On her fair face deep-settled grief appears,

And her mild eyes are bath'd in glist'ning tears;

Her careless ringlets, as a mourner's, flow

Adown her shoulders, and her breasts of snow:

A secret transport through the father ran,

While thus, in sighs, the royal bride began:—

"And know'st thou not, O warlike king," she cried,

"That furious Afric pours her peopled tide—

Her barb'rous nations, o'er the fields of Spain?

Morocco's lord commands the dreadful train.

Ne'er since the surges bath'd the circling coast,

Beneath one standard march'd so dread a host:

Such the dire fierceness of their brutal rage,

Pale are our bravest youth as palsied age.

By night our fathers' shades confess their fear,[248]

Their shrieks of terror from the tombs we hear:

To stem the rage of these unnumber'd bands,

Alone, O sire, my gallant husband stands;

His little host alone their breasts oppose

To the barb'd darts of Spain's innum'rous foes:

Then haste, O monarch, thou whose conqu'ring spear

Has chill'd Malucca's[249] sultry waves with fear:

Haste to the rescue of distress'd Castile,

(Oh! be that smile thy dear affection's seal!)

And speed, my father, ere my husband's fate

Be fix'd, and I, deprived of regal state,

Be left in captive solitude forlorn,

My spouse, my kingdom, and my birth to mourn."

In tears, and trembling, spoke the filial queen.

So, lost in grief, was lovely Venus[250] seen,

When Jove, her sire, the beauteous mourner pray'd

To grant her wand'ring son the promis'd aid.

Great Jove was mov'd to hear the fair deplore,

Gave all she ask'd, and griev'd she ask'd no more.

So griev'd Alonzo's noble heart. And now

The warrior binds in steel his awful brow;

The glitt'ring squadrons march in proud array,

On burnish'd shields the trembling sunbeams play:

The blaze of arms the warlike rage inspires,

And wakes from slothful peace the hero's fires.

With trampling hoofs Evora's plains rebound,

And sprightly neighings echo far around;

Far on each side the clouds of dust arise,

The drum's rough rattling rolls along the skies;

The trumpet's shrilly clangor sounds alarms,

And each heart burns, and ardent, pants for arms.

Where their bright blaze the royal ensigns pour'd,

High o'er the rest the great Alonzo tower'd;

High o'er the rest was his bold front admir'd,

And his keen eyes new warmth, new force inspir'd.

Proudly he march'd, and now, in Tarif's plain

The two Alonzos join their martial train:

Right to the foe, in battle-rank updrawn,

They pause—the mountain and the wide-spread lawn

Afford not foot-room for the crowded foe:

Aw'd with the horrors of the lifted blow

Pale look'd our bravest heroes. Swell'd with pride,

The foes already conquer'd Spain divide,

And, lordly o'er the field the promis'd victors stride.

So, strode in Elah's vale the tow'ring height

Of Gath's proud champion;[251] so, with pale affright,

The Hebrews trembled, while with impious pride

The huge-limb'd foe the shepherd boy[252] defied:

The valiant boy advancing, fits the string,

And round his head he whirls the sounding sling;

The monster staggers with the forceful wound,

And his huge bulk lies groaning on the ground.

Such impious scorn the Moor's proud bosom swell'd,

When our thin squadrons took the battle-field;

Unconscious of the Power who led us on,

That Power whose nod confounds th' eternal throne;

Led by that Power, the brave Castilian bar'd

The shining blade, and proud Morocco dar'd

His conqu'ring brand the Lusian hero drew,

And on Granada's sons resistless flew;
The spear-staffs crash, the splinters hiss around,
And the broad bucklers rattle on the ground:
With piercing shrieks the Moors their prophet's name,
And ours, their guardian saint, aloud acclaim.
Wounds gush on wounds, and blows resound to blows
A lake of blood the level plain o'erflows;
The wounded, gasping in the purple tide,
Now find the death the sword but half supplied.
Though wove[253] and quilted by their ladies' hands,
Vain were the mail-plates of Granada's bands.
With such dread force the Lusian rush'd along,
Steep'd in red carnage lay the boastful throng.
Yet now, disdainful of so light a prize,
Fierce o'er the field the thund'ring hero flies;
And his bold arm the brave Castilian joins
In dreadful conflict with the Moorish lines.

The parting sun now pour'd the ruddy blaze,
And twinkling Vesper shot his silv'ry rays
Athwart the gloom, and clos'd the glorious day,
When, low in dust, the strength of Afric lay.
Such dreadful slaughter of the boastful Moor
Never on battle-field was heap'd before;
Not he whose childhood vow'd[254] eternal hate
And desp'rate war against the Roman state:
Though three strong coursers bent beneath the weight
Of rings of gold (by many a Roman knight,
Erewhile, the badge of rank distinguish'd, worn),

From their cold hands at Cannæ's[255] slaughter torn;

Not his dread sword bespread the reeking plain

With such wide streams of gore, and hills of slain;

Nor thine, O Titus, swept from Salem's land

Such floods of ghosts, rolled down to death's dark strand;

Though, ages ere she fell, the prophets old

The dreadful scene of Salem's fall foretold,

In words that breathe wild horror: nor the shore,

When carnage chok'd the stream, so smok'd with gore,

When Marius' fainting legions drank the flood,

Yet warm, and purpled with Ambronian[256] blood;

Not such the heaps as now the plains of Tarif strew'd.

While glory, thus, Alonzo's name adorn'd,

To Lisbon's shores the happy chief return'd,

In glorious peace and well-deserv'd repose,

His course of fame, and honour'd age to close.

When now, O king, a damsel's fate[257] severe,

A fate which ever claims the woeful tear,

Disgraced his honours——On the nymph's 'lorn head

Relentless rage its bitterest rancour shed:

Yet, such the zeal her princely lover bore,

Her breathless corse the crown of Lisbon wore.

'Twas thou, O Love, whose dreaded shafts control

The hind's rude heart, and tear the hero's soul;

Thou, ruthless power, with bloodshed never cloy'd,

'Twas thou thy lovely votary destroy'd.

Thy thirst still burning for a deeper woe,

In vain to thee the tears of beauty flow;

The breast that feels thy purest flames divine,
With spouting gore must bathe thy cruel shrine.
Such thy dire triumphs!—Thou, O nymph, the while,
Prophetic of the god's unpitying guile,
In tender scenes by love-sick fancy wrought,
By fear oft shifted, as by fancy brought,
In sweet Mondego's ever-verdant bowers,
Languish'd away the slow and lonely hours:
While now, as terror wak'd thy boding fears,
The conscious stream receiv'd thy pearly tears;
And now, as hope reviv'd the brighter flame,
Each echo sigh'd thy princely lover's name.
Nor less could absence from thy prince remove
The dear remembrance of his distant love:
Thy looks, thy smiles, before him ever glow,
And o'er his melting heart endearing flow:
By night his slumbers bring thee to his arms,
By day his thoughts still wander o'er thy charms:
By night, by day, each thought thy loves employ,
Each thought the memory, or the hope, of joy.
Though fairest princely dames invok'd his love,
No princely dame his constant faith could move:
For thee, alone, his constant passion burn'd,
For thee the proffer'd royal maids he scorn'd.
Ah, hope of bliss too high—the princely dames
Refus'd, dread rage the father's breast inflames;
He, with an old man's wintry eye, surveys
The youth's fond love, and coldly with it weighs
The people's murmurs of his son's delay

To bless the nation with his nuptial day.

(Alas, the nuptial day was past unknown,

Which, but when crown'd, the prince could dare to own.)

And, with the fair one's blood, the vengeful sire

Resolves to quench his Pedro's faithful fire.

Oh, thou dread sword, oft stain'd with heroes' gore,

Thou awful terror of the prostrate Moor,

What rage could aim thee at a female breast,

Unarm'd, by softness and by love possess'd!

Dragg'd from her bower, by murd'rous ruffian hands,

Before the frowning king fair Inez stands;

Her tears of artless innocence, her air

So mild, so lovely, and her face so fair,

Mov'd the stern monarch; when, with eager zeal,

Her fierce destroyers urg'd the public weal;

Dread rage again the tyrant's soul possess'd,

And his dark brow his cruel thoughts confess'd;

O'er her fair face a sudden paleness spread,

Her throbbing heart with gen'rous anguish bled,

Anguish to view her lover's hopeless woes,

And all the mother in her bosom rose.

Her beauteous eyes, in trembling tear-drops drown'd,

To heaven she lifted (for her hands were bound);[258]

Then, on her infants turn'd the piteous glance,

The look of bleeding woe; the babes advance,

Smiling in innocence of infant age,

Unaw'd, unconscious of their grandsire's rage;

To whom, as bursting sorrow gave the flow,

The native heart-sprung eloquence of woe,
The lovely captive thus:—"O monarch, hear,
If e'er to thee the name of man was dear,
If prowling tigers, or the wolf's wild brood
(Inspir'd by nature with the lust of blood),
Have yet been mov'd the weeping babe to spare,
Nor left, but tended with a nurse's care,
As Rome's great founders[259] to the world were given;
Shalt thou, who wear'st the sacred stamp of Heaven,
The human form divine, shalt thou deny
That aid, that pity, which e'en beasts supply!
Oh, that thy heart were, as thy looks declare,
Of human mould, superfluous were my prayer;
Thou couldst not, then, a helpless damsel slay,
Whose sole offence in fond affection lay,
In faith to him who first his love confess'd,
Who first to love allur'd her virgin breast.
In these my babes shalt thou thine image see,
And, still tremendous, hurl thy rage on me?
Me, for their sakes, if yet thou wilt not spare,
Oh, let these infants prove thy pious care![260]
Yet, Pity's lenient current ever flows
From that brave breast where genuine valour glows;
That thou art brave, let vanquish'd Afric tell,
Then let thy pity o'er mine anguish swell;
Ah, let my woes, unconscious of a crime,
Procure mine exile to some barb'rous clime:
Give me to wander o'er the burning plains
Of Libya's deserts, or the wild domains

Of Scythia's snow-clad rocks, and frozen shore;

There let me, hopeless of return, deplore:

Where ghastly horror fills the dreary vale,

Where shrieks and howlings die on every gale,

The lion's roaring, and the tiger's yell,

There, with mine infant race, consign'd to dwell,

There let me try that piety to find,

In vain by me implor'd from human kind:

There, in some dreary cavern's rocky womb,

Amid the horrors of sepulchral gloom,

For him whose love I mourn, my love shall glow,

The sigh shall murmur, and the tear shall flow:

All my fond wish, and all my hope, to rear

These infant pledges of a love so dear,

Amidst my griefs a soothing glad employ,

Amidst my fears a woeful, hopeless joy."

In tears she utter'd—as the frozen snow

Touch'd by the spring's mild ray, begins to flow,

So, just began to melt his stubborn soul,

As mild-ray'd Pity o'er the tyrant stole;

But destiny forbade: with eager zeal

(Again pretended for the public weal),

Her fierce accusers urg'd her speedy doom;

Again, dark rage diffus'd its horrid gloom

O'er stern Alonzo's brow: swift at the sign,

Their swords, unsheath'd, around her brandish'd shine.

O foul disgrace, of knighthood lasting stain,

By men of arms a helpless lady[261] slain!

Thus Pyrrhus,[262] burning with unmanly ire,

Fulfilled the mandate of his furious sire;

Disdainful of the frantic matron's[263] prayer,

On fair Polyxena, her last fond care,

He rush'd, his blade yet warm with Priam's gore,

And dash'd the daughter on the sacred floor;

While mildly she her raving mother eyed,

Resign'd her bosom to the sword, and died.

Thus Inez, while her eyes to heaven appeal,

Resigns her bosom to the murd'ring steel:

That snowy neck, whose matchless form sustain'd

The loveliest face where all the graces reign'd,

Whose charms so long the gallant prince enflam'd,

That her pale corse was Lisbon's queen[264] proclaim'd,

That snowy neck was stain'd with spouting gore,

Another sword her lovely bosom tore.

The flowers that glisten'd with her tears bedew'd,

Now shrunk and languish'd with her blood embru'd.

As when a rose, ere-while of bloom so gay,

Thrown from the careless virgin's breast away,

Lies faded on the plain, the living red,

The snowy white, and all its fragrance fled;

So from her cheeks the roses died away,

And pale in death the beauteous Inez lay:

With dreadful smiles, and crimson'd with her blood,

Round the wan victim the stern murd'rers stood,

Unmindful of the sure, though future hour,

Sacred to vengeance and her lover's power.

O Sun, couldst thou so foul a crime behold,

Nor veil thine head in darkness, as of old[265]

A sudden night unwonted horror cast

O'er that dire banquet, where the sire's repast

The son's torn limbs supplied!—Yet you, ye vales!

Ye distant forests, and ye flow'ry dales!

When pale and sinking to the dreadful fall,

You heard her quiv'ring lips on Pedro call;

Your faithful echoes caught the parting sound,

And Pedro! Pedro! mournful, sigh'd around.

Nor less the wood-nymphs of Mondego's groves

Bewail'd the memory of her hapless loves:

Her griefs they wept, and, to a plaintive rill

Transform'd their tears, which weeps and murmurs still.

To give immortal pity to her woe

They taught the riv'let through her bowers to flow,

And still, through violet-beds, the fountain pours

Its plaintive wailing, and is named Amours.[266]

Nor long her blood for vengeance cried in vain:

Her gallant lord begins his awful reign,

In vain her murd'rers for refuge fly,

Spain's wildest hills no place of rest supply.

The injur'd lover's and the monarch's ire,

And stern-brow'd Justice in their doom conspire:

In hissing flames they die, and yield their souls in fire.[267]

Nor this alone his stedfast soul display'd:

Wide o'er the land he wav'd the awful blade

Of red-arm'd Justice. From the shades of night
He dragg'd the foul adulterer to light:
The robber from his dark retreat was led,
And he who spilt the blood of murder, bled.
Unmov'd he heard the proudest noble plead;
Where Justice aim'd her sword, with stubborn speed
Fell the dire stroke. Nor cruelty inspir'd,
Noblest humanity his bosom fir'd.
The caitiff, starting at his thoughts, repress'd
The seeds of murder springing in his breast.
His outstretch'd arm the lurking thief withheld,
For fix'd as fate he knew his doom was seal'd.
Safe in his monarch's care the ploughman reap'd,
And proud oppression coward distance kept.
Pedro the Just[268] the peopled towns proclaim,
And every field resounds her monarch's name.

Of this brave prince the soft degen'rate son,
Fernando the Remiss, ascends the throne.
With arm unnerv'd the listless soldier lay
And own'd the influence of a nerveless sway:
The stern Castilian drew the vengeful brand,
And strode proud victor o'er the trembling land.
How dread the hour, when injur'd heaven, in rage,
Thunders its vengeance on a guilty age!
Unmanly sloth the king, the nation stain'd;
And lewdness, foster'd by the monarch, reign'd:
The monarch own'd that first of crimes unjust,
The wanton revels of adult'rous lust:

Such was his rage for beauteous[269] Leonore,

Her from her husband's widow'd arms he tore:

Then with unbless'd, unhallow'd nuptials stain'd

The sacred altar, and its rites profan'd.

Alas! the splendour of a crown, how vain,

From Heaven's dread eye to veil the dimmest stain!

To conqu'ring Greece, to ruin'd Troy, what woes,

What ills on ills, from Helen's rape arose!

Let Appius own, let banish'd Tarquin tell

On their hot rage what heavy vengeance fell.

One female, ravish'd, Gibeah's streets[270] beheld,

O'er Gibeah's streets the blood of thousands swell'd

In vengeance of the crime; and streams of blood

The guilt of Zion's sacred bard[271] pursued.

Yet Love, full oft, with wild delirium blinds,

And fans his basest fires in noblest minds;

The female garb the great Alcides[272] wore,

And for his Omphăa le the distaff[273] bore.

For Cleopatra's frown the world was lost:

The Roman terror, and the Punic boast,

Cannæ's great victor,[274] for a harlot's smile,

Resign'd the harvest of his glorious toil.

And who can boast he never felt the fires,

The trembling throbbings of the young desires,

When he beheld the breathing roses glow,

And the soft heavings of the living snow;

The waving ringlets of the auburn hair,

And all the rapt'rous graces of the fair!

Oh! what defence, if fix'd on him, he spy

The languid sweetness of the stedfast eye!

Ye who have felt the dear, luxurious smart,

When angel-charms oppress the powerless heart,

In pity here relent the brow severe,

And o'er Fernando's weakness drop the tear.

To conclude the notes on this book, it may not be unnecessary to observe that Camoëns, in this episode, has happily adhered to a principal rule of the Epopea. To paint the manners and characters of the age in which the action is placed, is as requisite in the epic poem as it is to preserve the unity of the character of an individual. That gallantry of bravery and romantic cast of the military adventures, which characterised the Spaniards and Portuguese during the Moorish wars, is happily supported by Camoëns in its most just and striking colours. In storming the citadel of Arzila, the Count de Marialva, a brave old officer, lost his life. The king, leading his only son, the Prince Don Juan, to the body of the count, while the blood yet streamed from his wounds: "Behold," he cried, "that great man! May God grant you, my son, to imitate his virtues. May your honour, like his, be complete!"

END OF THE THIRD BOOK.

BOOK IV.

THE ARGUMENT.

STATE OF PORTUGAL ON THE DEATH OF DOM FERNANDO.

Beatrice, daughter of Fernando, not acknowledged by the Portuguese, the throne is occupied by Don John, a natural brother of Fernando. A Spanish prince having married Beatrice, the Spaniards invade Portugal, which they claim by right of marriage. The Portuguese, divided in council, are harangued in an eloquent speech by Don Nuño Alvarez Pereyra; he rallies the nobility around the king, who conquers the Castilians on the gory field of Aljubarota. Nuño Alvarez, following up his victory, penetrates as far as Seville, where he dictates the terms of peace to the haughty Spaniards. Don John carries war against the Moors into Africa. His son, Edward, renews hostilities with the African Moors: his brother, Don Fernando, surnamed the Inflexible, taken prisoner, prefers death in captivity to the surrender of Ceuta to the Moors, as the price of his ransom. Alfonso V. succeeds to the throne of Portugal; is victorious over the Moors, but conquered by the Castilians. John II., the thirteenth king of Portugal, sends out adventurers to find a way, by land, to India; they perish at the mouth of the Indus. Emmanuel, succeeding to the throne, resolves on continuing the discoveries of his predecessors. The rivers Indus and Ganges, personified, appear in a vision to Emmanuel, who, in consequence, makes choice of Vasco de Gama to command an expedition to the East.

AS the toss'd vessel on the ocean rolls,

When dark the night, and loud the tempest howls,

When the 'lorn mariner in every wave

That breaks and gleams, forebodes his wat'ry grave;

But when the dawn, all silent and serene,

With soft-pac'd ray dispels the shades obscene,

With grateful transport sparkling in each eye,

The joyful crew the port of safety spy;

Such darkling tempests, and portended fate,

While weak Fernando liv'd, appall'd the state;

Such when he died, the peaceful morning rose,

The dawn of joy, and sooth'd the public woes.

As blazing glorious o'er the shades of night,

Bright in his east breaks forth the lord of light,

So, valiant John with dazzling blaze appears,

And, from the dust his drooping nation rears.

Though sprung from youthful passion's wanton loves,[275]

Great Pedro's son in noble soul he proves;

And Heaven announc'd him king by right divine;—

A cradled infant gave the wondrous sign.[276]

Her tongue had never lisp'd the mother's name,

No word, no mimic sound her lips could frame,

When Heaven the miracle of speech inspir'd:

She raised her little hands, with rapture fir'd,

"Let Portugal," she cried, "with joy proclaim

The brave Don John, and own her monarch's name."

The burning fever of domestic rage
Now wildly rav'd, and mark'd the barb'rous age;
Through every rank the headlong fury ran,
And first, red slaughter in the court began.
Of spousal vows, and widow'd bed defil'd,
Loud fame the beauteous Leonore revil'd.
The adult'rous noble in her presence bled,
And, torn with wounds, his num'rous friends lay dead.
No more those ghastly, deathful nights amaze,
When Rome wept tears of blood in Scylla's days:
More horrid deeds Ulysses' towers[277] beheld:
Each cruel breast, where rankling envy swell'd,
Accus'd his foe as minion of the queen;
Accus'd, and murder closed the dreary scene.
All holy ties the frantic transport brav'd,
Nor sacred priesthood, nor the altar sav'd.
Thrown from a tower, like Hector's son of yore,
The mitred head[278] was dash'd with brains and gore.
Ghastly with scenes of death, and mangled limbs,
And, black with clotted blood, each pavement swims.

With all the fierceness of the female ire,
When rage and grief to tear the breast conspire,
The queen beheld her power, her honours lost,[279]
And ever, when she slept, th' adult'rer's ghost,
All pale, and pointing at his bloody shroud,
Seem'd ever for revenge to scream aloud.

173

Castile's proud monarch to the nuptial bed,

In happier days, her royal daughter[280] led.

To him the furious queen for vengeance cries,

Implores to vindicate his lawful prize,

The Lusian sceptre, his by spousal right;

The proud Castilian arms, and dares the fight.

To join his standard as it waves along,

The warlike troops from various regions throng:

Those who possess the lands by Rodrick given,[281]

What time the Moor from Turia's banks was driven;

That race who joyful smile at war's alarms,

And scorn each danger that attends on arms;

Whose crooked ploughshares Leon's uplands tear,

Now, cas'd in steel, in glitt'ring arms appear,

Those arms erewhile so dreadful to the Moor:

The Vandals glorying in their might of yore

March on; their helms, and moving lances gleam

Along the flow'ry vales of Betis' stream:

Nor stay'd the Tyrian islanders[282] behind,

On whose proud ensigns, floating on the wind,

Alcides' pillars[283] tower'd: Nor wonted fear

Withheld the base Galician's sordid spear;

Though, still, his crimson seamy scars reveal

The sure-aimed vengeance of the Lusian steel.

Where, tumbling down Cuenca's mountain side,

The murm'ring Tagus rolls his foamy tide,

Along Toledo's lawns, the pride of Spain,

Toledo's warriors join the martial train:

Nor less the furious lust of war inspires

The Biscayneer,[284] and wakes his barb'rous fires,

Which ever burn for vengeance, if the tongue

Of hapless stranger give the fancied wrong.

Nor bold Asturia, nor Guipuscoa's shore,

Famed for their steely wealth, and iron ore,

Delay'd their vaunting squadrons; o'er the dales

Cas'd in their native steel, and belted mails,

Blue gleaming from afar, they march along,

And join, with many a spear, the warlike throng.

As thus, wide sweeping o'er the trembling coast,

The proud Castilian leads his num'rous host;

The valiant John for brave defence prepares,

And, in himself collected, greatly dares:

For such high valour in his bosom glow'd,

As Samson's locks[285] by miracle bestow'd:

Safe, in himself resolv'd, the hero stands,

Yet, calls the leaders of his anxious bands:

The council summon'd, some with prudent mien,

And words of grave advice their terrors screen.

By sloth debas'd, no more the ancient fire

Of patriot loyalty can now inspire;

And each pale lip seem'd opening to declare

For tame submission, and to shun the war;

When glorious Nunio, starting from his seat,

Claim'd every eye, and clos'd the cold debate:

Singling his brothers from the dastard train,

His rolling looks, that flash'd with stern disdain,

On them he fix'd, then snatch'd his hilt in ire,

While his bold speech[286] bewray'd the soldier's fire,

Bold and unpolish'd; while his burning eyes

Seem'd as he dar'd the ocean, earth, and skies.

"Heavens! shall the Lusian nobles tamely yield!

Oh, shame! and yield, untried, the martial field!

That land whose genius, as the god of war,

Was own'd, where'er approach'd her thund'ring car;

Shall now her sons their faith, their love deny,

And, while their country sinks, ignobly fly;

Ye tim'rous herd, are ye the genuine line

Of those illustrious shades, whose rage divine,

Beneath great Henry's standards aw'd the foe,

For whom ye tremble and would stoop so low!

That foe, who, boastful now, then basely fled,

When your undaunted sires the hero led,

When seven bold earls, in chains, the spoil adorn'd,

And proud Castile through all her kindreds mourn'd,

Castile, your awful dread—yet, conscious, say,

When Diniz reign'd, when his bold son bore sway,

By whom were trodden down the bravest bands

That ever march'd from proud Castilia's lands?

'Twas your brave sires—and has one languid reign

Fix'd in your tainted souls so deep a stain,

That now, degen'rate from your noble sires,

The last dim spark of Lusian flame expires?

Though weak Fernando reign'd, in war unskill'd,

A godlike king now calls you to the field.

Oh! could like his, your mounting valour glow,

176

Vain were the threat'nings of the vaunting foe.
Not proud Castile, oft by your sires o'erthrown,
But ev'ry land your dauntless rage should own.
Still, if your hands, benumb'd by female fear,
Shun the bold war, hark! on my sword I swear,
Myself alone the dreadful war shall wage,
Mine be the fight"—and, trembling with the rage
Of val'rous fire, his hand half-drawn display'd
The awful terror of his shining blade,—
"I and my vassals dare the dreadful shock;
My shoulders never to a foreign yoke
Shall bend; and, by my sov'reign's wrath I vow,
And, by that loyal faith renounc'd by you,
My native land unconquer'd shall remain,
And all my monarch's foes shall heap the plain."

The hero paus'd—'Twas thus the youth of Rome,
The trembling few who 'scaped the bloody doom
That dy'd with slaughter Cannæ's purple field,
Assembled stood, and bow'd their necks to yield;
When nobly rising, with a like disdain,
The young Cornelius rag'd, nor rag'd in vain:[287]
On his dread sword his daunted peers he swore,
(The reeking blade yet black with Punic gore)
While life remain'd their arms for Rome to wield,
And, but with life, their conquer'd arms to yield.
Such martial rage brave Nunio's mien inspir'd;
Fear was no more: with rapt'rous ardour fir'd,
"To horse, to horse!" the gallant Lusians cried;

Rattled the belted mails on every side,

The spear-staff trembled; round their necks they wav'd

Their shining falchions, and in transport rav'd,

"The king our guardian!"—loud their shouts rebound,

And the fierce commons echo back the sound.

The mails, that long in rusting peace had hung,

Now on the hammer'd anvils hoarsely rung:

Some, soft with wool, the plumy helmets line,

And some the breast-plate's scaly belts entwine:

The gaudy mantles some, and scarfs prepare,

Where various lightsome colours gaily flare;

And golden tissue, with the warp enwove,

Displays the emblems of their youthful love.

The valiant John, begirt with warlike state,

Now leads his bands from fair Abrantes' gate;

Whose lawns of green the infant Tagus laves,

As from his spring he rolls his cooly waves.

The daring van, in Nunio's care, could boast

A general worthy of th' unnumber'd host,

Whose gaudy banners trembling Greece defied,

When boastful Xerxes lash'd the Sestian[288] tide:

Nunio, to proud Castile as dread a name,

As erst to Gaul and Italy the fame

Of Attila's impending rage. The right

Brave Roderic led, a chieftain train'd in fight;

Before the left the bold Almada rode;

And, proudly waving o'er the centre, nod

The royal ensigns, glitt'ring from afar,

Where godlike John inspires and leads the war.

'Twas now the time, when from the stubbly plain
The lab'ring hinds had borne the yellow grain;
The purple vintage heap'd the foamy tun,
And fierce, and red, the sun of August shone;
When from the gate the squadrons march along:
Crowds press'd on crowds, the walls and ramparts throng.
Here the sad mother rends her hoary hair,
While hope's fond whispers struggle with despair:
The weeping spouse to Heaven extends her hands:
And, cold with dread, the modest virgin stands,
Her earnest eyes, suffus'd with trembling dew,
Far o'er the plain the plighted youth pursue:
And prayers, and tears, and all the female wail,
And holy vows, the throne of Heaven assail.

Now each stern host full front to front appears,
And one joint shout heaven's airy concave tears:
A dreadful pause ensues, while conscious pride
Strives on each face the heart-felt doubt to hide.
Now wild, and pale, the boldest face is seen;
With mouth half open, and disorder'd mien,
Each warrior feels his creeping blood to freeze,
And languid weakness trembles in the knees.
And now, the clangor of the trumpet sounds,
And the rough rattling of the drum rebounds:
The fife's shrill whistling cuts the gale, on high
The flourish'd ensigns shine, with many a dye

Of blazing splendour: o'er the ground they wheel

And choose their footing, when the proud Castile

Bids sound the horrid charge; loud bursts the sound,

And loud Artabro's rocky cliffs rebound:

The thund'ring roar rolls round on every side,

And trembling, sinks Guidana's[289] rapid tide;

The slow-pac'd Durius[290] rushes o'er the plain,

And fearful Tagus hastens to the main:

Such was the tempest of the dread alarms,

The babes that prattled in their nurses' arms

Shriek'd at the sound: with sudden cold impress'd,

The mothers strain'd their infants to the breast,

And shook with horror. Now, far round, begin

The bow-strings' whizzing, and the brazen[291] din

Of arms on armour rattling; either van

Are mingled now, and man oppos'd to man:

To guard his native fields the one inspires,

And one the raging lust of conquest fires:

Now with fix'd teeth, their writhing lips of blue,

Their eye-balls glaring of the purple hue,

Each arm strains swiftest to impel the blow;

Nor wounds they value now, nor fear they know,

Their only passion to offend the foe.

Before his troops the glorious Nunio rode:

That land, the proud invaders claim'd, he sows

With their spilt blood, and with their corpses strews;

Their forceful volleys now the cross-bows pour,

The clouds are darken'd with the arrowy shower;

The white foam reeking o'er their wavy mane,

The snorting coursers rage, and paw the plain;

Beat by their iron hoofs, the plain rebounds,

As distant thunder through the mountains sounds:

The pond'rous spears crash, splint'ring far around;

The horse and horsemen flounder on the ground;

The ground groans, with the sudden weight oppress'd,

And many a buckler rings on many a crest.

Where, wide around, the raging Nunio's sword

With furious sway the bravest squadrons gor'd,

The raging foes in closer ranks advance,

And his own brothers shake the hostile lance.[292]

Oh, horrid sight! yet not the ties of blood,

Nor yearning memory his rage withstood;

With proud disdain his honest eyes behold

Whoe'er the traitor, who his king has sold.

Nor want there others in the hostile band

Who draw their swords against their native land;

And, headlong driv'n, by impious rage accurs'd,

In rank were foremost, and in fight the first.

So, sons and fathers, by each other slain,

With horrid slaughter dyed Pharsalia's[293] plain.

Ye dreary ghosts, who now for treasons foul,

Amidst the gloom of Stygian darkness howl;

Thou Catiline, and, stern Sertorius, tell

Your brother shades, and soothe the pains of hell;

With triumph tell them, some of Lusian race

Like you have earn'd the traitor's foul disgrace.

As waves on waves, the foes' increasing weight

Bears down our foremost ranks, and shakes the fight;

Yet, firm and undismay'd great Nunio stands,

And braves the tumult of surrounding bands.

So, from high Ceuta's[294] rocky mountains stray'd,

The ranging lion braves the shepherd's shade;

The shepherds hast'ning o'er the Tetuan[295] plain,

With shouts surround him, and with spears restrain:

He stops, with grinning teeth his breath he draws,

Nor is it fear, but rage, that makes him pause;

His threat'ning eyeballs burn with sparkling fire,

And, his stern heart forbids him to retire:

Amidst the thickness of the spears he flings,

So, midst his foes, the furious Nunio springs:

The Lusian grass with foreign gore distain'd,

Displays the carnage of the hero's hand.

[An ample shield the brave Giraldo bore,

Which from the vanquish'd Perez' arm he tore;

Pierc'd through that shield, cold death invades his eye,

And dying Perez saw his victor die.

Edward and Pedro, emulous of fame,

The same their friendship, and their youth the same,

Through the fierce Brigians[296] hew'd their bloody way,

Till, in a cold embrace, the striplings lay.

Lopez and Vincent rush'd on glorious death,

And, midst their slaughter'd foes, resign'd their breath.

Alonzo, glorying in his youthful might,

Spurr'd his fierce courser through the stagg'ring fight:

Shower'd from the dashing hoofs, the spatter'd gore

Flies round; but, soon the rider vaunts no more:

Five Spanish swords the murm'ring ghosts atone,

Of five Castilians by his arm o'erthrown.

Transfix'd with three Iberian spears, the gay,

The knightly lover, young Hilario lay:

Though, like a rose, cut off in op'ning bloom,

The hero weeps not for his early doom;

Yet, trembling in his swimming eye appears

The pearly drop, while his pale cheek he rears;

To call his lov'd Antonia's name he tries,

The name half utter'd, down he sinks, and dies.][297]

Now through his shatter'd ranks the monarch strode,

And now before his rallied squadrons rode:

Brave Nunio's danger from afar he spies,

And instant to his aid impetuous flies.

So, when returning from the plunder'd folds,

The lioness her empty den beholds,

Enrag'd she stands, and list'ning to the gale,

She hears her whelps low howling in the vale;

The living sparkles flashing from her eyes,

To the Massylian[298] shepherd-tents she flies;

She groans, she roars, and echoing far around

The seven twin-mountains tremble at the sound:

So, rag'd the king, and, with a chosen train,

He pours resistless o'er the heaps of slain.

"Oh, bold companions of my toils," he cries,

"Our dear-lov'd freedom on our lances lies;

Behold your friend, your monarch leads the way,

183

And dares the thickest of the iron fray.
Say, shall the Lusian race forsake their king,
Where spears infuriate on the bucklers ring!"

He spoke; then four times round his head he whirl'd
His pond'rous spear, and midst the foremost hurl'd;
Deep through the ranks the forceful weapon pass'd,
And many a gasping warrior sigh'd his last.[299]
With noble shame inspir'd, and mounting rage,
His bands rush on, and foot to foot engage;
Thick bursting sparkles from the blows aspire;
Such flashes blaze, their swords seem dipp'd in fire;[300]
The belts of steel and plates of brass are riv'n,
And wound for wound, and death for death is giv'n.

The first in honour of Saint Jago's band,[301]
A naked ghost now sought the gloomy strand;
And he of Calatrave, the sov'reign knight,
Girt with whole troops his arm had slain in fight,
Descended murm'ring to the shades of night.
Blaspheming Heaven, and gash'd with many a wound,
Brave Nunio's rebel kindred gnaw'd the ground.
And curs'd their fate, and died. Ten thousand more
Who held no title and no office bore,
And nameless nobles who, promiscuous fell,
Appeas'd that day the foaming dog of hell.[302]
Now, low the proud Castilian standard lies
Beneath the Lusian flag; a vanquish'd prize.
With furious madness fired, and stern disdain,

The fierce Iberians[303] to the fight again
Rush headlong; groans and yellings of despair
With horrid uproar rend the trembling air.
Hot boils the blood, thirst burns, and every breast
Pants, every limb, with fainty weight oppress'd,
Slow now obeys the will's stern ire, and slow
From every sword descends the feeble blow:
Till rage grew languid, and tir'd slaughter found
No arm to combat, and no breast to wound.
Now from the field Castile's proud monarch flies,[304]
In wild dismay he rolls his madd'ning eyes,
And leads the pale-lipp'd flight, swift wing'd with fear,
As drifted smoke; at distance disappear,
The dusty squadrons of the scatter'd rear;
Blaspheming Heaven, they fly, and him who first
Forg'd murd'ring arms, and led to horrid wars accurs'd.

The festive days by heroes old ordain'd[305]
The glorious victor on the field remain'd.
The funeral rites, and holy vows he paid:
Yet, not the while the restless Nunio stay'd;
O'er Tago's waves his gallant bands he led,
And humbled Spain in every province bled:
Sevilia's standard on his spear he bore,
And Andalusia's ensigns, steep'd in gore.
Low in the dust, distress'd Castilia mourn'd,
And, bath'd in tears, each eye to Heav'n was turn'd;
The orphan's, widow's, and the hoary sire's;
And Heav'n relenting, quench'd the raging fires

Of mutual hate: from England's happy shore
The peaceful seas two lovely sisters bore.[306]
The rival monarchs to the nuptial bed,
In joyful hour, the royal virgins led,
And holy peace assum'd her blissful reign,
Again the peasant joy'd, the landscape smiled again.

But, John's brave breast to warlike cares inur'd,
With conscious shame the sloth of ease endu'rd,
When not a foe awak'd his a rage in Spain,
The valiant hero brav'd the foamy main;
The first, nor meanest, of our kings who bore
The Lusian thunders to the Afric shore.
O'er the wild waves the victor-banners flow'd,
Their silver wings a thousand eagles show'd;
And, proudly swelling to the whistling gales,
The seas were whiten'd with a thousand sails.
Beyond the columns by Alcides[307] plac'd
To bound the world, the zealous warrior pass'd.
The shrines of Hagar's race, the shrines of lust,
And moon-crown'd mosques lay smoking in the dust.
O'er Abyla's high steep his lance he rais'd,
On Ceuta's lofty towers his standard blaz'd:
Ceuta, the refuge of the traitor train,
His vassal now, insures the peace of Spain.

But ah, how soon the blaze of glory dies![308]
Illustrious John ascends his native skies.
His gallant offspring prove their genuine strain,

And added lands increase the Lusian reign.

Yet, not the first of heroes Edward shone
His happiest days long hours of evil own.
He saw, secluded from the cheerful day,
His sainted brother pine his years away.
O glorious youth, in captive chains, to thee
What suiting honours may thy land decree![309]
Thy nation proffer'd, and the foe with joy,
For Ceuta's towers, prepar'd to yield the boy;
The princely hostage nobly spurns the thought
Of freedom, and of life so dearly bought:
The raging vengeance of the Moors defies,
Gives to the clanking chains his limbs, and dies
A dreary prison-death. Let noisy fame
No more unequall'd hold her Codrus' name;
Her Regulus, her Curtius boast no more,
Nor those the honour'd Decian name who bore.
The splendour of a court, to them unknown,
Exchang'd for deathful Fate's most awful frown,
To distant times, through every land, shall blaze
The self-devoted Lusian's nobler praise.

Now, to the tomb the hapless king descends,
His son, Alonzo, brighter fate attends.
Alonzo! dear to Lusus' race the name;
Nor his the meanest in the rolls of fame.
His might resistless, prostrate Afric own'd,
Beneath his yoke the Mauritanians[310] groan'd,

And, still they groan beneath the Lusian sway.
'Twas his, in victor-pomp, to bear away
The golden apples from Hesperia's shore,
Which but the son of Jove had snatch'd before.
The palm, and laurel, round his temples bound,
Display'd his triumphs on the Moorish ground.
When proud Arzilla's strength, Alcazer's towers,
And Tingia, boastful of her num'rous powers,
Beheld their adamantine walls o'erturn'd,
Their ramparts levell'd, and their temples burn'd.
Great was the day: the meanest sword that fought
Beneath the Lusian flag such wonders wrought
As from the muse might challenge endless fame,
Though low their station, and untold their name.

Now, stung with wild ambition's madd'ning fires,
To proud Castilia's throne the king[311] aspires.
The Lord of Arragon, from Cadiz' walls,
And hoar Pyrene's[312] sides his legions calls;
The num'rous legions to his standard throng,
And war, with horrid strides, now stalks along.
With emulation fir'd, the prince[313] beheld
His warlike sire ambitious of the field;
Scornful of ease, to aid his arms he sped,
Nor sped in vain: The raging combat bled:
Alonzo's ranks with carnage gor'd, Dismay
Spread her cold wings, and shook his firm array;
To flight she hurried; while, with brow serene,
The martial boy beheld the deathful scene.

With curving movement o'er the field he rode,
Th' opposing troops his wheeling squadrons mow'd:
The purple dawn, and evening sun beheld
His tents encamp'd assert the conquer'd field.
Thus, when the ghost of Julius[314] hover'd o'er
Philippi's plain, appeas'd with Roman gore,
Octavius' legions left the field in flight,
While happier Marcus triumph'd in the fight.

When endless night had seal'd his mortal eyes,
And brave Alonzo's spirit sought the skies,
The second of the name, the valiant John,
Our thirteenth monarch, now ascends the throne.
To seize immortal fame, his mighty mind,
(What man had never dar'd before), design'd;
That glorious labour which I now pursue,
Through seas unsail'd to find the shores that view
The day-star, rising from his wat'ry bed,
The first grey beams of infant morning shed.
Selected messengers his will obey;
Through Spain and France they hold their vent'rous way.
Through Italy they reach the port that gave
The fair Parthenope[315] an honour'd grave;[316]
That shore which oft has felt the servile chain,
But, now smiles happy in the care of Spain.
Now, from the port the brave advent'rers bore,
And cut the billows of the Rhodian shore;
Now, reach the strand where noble Pompey[317] bled;
And now, repair'd with rest, to Memphis sped;

And now, ascending by the vales of Nile,

(Whose waves pour fatness o'er the grateful soil),

Through Ethiopia's peaceful dales they stray,

Where their glad eyes Messiah's rites[318] survey:

And now they pass the fam'd Arabian flood,

Whose waves of old in wondrous ridges stood,

While Israel's favour'd race the sable[319] bottom trod:

Behind them, glist'ning to the morning skies,

The mountains nam'd from Ishmael's offspring[320] rise;

Now, round their steps the blest Arabia spreads

Her groves of odour, and her balmy meads;

And every breast, inspir'd with glee, inhales

The grateful fragrance of Sabæa's gales:

Now, past the Persian gulf their route ascends

Where Tigris' wave with proud Euphrates blends;

Illustrious streams, where still the native shows

Where Babel's haughty tower unfinished rose:

From thence, through climes unknown, their daring course

Beyond where Trajan forced his way, they force;[321]

Carmanian hordes, and Indian tribes they saw,

And many a barb'rous rite, and many a law[322]

Their search explor'd; but, to their native shore,

Enrich'd with knowledge, they return'd no more.

The glad completion of the fate's decree,

Kind Heaven reserv'd, Emmanuel, for thee.

The crown, and high ambition of thy[323] sires,

To thee descending, wak'd thy latent fires,

And, to command the sea from pole to pole,

With restless wish inflam'd thy mighty soul.

Now, from the sky, the sacred light withdrawn,
O'er heaven's clear azure shone the stars of dawn,
Deep silence spread her gloomy wings around,
And human griefs were wrapp'd in sleep profound.
The monarch slumber'd on his golden bed,
Yet, anxious cares possess'd his thoughtful head;
His gen'rous soul, intent on public good,
The glorious duties of his birth review'd.
When, sent by Heaven, a sacred dream inspir'd
His lab'ring mind, and with its radiance fir'd:
High to the clouds his tow'ring head was rear'd,
New worlds, and nations fierce, and strange, appear'd;
The purple dawning o'er the mountains flow'd,
The forest-boughs with yellow splendour glow'd;
High, from the steep, two copious glassy streams
Roll'd down, and glitter'd in the morning beams;
Here, various monsters of the wild were seen,
And birds of plumage azure, scarlet, green:
Here, various herbs, and flow'rs of various bloom;
There, black as night, the forest's horrid gloom,
Whose shaggy brakes, by human step untrod,
Darken'd the glaring lion's dread abode.
Here, as the monarch fix'd his wond'ring eyes,
Two hoary fathers from the streams arise;
Their aspect rustic, yet, a reverend grace
Appear'd majestic on their wrinkled face:
Their tawny beards uncomb'd, and sweepy long,

Adown their knees in shaggy ringlets hung;

From every lock the crystal drops distil,

And bathe their limbs, as in a trickling rill;

Gay wreaths of flowers, of fruitage, and of boughs,

(Nameless in Europe), crown'd their furrow'd brows.

Bent o'er his staff, more silver'd o'er with years,

Worn with a longer way, the one appears;

Who now slow beck'ning with his wither'd hand,

As now advanc'd before the king they stand:—

"O thou, whom worlds to Europe yet unknown,

Are doom'd to yield, and dignify thy crown;

To thee our golden shores the Fates decree;

Our necks, unbow'd before, shall bend to thee.

Wide thro' the world resounds our wealthy fame;

Haste, speed thy prows, that fated wealth to claim.

From Paradise my hallow'd waters spring;

The sacred Ganges I, my brother king

Th' illustrious author[324] of the Indian name:

Yet, toil shall languish, and the fight shall flame;

Our fairest lawns with streaming gore shall smoke,

Ere yet our shoulders bend beneath the yoke;

But, thou shalt conquer: all thine eyes survey,

With all our various tribes, shall own thy sway."

He spoke; and, melting in a silv'ry stream,

Both disappear'd; when waking from his dream,

The wond'ring monarch, thrill'd with awe divine,

Weighs in his lofty thoughts the sacred sign.

Now, morning bursting from the eastern sky,

Spreads o'er the clouds the blushing rose's dye,

The nations wake, and, at the sov'reign's call,

The Lusian nobles crowd the palace hall.

The vision of his sleep the monarch tells;

Each heaving breast with joyful wonder swells:

"Fulfil," they cry: "the sacred sign obey;

And spread the canvas for the Indian sea."

Instant my looks with troubled ardour burn'd,

When, keen on me, his eyes the monarch turn'd:

What he beheld I know not, but I know,

Big swell'd my bosom with a prophet's glow:

And long my mind, with wondrous bodings fir'd,

Had to the glorious, dreadful toil aspir'd:

Yet, to the king, whate'er my looks betray'd,

My looks the omen of success display'd.

When with that sweetness in his mien express'd,

Which, unresisted, wins the gen'rous breast,

"Great are the dangers, great the toils," he cried,

"Ere glorious honours crown the victor's pride.

If in the glorious strife the hero fall,

He proves no danger could his soul appal;

And, but to dare so great a toil, shall raise

Each age's wonder, and immortal praise.

For this dread toil, new oceans to explore,

To spread the sail where sail ne'er flow'd before,

For this dread labour, to your valour due,

From all your peers I name, O Vasco,[325] you.

Dread as it is, yet light the task shall be

To you my Gama, as perform'd for me."

My heart could bear no more:—"Let skies on fire,

Let frozen seas, let horrid war conspire,

I dare them all," I cried, "and, but repine

That one poor life is all I can resign.

Did to my lot Alcides'[326] labours fall,

For you my joyful heart would dare them all;

The ghastly realms of death, could man invade,

For you my steps should trace the ghastly shade."

While thus, with loyal zeal, my bosom swell'd,

That panting zeal my prince with joy beheld:

Honour'd with gifts I stood, but, honour'd more

By that esteem my joyful sov'reign bore.

That gen'rous praise which fires the soul of worth,

And gives new virtues unexpected birth,

That praise, e'en now, my heaving bosom fires,

Inflames my courage, and each wish inspires.

Mov'd by affection, and allur'd by fame,

A gallant youth, who bore the dearest name,

Paulus, my brother, boldly su'd to share

My toils, my dangers, and my fate in war;

And, brave Coëllo urg'd the hero's claim

To dare each hardship, and to join our fame:

For glory both with restless ardour burn'd,

And silken ease for horrid danger spurn'd;

Alike renown'd in council, or in field,

The snare to baffle, or the sword to wield.
Through Lisbon's youth the kindling ardour ran,
And bold ambition thrill'd from man to man;
And each, the meanest of the vent'rous band,
With gifts stood honour'd by the sov'reign's hand.
Heavens! what a fury swell'd each warrior's breast,
When each, in turn, the smiling king address'd!
Fir'd by his words the direst toils they scorn'd,
And, with the horrid lust of danger fiercely burn'd.

With such bold rage the youth of Mynia glow'd,
When the first keel the Euxine surges plough'd;
When, bravely vent'rous for the golden fleece,
Orac'lous Argo[327] sail'd from wond'ring Greece.
Where Tago's yellow stream the harbour laves,
And slowly mingles with the ocean waves,
In warlike pride, my gallant navy rode,
And, proudly o'er the beach my soldiers strode.
Sailors and landsmen, marshall'd o'er the strand,
In garbs of various hue around me stand;
Each earnest, first to plight the sacred vow,
Oceans unknown, and gulfs untried to plough:
Then, turning to the ships their sparkling eyes,
With joy they heard the breathing winds arise;
Elate with joy, beheld the flapping sail,
And purple standards floating on the gale:
While each presag'd, that great as Argo's fame,
Our fleet should give some starry band a name.

Where foaming on the shore the tide appears,

A sacred fane its hoary arches rears:

Dim o'er the sea the ev'ning shades descend,

And, at the holy shrine, devout, we bend:

There, while the tapers o'er the altar blaze,

Our prayers, and earnest vows to Heav'n we raise.

"Safe through the deep, where every yawning wave

Still to the sailor's eye displays his grave;

Thro' howling tempests, and thro' gulfs untried,

O mighty God! be thou our watchful guide."

While kneeling thus, before the sacred shrine,

In holy faith's most solemn rite we join;

Our peace with Heav'n the bread of peace confirms,

And meek contrition ev'ry bosom warms:

Sudden, the lights extinguish'd, all around

Dread silence reigns, and midnight-gloom profound;

A sacred horror pants on every breath,

And each firm breast devotes itself to death,

An offer'd sacrifice, sworn to obey

My nod, and follow where I lead the way.

Now, prostrate round the hallow'd shrine we lie,[328]

Till rosy morn bespreads the eastern sky;

Then, breathing fix'd resolves, my daring mates

March to the ships, while pour'd from Lisbon's gates,

Thousands on thousands crowding, press along,

A woful, weeping, melancholy throng.

A thousand white-rob'd priests our steps attend,

And prayers, and holy vows to Heav'n ascend;

A scene so solemn, and the tender woe

Of parting friends, constrain'd my tears to flow.
To weigh our anchors from our native shore—
To dare new oceans never dar'd before—
Perhaps to see my native coast no more—
Forgive, O king, if as a man I feel,
I bear no bosom of obdurate steel.——
(The godlike hero here suppress'd the sigh,
And wip'd the tear-drop from his manly eye;
Then, thus resuming)—All the peopled shore
An awful, silent look of anguish wore;
Affection, friendship, all the kindred ties
Of spouse and parent languish'd in their eyes:
As men they never should again behold,
Self-offer'd victims to destruction sold,
On us they fix'd the eager look of woe,
While tears o'er ev'ry cheek began to flow;
When thus aloud, "Alas! my son, my son,"
A hoary sire exclaims, "oh! whither run,
My heart's sole joy, my trembling age's stay,
To yield thy limbs the dread sea-monster's prey!
To seek thy burial in the raging wave,
And leave me cheerless sinking to the grave!
Was it for this I watch'd thy tender years,
And bore each fever of a father's fears!
Alas, my boy!"—His voice is heard no more,
The female shriek resounds along the shore:
With hair dishevell'd, through the yielding crowd
A lovely bride springs on, and screams aloud;
"Oh! where, my husband, where to seas unknown,

Where wouldst thou fly, me and my love disown!

And wilt thou, cruel, to the deep consign

That valued life, the joy, the soul of mine!

And must our loves, and all the kindred train

Of rapt endearments, all expire in vain!

All the dear transports of the warm embrace,

When mutual love inspir'd each raptur'd face!

Must all, alas! be scatter'd in the wind,

Nor thou bestow one ling'ring look behind!"

Such, the 'lorn parents' and the spouses' woes,

Such, o'er the strand the voice of wailing rose;

From breast to breast the soft contagion crept,

Moved by the woful sound the children wept;

The mountain-echoes catch the big swoll'n sighs,

And, through the dales, prolong the matron's cries;

The yellow sands with tears are silver'd o'er,

Our fate the mountains and the beach deplore.

Yet, firm we march, nor turn one glance aside

On hoary parent, or on lovely bride.

Though glory fir'd our hearts, too well we knew

What soft affection, and what love could do.

The last embrace the bravest worst can bear:

The bitter yearnings of the parting tear

Sullen we shun, unable to sustain

The melting passion of such tender pain.

Now, on the lofty decks, prepar'd, we stand,

When, tow'ring o'er the crowd that veil'd the strand,

A reverend figure[329] fix'd each wond'ring eye,
And, beck'ning thrice, he wav'd his hand on high,
And thrice his hoary curls he sternly shook,
While grief and anger mingled in his look;
Then, to its height his falt'ring voice he rear'd,
And through the fleet these awful words were heard:[330]

"O frantic thirst of honour and of fame,
The crowd's blind tribute, a fallacious name;
What stings, what plagues, what secret scourges curs'd,
Torment those bosoms where thy pride is nurs'd!
What dangers threaten, and what deaths destroy
The hapless youth, whom thy vain gleams decoy!
By thee, dire tyrant of the noble mind,
What dreadful woes are pour'd on human kind:
Kingdoms and empires in confusion hurl'd,
What streams of gore have drench'd the hapless world!
Thou dazzling meteor, vain as fleeting air,
What new-dread horror dost thou now prepare!
High sounds thy voice of India's pearly shore,
Of endless triumphs and of countless store:
Of other worlds so tower'd thy swelling boast,
Thy golden dreams when Paradise was lost,
When thy big promise steep'd the world in gore,
And simple innocence was known no more.
And say, has fame so dear, so dazzling charms?
Must brutal fierceness, and the trade of arms,
Conquest, and laurels dipp'd in blood, be priz'd,
While life is scorn'd, and all its joys despis'd?

And say, does zeal for holy faith inspire

To spread its mandates, thy avow'd desire?

Behold the Hagarene[331] in armour stands,

Treads on thy borders, and the foe demands:

A thousand cities own his lordly sway,

A thousand various shores his nod obey.

Through all these regions, all these cities, scorn'd

Is thy religion, and thine altars spurn'd.

A foe renown'd in arms the brave require;

That high-plum'd foe, renown'd for martial fire,

Before thy gates his shining spear displays,

Whilst thou wouldst fondly dare the wat'ry maze,

Enfeebled leave thy native land behind,

On shores unknown a foe unknown to find.

Oh! madness of ambition! thus to dare

Dangers so fruitless, so remote a war!

That Fame's vain flattery may thy name adorn,

And thy proud titles on her flag be borne:

Thee, lord of Persia, thee, of India lord,

O'er Ethiopia's vast, and Araby ador'd!

"Curs'd be the man who first on floating wood,

Forsook the beach, and braved the treach'rous flood!

Oh! never, never may the sacred Nine,[332]

To crown his brows, the hallow'd wreath entwine;

Nor may his name to future times resound;

Oblivion be his meed, and hell profound!

Curs'd be the wretch, the fire of heaven who stole,

And with ambition first debauch'd the soul!

200

What woes, Prometheus,[333] walk the frighten'd earth!

To what dread slaughter has thy pride giv'n birth!

On proud Ambition's pleasing gales upborne,

One boasts to guide the chariot of the morn;

And one on treach'rous pinions soaring high,[334]

O'er ocean's waves dar'd sail the liquid sky:

Dash'd from their height they mourn'd their blighted aim;

One gives a river, one a sea the name!

Alas! the poor reward of that gay meteor, fame!

Yet, such the fury of the mortal race,

Though fame's fair promise ends in foul disgrace,

Though conquest still the victor's hope betrays,

The prize a shadow, or a rainbow-blaze,

Yet, still through fire and raging seas they run

To catch the gilded shade, and sink undone!"

END OF THE FOURTH BOOK.

BOOK V.

THE ARGUMENT.

Departure of the expedition under the command of Vasco de Gama (A.D. 1497). Mountains of Portugal, Cintra, Morocco. Madeira; the burning shores of the Desert of Zanhagan; passage of the Tropic; cold waters of the dark river Senegal. San Jago; pass the rocky coasts of Sierra Leone, the island of St. Thomas, the kingdom of Congo, watered by the great river Zaire. They cross the line and behold the magnificent constellation of the Southern Cross, not visible in the northern hemisphere. After a voyage of five months, with continued storms, they arrive in the latitude of the Cape. Apparition of Adamastor, the giant of the Cape of Storms. His prophecy. The King of Melinda confirms, by the tradition of his people, the weird story of the Cape-giant told him by Gama. Narrative of the voyage continued; arrival of the expedition at the Port of Good Promise; pass by the ports of Mozambique and Mombas, and arrive at Melinda.

WHILE on the beach the hoary father stood,

201

And spoke the murmurs of the multitude,

We spread the canvas to the rising gales,

The gentle winds distend the snowy sails.

As from our dear-lov'd native shore we fly

Our votive shouts, redoubled, rend the sky;

"Success, success!" far echoes o'er the tide,

While our broad hulks the foamy waves divide.

From Leo[335] now, the lordly star of day,

Intensely blazing, shot his fiercest ray;

When, slowly gliding from our wishful eyes,

The Lusian mountains mingled with the skies;

Tago's lov'd stream, and Cintra's[336] mountains cold

Dim fading now, we now no more behold;

And, still with yearning hearts our eyes explore,

Till one dim speck of land appears no more.

Our native soil now far behind, we ply

The lonely dreary waste of seas, and boundless sky

Through the wild deep our vent'rous navy bore,

Where but our Henry plough'd the wave before;[337]

The verdant islands, first by him descried,

We pass'd; and, now in prospect op'ning wide,

Far to the left, increasing on the view,

Rose Mauritania's[338] hills of paly blue:

Far to the right the restless ocean roar'd,

Whose bounding surges never keel explor'd:

If bounding shore (as reason deems) divide

The vast Atlantic from the Indian tide.[339]

Nam'd from her woods,[340] with fragrant bowers adorn'd,

From fair Madeira's purple coast we turn'd:[340]
Cyprus and Paphos' vales the smiling loves
Might leave with joy for fair Madeira's groves;
A shore so flow'ry, and so sweet an air,
Venus might build her dearest temple there.
Onward we pass Massilia's barren strand,
A waste of wither'd grass and burning sand;
Where his thin herds the meagre native leads,
Where not a riv'let laves the doleful meads;
Nor herds, nor fruitage deck the woodland maze;
O'er the wild waste the stupid ostrich strays,
In devious search to pick her scanty meal,
Whose fierce digestion gnaws the temper'd steel.
From the green verge, where Tigitania ends,
To Ethiopia's line the dreary wild extends.
Now, past the limit, which his course divides,[341]
When to the north the sun's bright chariot rides,
We leave the winding bays and swarthy shores,
Where Senegal's black wave impetuous roars;
A flood, whose course a thousand tribes surveys,
The tribes who blacken'd in the fiery blaze
When Phaëton, devious from the solar height,
Gave Afric's sons the sable hue of night.
And now, from far the Libyan cape is seen,
Now by my mandate named the Cape of Green;[342]
Where, midst the billows of the ocean, smiles
A flow'ry sister-train, the happy isles,[343]
Our onward prows the murm'ring surges lave;
And now, our vessels plough the gentle wave,

Where the blue islands, named of Hesper old,

Their fruitful bosoms to the deep unfold.

Here, changeful Nature shows her various face,

And frolics o'er the slopes with wildest grace:

Here, our bold fleet their pond'rous anchors threw,

The sickly cherish, and our stores renew.

From him, the warlike guardian pow'r of Spain,

Whose spear's dread lightning o'er th' embattled plain

Has oft o'erwhelm'd the Moors in dire dismay,

And fix'd the fortune of the doubtful day;

From him we name our station of repair,

And Jago's name that isle shall ever bear.

The northern winds now curl'd the black'ning main,

Our sails unfurl'd, we plough the tide again:

Round Afric's coast our winding course we steer,

Where, bending to the east, the shores appear.

Here Jalofo[344] its wide extent displays,

And vast Mandinga shows its num'rous bays;

Whose mountains' sides, though parch'd and barren, hold,

In copious store, the seeds of beamy gold.[345]

The Gambia here his serpent-journey takes,

And, thro' the lawns, a thousand windings makes;

A thousand swarthy tribes his current laves

Ere mix his waters with th' Atlantic waves.

The Gorgades we pass'd, that hated shore,[346]

Fam'd for its terrors by the bards of yore;

Where but one eye by Phorcus' daughters shar'd,

The 'lorn beholders into marble star'd;

Three dreadful sisters! down whose temples roll'd

Their hair of snakes in many a hissing fold,

And, scatt'ring horror o'er the dreary strand,

With swarms of vipers sow'd the burning sand.

Still to the south our pointed keels we guide,

And, thro' the austral gulf, still onward ride:

Her palmy forests mingling with the skies,

Leona's[347] rugg'd steep behind us flies;

The Cape of Palms[348] that jutting land we name,

Already conscious of our nation's[349] fame.

Where the vex'd waves against our bulwarks roar,

And Lusian towers o'erlook the bending shore:

Our sails wide swelling to the constant blast,

Now, by the isle from Thomas nam'd we pass'd;

And Congo's spacious realm before us rose,

Where copious Layra's limpid billow flows;

A flood by ancient hero never seen,

Where many a temple o'er the banks of green,[350]

Rear'd by the Lusian heroes, through the night

Of pagan darkness, pours the mental light.

O'er the wild waves, as southward thus we stray,

Our port unknown, unknown the wat'ry way,

Each night we see, impress'd with solemn awe,

Our guiding stars, and native skies withdraw,

In the wide void we lose their cheering beams,

Lower and lower still the pole-star gleams.

Till past the limit, where the car of day

Roll'd o'er our heads, and pour'd the downward ray:

We now disprove the faith of ancient lore;

Boötes shining car appears no more.

For here we saw Calisto's[351] star retire

Beneath the waves, unaw'd by Juno's ire.

Here, while the sun his polar journeys takes,

His visit doubled, double season makes;

Stern winter twice deforms the changeful year,

And twice the spring's gay flowers their honours rear.

Now, pressing onward, past the burning zone,

Beneath another heaven and stars unknown,

Unknown to heroes and to sages old,

With southward prows our pathless course we hold:

Here, gloomy night assumes a darker reign,

And fewer stars emblaze the heavenly plain;

Fewer than those that gild the northern pole,

And o'er our seas their glitt'ring chariots roll:

While nightly thus, the lonely seas we brave,

Another pole-star[352] rises o'er the wave:

Full to the south a shining cross[353] appears,

Our heaving breasts the blissful omen cheers:

Seven radiant stars compose the hallow'd sign

That rose still higher o'er the wavy brine.

Beneath this southern axle of the world

Never, with daring search, was flag unfurl'd;

Nor pilot knows if bounding shores are plac'd,

Or, if one dreary sea o'erflow the lonely waste.

While thus our keels still onward boldly stray'd,

Now toss'd by tempests, now by calms delay'd,

To tell the terrors of the deep untried,

What toils we suffer'd, and what storms defied;

What rattling deluges the black clouds pour'd,

What dreary weeks of solid darkness lower'd;

What mountain-surges mountain-surges lash'd,

What sudden hurricanes the canvas dash'd;

What bursting lightnings, with incessant flare,

Kindled, in one wide flame, the burning air;

What roaring thunders bellow'd o'er our head,

And seem'd to shake the reeling ocean's bed:

To tell each horror on the deep reveal'd,

Would ask an iron throat with tenfold vigour steel'd:[354]

Those dreadful wonders of the deep I saw,

Which fill the sailor's breast with sacred awe;

And which the sages, of their learning vain,

Esteem the phantoms of the dreamful brain:

That living fire, by seamen held divine,[355]

Of Heaven's own care in storms the holy sign,

Which, midst the horrors of the tempest plays,

And, on the blast's dark wings will gaily blaze;

These eyes distinct have seen that living fire

Glide through the storm, and round my sails aspire.

And oft, while wonder thrill'd my breast, mine eyes

To heaven have seen the wat'ry columns rise.

Slender, at first, the subtle fume appears,

And writhing round and round its volume rears:

Thick as a mast the vapour swells its size,

A curling whirlwind lifts it to the skies;

The tube now straightens, now in width extends,

And, in a hov'ring cloud, its summit ends:

Still, gulp on gulp in sucks the rising tide,

And now the cloud, with cumbrous weight supplied,

Full-gorg'd, and black'ning, spreads, and moves, more slow,

And waving trembles to the waves below.

Thus, when to shun the summer's sultry beam

The thirsty heifer seeks the cooling stream,

The eager horse-leech fixing on her lips,

Her blood with ardent throat insatiate sips,

Till the gorg'd glutton, swell'd beyond her size,

Drops from her wounded hold, and bursting, dies.

So, bursts the cloud, o'erloaded with its freight,

And the dash'd ocean staggers with the weight.

But say, ye sages, who can weigh the cause,

And trace the secret springs of nature's laws,

Say, why the wave, of bitter brine erewhile,

Should to the bosom of the deep recoil

Robb'd of its salt, and, from the cloud distil,

Sweet as the waters of the limpid[356] rill?

Ye sons of boastful wisdom, famed of yore,

Whose feet unwearied wander'd many a shore,

From nature's wonders to withdraw the veil,

Had you with me unfurl'd the daring sail,

Had view'd the wondrous scenes mine eyes survey'd,

What seeming miracles the deep display'd,

What secret virtues various nature show'd,

Oh! heaven! with what a fire your page had glow'd!

And now, since wand'ring o'er the foamy spray,

Our brave Armada held her vent'rous way,

Five times the changeful empress of the night
Had fill'd her shining horns with silver light,
When sudden, from the maintop's airy round,
"Land! land!" is echoed. At the joyful sound,
Swift to the crowded decks the bounding crew
On wings of hope and flutt'ring transport flew,
And each strain'd eye with aching sight explores
The wide horizon of the eastern shores:
As thin blue clouds the mountain summits rise,
And now, the lawns salute our joyful eyes;
Loud through the fleet the echoing shouts prevail,
We drop the anchor, and restrain the sail;
And now, descending in a spacious bay,
Wide o'er the coast the vent'rous soldiers stray,
To spy the wonders of the savage shore,
Where stranger's foot had never trod before.
I and my pilots, on the yellow sand,
Explore beneath what sky the shores expand.
That sage device, whose wondrous use proclaims
Th' immortal honour of its authors'[357] names,
The sun's height measured, and my compass scann'd,
The painted globe of ocean and of land.
Here we perceiv'd our vent'rous keels had past
Unharm'd the southern tropic's howling blast;
And now, approach'd dread Neptune's secret reign,
Where the stern power, as o'er the austral main
He rides, wide scatters from the polar star
Hail, ice, and snow, and all the wintry war.
While thus attentive on the beach we stood,

My soldiers, hast'ning from the upland wood,

Right to the shore a trembling negro brought,

Whom, on the forest-height, by force they caught,

As, distant wander'd from the cell of home,

He suck'd the honey from the porous comb.

Horror glar'd in his look, and fear extreme,

In mien more wild than brutal Polypheme:

No word of rich Arabia's tongue[358] he knew,

No sign could answer, nor our gems would view:

From garments strip'd with shining gold he turn'd,

The starry diamond and the silver spurn'd.

Straight at my nod are worthless trinkets brought;

Round beads of crystal, as a bracelet wrought,

A cap of red, and, dangling on a string,

Some little bells of brass before him ring:

A wide-mouth'd laugh confess'd his barb'rous joy,

And, both his hands he raised to grasp the toy.

Pleas'd with these gifts, we set the savage free,

Homeward he springs away, and bounds with glee.

Soon as the gleamy streaks of purple morn

The lofty forest's topmost boughs adorn,

Down the steep mountain's side, yet hoar with dew,

A naked crowd, and black as night their hue,

Come tripping to the shore: Their wishful eyes

Declare what tawdry trifles most they prize:

These to their hopes were given, and, void of fear

(Mild seem'd their manners, and their looks sincere),

A bold rash youth, ambitious of the fame

Of brave adventurer, Velosó his name,

Through pathless brakes their homeward steps attends,

And, on his single arm, for help depends.

Long was his stay: my earnest eyes explore,

When, rushing down the mountain to the shore

I mark'd him; terror urged his rapid strides,

And soon Coëllo's skiff the wave divides.

Yet, ere his friends advanc'd, the treach'rous foe

Trod on his latest steps, and aim'd the blow.

Moved by the danger of a youth so brave,

Myself now snatch'd an oar, and sprung to save:

When sudden, black'ning down the mountain's height,

Another crowd pursu'd his panting flight;

And, soon an arrowy, and a flinty shower

Thick o'er our heads the fierce barbarians pour.

Nor pour'd in vain; a feather'd arrow stood

Fix'd[359] in my leg, and drank the gushing blood.

Vengeance, as sudden, ev'ry wound repays,

Full on their fronts our flashing lightnings blaze;

Their shrieks of horror instant pierce the sky,

And, wing'd with fear, at fullest speed they fly.

Long tracks of gore their scatter'd flight betray'd,

And now, Velosó to the fleet convey'd,

His sportful mates his brave exploits demand,

And what the curious wonders of the land:

"Hard was the hill to climb, my valiant friend,

But oh! how smooth and easy to descend!

Well hast thou prov'd thy swiftness for the chase,

And shown thy matchless merit in the race!"

With look unmov'd the gallant youth replied,

"For you, my friends, my fleetest speed was tried;

'Twas you the fierce barbarians meant to slay;

For you I fear'd the fortune of the day;

Your danger great without mine aid I knew,

And, swift as lightning, to your rescue flew."[360]

He now the treason of the foe relates,

How, soon as past the mountain's upland straits,

They chang'd the colour of their friendly show,

And force forbade his steps to tread below:

How, down the coverts of the steepy brake

Their lurking stand a treach'rous ambush take;

On us, when speeding to defend his flight,

To rush, and plunge us in the shades of night;

Nor, while in friendship, would their lips unfold

Where India's ocean laved the orient shores of gold.

Now, prosp'rous gales the bending canvas swell'd;

From these rude shores our fearless course we held:

Beneath the glist'ning wave the god of day

Had now five times withdrawn the parting ray,

When o'er the prow a sudden darkness spread,

And, slowly floating o'er the mast's tall head

A black cloud hover'd: nor appear'd from far

The moon's pale glimpse, nor faintly twinkling star;

So deep a gloom the low'ring vapour cast,

Transfix'd with awe the bravest stood aghast.

Meanwhile, a hollow bursting roar resounds,

As when hoarse surges lash their rocky mounds;

Nor had the black'ning wave, nor frowning heav'n
The wonted signs of gath'ring tempest giv'n.
Amaz'd we stood. "O thou, our fortune's guide,
Avert this omen, mighty God!" I cried;
"Or, through forbidden climes adventurous stray'd,
Have we the secrets of the deep survey'd,
Which these wide solitudes of seas and sky
Were doom'd to hide from man's unhallow'd eye?
Whate'er this prodigy, it threatens more
Than midnight tempests, and the mingled roar,
When sea and sky combine to rock the marble shore."
I spoke, when rising through the darken'd air,
Appall'd, we saw a hideous phantom glare;
High and enormous o'er the flood he tower'd,
And 'thwart our way with sullen aspect lower'd:
An earthy paleness o'er his cheeks was spread,
Erect uprose his hairs of wither'd red;
Writhing to speak, his sable lips disclose,
Sharp and disjoin'd, his gnashing teeth's blue rows;
His haggard beard flow'd quiv'ring on the wind,
Revenge and horror in his mien combin'd;
His clouded front, by with'ring lightnings scar'd,
The inward anguish of his soul declar'd.
His red eyes, glowing from their dusky caves,
Shot livid fires: far echoing o'er the waves
His voice resounded, as the cavern'd shore
With hollow groan repeats the tempest's roar.
Cold gliding horrors thrill'd each hero's breast,
Our bristling hair and tott'ring knees confess'd

Wild dread, the while with visage ghastly wan,

His black lips trembling, thus the fiend began:—[361]

"O you, the boldest of the nations, fir'd

By daring pride, by lust of fame inspir'd,

Who, scornful of the bow'rs of sweet repose,

Through these my waves advance your fearless prows,

Regardless of the length'ning wat'ry way,

And all the storms that own my sov'reign sway,

Who, mid surrounding rocks and shelves explore

Where never hero brav'd my rage before;

Ye sons of Lusus, who with eyes profane

Have view'd the secrets of my awful reign,

Have pass'd the bounds which jealous Nature drew

To veil her secret shrine from mortal view;

Hear from my lips what direful woes attend,

And, bursting soon, shall o'er your race descend.

"With every bounding keel that dares my rage,

Eternal war my rocks and storms shall wage,

The next proud fleet[362] that through my drear domain,

With daring search shall hoist the streaming vane,

That gallant navy, by my whirlwinds toss'd,

And raging seas, shall perish on my coast:

Then he, who first my secret reign descried,

A naked corpse, wide floating o'er the tide,

Shall drive—— Unless my heart's full raptures fail,

O Lusus! oft shalt thou thy children wail;

Each year thy shipwreck'd sons shalt thou deplore,

Each year thy sheeted masts shall strew my shore.

"With trophies plum'd behold a hero come,[363]
Ye dreary wilds, prepare his yawning tomb.
Though smiling fortune bless'd his youthful morn,
Though glory's rays his laurell'd brows adorn,
Full oft though he beheld with sparkling eye
The Turkish moons[364] in wild confusion fly,
While he, proud victor, thunder'd in the rear,
All, all his mighty fame shall vanish here.
Quiloa's sons, and thine, Mombaz, shall see
Their conqueror bend his laurell'd head to me;
While, proudly mingling with the tempest's sound,
Their shouts of joy from every cliff rebound.

"The howling blast, ye slumb'ring storms prepare,
A youthful lover, and his beauteous fair,
Triumphant sail from India's ravag'd land;
His evil angel leads him to my strand.
Through the torn hulk the dashing waves shall roar,
The shatter'd wrecks shall blacken all my shore.
Themselves escaped, despoil'd by savage hands,
Shall, naked, wander o'er the burning sands,
Spar'd by the waves far deeper woes to bear,
Woes, e'en by me, acknowledg'd with a tear.
Their infant race, the promis'd heirs of joy,
Shall now, no more, a hundred hands employ;
By cruel want, beneath the parents' eye,
In these wide wastes their infant race shall die;

Through dreary wilds, where never pilgrim trod,
Where caverns yawn, and rocky fragments nod,
The hapless lover and his bride shall stray,
By night unshelter'd, and forlorn by day.
In vain the lover o'er the trackless plain
Shall dart his eyes, and cheer his spouse in vain.
Her tender limbs, and breast of mountain snow,
Where, ne'er before, intruding blast might blow,
Parch'd by the sun, and shrivell'd by the cold
Of dewy night, shall he, fond man, behold.
Thus, wand'ring wide, a thousand ills o'erpast,
In fond embraces they shall sink at last;
While pitying tears their dying eyes o'erflow,
And the last sigh shall wail each other's woe.[365]

"Some few, the sad companions of their fate,
Shall yet survive, protected by my hate,
On Tagus' banks the dismal tale to tell,
How, blasted by my frown, your heroes fell."

He paus'd, in act still further to disclose
A long, a dreary prophecy of woes:
When springing onward, loud my voice resounds,
And midst his rage the threat'ning shade confounds.
"What art thou, horrid form, that rid'st the air?
By Heaven's eternal light, stern fiend, declare."
His lips he writhes, his eyes far round he throws,
And, from his breast, deep hollow groans arose,
Sternly askance he stood: with wounded pride

And anguish torn, "In me, behold," he cried,

While dark-red sparkles from his eyeballs roll'd,

"In me the Spirit of the Cape behold,

That rock, by you the Cape of Tempests nam'd,

By Neptune's rage, in horrid earthquakes fram'd,

When Jove's red bolts o'er Titan's offspring flam'd.

With wide-stretch'd piles I guard the pathless strand,

And Afric's southern mound, unmov'd, I stand:

Nor Roman prow, nor daring Tyrian oar

Ere dash'd the white wave foaming to my shore;

Nor Greece, nor Carthage ever spread the sail

On these my seas, to catch the trading gale.

You, you alone have dar'd to plough my main,

And, with the human voice, disturb my lonesome reign."

He spoke, and deep a lengthen'd sigh he drew,

A doleful sound, and vanish'd from the view:

The frighten'd billows gave a rolling swell,

And, distant far, prolong'd the dismal yell,

Faint, and more faint the howling echoes die,

And the black cloud dispersing, leaves the sky.

High to the angel-host, whose guardian care

Had ever round us watch'd, my hands I rear,

And Heaven's dread King implore: "As o'er our head

The fiend dissolv'd, an empty shadow fled;

So may his curses, by the winds of heav'n,

Far o'er the deep, their idle sport, be driv'n!"——

With sacred horror thrill'd, Melinda's lord

Held up the eager hand, and caught the word.

"Oh, wondrous faith of ancient days," he cries,

"Conceal'd in mystic lore and dark disguise!

Taught by their sires, our hoary fathers tell,

On these rude shores a giant-spectre fell,

What time, from heaven the rebel band were thrown:[366]

And oft the wand'ring swain has heard his moan.

While o'er the wave the clouded moon appears

To hide her weeping face, his voice he rears

O'er the wild storm. Deep in the days of yore,

A holy pilgrim trod the nightly shore;

Stern groans he heard; by ghostly spells controll'd,

His fate, mysterious, thus the spectre told:

'By forceful Titan's warm embrace compress'd,

The rock-ribb'd mother, Earth, his love confess'd:

The hundred-handed giant[367] at a birth,

And me, she bore, nor slept my hopes on earth;

My heart avow'd, my sire's ethereal flame;

Great Adamastor, then, my dreaded name.

In my bold brother's glorious toils engaged,

Tremendous war against the gods I waged:

Yet, not to reach the throne of heaven I try,

With mountain pil'd on mountain to the sky;

To me the conquest of the seas befel,

In his green realm the second Jove to quell.

Nor did ambition all my passions hold,

'Twas love that prompted an attempt so bold.

Ah me, one summer in the cool of day,

I saw the Nereids on the sandy bay,

With lovely Thetis from the wave, advance
In mirthful frolic, and the naked dance.
In all her charms reveal'd the goddess trod,
With fiercest fires my struggling bosom glow'd;
Yet, yet I feel them burning in my heart,
And hopeless, languish with the raging smart.
For her, each goddess of the heavens I scorn'd,
For her alone my fervent ardour burn'd.
In vain I woo'd her to the lover's bed,
From my grim form, with horror, mute she fled.
Madd'ning with love, by force I ween to gain
The silver goddess of the blue domain;
To the hoar mother of the Nereid band[368]
I tell my purpose, and her aid command:
By fear impell'd, old Doris tries to move,
And, win the spouse of Peleus to my love.
The silver goddess with a smile replies,
"What nymph can yield her charms a giant's prize!
Yet, from the horrors of a war to save,
And guard in peace our empire of the wave,
Whate'er with honour he may hope to gain,
That, let him hope his wish shall soon attain."
The promis'd grace infus'd a bolder fire,
And shook my mighty limbs with fierce desire.
But ah, what error spreads its dreadful night,
What phantoms hover o'er the lover's sight!
The war resign'd, my steps by Doris led,
While gentle eve her shadowy mantle spread,
Before my steps the snowy Thetis shone

In all her charms, all naked, and alone.

Swift as the wind with open arms I sprung,

And, round her waist with joy delirious clung:

In all the transports of the warm embrace,

A hundred kisses on her angel face,

On all its various charms my rage bestows,

And, on her cheek, my cheek enraptur'd glows.

When, oh, what anguish while my shame I tell!

What fix'd despair, what rage my bosom swell!

Here was no goddess, here no heav'nly charms,

A rugged mountain fill'd my eager arms,

Whose rocky top, o'erhung with matted brier,

Receiv'd the kisses of my am'rous fire.

Wak'd from my dream, cold horror freez'd my blood;

Fix'd as a rock, before the rock I stood;

"O fairest goddess of the ocean train,

Behold the triumph of thy proud disdain;

Yet why," I cried, "with all I wish'd decoy,

And, when exulting in the dream of joy,

A horrid mountain to mine arms convey!"

Madd'ning I spoke, and furious, sprung away.

Far to the south I sought the world unknown,

Where I, unheard, unscorn'd, might wail alone,

My foul dishonour, and my tears to hide,

And shun the triumph of the goddess' pride.

My brothers, now, by Jove's red arm o'erthrown,

Beneath huge mountains, pil'd on mountains groan;

And I, who taught each echo to deplore,

And tell my sorrows to the desert shore,

I felt the hand of Jove my crimes pursue,

My stiff'ning flesh to earthy ridges grew,

And my huge bones, no more by marrow warm'd,

To horrid piles, and ribs of rock transform'd,

Yon dark-brow'd cape of monstrous size became,

Where, round me still, in triumph o'er my shame,

The silv'ry Thetis bids her surges roar,

And waft my groans along the dreary shore.'"——

Melinda's monarch thus the tale pursu'd,

Of ancient faith, and Gama thus renew'd:—

Now, from the wave the chariot of the day,

Whirl'd by the fiery coursers, springs away,

When, full in view, the giant Cape appears,

Wide spreads its limbs, and high its shoulders rears;

Behind us, now, it curves the bending side,

And our bold vessels plough the eastern tide.

Nor long excursive off at sea we stand,

A cultur'd shore invites us to the land.

Here their sweet scenes the rural joys bestow,

And give our wearied minds a lively glow.[369]

The tenants of the coast, a festive band,

With dances meet us on the yellow sand;

Their brides on slow-pac'd oxen rode behind;

The spreading horns with flow'ry garlands twin'd,

Bespoke the dew-lapp'd beeves their proudest boast,

Of all their bestial store they valued most.

By turns the husbands, and the brides, prolong

The various measures of the rural song.

Now, to the dance the rustic reeds resound;

The dancers' heels, light-quiv'ring, beat the ground;

And now, the lambs around them bleating stray,

Feed from their hands, or, round them frisking play.

Methought I saw the sylvan reign of Pan,

And heard the music of the Mantuan swan:[370]

With smiles we hail them, and with joy behold

The blissful manners of the age of gold.

With that mild kindness, by their looks display'd,

Fresh stores they bring, with cloth of red repaid;

Yet, from their lips no word we knew could flow,

Nor sign of India's strand their hands bestow.

Fair blow the winds; again with sails unfurl'd

We dare the main, and seek the eastern world.

Now, round black Afric's coast our navy veer'd,

And, to the world's mid circle, northward steer'd:

The southern pole low to the wave declin'd,

We leave the isle of Holy Cross[371] behind:

That isle where erst a Lusian, when he pass'd

The tempest-beaten cape, his anchors cast,

And own'd his proud ambition to explore

The kingdoms of the morn could dare no more.

From thence, still on, our daring course we hold

Thro' trackless gulfs, whose billows never roll'd

Around the vessel's pitchy sides before;

Thro' trackless gulfs, where mountain surges roar,

For many a night, when not a star appear'd,

Nor infant moon's dim horns the darkness cheer'd;

For many a dreary night, and cheerless day,
In calms now fetter'd, now the whirlwind's play,
By ardent hope still fir'd, we forc'd our dreadful way.
Now, smooth as glass the shining waters lie,
No cloud, slow moving, sails the azure sky;
Slack from their height the sails unmov'd decline,
The airy streamers form the downward line;
No gentle quiver owns the gentle gale,
Nor gentlest swell distends the ready sail;
Fix'd as in ice, the slumb'ring prows remain,
And silence wide extends her solemn reign.
Now to the waves the bursting clouds descend,
And heaven and sea in meeting tempests blend;
The black-wing'd whirlwinds o'er the ocean sweep,
And from his bottom roars the stagg'ring deep.
Driv'n by the yelling blast's impetuous sway
Stagg'ring we bound, yet onward bound away:
And now, escaped the fury of the storm,
New danger threatens in a various form;
Though fresh the breeze the swelling canvas swell'd,
A current's headlong sweep our prows withheld:
The rapid force impress'd on every keel,
Backward, o'erpower'd, our rolling vessels reel:
When from their southern caves the winds, enraged,
In horrid conflict with the waves engaged;
Beneath the tempest groans each loaded mast,
And, o'er the rushing tide our bounding navy pass'd.[372]

Now shin'd the sacred morn, when from the east

Three kings[373] the holy cradled Babe address'd,
And hail'd him Lord of heaven: that festive day[374]
We drop our anchors in an opening bay;
The river from the sacred day we name,[375]
And stores, the wand'ring seaman's right, we claim:
Stores we receiv'd; our dearest hope in vain,
No word they utter'd could our ears retain;
Nought to reward our search for India's sound,
By word or sign our ardent wishes crown'd.[376]

Behold, O king, how many a shore we tried!
How many a fierce barbarian's rage defied!
Yet still, in vain, for India's shore we try,
The long-sought shores our anxious search defy.
Beneath new heavens, where not a star we knew,
Through changing climes, where poison'd air we drew;
Wandering new seas, in gulfs unknown, forlorn,
By labour weaken'd, and by famine worn;
Our food corrupted, pregnant with disease,
And pestilence on each expected breeze;
Not even a gleam of hope's delusive ray
To lead us onward through the devious way—
That kind delusion[377] which full oft has cheer'd
The bravest minds, till glad success appear'd;
Worn as we were, each night with dreary care,
Each day, with danger that increas'd despair;
Oh ! monarch, judge, what less than Lusian fire
Could still the hopeless scorn of fate inspire!
What less, O king, than Lusian faith withstand,

When dire despair and famine gave command
Their chief to murder, and with lawless power
Sweep Afric's seas, and every coast devour!
What more than men in wild despair still bold!
Those, more than men, in these my band behold!
Sacred to death, by death alone subdued,
These, all the rage of fierce despair withstood;[378]
Firm to their faith, though fondest hope no more
Could give the promise of their native shore!

Now, the sweet waters of the stream we leave,
And the salt waves our gliding prows receive:
Here to the left, between the bending shores,
Torn by the winds the whirling billow roars;
And boiling raves against the sounding coast,
Whose mines of gold Sofala's merchants boast:
Full to the gulf the show'ry south-winds howl,
Aslant, against the wind, our vessels roll:
Far from the land, wide o'er the ocean driv'n,
Our helms resigning to the care of heav'n,
By hope and fear's keen passions toss'd, we roam,
When our glad eyes beheld the surges foam
Against the beacons of a cultur'd bay,
Where sloops and barges cut the wat'ry way.
The river's opening breast some upward plied,
And some came gliding down the sweepy tide.
Quick throbs of transport heav'd in every heart
To view the knowledge of the seaman's art;
For here, we hop'd our ardent wish to gain,

To hear of India's strand, nor hop'd in vain.

Though Ethiopia's sable hue they bore

No look of wild surprise the natives wore:

Wide o'er their heads the cotton turban swell'd,

And cloth of blue the decent loins conceal'd.

Their speech, though rude and dissonant of sound,

Their speech a mixture of Arabian own'd.

Fernando, skill'd in all the copious store

Of fair Arabia's speech, and flow'ry lore,

In joyful converse heard the pleasing tale,

That, o'er these seas, full oft, the frequent sail,

And lordly vessels, tall as ours, appear'd,

Which, to the regions of the morning steer'd,

And, back returning, to the southmost land

Convey'd the treasures of the Indian strand;

Whose cheerful crews, resembling ours, display

The kindred face and colour of the day.[379]

Elate with joy we raise the glad acclaim,

And, "River of good signs,"[380] the port we name:

Then, sacred to the angel guide,[381] who led

The young Tobiah to the spousal bed,

And safe return'd him through the perilous way,

We rear a column[382] on the friendly bay.

Our keels, that now had steer'd through many a clime,

By shell-fish roughen'd, and incased with slime,

Joyful we clean, while bleating from the field

The fleecy dams the smiling natives yield:

But while each face an honest welcome shows,

And, big with sprightly hope, each bosom glows,

(Alas! how vain the bloom of human joy!

How soon the blasts of woe that bloom destroy!)

A dread disease its rankling horrors shed,

And death's dire ravage through mine army spread.

Never mine eyes such dreary sight beheld,

Ghastly the mouth and gums enormous swell'd;[383]

And instant, putrid like a dead man's wound,

Poisoned with fœtid steams the air around.

No sage physician's ever-watchful zeal,

No skilful surgeon's gentle hand to heal,

Were found: each dreary mournful hour we gave

Some brave companion to a foreign grave.

A grave, the awful gift of every shore!——

Alas! what weary toils with us they bore!

Long, long endear'd by fellowship in woe,

O'er their cold dust we give the tears to flow;

And, in their hapless lot forbode our own,

A foreign burial, and a grave unknown!

Now, deeply yearning o'er our deathful fate,

With joyful hope of India's shore elate,

We loose the hawsers and the sail expand,

And, upward coast the Ethiopian strand.

What danger threaten'd at Quiloa's isle,

Mozambique's treason, and Mombassa's guile:

What miracles kind Heav'n our guardian wrought,

Loud fame already to thine ears has brought:

Kind Heaven again that guardian care display'd,

And, to thy port our weary fleet convey'd,

Where thou, O king, Heaven's regent power below,

Bidd'st thy full bounty and thy truth to flow;

Health to the sick, and to the weary rest,

And sprightly hope reviv'd in every breast,

Proclaim thy gifts, with grateful joy repaid,

The brave man's tribute for the brave man's aid.

And now, in honour of thy fond command,

The glorious annals of my native land;

And what the perils of a route so bold,

So dread as ours, my faithful lips have told.

Then judge, great monarch, if the world before

Ere saw the prow such length of seas explore!

Nor sage Ulysses,[384] nor the Trojan[385] pride

Such raging gulfs, such whirling storms defied;

Nor one poor tenth of my dread course explor'd,

Though by the muse as demigods ador'd.

O thou whose breast all Helicon inflam'd,[386]

Whose birth seven vaunting cities proudly claim'd;

And thou whose mellow lute and rural song,[387]

In softest flow, led Mincio's waves along,

Whose warlike numbers, as a storm impell'd,

And Tiber's surges o'er his borders swell'd;

Let all Parnassus lend creative fire,

And all the Nine[388] with all their warmth inspire;

Your demigods conduct through every scene

Cold fear can paint, or wildest fancy feign;

The Syren's guileful lay, dire Circe's spell,[389]

And all the horrors of the Cyclop's cell;[390]

Bid Scylla's barking waves their mates o'erwhelm

And hurl the guardian pilot from the helm,[391]

Give sails and oars to fly the purple shore,

Where love of absent friend awakes no more;[392]

In all their charms display Calypso's smiles,

Her flow'ry arbours and her am'rous wiles;

In skins confin'd the blust'ring winds control,[393]

Or, o'er the feast bid loathsome harpies[394] prowl;

And lead your heroes through the dread abodes

Of tortur'd spectres and infernal[395] gods;

Give ev'ry flow'r that decks Aonia's hill

To grace your fables with divinest skill;

Beneath the wonders of my tale they fall,

Where truth, all unadorn'd and pure, exceeds them all.——

While thus, illustrious Gama charm'd their ears,

The look of wonder each Melindian wears,

And pleased attention witness'd the command

Of every movement of his lips, or hand.

The king, enraptur'd, own'd the glorious fame

Of Lisbon's monarchs and the Lusian name;

What warlike rage the victor-kings inspir'd!

Nor less their warriors' loyal faith admir'd.

Nor less his menial train, in wonder lost,

Repeat the gallant deeds that please them most,

Each to his mate; while, fix'd in fond amaze,

The Lusian features every eye surveys;

While, present to the view, by fancy brought,

Arise the wonders by the Lusians wrought,

And each bold feature to their wond'ring sight

Displays the raptur'd ardour of the fight.

Apollo now withdrew the cheerful day,

And left the western sky to twilight grey;

Beneath the wave he sought fair Thetis' bed,

And, to the shore Melinda's sov'reign sped.

What boundless joys are thine, O just Renown,

Thou hope of Virtue, and her noblest crown!

By thee the seeds of conscious worth are fir'd,

Hero by hero, fame by fame inspir'd:

Without thine aid how soon the hero dies!

By thee upborne, his name ascends the skies.

This Ammon[396] knew, and own'd his Homer's lyre

The noblest glory of Pelides' ire.[397]

This knew Augustus, and from Mantua's shade

To courtly ease the Roman bard convey'd;[398]

And soon exulting flow'd the song divine,

The noblest glory of the Roman line.

Dear was the Muse to Julius; ever dear

To Scipio, though the pond'rous, conquering spear

Roughen'd his hand, th' immortal pen he knew,

And, to the tented field the gentle Muses drew.

Each glorious chief of Greek or Latian line,

Or barb'rous race, adorn'd the Aonian shrine;

Each glorious name, e'er to the Muse endear'd.

Or woo'd the Muses, or, the Muse rever'd.

230

Alas, on Tago's hapless shores alone

The Muse is slighted, and her charms unknown;

For this, no Virgil here attunes the lyre,

No Homer here awakes the hero's fire.

On Tago's shores are Scipios, Cæsars born,

And Alexanders Lisbon's clime adorn;

But, Heaven has stamp'd them in a rougher mould,

Nor gave the polish to their genuine gold.

Careless and rude, or to be known or know,

In vain, to them, the sweetest numbers flow:

Unheard, in vain their native poet sings,

And cold neglect weighs down the Muse's wings,

Ev'n he whose veins the blood of Gama warms,[399]

Walks by, unconscious of the Muse's charms:

For him no Muse shall leave her golden loom,

No palm shall blossom, and no wreath shall bloom:

Yet, shall my labours and my cares be paid

By fame immortal, and by Gama's shade:

Him shall the song on ev'ry shore proclaim,

The first of heroes, first of naval fame.

Rude, and ungrateful, though my country be,

This proud example shall be taught by me—

"Where'er the hero's worth demands the skies,

To crown that worth some gen'rous bard shall rise!"

END OF THE FIFTH BOOK.

BOOK VI.

THE ARGUMENT.

Gama's long recital being concluded, the poet resumes the thread of his story in his own person. The Portuguese admiral enters into an alliance with the King of Melinda, assures him that the vessels of his nation will always in future anchor on his shores. Gama receives from the monarch a faithful pilot to conduct him to India. Bacchus now has recourse to Neptune, at whose palace the divinities of the sea assemble. The gods of the sea consent to let loose the winds and waves against the daring navigators. During the night the sailors on the watch relate to each other amusing stories. Veloso urges them to relate some proud feats of war. The history of the contest of the twelve knights of England with the twelve of Portugal is then told. A violent tempest assails the fleet. Vivid picture of a storm at sea. Gama addresses his prayer to God; and Venus, with her nymphs so captivates the storm-gods that a calm ensues. The boy at the mast-head raises a joyful cry of Land! re-echoed by the whole crew. The pilot informs the Portuguese that they are now approaching the kingdom of Calicut. The poet's reflections.

WITH heart sincere the royal pagan joy'd,

And hospitable rites each hour employ'd,

For much the king the Lusian band admir'd,

And, much their friendship and their aid desir'd;

Each hour the gay festivity prolongs,

Melindian dances, and Arabian songs;

Each hour in mirthful transport steals away,

By night the banquet, and the chase by day;

And now, the bosom of the deep invites,

And all the pride of Neptune's festive rites;

Their silken banners waving o'er the tide,

A jovial band, the painted galleys ride;

The net and angle various hands employ,

And Moorish timbrels sound the notes of joy.

Such was the pomp, when Egypt's beauteous[400] queen

Bade all the pride of naval show convene,

In pleasure's downy bosom, to beguile

Her love-sick warrior:[401] o'er the breast of Nile,

Dazzling with gold, the purple ensigns flow'd,
And to the lute the gilded barges row'd;
While from the wave, of many a shining hue,
The anglers' lines the panting fishes drew.

Now, from the West the sounding breezes blow,
And far the hoary flood was yet to plough:
The fountain and the field bestow'd their store,
And friendly pilots from the friendly shore,
Train'd in the Indian deep, were now aboard,
When Gama, parting from Melinda's lord,
The holy vows of lasting peace renew'd,
For, still the king for lasting friendship sued;
That Lusus' heroes in his port supplied,
And tasted rest, he own'd his dearest pride,
And vow'd, that ever while the seas they roam,
The Lusian fleets should find a bounteous home,
And, ever from the gen'rous shore receive
Whate'er his port, whate'er his land could give.[402]
Nor less his joy the grateful chief declar'd;
And now, to seize the valued hours prepar'd.
Full to the wind the swelling sails he gave,
And, his red prows divide the foamy wave:
Full to the rising sun the pilot steers,
And, far from shore through middle ocean bears.
The vaulted sky now widens o'er their heads,
Where first the infant morn his radiance sheds.
And now, with transport sparkling in his eyes,
Keen to behold the Indian mountains rise,

High on the decks each Lusian hero smiles,

And, proudly in his thoughts reviews his toils.

When the stern demon, burning with disdain,

Beheld the fleet triumphant plough the main:

The powers of heav'n, and heav'n's dread lord he knew,

Resolv'd in Lisbon glorious to renew

The Roman honours—raging with despair

From high Olympus' brow he cleaves the air,

On earth new hopes of vengeance to devise,

And sue that aid denied him in the skies;

Blaspheming Heav'n, he pierc'd the dread abode

Of ocean's lord, and sought the ocean's god.

Deep, where the bases of the hills extend,

And earth's huge ribs of rock enormous bend,

Where, roaring through the caverns, roll the waves

Responsive as the aërial tempest raves,

The ocean's monarch, by the Nereid train,

And wat'ry gods encircled, holds his reign.

Wide o'er the deep, which line could ne'er explore,

Shining with hoary sand of silver ore,

Extends the level, where the palace rears

Its crystal towers, and emulates the spheres;

So, starry bright, the lofty turrets blaze,

And, vie in lustre with the diamond's rays.

Adorn'd with pillars, and with roofs of gold,

The golden gates their massy leaves unfold:

Inwrought with pearl the lordly pillars shine,

The sculptur'd walls confess a hand divine.

Here, various colours in confusion lost,

Old Chaos' face and troubled image boast.

Here, rising from the mass, distinct and clear,

Apart, the four fair elements appear.

High o'er the rest ascends the blaze of fire,

Nor, fed by matter did the rays aspire,

But, glow'd ætherial, as the living flame,

Which, stol'n from heav'n, inspir'd the vital frame.

Next, all-embracing air was spread around,

Thin as the light, incapable of wound;

The subtle power the burning south pervades,

And penetrates the depth of polar shades.

Here, mother Earth, with mountains crown'd, is seen,

Her trees in blossom, and her lawns in green;

The lowing beeves adorn the clover vales,

The fleecy dams bespread the sloping dales;

Here, land from land the silver streams divide;

The sportive fishes through the crystal tide,

Bedropt with gold their shining sides display:

And here, old Ocean rolls his billows gray:

Beneath the moon's pale orb his current flows,

And, round the earth, his giant arms he throws.

Another scene display'd the dread alarms

Of war in heav'n, and mighty Jove in arms;

Here, Titan's race their swelling nerves distend

Like knotted oaks, and from their bases rend

And tower the mountains to the thund'ring sky,

While round their heads the forky lightnings fly;

Beneath huge Etna vanquish'd Typhon lies,[403]

And vomits smoke and fire against the darken'd skies.

Here, seems the pictur'd wall possess'd of life:
Two gods contending[404] in the noble strife,
The choicest boon to humankind to give,
Their toils to lighten, or their wants relieve:
While Pallas here appears to wave her hand,[405]
The peaceful olive's silver boughs expand:
Here, while the ocean's god indignant frown'd,
And rais'd his trident from the wounded ground,
As yet entangled in the earth, appears
The warrior horse; his ample chest he rears,
His wide red nostrils smoke, his eye-balls glare,
And his fore-hoofs, high pawing, smite the air.

Though wide, and various, o'er the sculptur'd stone[406]
The feats of gods, and godlike heroes shone;
On speed the vengeful demon views no more:
Forward he rushes through the golden door,
Where ocean's king, enclos'd with nymphs divine,
In regal state receives the king of wine:[407]
"O Neptune!" instant as he came, he cries,
"Here let my presence wake no cold surprise.
A friend I come, your friendship to implore
Against the Fates unjust, and Fortune's power;
Beneath whose shafts the great Celestials bow,
Yet ere I more, if more you wish to know,
The wat'ry gods in awful senate call,
For all should hear the wrong that touches all."
Neptune alarm'd, with instant speed commands
From ev'ry shore to call the wat'ry bands:

Triton, who boasts his high Neptunian race,

Sprung from the god by Salacé's[408] embrace,

Attendant on his sire the trumpet sounds,

Or, through the yielding waves, his herald, bounds:

Huge is his bulk, deform'd, and dark his hue;

His bushy beard, and hairs that never knew

The smoothing comb, of seaweed rank and long,

Around his breast and shoulders dangling hung,

And, on the matted locks black mussels clung;

A shell of purple on his head he bore,[409]

Around his loins no tangling garb he wore,

But all was cover'd with the slimy brood,

The snaily offspring of the unctuous flood;

And now, obedient to his dreadful sire,

High o'er the wave his brawny arms aspire;

To his black mouth his crooked shell applied,

The blast rebellows o'er the ocean wide:

Wide o'er their shores, where'er their waters flow,

The wat'ry powers the awful summons know;

And instant, darting to the palace hall,

Attend the founder of the Dardan wall;[410]

Old Father Ocean, with his num'rous race

Of daughters and of sons, was first in place.

Nereus and Doris, from whose nuptials sprung

The lovely Nereid train, for ever young,

Who people ev'ry sea on ev'ry strand,

Appear'd, attended with their filial band;

And changeful Proteus, whose prophetic mind[411]

The secret cause of Bacchus' rage divin'd,

Attending, left the flocks, his scaly charge,

To graze the bitter, weedy foam at large.

In charms of power the raging waves to tame,

The lovely spouse of ocean's sov'reign came.[412]

From Heaven and Vesta sprung the birth divine,

Her snowy limbs bright through the vestments shine.

Here, with the dolphin, who persuasive led

Her modest steps to Neptune's spousal bed,

Fair Amphitrité mov'd, more sweet, more gay

Than vernal fragrance, and the flowers of May;

Together with her sister-spouse she came,

The same their wedded lord, their love the same;

The same the brightness of their sparkling eyes,

Bright as the sun, and azure as the skies.

She, who, the rage of Athamas to shun,[414]

Plung'd in the billows with her infant son;

A goddess now, a god the smiling boy,

Together sped; and Glaucus lost to joy,[415]

Curs'd in his love by vengeful Circé's hate,

Attending, wept his Scylla's hapless fate.

And now, assembled in the hall divine,

The ocean gods in solemn council join;

The goddesses on pearl embroid'ry sat,

The gods, on sparkling crystal chairs of state,

And, proudly honour'd, on the regal throne,

Beside the ocean's lord, Thyoneus[416] shone.

High from the roof the living amber glows,[417]

High from the roof the stream of glory flows,

And, richer fragrance far around exhales
Than that which breathes on fair Arabia's gales.

Attention now, in list'ning silence waits:
The power, whose bosom rag'd against the Fates,
Rising, casts round his vengeful eyes, while rage
Spread o'er his brows the wrinkled seams of age.
"O thou," he cries, "whose birthright sov'reign sway,
From pole to pole, the raging waves obey;
Of human race 'tis thine to fix the bounds,
And fence the nations with thy wat'ry mounds:
And thou, dread power, O Father Ocean, hear,
Thou, whose wide arms embrace the world's wide sphere,
'Tis thine the haughtiest victor to restrain,
And bind each nation in its own domain:
And you, ye gods, to whom the seas are giv'n,
Your just partition with the gods of heav'n;
You who, of old unpunish'd never bore
The daring trespass of a foreign oar;
You who beheld, when Earth's dread offspring strove[418]
To scale the vaulted sky, the seat of Jove:
Indignant Jove deep to the nether world
The rebel band in blazing thunders hurl'd.
Alas! the great monition lost on you,
Supine you slumber, while a roving crew,
With impious search, explore the wat'ry way,
And, unresisted, through your empire stray:
To seize the sacred treasures of the main,
Their fearless prows your ancient laws disdain:

239

Where, far from mortal sight his hoary head

Old Ocean hides, their daring sails they spread,

And their glad shouts are echo'd where the roar

Of mounting billows only howl'd before.

In wonder, silent, ready Boreas[419] sees

Your passive languor, and neglectful ease;

Ready, with force auxiliar, to restrain

The bold intruders on your awful reign;

Prepar'd to burst his tempests, as of old,

When his black whirlwinds o'er the ocean roll'd,

And rent the Mynian[420] sails, whose impious pride

First brav'd their fury, and your power defied.

Nor deem that, fraudful, I my hope deny;

My darken'd glory sped me from the sky.

How high my honours on the Indian shore!

How soon these honours must avail no more!

Unless these rovers, who with doubled shame

To stain my conquests, bear my vassal's[421] name,

Unless they perish on the billowy way.

Then rouse, ye gods, and vindicate your sway.

The powers of heaven, in vengeful anguish, see

The tyrant of the skies, and Fate's decree;

The dread decree, that to the Lusian train

Consigns, betrays your empire of the main:

Say, shall your wrong alarm the high abodes?

Are men exalted to the rank of gods?

O'er you exalted, while in careless ease

You yield the wrested trident of the seas,

Usurp'd your monarchy, your honours stain'd,

Your birthright ravish'd, and your waves profan'd!
Alike the daring wrong to me, to you,
And, shall my lips in vain your vengeance sue!
This, this to sue from high Olympus bore———"
More he attempts, but rage permits no more.
Fierce, bursting wrath the wat'ry gods inspires,
And, their red eye-balls burn with livid fires:
Heaving and panting struggles evr'y breast,
With the fierce billows of hot ire oppress'd.
Twice from his seat divining Proteus rose,
And twice he shook, enrag'd, his sedgy brows:
In vain; the mandate was already giv'n,
From Neptune sent, to loose the winds of heav'n:
In vain; though prophecy his lips inspir'd,
The ocean's queen his silent lips requir'd.
Nor less the storm of headlong rage denies,
Or counsel to debate, or thought to rise.
And now, the God of Tempests swift unbinds
From their dark caves the various rushing winds:
High o'er the storm the power impetuous rides,
His howling voice the roaring tempest guides;
Right to the dauntless fleet their rage he pours,
And, first their headlong outrage tears the shores:
A deeper night involves the darken'd air,
And livid flashes through the mountains glare:
Uprooted oaks, with all their leafy pride,
Roll thund'ring down the groaning mountain's side;
And men and herds in clam'rous uproar run,
The rocking towers and crashing woods to shun.

241

While, thus, the council of the wat'ry state

Enrag'd, decreed the Lusian heroes' fate,

The weary fleet before the gentle gale

With joyful hope display'd the steady sail;

Thro' the smooth deep they plough'd the length'ning way;

Beneath the wave the purple car of day

To sable night the eastern sky resign'd,

And, o'er the decks cold breath'd the midnight wind.

All but the watch in warm pavilions slept,

The second watch the wonted vigils kept:

Supine their limbs, the mast supports the head,

And the broad yard-sail o'er their shoulders spread

A grateful cover from the chilly gale,

And sleep's soft dews their heavy eyes assail.

Languid against the languid power they strive,

And, sweet discourse preserves their thoughts alive.

When Leonardo, whose enamour'd thought

In every dream the plighted fair one sought—

"The dews of sleep what better to remove

Than the soft, woful, pleasing tales of love?"

"Ill-timed, alas!" the brave Veloso cries,

"The tales of love, that melt the heart and eyes.

The dear enchantments of the fair I know,

The fearful transport, and the rapturous woe:

But, with our state ill suits the grief or joy;

Let war, let gallant war our thoughts employ:

With dangers threaten'd, let the tale inspire

The scorn of danger, and the hero's fire."

His mates with joy the brave Veloso hear,

And, on the youth the speaker's toil confer.

The brave Veloso takes the word with joy,

"And truth," he cries, "shall these slow hours decoy.

The warlike tale adorns our nation's fame,

The twelve of England give the noble theme.

"When Pedro's gallant heir, the valiant John,

Gave war's full splendour to the Lusian throne,

In haughty England, where the winter spreads

His snowy mantle o'er the shining meads,[422]

The seeds of strife the fierce Erynnis sows;[423]

The baleful strife from court dissension rose.

With ev'ry charm adorn'd, and ev'ry grace,

That spreads its magic o'er the female face,

Twelve ladies shin'd the courtly train among,

The first, the fairest of the courtly throng;

But, Envy's breath revil'd their injur'd name,

And stain'd the honour of their virgin fame.

Twelve youthful barons own'd the foul report,

The charge at first, perhaps, a tale of sport.

Ah, base the sport that lightly dares defame

The sacred honour of a lady's name!

What knighthood asks the proud accusers yield,

And, dare the damsels' champions to the field.[424]

'There let the cause, as honour wills, be tried,

And, let the lance and ruthless sword decide.'

The lovely dames implore the courtly train,

With tears implore them, but implore in vain.

So fam'd, so dreaded tower'd each boastful knight,

The damsels' lovers shunn'd the proffer'd fight.

Of arm unable to repel the strong,

The heart's each feeling conscious of the wrong,

When, robb'd of all the female breast holds dear,

Ah Heaven, how bitter flows the female tear!

To Lancaster's bold duke the damsels sue;

Adown their cheeks, now paler than the hue

Of snowdrops trembling to the chilly gale,

The slow-pac'd crystal tears their wrongs bewail.

When down the beauteous face the dew-drop flows,

What manly bosom can its force oppose!

His hoary curls th' indignant hero shakes,

And, all his youthful rage restor'd, awakes:

'Though loth,' he cries, 'to plunge my bold compeers

In civil discord, yet, appease your tears:

From Lusitania'—for, on Lusian ground

Brave Lancaster had strode with laurel crown'd;

Had mark'd how bold the Lusian heroes shone,

What time he claim'd the proud Castilian throne,[425]

How matchless pour'd the tempest of their might,

When, thund'ring at his side, they rul'd the fight:

Nor less their ardent passion for the fair,

Gen'rous and brave, he view'd with wond'ring care,

When, crown'd with roses, to the nuptial bed

The warlike John his lovely daughter led—

'From Lusitania's clime,' the hero cries,

'The gallant champions of your fame shall rise.

Their hearts will burn (for well their hearts I know)

To pour your vengeance on the guilty foe.

Let courtly phrase the heroes' worth admire,

And, for your injur'd names, that worth require:

Let all the soft endearments of the fair,

And words that weep your wrongs, your wrongs declare.

Myself the heralds to the chiefs will send,

And to the king, my valiant son, commend.'

He spoke; and twelve of Lusian race he names

All noble youths, the champions of the dames.

The dames, by lot, their gallant champions choose,[426]

And each her hero's name, exulting, views.

Each in a various letter hails her chief,

And, earnest for his aid, relates her grief:

Each to the king her courtly homage sends,

And valiant Lancaster their cause commends.

Soon as to Tagus' shores the heralds came,

Swift through the palace pours the sprightly flame

Of high-soul'd chivalry; the monarch glows

First on the listed field to dare the foes;

But regal state withheld. Alike their fires,

Each courtly noble to the toil aspires:

High on his helm, the envy of his peers,

Each chosen knight the plume of combat wears.

In that proud port, half circled by the wave,

Which Portugallia to the nation gave,

A deathless name,[427] a speedy sloop receives

The sculptur'd bucklers, and the clasping greaves,

The swords of Ebro, spears of lofty size,

And breast-plates, flaming with a thousand dyes,

Helmets high plum'd, and, pawing for the fight,

Bold steeds, whose harness shone with silv'ry light

Dazzling the day. And now, the rising gale

Invites the heroes, and demands the sail,

When brave Magricio thus his peers address'd,

'Oh, friends in arms, of equal powers confess'd,

Long have I hop'd through foreign climes to stray,

Where other streams than Douro wind their way;

To note what various shares of bliss and woe

From various laws and various customs flow;

Nor deem that, artful, I the fight decline;

England shall know the combat shall be mine.

By land I speed, and, should dark fate prevent,

(For death alone shall blight my firm intent),

Small may the sorrow for my absence be,

For yours were conquest, though unshar'd by me.

Yet, something more than human warms my breast,

And sudden whispers,[428] In our fortunes blest,

Nor envious chance, nor rocks, nor whelmy tide,

Shall our glad meeting at the list divide.'

"He said; and now, the rites of parting friends

Sufficed, through Leon and Castile he bends.

On many a field, enrapt, the hero stood,

And the proud scenes of Lusian conquest view'd.

Navarre he pass'd, and pass'd the dreary wild,

Where rocks on rocks o'er yawning glens are pil'd;

The wolf's dread range, where, to the ev'ning skies

In clouds involv'd, the cold Pyrenians rise.

Through Gallia's flow'ry vales, and wheaten plains

He strays, and Belgia now his steps detains.

There, as forgetful of his vow'd intent,

In various cares the fleeting days he spent:

His peers, the while, direct to England's strand,

Plough the chill northern wave; and now, at land,

Adorn'd in armour, and embroid'ry gay,

To lordly London hold the crowded way:

Bold Lancaster receives the knights with joy;

The feast, and warlike song each hour employ.

The beauteous dames, attending, wake their fire,

With tears enrage them, and with smiles inspire.

And now, with doubtful blushes rose the day,

Decreed the rites of wounded fame to pay.

The English monarch gives the listed bounds,

And, fix'd in rank, with shining spears surrounds.

Before their dames the gallant knights advance,

(Each like a Mars), and shake the beamy lance:

The dames, adorn'd in silk and gold, display

A thousand colours glitt'ring to the day:

Alone in tears, and doleful mourning, came,

Unhonour'd by her knight, Magricio's dame.

'Fear not our prowess,' cry the bold eleven,

'In numbers, not in might, we stand uneven.

More could we spare, secure of dauntless might,

When for the injur'd female name we fight.'

"Beneath a canopy of regal state,

High on a throne, the English monarch sat,

All round, the ladies and the barons bold,

Shining in proud array, their stations hold.

Now, o'er the theatre the champions pour,

And facing three to three, and four to four,

Flourish their arms in prelude. From the bay

Where flows the Tagus to the Indian sea,

The sun beholds not, in his annual race,

A twelve more sightly, more of manly grace

Than tower'd the English knights. With frothing jaws,

Furious, each steed the bit restrictive gnaws,

And, rearing to approach the rearing foe,

Their wavy manes are dash'd with foamy snow:

Cross-darting to the sun a thousand rays,

The champions' helmets as the crystal blaze.

Ah now, the trembling ladies' cheeks how wan!

Cold crept their blood; when, through the tumult ran

A shout, loud gath'ring; turn'd was ev'ry eye

Where rose the shout, the sudden cause to spy.

And lo, in shining arms a warrior rode,

With conscious pride his snorting courser trod;

Low to the monarch, and the dames he bends,

And now, the great Magricio joins his friends.

With looks that glow'd, exulting rose the fair,

Whose wounded honour claim'd the hero's care.

Aside the doleful weeds of mourning thrown,

In dazzling purple, and in gold she shone.

Now, loud the signal of the fight rebounds,

Quiv'ring the air, the meeting shock resounds

Hoarse, crashing uproar; griding splinters spring

Far round, and bucklers dash'd on bucklers ring.

Their swords flash lightning; darkly reeking o'er

The shining mail-plates flows the purple gore.

Torn by the spur, the loosen'd reins at large,

Furious, the steeds in thund'ring plunges charge;

Trembles beneath their hoofs the solid ground,

And, thick the fiery sparkles flash around,

A dreadful blaze! With pleasing horror thrill'd,

The crowd behold the terrors of the field.

Here, stunn'd and stagg'ring with the forceful blow,

A bending champion grasps the saddle-bow;

Here, backward bent, a falling knight reclines,

His plumes, dishonour'd, lash the courser's loins.

So, tir'd and stagger'd toil'd the doubtful fight,

When great Magricio, kindling all his might,

Gave all his rage to burn: with headlong force,

Conscious of victory, his bounding horse

Wheels round and round the foe; the hero's spear

Now on the front, now flaming on the rear,

Mows down their firmest battle; groans the ground

Beneath his courser's smiting hoofs: far round

The cloven helms and splinter'd shields resound.

Here, torn and trail'd in dust the harness gay,

From the fall'n master springs the steed away;

Obscene with dust and gore, slow from the ground

Rising, the master rolls his eyes around,

Pale as a spectre on the Stygian coast,

In all the rage of shame confus'd, and lost:

Here, low on earth, and o'er the riders thrown,

The wallowing coursers and the riders groan:

Before their glimm'ring vision dies the light,

And, deep descends the gloom of death's eternal night.

They now who boasted, 'Let the sword decide,'

Alone in flight's ignoble aid confide:

Loud to the skies the shout of joy proclaims

The spotless honour of the ladies' names.

"In painted halls of state, and rosy bowers,

The twelve brave Lusians crown the festive hours.

Bold Lancaster the princely feast bestows,

The goblet circles, and the music flows;

And ev'ry care, the transport of their joy,

To tend the knights the lovely dames employ;

The green-bough'd forests by the lawns of Thames

Behold the victor-champions, and the dames

Rouse the tall roe-buck o'er the dews of morn,

While, through the dales of Kent resounds the bugle-horn.

The sultry noon the princely banquet owns,

The minstrel's song of war the banquet crowns:

And, when the shades of gentle ev'ning fall,

Loud with the dance resounds the lordly hall:

The golden roofs, while Vesper shines, prolong

The trembling echoes of the harp and song.

Thus pass'd the days on England's happy strand,

Till the dear mem'ry of their natal land

Sigh'd for the banks of Tagus. Yet, the breast

Of brave Magricio spurns the thoughts of rest.

In Gaul's proud court he sought the listed plain,

In arms, an injur'd lady's knight again.

As Rome's Corvinus[429] o'er the field he strode,

And, on the foe's huge cuirass proudly trod.

No more by tyranny's proud tongue revil'd,

The Flandrian countess on her hero smil'd.[430]

The Rhine another pass'd, and prov'd his might,[431]

A fraudful German dar'd him to the fight.

Strain'd in his grasp, the fraudful boaster fell——"

Here sudden stopp'd the youth; the distant yell

Of gath'ring tempest sounded in his ears,

Unheard, unheeded by his list'ning peers.

Earnest, at full, they urge him to relate

Magricio's combat, and the German's fate.

When, shrilly whistling through the decks, resounds

The master's call, and loud his voice rebounds:

Instant from converse, and from slumber, start

Both bands, and instant to their toils they dart.

"Aloft, oh speed, down, down the topsails!" cries

The master: "sudden from my earnest eyes

Vanish'd the stars; slow rolls the hollow sigh,

The storm's dread herald." To the topsails fly

The bounding youths, and o'er the yardarms whirl

The whizzing ropes, and swift the canvas furl;

When, from their grasp the bursting tempests bore

The sheets half-gather'd, and in fragments tore.

"Strike, strike the mainsail!" loud again he rears

His echoing voice; when, roaring in their ears,

As if the starry vault, by thunders riv'n,

Rush'd downward to the deep the walls of heav'n,

With headlong weight a fiercer blast descends,

And, with sharp whirring crash, the mainsail rends;

Loud shrieks of horror through the fleet resound;

Bursts the torn cordage; rattle far around

The splinter'd yardarms; from each bending mast,

In many a shred, far streaming on the blast

The canvas floats; low sinks the leeward side,

O'er the broad vessels rolls the swelling tide:

"Oh strain each nerve!" the frantic pilot cries—

"Oh now!"—and instant every nerve applies,

Tugging what cumbrous lay, with strainful force;

Dash'd by the pond'rous loads, the surges hoarse

Roar in new whirls: the dauntless soldiers ran

To pump, yet, ere the groaning pump began

The wave to vomit, o'er the decks o'erthrown

In grovelling heaps, the stagger'd soldiers groan:

So rolls the vessel, not the boldest three,

Of arm robustest, and of firmest knee,

Can guide the starting rudder; from their hands

The helm bursts; scarce a cable's strength commands

The stagg'ring fury of its starting bounds,

While to the forceful, beating surge resounds

The hollow crazing hulk: with kindling rage

The adverse winds the adverse winds engage,

As, from its base of rock their banded power

Strove in the dust to strew some lordly tower,

Whose dented battlements in middle sky

Frown on the tempest and its rage defy;

So, roar'd the winds: high o'er the rest upborne

On the wide mountain-wave's slant ridge forlorn,

At times discover'd by the lightnings blue,

Hangs Gama's lofty vessel, to the view

Small as her boat; o'er Paulus' shatter'd prore

Falls the tall mainmast, prone, with crashing roar;

Their hands, yet grasping their uprooted hair,

The sailors lift to heaven in wild despair,

The Saviour-God each yelling voice implores.

Nor less from brave Coello's war-ship pours

The shriek, shrill rolling on the tempest's wings:

Dire as the bird of death at midnight sings

His dreary howlings in the sick man's ear,

The answ'ring shriek from ship to ship they hear.

Now, on the mountain-billows upward driv'n,

The navy mingles with the clouds of heav'n;

Now, rushing downward with the sinking waves,

Bare they behold old Ocean's vaulty caves.

The eastern blast against the western pours,

Against the southern storm the northern roars:

From pole to pole the flashy lightnings glare,

One pale, blue, twinkling sheet enwraps the air;

In swift succession now the volleys fly,

Darted in pointed curvings o'er the sky;

And, through the horrors of the dreadful night,

O'er the torn waves they shed a ghastly light;

The breaking surges flame with burning red,

Wider, and louder still the thunders spread,

As if the solid heav'ns together crush'd,

Expiring worlds on worlds expiring rush'd,

And dim-brow'd Chaos struggled to regain

The wild confusion of his ancient reign.

Not such the volley when the arm of Jove

From heav'n's high gates the rebel Titans drove;

Not such fierce lightnings blaz'd athwart the flood,

When, sav'd by Heaven, Deucalion's vessel rode

High o'er the delug'd hills. Along the shore

The halcyons, mindful of their fate, deplore;[432]

As beating round, on trembling wings they fly,

Shrill through the storm their woful clamours die.

So, from the tomb, when midnight veils the plains,

With shrill, faint voice, th' untimely ghost complains.[433]

The am'rous dolphins to their deepest caves

In vain retreat, to fly the furious waves;

High o'er the mountain-capes the ocean flows,

And tears the aged forests from their brows:

The pine and oak's huge, sinewy roots uptorn,

And, from their beds the dusky sands upborne

On the rude whirlings of the billowy sweep,

Imbrown the surface of the boiling deep.

High to the poop the valiant Gama springs,

And all the rage of grief his bosom wrings,

Grief to behold, the while fond hope enjoy'd

The meed of all his toils, that hope destroy'd.

In awful horror lost, the hero stands,

And rolls his eyes to heav'n, and spreads his hands,

While to the clouds his vessel rides the swell,

And now, her black keel strikes the gates of hell;

"O Thou," he cries, "whom trembling heav'n obeys,
Whose will the tempest's furious madness sways,
Who, through the wild waves, ledd'st Thy chosen race,
While the high billows stood like walls of brass:[434]
O Thou, while ocean bursting o'er the world
Roar'd o'er the hills, and from the sky down hurl'd
Rush'd other headlong oceans; oh, as then
The second father of the race of men[435]
Safe in Thy care the dreadful billows rode,
Oh! save us now, be now the Saviour-God!
Safe in Thy care, what dangers have we pass'd!
And shalt Thou leave us, leave us now at last
To perish here—our dangers and our toils
To spread Thy laws unworthy of Thy smiles;
Our vows unheard? Heavy with all thy weight,
Oh horror, come! and come, eternal night!"

He paus'd;—then round his eyes and arms he threw
In gesture wild, and thus: "Oh happy you!
You, who in Afric fought for holy faith,
And, pierc'd with Moorish spears, in glorious death
Beheld the smiling heav'ns your toils reward,
By your brave mates beheld the conquest shar'd;
Oh happy you, on every shore renown'd!
Your vows respected, and your wishes crown'd."

He spoke; redoubled rag'd the mingled blasts;
Through the torn cordage and the shatter'd masts
The winds loud whistled, fiercer lightnings blaz'd,

And louder roars the doubled thunders rais'd,

The sky and ocean blending, each on fire,

Seem'd as all Nature struggled to expire.

When now, the silver star of Love appear'd,[436]

Bright in the east her radiant front she rear'd;

Fair, through the horrid storm, the gentle ray

Announc'd the promise of the cheerful day;

From her bright throne Celestial Love beheld

The tempest burn, and blast on blast impell'd:

"And must the furious demon still," she cries,

"Still urge his rage, nor all the past suffice!

Yet, as the past, shall all his rage be vain——"

She spoke, and darted to the roaring main;

Her lovely nymphs she calls, the nymphs obey,

Her nymphs the virtues who confess her sway;

Round ev'ry brow she bids the rose-buds twine,

And ev'ry flower adown the locks to shine,

The snow-white lily, and the laurel green,

And pink and yellow as at strife be seen.

Instant, amid their golden ringlets strove

Each flow'ret, planted by the hand of Love;

At strife, who first th' enamour'd powers to gain,

Who rule the tempests and the waves restrain:

Bright as a starry band the Nereids shone,

Instant old Eolus' sons their presence[437] own;

The winds die faintly, and, in softest sighs,

Each at his fair one's feet desponding lies:

The bright Orithia, threatening, sternly chides

The furious Boreas, and his faith derides;

The furious Boreas owns her powerful bands:

Fair Galatea, with a smile commands

The raging Notus, for his love, how true,

His fervent passion and his faith she knew.

Thus, every nymph her various lover chides;

The silent winds are fetter'd by their brides;

And, to the goddess of celestial loves,

Mild as her look, and gentle as her doves,

In flow'ry bands are brought. Their am'rous flame

The queen approves, and "ever burn the same,"

She cries, and joyful on the nymphs' fair hands,

Th' Eolian race receive the queen's commands,

And vow, that henceforth her Armada's sails

Should gently swell with fair propitious gales.[438]

Now, morn, serene, in dappled grey arose

O'er the fair lawns where murm'ring Ganges flows;

Pale shone the wave beneath the golden beam,

Blue, o'er the silver flood, Malabria's mountains gleam;

The sailors on the main-top's airy round,

"Land, land!" aloud with waving hands resound;

Aloud the pilot of Melinda cries,

"Behold, O chief, the shores of India rise!"

Elate, the joyful crew on tip-toe trod,

And every breast with swelling raptures glow'd;

Gama's great soul confess'd the rushing swell,

Prone on his manly knees the hero fell;

"O bounteous heav'n!" he cries, and spreads his hands

To bounteous heav'n, while boundless joy commands

No further word to flow. In wonder lost,

As one in horrid dreams through whirlpools toss'd,

Now, snatch'd by demons, rides the flaming air,

And howls, and hears the howlings of despair;

Awak'd, amaz'd, confus'd with transport glows,

And, trembling still, with troubled joy o'erflows;

So, yet affected with the sickly weight

Left by the horrors of the dreadful night,

The hero wakes, in raptures to behold

The Indian shores before his prows unfold:

Bounding, he rises, and, with eyes on fire,

Surveys the limits of his proud desire.

O glorious chief, while storms and oceans rav'd,

What hopeless toils thy dauntless valour brav'd!

By toils like thine the brave ascend to heav'n,

By toils like thine immortal fame is giv'n.

Not he, who daily moves in ermine gown,

Who nightly slumbers on the couch of down;

Who proudly boasts through heroes old to trace

The lordly lineage of his titled race;

Proud of the smiles of every courtier lord,

A welcome guest at every courtier's board;

Not he, the feeble son of ease, may claim

Thy wreath, O Gama, or may hope thy fame.

'Tis he, who nurtur'd on the tented field,

From whose brown cheek each tint of fear expell'd,

With manly face unmov'd, secure, serene,

Amidst the thunders of the deathful scene,

From horror's mouth dares snatch the warrior's crown,

His own his honours, all his fame his own:

Who, proudly just to honour's stern commands,

The dogstar's rage on Afric's burning sands,

Or the keen air of midnight polar skies,

Long watchful by the helm, alike defies:

Who, on his front, the trophies of the wars,

Bears his proud knighthood's badge, his honest scars;

Who, cloth'd in steel, by thirst, by famine worn,

Through raging seas by bold ambition borne,

Scornful of gold, by noblest ardour fir'd,

Each wish by mental dignity inspir'd,

Prepar'd each ill to suffer, or to dare,

To bless mankind, his great, his only care;

Him whom her son mature Experience owns,

Him, him alone Heroic Glory crowns.

Once more the translator is tempted to confess his opinion, that the contrary practice of Homer and Virgil affords, in reality, no reasonable objection against the exclamatory exuberances of Camoëns. Homer, though the father of the epic poem, has his exuberances, which violently trespass against the first rule of the epopea, the unity of the action. A rule which, strictly speaking, is not outraged by the digressive exclamations of Camoëns. The one now before us, as the severest critic must allow, is happily adapted to the subject of the book. The great dangers which the hero had hitherto encountered are particularly described. He is afterwards brought in safety to the Indian shore, the object of his ambition, and of all his toils. The exclamation, therefore, on the grand hinge of the poem has its propriety, and discovers the warmth of its author's genius. It must also please, as it is strongly characteristic of the temper of our military poet. The manly contempt with which he speaks of the luxurious, inactive courtier, and the delight and honour with which he talks of the toils of the soldier, present his own active life to the reader of sensibility. His campaigns in Africa, where in a gallant attack he lost an eye, his dangerous life at sea, and the military fatigues, and the battles in which he bore an honourable share in India, rise to our idea, and possess us with an esteem and admiration of our martial poet, who thus could look back with a gallant enthusiasm (though his modesty does not mention himself) on all the hardships he had endured; who thus could bravely esteem the dangers to which he had been exposed, and by which he had severely suffered, as the most desirable occurrences of his life, and the ornament of his name.

END OF THE SIXTH BOOK.

BOOK VII.

THE ARGUMENT.

The poet, having expatiated on the glorious achievements of the Portuguese, describes the Germans, English, French, and Italians, reproaching them for their profane wars and luxury, while they ought to have been employed in opposing the enemies of the Christian faith. He then describes the western peninsula of India—the shores of Malabar—and Calicut, the capital of the Zamorim, where Gama had landed. Monsaide, a Moor of Barbary, is met with, who addresses Gama in Spanish, and offers to serve him as interpreter, Monsaide gives him a particular account of everything in India. The Zamorim invites Gama to an audience. The catual, or prime minister, with his officers, visits the ships, and embraces the opportunity of asking Gama to relate to him the history of Portugal.

HAIL glorious chief![439] where never chief before

Forc'd his bold way, all hail on India's shore!

And hail, Ye Lusian heroes, fair and wide

What groves of palm, to haughty Rome denied,

For you by Ganges' length'ning banks unfold!

What laurel-forests on the shores of gold

For you their honours ever verdant rear,

Proud, with their leaves, to twine the Lusian spear!

Ah Heav'n! what fury Europe's sons controls!

What self-consuming discord fires their souls!

'Gainst her own breast her sword Germania turns,

Through all her states fraternal rancour burns;[440]

Some, blindly wand'ring, holy faith disclaim,[441]

And, fierce through all, wild rages civil flame.

High sound the titles of the English crown,

"King of Jerusalem,"[442] his old renown!

Alas, delighted with an airy name,

The thin, dim shadow of departed fame,

England's stern monarch, sunk in soft repose,

Luxurious riots mid his northern snows:

Or, if the starting burst of rage succeed,

His brethren are his foes, and Christians bleed;

While Hagar's brutal race his titles stain,

In weeping Salem unmolested reign,

And with their rites impure her holy shrines profane.

And thou, O Gaul,[443] with gaudy trophies plum'd.

"Most Christian" nam'd; alas, in vain assum'd!

What impious lust of empire steels thy breast[444]

From their just lords the Christian lands to wrest!

While holy faith's hereditary foes[445]

Possess the treasures where Cynifio flows;[446]

And all secure, behold their harvests smile

In waving gold along the banks of Nile.

And thou, O lost to glory, lost to fame,

Thou dark oblivion of thy ancient name,

By every vicious luxury debas'd,

Each noble passion from thy breast eras'd,

Nerveless in sloth, enfeebling arts thy boast,

O Italy, how fall'n, how low, how lost![447]

In vain, to thee, the call of glory sounds,

Thy sword alone thy own soft bosom wounds.

Ah, Europe's sons, ye brother-powers, in you

The fables old of Cadmus[448] now are true;

Fierce rose the brothers from the dragon teeth,

And each fell, crimson'd with a brother's death.

So, fall the bravest of the Christian name,[449]

While dogs unclean[450] Messiah's lore blaspheme,

And howl their curses o'er the holy tomb,

While to the sword the Christian race they doom.

From age to age, from shore to distant shore,

By various princes led, their legions pour;

United all in one determin'd aim,

From ev'ry land to blot the Christian name.

Then wake, ye brother-powers, combin'd awake,

And, from the foe the great example take.

If empire tempt ye, lo, the East expands,

Fair and immense, her summer-garden lands:

There, boastful Wealth displays her radiant store;

Pactol and Hermus' streams, o'er golden ore,

Roll their long way; but, not for you they flow,

Their treasures blaze on the stern sultan's brow:

For him Assyria plies the loom of gold,

And Afric's sons their deepest mines unfold

To build his haughty throne. Ye western powers,

To throw the mimic bolt of Jove is yours,

Yours all the art to wield the arms of fire,

Then, bid the thunders of the dreadful tire

Against the walls of dread Byzantium[451] roar,

Till, headlong driven from Europe's ravish'd shore

To their cold Scythian wilds, and dreary dens,

By Caspian mountains, and uncultur'd fens,

(Their fathers' seats beyond the Wolgian Lake,[452])

The barb'rous race of Saracen betake.

And hark, to you the woful Greek exclaims;

The Georgian fathers and th' Armenian dames,

Their fairest offspring from their bosoms torn,

(A dreadful tribute!)[453] loud imploring mourn.

Alas, in vain! their offspring captive led,

In Hagar's[454] sons' unhallow'd temples bred,

To rapine train'd, arise a brutal host,

The Christian terror, and the Turkish boast.

Yet sleep, ye powers of Europe, careless sleep,

To you in vain your eastern brethren weep;

Yet, not in vain their woe-wrung tears shall sue,

Though small the Lusian realms, her legions few,

The guardian oft by Heav'n ordain'd before,

The Lusian race shall guard Messiah's lore.

When Heav'n decreed to crush the Moorish foe

Heav'n gave the Lusian spear to strike the blow.

When Heav'n's own laws o'er Afric's shores were heard,

The sacred shrines the Lusian heroes rear'd;[455]

Nor shall their zeal in Asia's bounds expire,

Asia, subdu'd, shall fume with hallow'd fire.

When the red sun the Lusian shore forsakes,

And on the lap of deepest west[456] awakes,

O'er the wild plains, beneath unincens'd skies

The sun shall view the Lusian altars rise.

And, could new worlds by human step be trod,

Those worlds should tremble at the Lusian nod.[457]

And now, their ensigns blazing o'er the tide,
On India's shore the Lusian heroes ride.
High to the fleecy clouds resplendent far
Appear the regal towers of Malabar,
Imperial Calicut,[458] the lordly seat
Of the first monarch of the Indian state.
Right to the port the valiant Gama bonds,
With joyful shouts, a fleet of boats attends:
Joyful, their nets they leave and finny prey,
And, crowding round the Lusians, point the way.
A herald now, by Vasco's high command
Sent to the monarch, treads the Indian strand;
The sacred staff he bears, in gold he shines,
And tells his office by majestic signs.
As, to and fro, recumbent to the gale,
The harvest waves along the yellow dale,
So, round the herald press the wond'ring throng,
Recumbent waving as they pour along,
And much his manly port and strange attire,
And much his fair and ruddy hue admire:
When, speeding through the crowd, with eager haste,
And honest smiles, a son of Afric press'd;
Enrapt with joy the wond'ring herald hears
Castilia's manly tongue salute his ears.[459]
"What friendly angel from thy Tago's shore
Has led thee hither?" cries the joyful Moor.
Then, hand in hand (the pledge of faith) conjoin'd—

"Oh joy beyond the dream of hope to find,
To hear a kindred voice," the Lusian cried,
"Beyond unmeasur'd gulfs and seas untried;
Untried, before our daring keels explor'd
Our fearless way! O Heav'n, what tempests roar'd,
While, round the vast of Afric's southmost land,
Our eastward bowsprits sought the Indian strand!"
Amaz'd, o'erpower'd, the friendly stranger stood—
"A path now open'd through the boundless flood!
The hope of ages, and the dread despair,
Accomplish'd now, and conquer'd!"—Stiff his hair
Rose thrilling, while his lab'ring thoughts pursued
The dreadful course by Gama's fate subdued.
Homeward, with gen'rous warmth o'erflow'd, he leads
The Lusian guest, and swift the feast succeeds;
The purple grape, and golden fruitage smile;
And each choice viand of the Indian soil
Heap'd o'er the board, the master's zeal declare;
The social feast the guest and master share:
The sacred pledge of eastern faith[460] approv'd,
By wrath unalter'd, and by wrong unmov'd.
Now, to the fleet the joyful herald bends,
With earnest pace the Heav'n-sent friend attends:
Now, down the river's sweepy stream they glide,
And now, their pinnace cuts the briny tide:
The Moor, with transport sparkling in his eyes,
The well-known make of Gama's navy spies,
The bending bowsprit, and the mast so tall,
The sides black, frowning as a castle wall,

265

The high-tower'd stern, the lordly nodding prore,

And the broad standard slowly waving o'er

The anchor's moony[461] fangs. The skiff he leaves,

Brave Gama's deck his bounding step receives;

And, "Hail!" he cries: in transport Gama sprung,

And round his neck with friendly welcome hung;

Enrapt, so distant o'er the dreadful main,

To hear the music of the tongue of Spain.

And now, beneath a painted shade of state,

Beside the admiral, the stranger sat.

Of India's clime, the natives, and the laws,

What monarch sways them, what religion awes?

Why from the tombs devoted to his sires

The son so far? the valiant chief inquires.

In act to speak the stranger waves his hand,

The joyful crew in silent wonder stand,

Each gently pressing on, with greedy ear,

As erst the bending forests stoop'd to hear

In Rhodope,[462] when Orpheus' heavenly strain,

Deplor'd his lost Eurydice in vain;

While, with a mien that gen'rous friendship won

From ev'ry heart, the stranger thus began:—

"Your glorious deeds, ye Lusians, well I know,

To neighb'ring earth the vital air I owe;

Yet—though my faith the Koran's lore revere;

So taught my sires; my birth at proud Tangier,

A hostile clime to Lisbon's awful name—

I glow, enraptur'd, o'er the Lusian fame;

Proud though your nation's warlike glories shine,

These proudest honours yield, O chief, to thine;

Beneath thy dread achievements low they fall,

And India's shore, discover'd, crowns them all.

Won by your fame, by fond affection sway'd,

A friend I come, and offer friendship's aid.

As, on my lips Castilia's language glows,

So, from my tongue the speech of India flows:

Mozaide my name, in India's court belov'd,

For honest deeds (but time shall speak) approv'd.

When India's monarch greets his court again,

(For now the banquet on the tented plain:

And sylvan chase his careless hours employ),[463]

When India's mighty lord, with wond'ring joy,

Shall hail you welcome on his spacious shore

Through oceans never plough'd by keel before,

Myself shall glad interpreter attend,

Mine ev'ry office of the faithful friend.

Ah! but a stream, the labour of the oar,

Divides my birthplace from your native shore;

On shores unknown, in distant worlds, how sweet

The kindred tongue, the kindred face, to greet!

Such now my joy; and such, O Heav'n, be yours!

Yes, bounteous Heav'n your glad success secures.

Till now impervious, Heav'n alone subdued

The various horrors of the trackless flood:

Heav'n sent you here for some great work divine,

And Heav'n inspires my breast your sacred toils to join.

"Vast are the shores of India's wealthful soil;
Southward sea-girt she forms a demi-isle:
His cavern'd cliffs with dark-brow'd forests crown'd,
Hemodian Taurus[464] frowns her northern bound:
From Caspia's lake th' enormous mountain[464] spreads,
And, bending eastward, rears a thousand heads:
Far to extremest sea the ridges thrown,
By various names, through various tribes are known:
Here down the waste of Taurus' rocky side
Two infant rivers pour the crystal tide,
Indus the one, and one the Ganges nam'd,
Darkly of old through distant nations fam'd:
One eastward curving holds his crooked way,
One to the west gives his swoll'n tide to stray:
Declining southward many a land they lave,
And, widely swelling, roll the sea-like wave,
Till the twin offspring of the mountain sire
Both in the Indian deep engulf'd expire:
Between these streams, fair smiling to the day,
The Indian lands their wide domains display,
And many a league, far to the south they bend,
From the broad region where the rivers end,
Till, where the shores to Ceylon's isle oppose,
In conic form the Indian regions close.
To various laws the various tribes incline,
And various are the rites esteem'd divine:
Some, as from Heav'n, receive the Koran's lore,
Some the dread monsters of the wild adore;
Some bend to wood and stone the prostrate head,

And rear unhallow'd altars to the dead.

By Ganges' banks, as wild traditions tell,[465]

Of old the tribes liv'd healthful by the smell;

No food they knew, such fragrant vapours rose

Rich from the flow'ry lawns where Ganges flows:

Here now the Delhian, and the fierce Pathàn,

Feed their fair flocks; and here, a heathen clan,

Stern Dekhan's sons the fertile valleys till,

A clan, whose hope to shun eternal ill,

Whose trust from ev'ry stain of guilt to save,

Is fondly plac'd in Ganges' holy wave;[466]

If to the stream the breathless corpse be giv'n

They deem the spirit wings her way to heav'n.

Here by the mouths, where hallow'd Ganges ends,

Bengala's beauteous Eden wide extends,

Unrivall'd smile her fair luxurious vales:

And here Cambaya[467] spreads her palmy dales;

A warlike realm, where still the martial race

From Porus,[468] fam'd of yore, their lineage trace.

Narsinga[469] here displays her spacious line,

In native gold her sons and ruby shine:

Alas, how vain! these gaudy sons of fear,

Trembling, bow down before each hostile spear.

And now, behold!"—and while he spoke he rose,

Now, with extended arm, the prospect shows,—

"Behold these mountain tops of various size

Blend their dim ridges with the fleecy skies:

Nature's rude wall, against the fierce Canar[470]

They guard the fertile lawns of Malabar.

Here, from the mountain to the surgy main,

Fair as a garden, spreads the smiling plain:

And lo, the empress of the Indian powers,

Their lofty Calicut, resplendent towers;

Hers ev'ry fragrance of the spicy shore,

Hers ev'ry gem of India's countless store:

Great Samoreem, her lord's imperial style,

The mighty lord of India's utmost soil:

To him the kings their duteous tribute pay,

And, at his feet, confess their borrow'd sway.

Yet higher tower'd the monarchs ancients boast,

Of old one sov'reign rul'd the spacious coast.

A votive train, who brought the Koran's lore,

(What time great Perimal the sceptre bore),

From blest Arabia's groves to India came;

Life were their words, their eloquence a flame

Of holy zeal: fir'd by the powerful strain,

The lofty monarch joins the faithful train,

And vows, at fair Medina's[471] shrine, to close

His life's mild eve in prayer, and sweet repose.

Gifts he prepares to deck the prophet's tomb,

The glowing labours of the Indian loom,

Orissa's spices, and Golconda's gems;

Yet, e'er the fleet th' Arabian ocean stems,

His final care his potent regions claim,

Nor his the transport of a father's name:

His servants, now, the regal purple wear,

And, high enthron'd, the golden sceptres bear.

Proud Cochim one, and one fair Chalé sways,

The spicy isle another lord obeys;

Coulam and Cananoor's luxurious fields,

And Cranganore to various lords he yields.

While these, and others thus the monarch grac'd,

A noble youth his care unmindful pass'd:

Save Calicut, a city poor and small,

Though lordly now, no more remain'd to fall:

Griev'd to behold such merit thus repaid,

The sapient youth the 'king of kings' he made,

And, honour'd with the name, great Zamoreem,

The lordly, titled boast of power supreme.

And now, great Perimal[472] resigns his reign,

The blissful bowers of Paradise to gain:

Before the gale his gaudy navy flies,

And India sinks for ever from his eyes.

And soon to Calicut's commodious port

The fleets, deep-edging with the wave, resort:

Wide o'er the shore extend the warlike piles,

And all the landscape round luxurious smiles.

And now, her flag to ev'ry gale unfurl'd,

She towers, the empress of the eastern world:

Such are the blessings sapient kings bestow,

And from thy stream such gifts, O Commerce, flow.

"From that sage youth, who first reign'd 'king of kings,'

He now who sways the tribes of India springs.

Various the tribes, all led by fables vain,

Their rites the dotage of the dreamful brain.

All, save where Nature whispers modest care,

Naked, they blacken in the sultry air.

The haughty nobles and the vulgar race

Never must join the conjugal embrace;

Nor may the stripling, nor the blooming maid,

(Oh, lost to joy, by cruel rites betray'd!)

To spouse of other than their father's art,

At Love's connubial shrine unite the heart:

Nor may their sons (the genius and the view

Confin'd and fetter'd) other art pursue.

Vile were the stain, and deep the foul disgrace,

Should other tribe touch one of noble race;

A thousand rites, and washings o'er and o'er,

Can scarce his tainted purity restore.

Poleas[473] the lab'ring lower clans are nam'd:

By the proud Nayres the noble rank is claim'd;

The toils of culture, and of art they scorn,

The warrior's plumes their haughty brows adorn;

The shining falchion brandish'd in the right,

Their left arm wields the target in the fight;

Of danger scornful, ever arm'd they stand

Around the king, a stern barbarian band.

Whate'er in India holds the sacred name

Of piety or lore, the Brahmins claim:

In wildest rituals, vain and painful, lost,

Brahma,[474] their founder, as a god they boast.[475]

To crown their meal no meanest life expires,

Pulse, fruit, and herbs alone their board requires:

Alone, in lewdness riotous and free,

No spousal ties withhold, and no degree:

Lost to the heart-ties, to his neighbour's arms,
The willing husband yields his spouse's charms:
In unendear'd embraces free they blend;
Yet, but the husband's kindred may ascend
The nuptial couch: alas, too blest, they know
Nor jealousy's suspense, nor burning woe;
The bitter drops which oft from dear affection flow.
But, should my lips each wond'rous scene unfold,
Which your glad eyes will soon amaz'd behold,
Oh, long before the various tale could run,
Deep in the west would sink yon eastern sun.
In few, all wealth from China to the Nile,
All balsams, fruit, and gold on India's bosom smile."

While thus, the Moor his faithful tale reveal'd,
Wide o'er the coast the voice of Rumour swell'd;
As, first some upland vapour seems to float
Small as the smoke of lonely shepherd cote,
Soon o'er the dales the rolling darkness spreads,
And wraps in hazy clouds the mountain heads,
The leafless forest and the utmost lea;
And wide its black wings hover o'er the sea:
The tear-dropp'd bough hangs weeping in the vale,
And distant navies rear the mist-wet sail.
So, Fame increasing, loud and louder grew,
And to the sylvan camp resounding flew:
"A lordly band," she cries, "of warlike mien,
Of face and garb in India never seen,
Of tongue unknown, through gulfs undar'd before,

Unknown their aim, have reach'd the Indian shore."

To hail their chief the Indian lord prepares,

And to the fleet he sends his banner'd Nayres:

As to the bay the nobles press along,

The wond'ring city pours th' unnumber'd throng.

And now brave Gama, and his splendid train,

Himself adorn'd in all the pride of Spain,

In gilded barges slowly bend to shore,

While to the lute the gently falling oar

Now, breaks the surges of the briny tide,

And now, the strokes the cold fresh stream divide.

Pleas'd with the splendour of the Lusian band,

On every bank the crowded thousands stand.

Begirt with, high-plum'd nobles, by the flood

The first great minister of India stood,

The Catual[476] his name in India's tongue:

To Gama swift the lordly regent sprung;

His open arms the valiant chief enfold,

And now he lands him on the shore of gold:

With pomp unwonted India's nobles greet

The fearless heroes of the warlike fleet.

A couch on shoulders borne, in India's mode,

(With gold the canopy and purple glow'd),

Receives the Lusian captain; equal rides

The lordly catual, and onward guides,

While Gama's train, and thousands of the throng

Of India's sons, encircling, pour along.

To hold discourse in various tongues they try;

In vain; the accents unremember'd die,

Instant as utter'd. Thus, on Babel's plain

Each builder heard his mate, and heard in vain.

Gama the while, and India's second lord,

Hold glad responses, as the various word

The faithful Moor unfolds. The city gate

They pass'd, and onward, tower'd in sumptuous state,

Before them now the sacred temple rose;

The portals wide the sculptur'd shrines disclose.

The chiefs advance, and, enter'd now, behold

The gods of wood, cold stone, and shining gold;

Various of figure, and of various face,

As the foul demon will'd the likeness base.

Taught to behold the rays of godhead shine

Fair imag'd in the human face divine,

With sacred horror thrill'd, the Lusians view'd

The monster forms, Chimera-like, and rude.[477]

Here, spreading horns a human visage bore,

So, frown'd stern Jove in Lybia's fane of yore.

One body here two various faces rear'd;

So, ancient Janus o'er his shrine appear'd.

A hundred arms another brandish'd wide;

So, Titan's son[478] the race of heaven defied.

And here, a dog his snarling tusks display'd;

Anubis, thus in Memphis' hallow'd shade

Grinn'd horrible. With vile prostrations low

Before these shrines the blinded Indians bow.[479]

And now, again the splendid pomp proceeds;

To India's lord the haughty regent leads.

To view the glorious leader of the fleet

Increasing thousands swell o'er every street;

High o'er the roofs the struggling youths ascend,

The hoary fathers o'er the portals bend,

The windows sparkle with the glowing blaze

Of female eyes, and mingling diamond's rays.

And now, the train with solemn state and slow,

Approach the royal gate, through many a row

Of fragrant wood-walks, and of balmy bowers,

Radiant with fruitage, ever gay with flowers.

Spacious the dome its pillar'd grandeur spread,

Nor to the burning day high tower'd the head;

The citron groves around the windows glow'd,

And branching palms their grateful shade bestow'd;

The mellow light a pleasing radiance cast;

The marble walls Dædalian sculpture grac'd

Here India's fate,[480] from darkest times of old,

The wondrous artist on the stone enroll'd;

Here, o'er the meadows, by Hydaspes' stream,

In fair array the marshall'd legions seem:

A youth of gleeful eye the squadrons led,

Smooth was his cheek, and glow'd with purest red:

Around his spear the curling vine-leaves wav'd;

And, by a streamlet of the river lav'd,

Behind her founder, Nysa's walls were rear'd;[481]

So breathing life the ruddy god appear'd,

Had Semele beheld the smiling boy,[482]

The mother's heart had proudly heav'd with joy.

Unnumber'd here, were seen th' Assyrian throng,

That drank whole rivers as they march'd along:

Each eye seem'd earnest on their warrior queen,[483]

High was her port, and furious was her mien;

Her valour only equall'd by her lust;

Fast by her side her courser paw'd the dust,

Her son's vile rival; reeking to the plain

Fell the hot sweat-drops as he champ'd the rein.

And here display'd, most glorious to behold,

The Grecian banners, op'ning many a fold,

Seem'd trembling on the gale; at distance far

The Ganges lav'd the wide-extended war.

Here, the blue marble gives the helmets' gleam;

Here, from the cuirass shoots the golden beam.

A proud-eyed youth, with palms unnumber'd gay,

Of the bold veterans led the brown array;

Scornful of mortal birth enshrin'd he rode,

Call'd Jove his father,[484] and assum'd the god.

While dauntless Gama and his train survey'd

The sculptur'd walls, the lofty regent said:

"For nobler wars than these you wond'ring see

That ample space th' eternal fates decree:

Sacred to these th' unpictur'd wall remains,

Unconscious yet of vanquish'd India's chains.

Assur'd we know the awful day shall come,

Big with tremendous fate, and India's doom.

The sons of Brahma, by the god their sire

Taught to illume the dread divining fire,

From the drear mansions of the dark abodes

Awake the dead, or call th' infernal gods;

Then, round the flame, while glimm'ring ghastly blue,

Behold the future scene arise to view.

The sons of Brahma, in the magic hour,

Beheld the foreign foe tremendous lower;

Unknown their tongue, their face, and strange attire,

And their bold eye-balls burn'd with warlike ire:

They saw the chief o'er prostrate India rear

The glitt'ring terrors of his awful spear.

But, swift behind these wint'ry days of woe

A spring of joy arose in liveliest glow,

Such gentle manners, leagued with wisdom, reign'd

In the dread victors, and their rage restrain'd.

Beneath their sway majestic, wise, and mild,

Proud of her victors' laws, thrice happier India smil'd.

So, to the prophets of the Brahmin train

The visions rose, that never rose in vain."

The regent ceas'd; and now, with solemn pace,

The chiefs approach the regal hall of grace.

The tap'stried walls with gold were pictur'd o'er,

And flow'ry velvet spread the marble floor.[485]

In all the grandeur of the Indian state,

High on a blazing couch, the monarch sat,

With starry gems the purple curtains shin'd,

And ruby flowers and golden foliage twin'd

Around the silver pillars: high o'er head

The golden canopy its radiance shed:

Of cloth of gold the sov'reign's mantle shone,

And, his high turban flam'd with precious stone

Sublime and awful was his sapient mien,
Lordly his posture, and his brow serene.
A hoary sire, submiss on bended knee,
(Low bow'd his head), in India's luxury,
A leaf,[486] all fragrance to the glowing taste,
Before the king each little while replac'd.
The patriarch Brahmin (soft and slow he rose),
Advancing now, to lordly Gama bows,
And leads him to the throne; in silent state
The monarch's nod assigns the captain's seat;
The Lusian train in humbler distance stand:
Silent, the monarch eyes the foreign band
With awful mien; when valiant Gama broke
The solemn pause, and thus majestic spoke:—

"From where the crimson sun of ev'ning laves
His blazing chariot in the western waves,
I come, the herald of a mighty king,
And, holy vows of lasting friendship bring
To thee, O monarch, for resounding Fame
Far to the west has borne thy princely name;
All India's sov'reign thou! Nor deem I sue,
Great as thou art, the humble suppliant's due.
Whate'er from western Tagus to the Nile,
Inspires the monarch's wish, the merchant's toil,
From where the north-star gleams o'er seas of frost,
To Ethiopia's utmost burning coast,
Whate'er the sea, whate'er the land bestows,
In my great monarch's realm unbounded flows.

Pleas'd thy high grandeur and renown to hear,
My sov'reign offers friendship's bands sincere:
Mutual he asks them, naked of disguise,
Then, every bounty of the smiling skies
Shower'd on his shore and thine, in mutual flow,
Shall joyful Commerce on each shore bestow.
Our might in war, what vanquish'd nations fell
Beneath our spear, let trembling Afric tell;
Survey my floating towers, and let thine ear,
Dread as it roars, our battle-thunder hear.
If friendship then thy honest wish explore,
That dreadful thunder on thy foes shall roar.
Our banners o'er the crimson field shall sweep,
And our tall navies ride the foamy deep,
Till not a foe against thy land shall rear
Th' invading bowsprit, or the hostile spear:
My king, thy brother, thus thy wars shall join,
The glory his, the gainful harvest thine."

Brave Gama spake; the pagan king replies,
"From lands which now behold the morning rise,
While eve's dim clouds the Indian sky enfold,
Glorious to us an offer'd league we hold.
Yet shall our will in silence rest unknown,
Till what your land, and who the king you own,
Our council deeply weigh. Let joy the while,
And the glad feast, the fleeting hours beguile.
Ah! to the wearied mariner, long toss'd
O'er briny waves, how sweet the long-sought coast!

The night now darkens; on the friendly shore
Let soft repose your wearied strength restore,
Assur'd an answer from our lips to bear,
Which, not displeas'd, your sov'reign lord shall hear.
More now we add not."[487] From the hall of state
Withdrawn, they now approach the regent's gate;
The sumptuous banquet glows; all India's pride
Heap'd on the board the royal feast supplied.
Now, o'er the dew-drops of the eastern lawn
Gleam'd the pale radiance of the star of dawn,
The valiant Gama on his couch repos'd,
And balmy rest each Lusian eye-lid clos'd:
When the high catual, watchful to fulfil
The cautious mandates of his sov'reign's will,
In secret converse with the Moor retires;
And, earnest, much of Lusus' sons inquires;
What laws, what holy rites, what monarch sway'd
The warlike race? When thus the just Mozaide:—

"The land from whence these warriors well I know,
(To neighb'ring earth my hapless birth I owe)
Illustrious Spain, along whose western shores
Grey-dappled eve the dying twilight pours.—
A wondrous prophet gave their holy lore,
The godlike seer a virgin mother bore,
Th' Eternal Spirit on the human race
(So be they taught) bestow'd such awful grace.
In war unmatch'd, they rear the trophied crest:
What terrors oft have thrill'd my infant breast[488]

When their brave deeds my wond'ring fathers told;

How from the lawns, where, crystalline and cold,

The Guadiana rolls his murm'ring tide,

And those where, purple by the Tago's side,

The length'ning vineyards glisten o'er the field,

Their warlike sires my routed sires expell'd:

Nor paus'd their rage; the furious seas they brav'd,

Nor loftiest walls, nor castled mountains saved;

Round Afric's thousand bays their navies rode,

And their proud armies o'er our armies trod.

Nor less, let Spain through all her kingdoms own,

O'er other foes their dauntless valour shone:

Let Gaul confess, her mountain-ramparts wild,

Nature in vain the hoar Pyrenians pil'd.

No foreign lance could e'er their rage restrain,

Unconquer'd still the warrior race remain.

More would you hear, secure your care may trust

The answer of their lips, so nobly just,

Conscious of inward worth, of manners plain,

Their manly souls the gilded lie disdain.

Then, let thine eyes their lordly might admire,

And mark the thunder of their arms of fire:

The shore, with trembling, hears the dreadful sound,

And rampir'd walls lie smoking on the ground.

Speed to the fleet; their arts, their prudence weigh,

How wise in peace, in war how dread, survey."

With keen desire the craftful pagan burn'd

Soon as the morn in orient blaze return'd,

To view the fleet his splendid train prepares;

And now, attended by the lordly Nayres,

The shore they cover, now the oarsmen sweep

The foamy surface of the azure deep:

And now, brave Paulus gives the friendly hand,

And high on Gama's lofty deck they stand.

Bright to the day the purple sail-cloths glow,

Wide to the gale the silken ensigns flow;

The pictur'd flags display the warlike strife;

Bold seem the heroes, as inspir'd by life.

Here, arm to arm, the single combat strains,

Here, burns the combat on the tented plains

General and fierce; the meeting lances thrust,

And the black blood seems smoking on the dust.

With earnest eyes the wond'ring regent views

The pictur'd warriors, and their history sues.

But now the ruddy juice, by Noah found,[489]

In foaming goblets circled swiftly round,

And o'er the deck swift rose the festive board;

Yet, smiling oft, refrains the Indian lord:

His faith forbade with other tribe to join

The sacred meal, esteem'd a rite divine.[490]

In bold vibrations, thrilling on the ear,

The battle sounds the Lusian trumpets rear;

Loud burst the thunders of the arms of fire,

Slow round the sails the clouds of smoke aspire,

And rolling their dark volumes o'er the day

The Lusian war, in dreadful pomp, display.

In deepest thought the careful regent weigh'd

The pomp and power at Gama's nod bewray'd;

Yet, seem'd alone in wonder to behold

The glorious heroes, and the wars half told

In silent poesy.—Swift from the board

High crown'd with wine, uprose the Indian lord;

Both the bold Gamas, and their gen'rous peer,

The brave Coello, rose, prepar'd to hear

Or, ever courteous, give the meet reply:

Fix'd and inquiring was the regent's eye:

The warlike image of a hoary sire,

Whose name shall live till earth and time expire,

His wonder fix'd, and more than human glow'd

The hero's look; his robes of Grecian mode;

A bough, his ensign, in his right he wav'd,

A leafy bough.—But I, fond man depraved!

Where would I speed, as madd'ning in a dream,

Without your aid, ye Nymphs of Tago's stream!

Or yours, ye Dryads of Mondego's bowers!

Without your aid how vain my wearied powers!

Long yet, and various lies my arduous way

Through low'ring tempests and a boundless sea.

Oh then, propitious hear your son implore,

And guide my vessel to the happy shore.

Ah! see how long what perilous days, what woes

On many a foreign coast around me rose,

As, dragg'd by Fortune's chariot-wheels along,

I sooth'd my sorrows with the warlike song:[491]

Wide ocean's horrors length'ning now around,

And, now my footsteps trod the hostile ground;

Yet, mid each danger of tumultuous war

Your Lusian heroes ever claim'd my care:

As Canace[492] of old, ere self-destroy'd,

One hand the pen, and one the sword employ'd,

Degraded now, by poverty abhorr'd,

The guest dependent at the lordling's board:

Now blest with all the wealth fond hope could crave,

Soon I beheld that wealth beneath the wave

For ever lost;[493] myself escap'd alone,

On the wild shore all friendless, hopeless, thrown;

My life, like Judah's heaven-doom'd king of yore,[494]

By miracle prolong'd; yet not the more

To end my sorrows: woes succeeding woes

Belied my earnest hopes of sweet repose:

In place of bays around my brows to shed

Their sacred honours, o'er my destin'd head

Foul Calumny proclaim'd the fraudful tale,

And left me mourning in a dreary jail.[495]

Such was the meed, alas! on me bestow'd,

Bestow'd by those for whom my numbers glow'd,

By those who to my toils their laurel honours ow'd.

Ye gentle nymphs of Tago's rosy bowers,

Ah, see what letter'd patron-lords are yours!

Dull as the herds that graze their flow'ry dales,

To them in vain the injur'd muse bewails:

No fost'ring care their barb'rous hands bestow,

Though to the muse their fairest fame they owe.

Ah, cold may prove the future priest of fame

Taught by my fate: yet, will I not disclaim

Your smiles, ye muses of Mondego's shade;

Be still my dearest joy your happy aid!

And hear my vow: Nor king, nor loftiest peer

Shall e'er from me the song of flatt'ry hear;

Nor crafty tyrant, who in office reigns,

Smiles on his king, and binds the land in chains;

His king's worst foe: nor he whose raging ire,

And raging wants, to shape his course, conspire;

True to the clamours of the blinded crowd,

Their changeful Proteus, insolent and loud:

Nor he whose honest mien secures applause,

Grave though he seem, and father of the laws,

Who, but half-patriot, niggardly denies

Each other's merit, and withholds the prize:

Who spurns the muse,[496] nor feels the raptur'd strain,

Useless by him esteem'd, and idly vain:

For him, for these, no wreath my hand shall twine;

On other brows th' immortal rays shall shine:

He who the path of honour ever trod,

True to his king, his country, and his God,

On his blest head my hands shall fix the crown

Wove of the deathless laurels of renown.

END OF THE SEVENTH BOOK.

BOOK VIII.

THE ARGUMENT.

Description of the pictures, given by Paulus. The heroes of Portugal, from Lusus, one of the companions of Bacchus (who gave his name to Portugal), and Ulysses, the founder of Lisbon, down to Don Pedro and Don Henrique (Henry), the conquerors of Ceuta, are all represented in the portraits of Gama, and are characterized by appropriate verses. Meanwhile the zamorim has recourse to the oracles of his false gods, who make him acquainted with the future dominion of the Portuguese over India, and the consequent ruin of his empire. The Mohammedan Arabs conspire against the Portuguese. The zamorim questions the truth of Gama's statement, and charges him with being captain of a band of pirates. Gama is obliged to give up to the Indians the whole of his merchandise as ransom, when he obtains permission to re-embark. He seizes several merchants of Calicut, whom he detains on board his ship as hostages for his two factors, who were on land to sell his merchandise. He afterwards liberates the natives, whom he exchanges for his two companions. In Mickle's translation this portion of the original is omitted, and the factors are released in consequence of a victory gained by Gama.

WITH eye unmov'd the silent Catual[497] view'd

The pictur'd sire[498] with seeming life endu'd;

A verdant vine-bough waving in his right,

Smooth flow'd his sweepy beard of glossy white,

When thus, as swift the Moor unfolds the word,

The valiant Paulus to the Indian lord:—

"Bold though these figures frown, yet bolder far

These godlike heroes shin'd in ancient war.

In that hoar sire, of mien serene, august,

Lusus behold, no robber-chief unjust;

His cluster'd bough—the same which Bacchus bore[499]—

He waves, the emblem of his care of yore;

The friend of savage man, to Bacchus dear,

The son of Bacchus, or the bold compeer,

What time his yellow locks with vine-leaves curl'd,

The youthful god subdued the savage world,

Bade vineyards glisten o'er the dreary waste,

And humaniz'd the nations as he pass'd.

Lusus, the lov'd companion of the god,

In Spain's fair bosom fix'd his last abode,

Our kingdom founded, and illustrious reign'd

In those fair lawns, the bless'd Elysium feign'd,[500]

Where, winding oft, the Guadiana roves,

And Douro murmurs through, the flow'ry groves.

Here, with his bones, he left his deathless fame,

And Lusitania's clime shall ever bear his name.

That other chief th' embroider'd silk displays,

Toss'd o'er the deep whole years of weary days,

On Tago's banks, at last, his vows he paid:

To wisdom's godlike power, the Jove-born maid,[501]

Who fir'd his lips with eloquence divine,

On Tago's banks he rear'd the hallow'd shrine.

Ulysses he, though fated to destroy,

On Asian ground, the heav'n-built towers of Troy,[502]

On Europe's strand, more grateful to the skies,

He bade th' eternal walls of Lisbon rise."[503]

"But who that godlike terror of the plain,

Who strews the smoking field with heaps of slain?

What num'rous legions fly in dire dismay,

Whose standards wide the eagle's wings display?"

The pagan asks: the brother chief[504] replies:—

"Unconquer'd deem'd, proud Rome's dread standard flies,

His crook thrown by, fir'd by his nation's woes,

The hero-shepherd Viriatus rose;

His country sav'd proclaim'd his warlike fame,

And Rome's wide empire trembled at his name.

That gen'rous pride which Rome to Pyrrhus bore,[505]

To him they show'd not; for they fear'd him more.

Not on the field o'ercome by manly force,

Peaceful he slept; and now, a murder'd corse,

By treason slain, he lay. How stern, behold,

That other hero, firm, erect, and bold:

The power by which he boasted he divin'd,

Beside him pictur'd stands, the milk-white hind:

Injur'd by Rome, the stern Sertorius fled

To Tago's shore, and Lusus' offspring led;

Their worth he knew; in scatter'd flight he drove

The standards painted with the birds of Jove.

And lo, the flag whose shining colours own

The glorious founder of the Lusian throne!

Some deem the warrior of Hungarian race,[506]

Some from Lorraine the godlike hero trace.

From Tagus' banks the haughty Moor expell'd,

Galicia's sons, and and Leon's warriors quell'd,

To weeping Salem's[507] ever-hallow'd meads,

His warlike bands the holy Henry leads;

By holy war to sanctify his crown,

And, to his latest race, auspicious waft it down."

"And who this awful chief?" aloud exclaims

The wond'ring regent. "O'er the field he flames

In dazzling steel; where'er he bends his course

The battle sinks beneath his headlong force:

Against his troops, though few, the num'rous foes

In vain their spears and tow'ry walls oppose.

With smoking blood his armour sprinkled o'er,

High to the knees his courser paws in gore:

O'er crowns and blood-stain'd ensigns scatter'd round

He rides; his courser's brazen hoofs resound."

"In that great chief," the second Gama cries,

"The first Alonzo[508] strikes thy wond'ring eyes.

From Lusus' realm the pagan Moors he drove;

Heav'n, whom he lov'd, bestow'd on him such love,

Beneath him, bleeding of its mortal wound,

The Moorish strength lay prostrate on the ground.

Nor Ammon's son, nor greater Julius dar'd

With troops so few, with hosts so num'rous warr'd:

Nor less shall Fame the subject heroes own:

Behold that hoary warrior's rageful frown!

On his young pupil's flight[509] his burning eyes

He darts, and, 'Turn thy flying host,' he cries,

'Back to the field!' The vet'ran and the boy

Back to the field exult with furious joy:

Their ranks mow'd down, the boastful foe recedes,

The vanquish'd triumph, and the victor bleeds.

Again, that mirror of unshaken faith,

Egaz behold, a chief self-doom'd to death.[510]

Beneath Castilia's sword his monarch lay;

Homage he vow'd his helpless king should pay;

His haughty king reliev'd, the treaty spurns,

With conscious pride the noble Egaz burns;

His comely spouse and infant race he leads,

Himself the same, in sentenced felons' weeds,

Around their necks the knotted halters bound,

With naked feet they tread the flinty ground;

And, prostrate now before Castilia's throne,

Their offer'd lives their monarch's pride atone.

Ah Rome! no more thy gen'rous consul boast.[511]

Whose 'lorn submission sav'd his ruin'd host:

No father's woes assail'd his stedfast mind;

The dearest ties the Lusian chief resign'd.

"There, by the stream, a town besieged behold,

The Moorish tents the shatter'd walls enfold.

Fierce as the lion from the covert springs,

When hunger gives his rage the whirlwind's wings;

From ambush, lo, the valiant Fuaz pours,

And whelms in sudden rout th'astonish'd Moors.

The Moorish king[512] in captive chains he sends;

And, low at Lisbon's throne, the royal captive bends.

Fuaz again the artist's skill displays;

Far o'er the ocean shine his ensign's rays:

In crackling flames the Moorish galleys fly,

And the red blaze ascends the blushing sky:

O'er Avila's high steep the flames aspire,

And wrap the forests in a sheet of fire:

There seem the waves beneath the prows to boil;

And distant, far around for many a mile,

The glassy deep reflects the ruddy blaze;

Far on the edge the yellow light decays,

And blends with hov'ring blackness. Great and dread

Thus shone the day when first the combat bled,

The first our heroes battled on the main,

The glorious prelude of our naval reign,

Which, now the waves beyond the burning zone,

And northern Greenland's frost-bound billows own.

Again behold brave Fuaz dares the fight!

O'erpower'd he sinks beneath the Moorish might;

Smiling in death the martyr-hero lies,

And lo, his soul triumphant mounts the skies.

Here now, behold, in warlike pomp portray'd,

A foreign navy brings the pious aid.[513]

Lo, marching from the decks the squadrons spread,

Strange their attire, their aspect firm and dread.

The holy cross their ensigns bold display,

To Salem's aid they plough'd the wat'ry way:

Yet first, the cause the same, on Tago's shore

They dye their maiden swords in pagan gore.

Proud stood the Moor on Lisbon's warlike towers,

From Lisbon's walls they drive the Moorish powers:

Amid the thickest of the glorious fight,

Lo, Henry falls, a gallant German knight,

A martyr falls: that holy tomb behold,

There waves the blossom'd palm, the boughs of gold:

O'er Henry's grave the sacred plant arose,

And from the leaves,[514] Heav'n's gift, gay health redundant flows.

"Aloft, unfurl!" the valiant Paulus cries.

Instant, new wars on new-spread ensigns rise

"In robes of white behold a priest advance![515]

His sword in splinters smites the Moorish lance:

Arronchez won revenges Lira's fall:

And lo, on fair Savilia's batter'd wall,

How boldly calm, amid the crashing spears,

That hero-form the Lusian standard rears.

There bleeds the war on fair Vandalia's plain:

Lo, rushing through the Moors, o'er hills of slain

The hero rides, and proves by genuine claim

The son of Egas,[516] and his worth the same.

Pierc'd by his dart the standard-bearer dies;

Beneath his feet the Moorish standard lies:

High o'er the field, behold the glorious blaze!

The victor-youth the Lusian flag displays.

Lo, while the moon through midnight azure rides,

From the high wall adown his spear-staff glides

The dauntless Gerald:[517] in his left he bears

Two watchmen's heads, his right the falchion rears:

The gate he opens, swift from ambush rise

His ready bands, the city falls his prize:

Evora still the grateful honour pays,

Her banner'd flag the mighty deed displays:

There frowns the hero; in his left he bears

The two cold heads, his right the falchion rears.

Wrong'd by his king,[518] and burning for revenge,

Behold his arms that proud Castilian change;

The Moorish buckler on his breast he bears,

And leads the fiercest of the pagan spears.

Abrantes falls beneath his raging force,

And now to Tagus bends his furious course.

Another fate he met on Tagus' shore,

Brave Lopez from his brows the laurels tore;

His bleeding army strew'd the thirsty ground,

And captive chains the rageful leader bound.

Resplendent far that holy chief behold!

Aside he throws the sacred staff of gold,

And wields the spear of steel. How bold advance

The num'rous Moors, and with the rested lance

Hem round the trembling Lusians. Calm and bold

Still towers the priest, and lo, the skies unfold:[519]

Cheer'd by the vision, brighter than the day,

The Lusians trample down the dread array

Of Hagar's legions: on the reeking plain

Low, with their slaves, four haughty kings lie slain.

In vain Alcazar rears her brazen walls,

Before his rushing host Alcazar falls.

There, by his altar, now the hero shines,

And, with the warrior's palm, his mitre twines.

That chief behold: though proud Castilia's host

He leads, his birth shall Tagus ever boast.

As a pent flood bursts headlong o'er the strand

So pours his fury o'er Algarbia's land:

Nor rampir'd town, nor castled rock afford

The refuge of defence from Payo's sword.

By night-veil'd art proud Sylves falls his prey,

And Tavila's high, walls, at middle day,

Fearless he scales: her streets in blood deplore

The seven brave hunters murder'd by the Moor.[520]

These three bold knights how dread![521] Thro' Spain and France

At joust and tourney with the tilted lance

Victors they rode: Castilia's court beheld

Her peers o'erthrown; the peers with rancour swell'd:

The bravest of the three their swords surround;

Brave Ribeir strews them vanquish'd o'er the ground.

Now let thy thoughts, all wonder and on fire,

That darling son of warlike Fame admire.

Prostrate at proud Castilia's monarch's feet

His land lies trembling: lo, the nobles meet:

Softly they seem to breathe, and forward bend

The servile neck; each eye distrusts his friend;

Fearful each tongue to speak; each bosom cold:

When, colour'd with stern rage, erect and bold,

The hero rises: 'Here no foreign throne

Shall fix its base; my native king alone

Shall reign.' Then, rushing to the fight, he leads;

Low, vanquish'd in the dust, Castilia bleeds.

Where proudest hope might deem it vain to dare,

God led him on, and crown'd the glorious war.

Though fierce, as num'rous, are the hosts that dwell

By Betis' stream, these hosts before him fell.

The fight behold: while absent from his bands,

Press'd on the step of flight his army stands,

To call the chief a herald speeds away:

Low, on his knees, the gallant chief survey!

He pours his soul, with lifted hands implores,

And Heav'n's assisting arm, inspir'd, adores.

Panting, and pale, the herald urges speed:

With holy trust of victory decreed,

Careless he answers, 'Nothing urgent calls:'

And soon the bleeding foe before him falls.

To Numa, thus, the pale patricians fled—

'The hostile squadrons o'er the kingdom spread!'
They cry; unmov'd, the holy king replies—
'And I, behold, am off'ring sacrifice!'[522]
Earnest, I see thy wond'ring eyes inquire
Who this illustrious chief, his country's sire?
The Lusian Scipio well might speak his fame,
But nobler Nunio shines a greater name:[523]
On earth's green bosom, or on ocean grey,
A greater never shall the sun survey.

"Known by the silver cross, and sable shield,
Two Knights of Malta[524] there command the field;
From Tago's banks they drive the fleecy prey,
And the tir'd ox lows on his weary way:
When, as the falcon through the forest glade
Darts on the lev'ret, from the brown-wood shade
Darts Roderic on their rear; in scatter'd flight
They leave the goodly herds the victor's right.
Again, behold, in gore he bathes his sword;
His captive friend,[525] to liberty restor'd,
Glows to review the cause that wrought his woe,
The cause, his loyalty, as taintless snow.
Here treason's well-earn'd meed allures thine eyes,[526]
Low, grovelling in the dust, the traitor dies;
Great Elvas gave the blow. Again, behold,
Chariot and steed in purple slaughter roll'd:
Great Elvas triumphs; wide o'er Xeres' plain
Around him reeks the noblest blood of Spain.

"Here Lisbon's spacious harbour meets the view:
How vast the foe's, the Lusian fleet how few!
Castile's proud war-ships, circling round, enclose
The Lusian galleys; through their thund'ring rows,
Fierce pressing on, Pereira fearless rides,
His hook'd irons grasp the adm'ral's sides:
Confusion maddens: on the dreadless knight
Castilia's navy pours its gather'd might:
Pereira dies, their self-devoted prey,
And safe the Lusian galleys speed away.[527]

"Lo, where the lemon-trees from yon green hill
Throw their cool shadows o'er the crystal rill;
There twice two hundred fierce Castilian foes
Twice eight, forlorn, of Lusian race enclose;
Forlorn they seem; but taintless flow'd their blood
From those three hundred who of old withstood;
Withstood, and from a thousand Romans tore
The victor-wreath, what time the shepherd[528] bore
The leader's staff of Lusus: equal flame
Inspir'd these few,[529] their victory the same.
Though twenty lances brave each single spear,
Never the foes superior might to fear
Is our inheritance, our native right,
Well tried, well prov'd in many a dreadful fight.

"That dauntless earl behold; on Libya's coast,
Far from the succour of the Lusian host,[530]
Twice hard besieg'd, he holds the Ceutan towers

Against the banded might of Afric's powers.

That other earl;[531]—behold the port he bore,

So, trod stern Mars on Thracia's hills of yore.

What groves of spears Alcazar's gates surround!

There Afric's nations blacken o'er the ground.

A thousand ensigns, glitt'ring to the day,

The waning moon's slant silver horns display.

In vain their rage; no gate, no turret falls,

The brave De Vian guards Alcazar's walls.

In hopeless conflict lost his king appears;

Amid the thickest of the Moorish spears

Plunges bold Vian: in the glorious strife

He dies, and dying saves his sov'reign's life.

"Illustrious, lo, two brother-heroes shine,[532]

Their birth, their deeds, adorn the royal line;

To ev'ry king of princely Europe known,

In ev'ry court the gallant Pedro shone.

The glorious Henry[533]—kindling at his name

Behold my sailors' eyes all sparkle flame!

Henry the chief, who first, by Heav'n inspir'd,

To deeds unknown before, the sailor fir'd,

The conscious sailor left the sight of shore,

And dar'd new oceans, never plough'd before.

The various wealth of ev'ry distant land

He bade his fleets explore, his fleets command.

The ocean's great discoverer he shines;

Nor less his honours in the martial lines:

The painted flag the cloud-wrapt siege displays,

There Ceuta's rocking wall its trust betrays.
Black yawns the breach; the point of many a spear
Gleams through the smoke; loud shouts astound the ear.
Whose step first trod the dreadful pass? Whose sword
Hew'd its dark way, first with the foe begor'd?
'Twas thine, O glorious Henry, first to dare
The dreadful pass, and thine to close the war.
Taught by his might, and humbled in her gore,
The boastful pride of Afric tower'd no more.

"Num'rous though these, more num'rous warriors shine
Th' illustrious glory of the Lusian line.
But ah, forlorn, what shame to barb'rous pride![534]
Friendless the master of the pencil died;
Immortal fame his deathless labours gave;
Poor man, he sunk neglected to the grave!"

The gallant Paulus faithful thus explain'd
The various deeds the pictur'd flags contain'd.
Still o'er and o'er, and still again untir'd,
The wond'ring regent of the wars inquir'd:
Still wond'ring, heard the various pleasing tale,
Till o'er the decks cold sigh'd the ev'ning gale:
The falling darkness dimm'd the eastern shore,
And twilight hover'd o'er the billows hoar
Far to the west, when, with his noble band,
The thoughtful regent sought his native strand.

O'er the tall mountain-forest's waving boughs

Aslant, the new moon's slender horns arose;

Near her pale chariot shone a twinkling star,

And, save the murm'ring of the wave afar,

Deep-brooding silence reign'd; each labour clos'd,

In sleep's soft arms the sons of toil repos'd.

And now, no more the moon her glimpses shed,

A sudden, black-wing'd cloud the sky o'erspread,

A sullen murmur through the woodland groan'd,

In woe-swoll'n sighs the hollow winds bemoan'd:

Borne on the plaintive gale, a patt'ring shower

Increas'd the horrors of the evil hour.

Thus, when the God of earthquakes rocks the ground,

He gives the prelude in a dreary sound;

O'er nature's face a horrid gloom he throws,

With dismal note the cock unusual crows,

A shrill-voic'd howling trembles thro' the air,

As passing ghosts were weeping in despair;

In dismal yells the dogs confess their fear,

And shiv'ring, own some dreadful presence near.

So, lower'd the night, the sullen howl the same,

And, 'mid the black-wing'd gloom, stern Bacchus came;

The form, and garb of Hagar's son he took,

The ghost-like aspect, and the threat'ning look.[535]

Then, o'er the pillow of a furious priest,

Whose burning zeal the Koran's lore profess'd,

Reveal'd he stood, conspicuous in a dream,

His semblance shining, as the moon's pale gleam:

"And guard," he cries, "my son, O timely guard,

Timely defeat the dreadful snare prepar'd:

And canst thou, careless, unaffected, sleep,

While these stern, lawless rovers of the deep

Fix on thy native shore a foreign throne,

Before whose steps thy latest race shall groan!"

He spoke; cold horror shook the Moorish priest;

He wakes, but soon reclines in wonted rest:

An airy phantom of the slumb'ring brain

He deem'd the vision; when the fiend again,

With sterner mien, and fiercer accent spoke:

"Oh faithless! worthy of the foreign yoke!

And know'st thou not thy prophet sent by Heav'n,

By whom the Koran's sacred lore was giv'n,

God's chiefest gift to men: and must I leave

The bowers of Paradise, for you to grieve,

For you to watch, while, thoughtless of your woe,

Ye sleep, the careless victims of the foe;

The foe, whose rage will soon with cruel joy,

If unoppos'd, my sacred shrines destroy?

Then, while kind Heav'n th'auspicious hour bestows,

Let ev'ry nerve their infant strength oppose.

When, softly usher'd by the milky dawn,

The sun first rises[536] o'er the daisied lawn,

His silver lustre, as the shining dew

Of radiance mild, unhurt the eye may view:

But, when on high the noon-tide flaming rays

Give all the force of living fire to blaze,

A giddy darkness strikes the conquer'd sight,

That dares, in all his glow, the lord of light.

Such, if on India's soil the tender shoot

Of these proud cedars fix the stubborn root,

Such, shall your power before them sink decay'd.

And India's strength shall wither in their shade."

He spoke; and, instant from his vot'ry's bed

Together with repose, the demon fled;

Again cold horror shook the zealot's frame,

And all his hatred of Messiah's name

Burn'd in his venom'd heart, while, veil'd in night,

Right to the palace sped the demon's flight.

Sleepless the king he found, in dubious thought;

His conscious fraud a thousand terrors brought:

All gloomy as the hour, around him stand,

With haggard looks, the hoary Magi band:[537]

To trace what fates on India's wide domain

Attend the rovers from unheard-of Spain,

Prepar'd, in dark futurity, to prove

The hell-taught rituals of infernal Jove:

Mutt'ring their charms, and spells of dreary sound,

With naked feet they beat the hollow ground;

Blue gleams the altar's flame along the walls,

With dismal, hollow groans the victim falls;

With earnest eyes the priestly band explore

The entrails, throbbing in the living gore.

And lo, permitted by the power divine,

The hov'ring demon gives the dreadful sign.[538]

Here furious War her gleamy falchion draws,

Here lean-ribb'd Famine writhes her falling jaws;

Dire as the fiery pestilential star

Darting his eyes, high on his trophied car,

Stern Tyranny sweeps wide o'er India's ground;

On vulture-wings fierce Rapine hovers round;

Ills after ills, and India's fetter'd might,

Th'eternal yoke.[539] Loud shrieking at the sight,

The starting wizards from the altar fly,

And silent horror glares in ev'ry eye:

Pale stands the monarch, lost in cold dismay,

And, now impatient, waits the ling'ring day.

With gloomy aspect rose the ling'ring dawn,

And dropping tears flow'd slowly o'er the lawn;

The Moorish priest, with fear and vengeance fraught,

Soon as the light appear'd his kindred sought;

Appall'd, and trembling with ungen'rous fear,

In secret council met, his tale they hear;

As, check'd by terror or impell'd by hate,

Of various means they ponder and debate,

Against the Lusian train what arts employ,

By force to slaughter, or by fraud destroy;

Now black, now pale, their bearded cheeks appear,

As boiling rage prevails, or boding fear;

Beneath their shady brows, their eye-balls roll,

Nor one soft gleam bespeaks the gen'rous soul;

Through quiv'ring lips they draw their panting breath.

While their dark fraud decrees the works of death;

Nor unresolv'd the power of gold to try

Swift to the lordly catual's gate they hie.—

Ah, what the wisdom, what the sleepless care

Efficient to avoid the traitor's snare;

What human power can give a king to know

The smiling aspect of the lurking foe!

So let the tyrant plead.[540]—The patriot king

Knows men, knows whence the patriot virtues spring;

From inward worth, from conscience firm and bold,

(Not from the man whose honest name is sold),

He hopes that virtue, whose unalter'd weight

Stands fix'd, unveering with the storms of state.

Lur'd was the regent with the Moorish gold,

And now agreed their fraudful course to hold,

Swift to the king the regent's steps they tread;

The king they found o'erwhelm'd in sacred dread.

The word they take, their ancient deeds relate,

Their ever faithful service of the state;[541]

"For ages long, from shore to distant shore

For thee our ready keels the traffic bore:

For thee we dar'd each horror of the wave;

Whate'er thy treasures boast our labours gave.

And wilt thou now confer our long-earn'd due,

Confer thy favour on a lawless crew?

The race they boast, as tigers of the wold

Bear that proud sway, by justice uncontroll'd.

Yet, for their crimes, expell'd that bloody home,

These, o'er the deep, rapacious plund'rers roam.

Their deeds we know; round Afric's shores they came,

And spread, where'er they pass'd, devouring flame;

Mozambique's towers, enroll'd in sheets of fire,

Blaz'd to the sky, her own funereal pyre.

Imperial Calicut shall feel the same,

And these proud state-rooms feed the funeral flame;

While many a league far round, their joyful eyes

Shall mark old ocean reddening to the skies.

Such dreadful fates, o'er thee, O king, depend,

Yet, with thy fall our fate shall never blend:

Ere o'er the east arise the second dawn

Our fleets, our nation from thy land withdrawn,

In other climes, beneath a kinder reign

Shall fix their port: yet may the threat be vain!

If wiser thou with us thy powers employ,

Soon shall our powers the robber-crew destroy.

By their own arts and secret deeds o'ercome,

Here shall they meet the fate escaped at home."

While thus the priest detain'd the monarch's ear,

His cheeks confess'd the quiv'ring pulse of fear.

Unconscious of the worth that fires the brave,

In state a monarch, but in heart a slave,

He view'd brave Vasco, and his gen'rous train,

As his own passions stamp'd the conscious stain:

Nor less his rage the fraudful regent fir'd;

And valiant Gama's fate was now conspir'd.

Ambassadors from India Gama sought,

And oaths of peace, for oaths of friendship brought;

The glorious tale, 'twas all he wish'd, to tell;

So Ilion's[542] fate was seal'd when Hector fell.

Again convok'd before the Indian throne,

The monarch meets him with a rageful frown;

"And own," he cries, "the naked truth reveal,

Then shall my bounteous grace thy pardon seal.

Feign'd is the treaty thou pretend'st to bring:

No country owns thee, and thou own'st no king.

Thy life, long roving o'er the deep, I know—

A lawless robber, every man thy foe.

And think'st thou credit to thy tale to gain?

Mad were the sov'reign, and the hope were vain,

Through ways unknown, from utmost western shore,

To bid his fleets the utmost east explore.

Great is thy monarch, so thy words declare;

But sumptuous gifts the proof of greatness bear:

Kings thus to kings their empire's grandeur show;

Thus prove thy truth, thus we thy truth allow.

If not, what credence will the wise afford?

What monarch trust the wand'ring seaman's word?

No sumptuous gift thou bring'st.[543]—Yet, though some crime

Has thrown thee, banish'd from thy native clime,

(Such oft of old the hero's fate has been),

Here end thy toils, nor tempt new fates unseen:

Each land the brave man nobly calls his home:

Or if, bold pirates, o'er the deep you roam,

Skill'd the dread storm to brave, O welcome here!

Fearless of death, or shame, confess sincere:

My name shall then thy dread protection be,

My captain thou, unrivall'd on the sea."

Oh now, ye Muses, sing what goddess fir'd

Gama's proud bosom, and his lips inspir'd.

Fair Acidalia, love's celestial queen,[544]

The graceful goddess of the fearless mien,

Her graceful freedom on his look bestow'd,

And all collected in his bosom glow'd.

"Sov'reign," he cries, "oft witness'd, well I know

The rageful falsehood of the Moorish foe:

Their fraudful tales, from hatred bred, believ'd,

Thine ear is poison'd, and thine eye deceiv'd.

What light, what shade the courtier's mirror gives,

That light, that shade the guarded king receives.

Me hast thou view'd in colours not mine own,

Yet, bold I promise shall my truth be known.

If o'er the seas a lawless pest I roam,

A blood-stain'd exile from my native home,

How many a fertile shore and beauteous isle,

Where Nature's gifts, unclaim'd, unbounded, smile,

Mad have I left, to dare the burning zone,

And all the horrors of the gulfs unknown

That roar beneath the axle of the world.

Where ne'er before was daring sail unfurl'd!

And have I left these beauteous shores behind,

And have I dar'd the rage of ev'ry wind,

That now breath'd fire, and now came wing'd with frost,

Lur'd by the plunder of an unknown coast?

Not thus the robber leaves his certain prey

For the gay promise of a nameless day.

Dread and stupendous, more than death-doom'd man

Might hope to compass, more than wisdom plan,

To thee my toils, to thee my dangers rise:

Ah! Lisbon's kings behold with other eyes.

Where virtue calls, where glory leads the way,

No dangers move them, and no toils dismay.

Long have the kings of Lusus' daring race

Resolv'd the limits of the deep to trace,

Beneath the morn to ride the furthest waves,

And pierce the farthest shore old Ocean laves.

Sprung from the prince,[545] before whose matchless power

The strength of Afric wither'd as a flower

Never to bloom again, great Henry shone,

Each gift of nature and of art his own;

Bold as his sire, by toils on toils untir'd,

To find the Indian shore his pride aspir'd.

Beneath the stars that round the Hydra shine,

And where fam'd Argo hangs the heav'nly sign,

Where thirst and fever burn on ev'ry gale

The dauntless Henry rear'd the Lusian sail.

Embolden'd by the meed that crown'd his toils,

Beyond the wide-spread shores and num'rous isles,

Where both the tropics pour the burning day,

Succeeding heroes forc'd th' exploring way;

That race which never view'd the Pleiad's car,

That barb'rous race beneath the southern star,

Their eyes beheld.—Dread roar'd the blast—the wave

Boils to the sky, the meeting whirlwinds rave

O'er the torn heav'ns; loud on their awe-struck ear

Great Nature seem'd to call, 'Approach not here!'

At Lisbon's court they told their dread escape,

And from her raging tempests, nam'd the Cape.[546]

'Thou southmost point,' the joyful king exclaim'd,

'Cape of Good Hope, be thou for ever nam'd!

Onward my fleets shall dare the dreadful way,

And find the regions of the infant day.'

In vain the dark and ever-howling blast

Proclaim'd, 'This ocean never shall be past;'

Through that dread ocean, and the tempests' roar,

My king commanded, and my course I bore.

The pillar thus of deathless fame, begun

By other chiefs,[547] beneath the rising sun

In thy great realm, now to the skies I raise,

The deathless pillar of my nation's praise.

Through these wild seas no costly gift I brought;

Thy shore alone and friendly peace I sought.

And yet to thee the noblest gift I bring

The world can boast—the friendship of my king.

And mark the word, his greatness shall appear

When next my course to India's strand I steer,

Such proofs I'll bring as never man before

In deeds of strife, or peaceful friendship bore.

Weigh now my words, my truth demands the light,

For truth shall ever boast, at last, resistless might."

Boldly the hero spake with brow severe,

Of fraud alike unconscious, as of fear:

His noble confidence with truth impressed

Sunk deep, unwelcome, in the monarch's breast,
Nor wanting charms his avarice to gain
Appear'd the commerce of illustrious Spain.
Yet, as the sick man loathes the bitter draught,
Though rich with health he knows the cup comes fraught;
His health without it, self-deceiv'd, he weighs,
Now hastes to quaff the drug, and now delays;
Reluctant thus, as wav'ring passion veer'd,
The Indian lord the dauntless Gama heard:
The Moorish threats yet sounding in his ear,
He acts with caution, and is led by fear.
With solemn pomp he bids his lords prepare
The friendly banquet; to the regent's care
Commends brave Gama, and with pomp retires:
The regent's hearths awake the social fires;
Wide o'er the board the royal feast is spread,
And, fair embroidered, shines De Gama's bed.
The regent's palace high o'erlook'd the bay
Where Gama's black-ribb'd fleet at anchor lay.[548]

Ah, why the voice of ire and bitter woe
O'er Tago's banks, ye nymphs of Tagus, show?
The flow'ry garlands from your ringlets torn,
Why wand'ring wild with trembling steps forlorn?
The demon's rage you saw, and mark'd his flight
To the dark mansions of eternal night:
You saw how, howling through the shades beneath,
He wak'd new horrors in the realms of death.
What trembling tempests shook the thrones of hell,

And groan'd along her caves, ye muses, tell.

The rage of baffled fraud, and all the fire

Of powerless hate, with tenfold flames conspire;

From ev'ry eye the tawny lightnings glare,

And hell, illumin'd by the ghastly flare,

(A drear blue gleam), in tenfold horror shows

Her darkling caverns; from his dungeon rose

Hagar's stern son: pale was his earthy hue,

And from his eye-balls flash'd the lightnings blue;

Convuls'd with rage the dreadful shade demands

The last assistance of th' infernal bands.

As when the whirlwinds, sudden bursting, bear

Th' autumnal leaves high floating through the air;

So, rose the legions of th' infernal state,

Dark Fraud, base Art, fierce Rage, and burning Hate:

Wing'd by the Furies to the Indian strand

They bend; the demon leads the dreadful band,

And, in the bosoms of the raging Moors

All their collected, living strength he pours.

One breast alone against his rage was steel'd,

Secure in spotless Truth's celestial shield.

One evening past, another evening clos'd,

The regent still brave Gama's suit oppos'd;

The Lusian chief his guarded guest detain'd,

With arts on arts, and vows of friendship feign'd.

His fraudful art, though veil'd in deep disguise,

Shone bright to Gama's manner-piercing eyes.

As in the sun's bright[549] beam the gamesome boy

Plays with the shining steel or crystal toy,

Swift and irregular, by sudden starts,

The living ray with viewless motion darts,

Swift o'er the wall, the floor, the roof, by turns

The sun-beam dances, and the radiance burns:

In quick succession, thus, a thousand views

The sapient Lusian's lively thought pursues;

Quick as the lightning ev'ry view revolves,

And, weighing all, fix'd are his dread resolves.

O'er India's shore the sable night descends,

And Gama, now, secluded from his friends,

Detain'd a captive in the room of state,

Anticipates in thought to-morrow's fate;

For just Mozaide no gen'rous care delays,

And Vasco's trust with friendly toils repays.

END OF THE EIGHTH BOOK.

BOOK IX.

THE ARGUMENT.

The liberation of Gama's factors is effected by a great victory over the Moorish fleet, and by the bombardment of Calicut. Gama returns in consequence to his ships, and weighs anchor to return to Europe with the news of his great discoveries. Camoëns then introduces a very singular, but agreeable episode, recounting the love adventures of his heroes in one of the islands of the ocean. Venus, in search of her son, journeys through all his realms to implore his aid, and at length arrives at the spot where Love's artillery and arms are forged. Venus intercedes with her son in favour of the Portuguese. The island of Love, like that of Delos, floats on the ocean. It is then explained by the poet that these seeming realities are only allegorical.

RED[550] rose the dawn; roll'd o'er the low'ring sky,

The scattering clouds of tawny purple fly.

While yet the day-spring struggled with the gloom,

312

The Indian monarch sought the regent's dome.
In all the luxury of Asian state,
High on a star-gemm'd couch the monarch sat:
Then on th' illustrious captive, bending down
His eyes, stern darken'd with a threat'ning frown,
"Thy truthless tale," he cries, "thy art appears,
Confess'd inglorious by thy cautious fears.
Yet, still if friendship, honest, thou implore,
Yet now command thy vessels to the shore:
Gen'rous, as to thy friends, thy sails resign,
My will commands it, and the power is mine:
In vain thy art, in vain thy might withstands,
Thy sails, and rudders too, my will demands:[551]
Such be the test, thy boasted truth to try,
Each other test despis'd, I fix'd deny.
And has my regent sued two days in vain!
In vain my mandate, and the captive chain!
Yet not in vain, proud chief, ourself shall sue
From thee the honour to my friendship due:
Ere force compel thee, let the grace be thine,
Our grace permits it, freely to resign,
Freely to trust our friendship, ere too late
Our injur'd honour fix thy dreadful fate."

While thus he spake, his changeful look declar'd
In his proud breast what starting passions warr'd.
No feature mov'd on Gama's face was seen;
Stern he replies, with bold yet anxious mien,
"In me my sov'reign represented see,

His state is wounded, and he speaks in me;
Unaw'd by threats, by dangers uncontroll'd,
The laws of nations bid my tongue be bold.
No more thy justice holds the righteous scale,
The arts of falsehood and the Moors prevail;
I see the doom my favour'd foes decree,
Yet, though in chains I stand, my fleet is free.
The bitter taunts of scorn the brave disdain;
Few be my words, your arts, your threats are vain.
My sov'reign's fleet I yield not to your sway;[552]
Safe shall my fleet to Lisboa's strand convey
The glorious tale of all the toils I bore,
Afric surrounded, and the Indian shore
Discover'd. These I pledg'd my life to gain,
These to my country shall my life maintain.
One wish alone my earnest heart desires,
The sole impassion'd hope my breast respires;
My finish'd labours may my sov'reign hear!
Besides that wish, nor hope I know, nor fear.
And lo, the victim of your rage I stand,
And bare my bosom to the murd'rer's hand."

With lofty mien he spake. In stern disdain,
"My threats," the monarch cries, "were never vain:
Swift give the sign."—Swift as he spake, appear'd
The dancing streamer o'er the palace rear'd;
Instant another ensign distant rose,
Where, jutting through the flood, the mountain throws
A ridge enormous, and on either side

Defends the harbours from the furious tide.
Proud on his couch th' indignant monarch sat,
And awful silence fill'd the room of state.
With secret joy the Moors, exulting, glow'd,
And bent their eyes where Gama's navy rode,
Then, proudly heav'd with panting hope, explore
The wood-crown'd upland of the bending shore.
Soon o'er the palms a mast's tall pendant flows,
Bright to the sun the purple radiance glows;
In martial pomp, far streaming to the skies,
Vanes after vanes in swift succession rise,
And, through the opening forest-boughs of green,
The sails' white lustre moving on is seen;
When sudden, rushing by the point of land
The bowsprits nod, and wide the sails expand;
Full pouring on the sight, in warlike pride,
Extending still the rising squadrons ride:
O'er every deck, beneath the morning rays,
Like melted gold, the brazen spear-points blaze;
Each prore surrounded with a hundred oars,
Old Ocean boils around the crowded prores:
And, five times now in number Gama's might,
Proudly their boastful shouts provoke the fight;
Far round the shore the echoing peal rebounds,
Behind the hill an answ'ring shout resounds:
Still by the point new-spreading sails appear,
Till seven times Gama's fleet concludes the rear.
Again the shout triumphant shakes the bay;
Form'd as a crescent, wedg'd in firm array,

Their fleet's wide horns the Lusian ships enclasp,
Prepar'd to crush them in their iron grasp.
Shouts echo shouts.—With stern, disdainful eyes
The Indian king to manly Gama cries,
"Not one of thine on Lisboa's shore shall tell
The glorious tale, how bold thy heroes fell."
With alter'd visage, for his eyes flash'd fire,
"God sent me here, and God's avengeful ire
Shall blast thy perfidy," great Vasco cried,
"And humble in the dust thy wither'd pride."
A prophet's glow inspir'd his panting breast,
Indignant smiles the monarch's scorn confess'd.
Again deep silence fills the room of state,
And the proud Moors, secure, exulting wait:
And now inclasping Gama's in a ring,
Their fleet sweeps on.—Loud whizzing from the string
The black-wing'd arrows float along the sky,
And rising clouds the falling clouds supply.
The lofty crowding spears that bristling stood
Wide o'er the galleys as an upright wood,
Bend sudden, levell'd for the closing fight,
The points, wide-waving, shed a gleamy light.
Elate with joy the king his aspect rears,
And valiant Gama, thrill'd with transport, hears
His drums' bold rattling raise the battle sound;
Echo, deep-ton'd, hoarse, vibrates far around;
The shiv'ring trumpets tear the shrill-voic'd air,
Quiv'ring the gale, the flashing lightnings flare,
The smoke rolls wide, and sudden bursts the roar,

The lifted waves fall trembling, deep the shore

Groans; quick and quicker blaze embraces blaze

In flashing arms; louder the thunders raise

Their roaring, rolling o'er the bended skies

The burst incessant; awe-struck Echo dies

Falt'ring and deafen'd; from the brazen throats,

Cloud after cloud, enroll'd in darkness, floats,

Curling their sulph'rous folds of fiery blue,

Till their huge volumes take the fleecy hue,

And roll wide o'er the sky; wide as the sight

Can measure heav'n, slow rolls the cloudy white:

Beneath, the smoky blackness spreads afar

Its hov'ring wings, and veils the dreadful war

Deep in its horrid breast; the fierce red glare,

Cheq'ring the rifted darkness, fires the air,

Each moment lost and kindled, while around,

The mingling thunders swell the lengthen'd sound.

When piercing sudden through the dreadful roar

The yelling shrieks of thousands strike the shore:

Presaging horror through the monarch's breast

Crept cold; and gloomy o'er the distant east,

Through Gata's hills[553] the whirling tempest sigh'd,

And westward sweeping to the blacken'd tide,

Howl'd o'er the trembling palace as it past,

And o'er the gilded walls a gloomy twilight cast;

Then, furious, rushing to the darken'd bay,[554]

Resistless swept the black-wing'd night away,

With all the clouds that hover'd o'er the fight,

And o'er the weary combat pour'd the light.

As by an Alpine mountain's pathless side

Some traveller strays, unfriended of a guide;

If o'er the hills the sable night descend,

And gath'ring tempest with the darkness blend,

Deep from the cavern'd rocks beneath, aghast

He hears the howling of the whirlwind's blast;

Above, resounds the crash, and down the steep

Some rolling weight groans on with found'ring sweep;

Aghast he stands, amid the shades of night,

And all his soul implores the friendly light:

It comes; the dreadful lightning's quiv'ring blaze

The yawning depth beneath his lifted step betrays;

Instant unmann'd, aghast in horrid pain,

his knees no more their sickly weight sustain;

Powerless he sinks, no more his heart-blood flows;

So sunk the monarch, and his heart-blood froze;

So sunk he down, when o'er the clouded bay

The rushing whirlwind pour'd the sudden day:

Disaster's giant arm in one wide sweep

Appear'd, and ruin blacken'd o'er the deep;

The sheeted masts drove floating o'er the tide,

And the torn hulks roll'd tumbling on the side;

Some shatter'd plank each heaving billow toss'd,

And, by the hand of Heav'n, dash'd on the coast

Groan'd prores ingulf'd; the lashing surges rave

O'er the black keels upturn'd, the swelling wave

Kisses the lofty mast's reclining head;

And, far at sea, some few torn galleys fled.

Amid the dreadful scene triumphant rode

The Lusian war-ships, and their aid bestow'd:

Their speedy boats far round assisting ply'd,

Where plunging, struggling, in the rolling tide,

Grasping the shatter'd wrecks, the vanquish'd foes

Rear'd o'er the dashing waves their haggard brows.

No word of scorn the lofty Gama spoke,

Nor India's king the dreadful silence broke.

Slow pass'd the hour, when to the trembling shore,

In awful pomp, the victor-navy bore:

Terrific, nodding on, the bowsprits bend,

And the red streamers other war portend:

Soon bursts the roar; the bombs tremendous rise,

And trail their black'ning rainbows o'er the skies;

O'er Calicut's proud domes their rage they pour,

And wrap her temples in a sulph'rous shower.

'Tis o'er——In threat'ning silence rides the fleet:

Wild rage, and horror yell in ev'ry street;

Ten thousands pouring round the palace gate,

In clam'rous uproar wail their wretch'd fate:

While round the dome, with lifted hands, they kneel'd,

"Give justice, justice to the strangers yield——

Our friends, our husbands, sons, and fathers slain!

Happier, alas, than these that yet remain——

Curs'd be the counsels, and the arts unjust——

Our friends in chains——our city in the dust——

Yet, yet prevent——"

The silent Vasco saw

The weight of horror, and o'erpowering awe

That shook the Moors, that shook the regent's knees,
And sunk the monarch down. By swift degrees
The popular clamour rises. Lost, unmann'd,
Around the king the trembling council stand;
While, wildly glaring on each other's eyes,
Each lip in vain the trembling accent tries;
With anguish sicken'd, and of strength bereft,
Earnest each look inquires, What hope is left!
In all the rage of shame and grief aghast,
The monarch, falt'ring, takes the word at last:
"By whom, great chief, are these proud war-ships sway'd,
Are there thy mandates honour'd and obey'd?
Forgive, great chief, let gifts of price restrain
Thy just revenge. Shall India's gifts be vain!—
Oh spare my people and their doom'd abodes—
Prayers, vows, and gifts appease the injur'd gods:
Shall man deny? Swift are the brave to spare:
The weak, the innocent confess their care—
Helpless, as innocent of guile, to thee
Behold these thousands bend the suppliant knee—
Thy navy's thund'ring sides black to the land
Display their terrors—yet mayst thou command——"

O'erpower'd he paus'd. Majestic and serene
Great Vasco rose, then, pointing to the scene
Where bled the war, "Thy fleet, proud king, behold
O'er ocean and the strand in carnage roll'd!
So, shall this palace, smoking in the dust,
And yon proud city, weep thy arts unjust.

The Moors I knew, and, for their fraud prepar'd,

I left my fix'd command my navy's guard:[555]

Whate'er from shore my name or seal convey'd

Of other weight, that fix'd command forbade;

Thus, ere its birth destroy'd, prevented fell

What fraud might dictate, or what force compel.

This morn the sacrifice of Fraud I stood,

But hark, there lives the brother of my blood,

And lives the friend, whose cares conjoin'd control

These floating towers, both brothers of my soul.

'If thrice,' I said, 'arise the golden morn,

Ere to my fleet you mark my glad return,

Dark Fraud with all her Moorish arts withstands,

And force, or death withholds me from my bands:

Thus judge, and swift unfurl the homeward sail,

Catch the first breathing of the eastern gale,

Unmindful of my fate on India's shore:[556]

Let but my monarch know, I wish no more.'

Each, panting while I spoke, impatient cries,

The tear-drop bursting in their manly eyes,

'In all but one thy mandates we obey,

In one we yield not to thy gen'rous sway:

Without thee, never shall our sails return;

India shall bleed, and Calicut shall burn—

Thrice shall the morn arise; a flight of bombs

Shall then speak vengeance to their guilty domes:

Till noon we pause; then, shall our thunders roar,

And desolation sweep the treach'rous shore.'

Behold, proud king, their signal in the sky,

Near his meridian tower the sun rides high.
O'er Calicut no more the ev'ning shade
Shall spread her peaceful wings, my wrath unstaid;
Dire through the night her smoking dust shall gleam,
Dire thro' the night shall shriek the female scream."

"Thy worth, great chief," the pale-lipp'd regent cries,
"Thy worth we own: oh, may these woes suffice!
To thee each proof of India's wealth we send;
Ambassadors, of noblest race, attend——"
Slow as he falter'd, Gama caught the word,
"On terms I talk not, and no truce afford:
Captives enough shall reach the Lusian shore:
Once you deceiv'd me, and I treat no more.
E'en now my faithful sailors, pale with rage,
Gnaw their blue lips, impatient to engage;
Rang'd by their brazen tubes, the thund'ring band
Watch the first movement of my brother's hand;
E'en now, impatient, o'er the dreadful tire
They wave their eager canes betipp'd with fire;
Methinks my brother's anguish'd look I see,
The panting nostril and the trembling knee,
While keen he eyes the sun. On hasty strides,
Hurried along the deck, Coello chides
His cold, slow ling'ring, and impatient cries,
'Oh, give the sign, illume the sacrifice,
A brother's vengeance for a brother's blood——"

He spake; and stern the dreadful warrior stood;

So seem'd the terrors of his awful nod,

The monarch trembled as before a god;

The treach'rous Moors sank down in faint dismay,

And speechless at his feet the council lay:

Abrupt, with outstretched arms, the monarch cries,

"What yet——" but dar'd not meet the hero's eyes,

"What yet may save!"[557]—Great Vasco stern rejoins,

"Swift, undisputing, give th' appointed signs:

High o'er thy loftiest tower my flag display,

Me and my train swift to my fleet convey:

Instant command—behold the sun rides high——"

He spake, and rapture glow'd in ev'ry eye;

The Lusian standard o'er the palace flow'd,

Swift o'er the bay the royal barges row'd.

A dreary gloom a sudden whirlwind threw;

Amid the howling blast, enrag'd, withdrew

The vanquish'd demon. Soon, in lustre mild

As April smiles, the sun auspicious smil'd:

Elate with joy, the shouting thousands trod,

And Gama to his fleet triumphant rode.

Soft came the eastern gale on balmy wings:

Each joyful sailor to his labour springs;

Some o'er the bars their breasts robust recline,

And, with firm tugs, the rollers[558] from the brine,

Reluctant dragg'd, the slime-brown'd anchors raise;

Each gliding rope some nimble hand obeys;

Some bending o'er the yard-arm's length, on high,

With nimble hands, the canvas wings untie;

The flapping sails their wid'ning folds distend,

And measur'd, echoing shouts their sweaty toils attend.

Nor had the captives lost the leader's care,

Some to the shore the Indian barges bear;

The noblest few the chief detains, to own

His glorious deeds before the Lusian throne;

To own the conquest of the Indian shore:

Nor wanted ev'ry proof of India's store.

What fruits in Ceylon's fragrant woods abound,

With woods of cinnamon her hills are crown'd:

Dry'd in its flower, the nut of Banda's grove,

The burning pepper, and the sable clove;

The clove, whose odour on the breathing gale,

Far to the sea, Molucca's plains exhale;

All these, provided by the faithful Moor,

All these, and India's gems, the navy bore:

The Moor attends, Mozaide, whose zealous care

To Gama's eyes unveil'd each treach'rous snare:[559]

So burn'd his breast with Heav'n-illumin'd flame,

And holy rev'rence of Messiah's name.

O, favour'd African, by Heaven's own light

Call'd from the dreary shades of error's night!

What man may dare his seeming ills arraign,

Or what the grace of Heaven's designs explain!

Far didst thou from thy friends a stranger roam,

There wast thou call'd to thy celestial home.[560]

With rustling sound now swell'd the steady sail;

The lofty masts reclining to the gale,

On full-spread wings the navy springs away,

And, far behind them, foams the ocean grey:

Afar the less'ning hills of Gata fly,

And mix their dim blue summits with the sky:

Beneath the wave low sinks the spicy shore,

And, roaring through the tide, each nodding prore

Points to the Cape, great Nature's southmost bound,

The Cape of Tempests, now of Hope renown'd.

Their glorious tale on Lisboa's shore to tell

Inspires each bosom with a rapt'rous swell;

Now through their breasts the chilly tremors glide,

To dare once more the dangers dearly tried.—

Soon to the winds are these cold fears resign'd,

And all their country rushes on the mind;

How sweet to view their native land, how sweet

The father, brother, and the bride to greet!

While list'ning round the hoary parent's board

The wond'ring kindred glow at ev'ry word;

How sweet to tell what woes, what toils they bore,

The tribes, and wonders of each various shore!

These thoughts, the traveller's lov'd reward, employ,

And swell each bosom with unutter'd joy.[561]

The queen of love, by Heaven's eternal grace,

The guardian goddess of the Lusian race;

The queen of love, elate with joy, surveys

Her heroes, happy, plough the wat'ry maze:

Their dreary toils revolving in her thought,

And all the woes by vengeful Bacchus wrought;

These toils, these woes, her yearning cares employ,

To bathe, and balsam in the streams of joy.

Amid the bosom of the wat'ry waste,

Near where the bowers of Paradise were plac'd,[562]

An isle, array'd in all the pride of flowers,

Of fruits, of fountains, and of fragrant bowers,

She means to offer to their homeward prows,

The place of glad repast and sweet repose;

And there, before their raptur'd view, to raise

The heav'n-topp'd column of their deathless praise.

The goddess now ascends her silver car,

(Bright was its hue as love's translucent star);

Beneath the reins the stately birds,[563] that sing

Their sweet-ton'd death-song spread the snowy wing;

The gentle winds beneath her chariot sigh,

And virgin blushes purple o'er the sky:

On milk-white pinions borne, her cooing doves

Form playful circles round her as she moves;

And now their beaks in fondling kisses join,

In am'rous nods their fondling necks entwine.

O'er fair Idalia's bowers the goddess rode,

And by her altars sought Idalia's god:

The youthful bowyer of the heart was there;

His falling kingdom claim'd his earnest care.[564]

His bands he musters, through the myrtle groves

On buxom wings he trains the little loves.

Against the world, rebellious and astray,

He means to lead them, and resume his sway:

326

For base-born passions, at his shrine, 'twas told,

Each nobler transport of the breast controll'd.

A young Actæon,[565] scornful of his lore,

Morn after morn pursues the foamy boar,

In desert wilds, devoted to the chase;

Each dear enchantment of the female face

Spurn'd, and neglected. Him, enrag'd, he sees,

And sweet, and dread his punishment decrees.

Before his ravish'd sight, in sweet surprise,

Naked in all her charms, shall Dian rise;

With love's fierce flames his frozen heart shall burn,[566]

Coldly his suit, the nymph, unmov'd, shall spurn.

Of these lov'd dogs that now his passions sway,

Ah, may he never fall the hapless prey!

Enrag'd, he sees a venal herd, the shame

Of human race, assume the titled name;[567]

And each, for some base interest of his own,

With Flatt'ry's manna'd lips assail the throne.

He sees the men, whom holiest sanctions bind

To poverty, and love of human kind;

While, soft as drop the dews of balmy May,

Their words preach virtue, and her charms display,

He sees with lust of gold their eyes on fire,

And ev'ry wish to lordly state aspire;

He sees them trim the lamp at night's mid hour,

To plan new laws to arm the regal power;

Sleepless, at night's mid hour, to raze the laws,

The sacred bulwarks of the people's cause,

Fram'd ere the blood of hard-earn'd victory
On their brave fathers' helm-hack'd swords was dry.

Nor these alone; each rank, debas'd and rude,
Mean objects, worthless of their love, pursued:
Their passions thus rebellious to his lore,
The god decrees to punish and restore.
The little loves, light hov'ring in the air,
Twang their silk bow-strings, and their aims prepare:
Some on th' immortal anvils point the dart,
With power resistless to inflame the heart;
Their arrow heads they tip with soft desires,
And all the warmth of love's celestial fires;
Some sprinkle o'er the shafts the tears of woe,
Some store the quiver, some steel-spring the bow;
Each chanting as he works the tuneful strain
Of love's dear joys, of love's luxurious pain;
Charm'd was the lay to conquer and refine,
Divine the melody, the song divine.

Already, now, began the vengeful war,
The witness of the god's benignant care;
On the hard bosoms of the stubborn crowd[568]
An arrowy shower the bowyer train bestow'd;
Pierced by the whizzing shafts, deep sighs the air,
And answering sighs the wounds of love declare.
Though various featur'd, and of various hue,
Each nymph seems loveliest in her lover's view;
Fir'd by the darts, by novice archers sped,

Ten thousand wild, fantastic loves are bred:
In wildest dreams the rustic hind aspires,
And haughtiest lords confess the humblest fires.

The snowy swans of love's celestial queen
Now land her chariot on the shore of green;
One knee display'd, she treads the flow'ry strand,
The gather'd robe falls loosely from her hand;
Half-seen her bosom heaves the living snow,
And on her smiles the living roses glow.
The bowyer god,[569] whose subtle shafts ne'er fly
Misaim'd, in vain, in vain on earth or sky,
With rosy smiles the mother power receives;
Around her climbing, thick as ivy leaves,
The vassal loves in fond contention join
Who, first and most, shall kiss her hand divine.
Swift in her arms she caught her wanton boy,
And, "Oh, my son," she cries, "my pride, my joy!
Against thy might the dreadful Typhon fail'd,
Against thy shaft nor heav'n, nor Jove prevail'd;
Unless thine arrow wake the young desires,
My strength, my power, in vain each charm expires:
My son, my hope, I claim thy powerful aid,
Nor be the boon thy mother sues delay'd:
Where'er—so will th' eternal fates—where'er
The Lusian race the victor standards rear,
There shall my hymns resound, my altars flame,
And heav'nly Love her joyful lore proclaim.
My Lusian heroes, as my Romans, brave,

Long toss'd, long hopeless on the storm-torn wave,

Wearied and weak, at last on India's shore

Arriv'd, new toils, repose denied, they bore;

For Bacchus there with tenfold rage pursued

My dauntless sons, but now his might subdued,

Amid these raging seas, the scene of woes,

Theirs shall be now the balm of sweet repose;

Theirs ev'ry joy the noblest heroes claim,

The raptur'd foretaste of immortal fame.

Then, bend thy bow and wound the Nereid train,

The lovely daughters of the azure main;

And lead them, while they pant with am'rous fire,

Right to the isle which all my smiles inspire:

Soon shall my care that beauteous isle supply,

Where Zephyr, breathing love, on Flora's lap shall sigh.

There let the nymphs the gallant heroes meet,

And strew the pink and rose beneath their feet:

In crystal halls the feast divine prolong,

With wine nectareous and immortal song:

Let every nymph the snow-white bed prepare,

And, fairer far, resign her bosom there;

There, to the greedy riotous embrace

Resign each hidden charm with dearest grace.

Thus, from my native waves a hero line

Shall rise, and o'er the East illustrious shine;[570]

Thus, shall the rebel world thy prowess know,

And what the boundless joys our friendly powers bestow."

She said; and smiling view'd her mighty boy;

Swift to the chariot springs the god of joy;

His ivory bow, and arrows tipp'd with gold,

Blaz'd to the sun-beam as the chariot roll'd:

Their silver harness shining to the day,

The swans, on milk-white pinions, spring away,

Smooth gliding o'er the clouds of lovely blue;

And Fame[571] (so will'd the god) before them flew:

A giant goddess, whose ungovern'd tongue

With equal zeal proclaims or right or wrong;

Oft had her lips the god of love blasphem'd,

And oft with tenfold praise his conquests nam'd:

A hundred eyes she rolls with ceaseless care,

A thousand tongues what these behold declare:

Fleet is her flight, the lightning's wing she rides,

And, though she shifts her colours swift as glides

The April rainbow, still the crowd she guides.

And now, aloft her wond'ring voice she rais'd,

And, with a thousand glowing tongues, she prais'd

The bold discoverers of the eastern world—

In gentle swells the list'ning surges curl'd,

And murmur'd to the sounds of plaintive love

Along the grottoes where the Nereids rove.

The drowsy power on whose smooth easy mien

The smiles of wonder and delight are seen,

Whose glossy, simp'ring eye bespeaks her name,

Credulity, attends the goddess Fame.

Fir'd by the heroes' praise, the wat'ry gods,[572]

With ardent speed forsake their deep abodes;

Their rage by vengeful Bacchus rais'd of late,

Now stung remorse, and love succeeds to hate.

Ah, where remorse in female bosom bleeds,

The tend'rest love in all its glow succeeds.

When fancy glows, how strong, O Love, thy power!

Nor slipp'd the eager god the happy hour;

Swift fly his arrows o'er the billowy main,

Wing'd with his fires, nor flies a shaft in vain:

Thus, ere the face the lover's breast inspires,

The voice of fame awakes the soft desires.

While from the bow-string start the shafts divine,

His ivory moon's wide horns incessant join,

Swift twinkling to the view: and wide he pours,

Omnipotent in love, his arrowy showers.

E'en Thetis' self confess'd the tender smart,

And pour'd the murmurs of the wounded heart:

Soft o'er the billows pants the am'rous sigh;

With wishful languor melting on each eye

The love-sick nymphs explore the tardy sails

That waft the heroes on the ling'ring gales.

Give way, ye lofty billows, low subside,

Smooth as the level plain, your swelling pride,

Lo, Venus comes! Oh, soft, ye surges, sleep,

Smooth be the bosom of the azure deep,

Lo, Venus comes! and in her vig'rous train

She brings the healing balm of love-sick pain.

White as her swans,[573] and stately as they rear

Their snowy crests when o'er the lake they steer,

Slow moving on, behold, the fleet appears,

And o'er the distant billow onward steers.

The beauteous Nereids, flush'd in all their charms,

Surround the goddess of the soft alarms:

Right to the isle she leads the smiling train,

And all her arts her balmy lips explain;

The fearful languor of the asking eye,

The lovely blush of yielding modesty,

The grieving look, the sigh, the fav'ring smile,

And all th' endearments of the open wile,

She taught the nymphs—in willing breasts that heav'd

To hear her lore, her lore the nymphs receiv'd.

As now triumphant to their native shore

Through the wide deep the joyful navy bore,

Earnest the pilot's eyes sought cape or bay,

For long was yet the various wat'ry way;

Sought cape or isle, from whence their boats might bring

The healthful bounty of the crystal spring:

When sudden, all in nature's pride array'd,

The Isle of Love its glowing breast display'd.

O'er the green bosom of the dewy lawn

Soft blazing flow'd the silver of the dawn,

The gentle waves the glowing lustre share,

Arabia's balm was sprinkled o'er the air.

Before the fleet, to catch the heroes' view,

The floating isle fair Acidalia drew:

Soon as the floating verdure caught their sight,[574]

She fix'd, unmov'd, the island of delight.

So when in child-birth of her Jove-sprung load,

The sylvan goddess and the bowyer god,

In friendly pity of Latona's woes,[575]

Amid the waves the Delian isle arose.

And now, led smoothly o'er the furrow'd tide,

Right to the isle of joy the vessels glide:

The bay they enter, where on ev'ry hand,

Around them clasps the flower-enamell'd land;

A safe retreat, where not a blast may shake

Its flutt'ring pinions o'er the stilly lake.

With purple shells, transfus'd as marble veins,

The yellow sands celestial Venus stains.

With graceful pride three hills of softest green

Rear their fair bosoms o'er the sylvan scene;

Their sides embroider'd boast the rich array

Of flow'ry shrubs in all the pride of May;

The purple lotus and the snowy thorn,

And yellow pod-flowers ev'ry slope adorn.

From the green summits of the leafy hills

Descend, with murm'ring lapse, three limpid rills:

Beneath the rose-trees loit'ring, slow they glide,

Now, tumbles o'er some rock their crystal pride;

Sonorous now, they roll adown the glade,

Now, plaintive tinkle in the secret shade,

Now, from the darkling grove, beneath the beam

Of ruddy morn, like melted silver stream,

Edging the painted margins of the bowers,

And breathing liquid freshness on the flowers.

Here, bright reflected in the pool below,

The vermeil apples tremble on the bough;

Where o'er the yellow sands the waters sleep

The primros'd banks, inverted, dew-drops weep;

Where murm'ring o'er the pebbles purls the stream

The silver trouts in playful curvings gleam.

Long thus, and various, ev'ry riv'let strays,

Till closing, now, their long meand'ring maze,

Where in a smiling vale the mountains end,

Form'd in a crystal lake the waters blend:[576]

Fring'd was the border with a woodland shade,

In ev'ry leaf of various green array'd,

Each yellow-ting'd, each mingling tint between

The dark ash-verdure and the silv'ry green.

The trees, now bending forward, slowly shake

Their lofty honours o'er the crystal lake;

Now, from the flood the graceful boughs retire

With coy reserve, and now again admire

Their various liv'ries, by the summer dress'd,

Smooth-gloss'd and soften'd in the mirror's breast.

So, by her glass the wishful virgin stays,

And, oft retiring, steals the ling'ring gaze.

A thousand boughs aloft to heav'n display

Their fragrant apples, shining to the day;

The orange here perfumes the buxom air,

And boasts the golden hue of Daphne's hair.[577]

Near to the ground each spreading bough descends,

Beneath her yellow load the citron bends;

The fragrant lemon scents the cooly grove;

Fair as (when rip'ning for the days of love)

The virgin's breasts the gentle swell avow,

So, the twin fruitage swell on every bough.

Wild forest-trees the mountain sides array'd

With curling foliage and romantic shade:

Here spreads the poplar, to Alcides dear;

And dear to Phœbus, ever verdant here,

The laurel joins the bowers for ever green,

The myrtle bowers belov'd of beauty's queen.

To Jove the oak his wide-spread branches rears;

And high to heav'n the fragrant cedar bears;

Where through the glades appear the cavern'd rocks,

The lofty pine-tree waves her sable locks;

Sacred to Cybĕlē the whisp'ring pine

Loves the wild grottoes where the white cliffs shine;

Here towers the cypress, preacher to the wise,

Less'ning from earth her spiral honours rise,

Till, as a spear-point rear'd, the topmost spray

Points to the Eden of eternal day.

Here round her fost'ring elm the smiling vine,

In fond embraces, gives her arms to twine,

The num'rous clusters pendant from the boughs,

The green here glistens, here the purple glows;

For, here the genial seasons of the year

Danc'd hand in hand, no place for winter here;

His grisly visage from the shore expell'd,

United sway the smiling seasons held.

Around the swelling fruits of deep'ning red,

Their snowy hues the fragrant blossoms spread;

Between the bursting buds of lucid green

The apple's ripe vermilion blush is seen;

For here each gift Pomona's hand bestows

In cultur'd garden, free, uncultur'd flows,

The flavour sweeter, and the hue more fair,

Than e'er was foster'd by the hand of care.

The cherry here in shining crimson glows;

And, stain'd with lover's blood,[578] in pendent rows,

The bending boughs the mulberries o'erload;

The bending boughs caress'd by Zephyr nod.

The gen'rous peach, that strengthens in exile

Far from his native earth, the Persian soil,

The velvet peach, of softest glossy blue,

Hangs by the pomegranate of orange hue,

Whose open heart a brighter red displays

Than that which sparkles in the ruby's blaze.

Here, trembling with their weight, the branches bear,

Delicious as profuse, the tap'ring pear.

For thee, fair fruit, the songsters of the grove

With hungry bills from bower to arbour rove.

Ah, if ambitious thou wilt own the care

To grace the feast of heroes and the fair,

Soft let the leaves, with grateful umbrage, hide

The green-tinged orange of thy mellow side.

A thousand flowers of gold, of white and red,

Far o'er the shadowy vale[579] their carpets spread,

Of fairer tap'stry, and of richer bloom,

Than ever glow'd in Persia's boasted loom:

As glitt'ring rainbows o'er the verdure thrown,

O'er every woodland walk th' embroid'ry shone.

Here o'er the wat'ry mirror's lucid bed

Narcissus, self-enamour'd, hangs the head;

And here, bedew'd with love's celestial tears,

The woe-mark'd flower of slain Adonis rears[580]

Its purple head, prophetic of the reign

When lost Adonis shall revive again.

At strife appear the lawns and purpled skies,

Which from each other stole the beauteous dyes:[581]

The lawn in all Aurora's lustre glows,

Aurora steals the blushes of the rose,

The rose displays the blushes that adorn

The spotless virgin on the nuptial morn.

Zephyr and Flora emulous conspire

To breathe their graces o'er the field's attire;

The one gives healthful freshness, one the hue

Fairer than e'er creative pencil drew.

Pale as the love-sick hopeless maid they dye

The modest violet; from the curious eye

The modest violet turns her gentle head,

And, by the thorn, weeps o'er her lowly bed.

Bending beneath the tears of pearly dawn

The snow-white lily glitters o'er the lawn;

Low from the bough reclines the damask rose,

And o'er the lily's milk-white bosom glows.

Fresh in the dew, far o'er the painted dales,

Each fragrant herb her sweetest scent exhales.

The hyacinth bewrays the doleful Ai,[582]

And calls the tribute of Apollo's sigh;

Still on its bloom the mournful flower retains

The lovely blue that dy'd the stripling's veins.

Pomona, fir'd with rival envy, views
The glaring pride of Flora's darling hues;
Where Flora bids the purple iris spread,
She hangs the wilding's blossom white and red;
Where wild-thyme purples, where the daisy snows
The curving slopes, the melon's pride she throws;
Where by the stream the lily of the vale,
Primrose, and cowslip meek, perfume the gale,
Beneath the lily, and the cowslip's bell,
The scarlet strawberries luxurious swell.
Nor these alone the teeming Eden yields,
Each harmless bestial crops the flow'ry fields;
And birds of ev'ry note, and ev'ry wing,
Their loves responsive thro' the branches sing:
In sweet vibrations thrilling o'er the skies,
High pois'd in air, the lark his warbling tries;
The swan, slow sailing o'er the crystal lake,
Tunes his melodious note; from ev'ry brake
The glowing strain the nightingale returns,
And, in the bowers of love, the turtle mourns.
Pleas'd to behold his branching horns appear,
O'er the bright fountain bends the fearless deer;
The hare starts trembling from the bushy shade,
And, swiftly circling, crosses oft the glade.
Where from the rocks the bubbling founts distil,
The milk-white lambs come bleating down the hill;
The dappled heifer seeks the vales below,
And from the thicket springs the bounding doe.
To his lov'd nest, on fondly flutt'ring wings,

In chirping bill the little songster brings

The food untasted; transport thrills his breast;

'Tis nature's touch, 'tis instinct's heav'n-like feast.

Thus bower and lawn were deck'd with Eden's flowers,

And song and joy imparadis'd the bowers.

And soon the fleet their ready anchors threw:

Lifted on eager tip-toe at the view,

On nimble feet that bounded to the strand

The second Argonauts[583] elance to land.

Wide o'er the beauteous isle[584] the lovely fair

Stray through the distant glades, devoid of care.

From lowly valley and from mountain grove

The lovely nymphs renew the strains of love.

Here from the bowers that crown the plaintive rill

The solemn harp's melodious warblings thrill;

Here from the shadows of the upland grot

The mellow lute renews the swelling note.

As fair Diana, and her virgin train,

Some gaily ramble o'er the flow'ry plain,

In feign'd pursuit of hare or bounding roe,

Their graceful mien and beauteous limbs to show;

Now seeming careless, fearful now and coy,

(So, taught the goddess of unutter'd joy),

And, gliding through the distant glades, display

Each limb, each movement, naked as the day.

Some, light with glee, in careless freedom take

Their playful revels in the crystal lake;

One trembling stands no deeper than the knee

To plunge reluctant, while in sportful glee
Another o'er her sudden laves the tide;
In pearly drops the wishful waters glide,
Reluctant dropping from her breasts of snow;
Beneath the wave another seems to glow;
The am'rous waves her bosom fondly kiss'd,
And rose and fell, as panting, on her breast.
Another swims along with graceful pride,
Her silver arms the glist'ning waves divide,
Her shining sides the fondling waters lave,
Her glowing cheeks are brighten'd by the wave,
Her hair, of mildest yellow, flows from side
To side, as o'er it plays the wanton tide,
And, careless as she turns, her thighs of snow
Their tap'ring rounds in deeper lustre show.

Some gallant Lusians sought the woodland prey,
And, thro' the thickets, forc'd the pathless way;
Where some, in shades impervious to the beam,
Supinely listen'd to the murm'ring stream:
When sudden, through the boughs, the various dyes
Of pink, of scarlet, and of azure rise,
Swift from the verdant banks the loit'rers spring,
Down drops the arrow from the half-drawn string:
Soon they behold 'twas not the rose's hue,
The jonquil's yellow, nor the pansy's blue:
Dazzling the shades the nymphs appear—the zone
And flowing scarf in gold and azure shone.
Naked as Venus stood in Ida's bower,

Some trust the dazzling charms of native power;

Through the green boughs and darkling shades they show

The shining lustre of their native snow,

And every tap'ring, every rounded swell

Of thigh, of bosom, as they glide, reveal.

As visions, cloth'd in dazzling white, they rise,

Then steal unnoted from the flurried eyes:

Again apparent, and again, withdrawn,

They shine and wanton o'er the smiling lawn.

Amaz'd and lost in rapture of surprise,

"All joy, my friends!" the brave Veloso cries,

"Whate'er of goddesses old fable told,

Or poet sung of sacred groves, behold.

Sacred to goddesses divinely bright

These beauteous forests own their guardian might.

From eyes profane, from ev'ry age conceal'd,

To us, behold, all Paradise reveal'd!

Swift let us try if phantoms of the air,

Or living charms, appear divinely fair!"

Swift at the word the gallant Lusians bound,

Their rapid footsteps scarcely touch the ground;

Through copse, through brake, impatient of their prey,

Swift as the wounded deer, they spring away:

Fleet through the winding shades, in rapid flight,

The nymphs, as wing'd with terror, fly their sight;

Fleet though they fled, the mild reverted eye

And dimpling smile their seeming fear deny.

Fleet through the shades in parted rout they glide:

If winding path the chosen pairs divide,

Another path by sweet mistake betrays,
And throws the lover on the lover's gaze:
If dark-brow'd bower conceal the lovely fair,
The laugh, the shriek, confess the charmer there.

Luxurious here the wanton zephyrs toy,
And ev'ry fondling fav'ring art employ.
Fleet as the fair ones speed, the busy gale
In wanton frolic lifts the trembling veil;
White though the veil, in fairer brighter glow,
The lifted robe displays the living snow:
Quick flutt'ring on the gale the robe conceals,
Then instant to the glance each charm reveals;
Reveals, and covers from the eyes on fire,
Reveals, and with the shade inflames desire.
One, as her breathless lover hastens on,
With wily stumble sudden lies o'erthrown;
Confus'd, she rises with a blushing smile;
The lover falls the captive of her guile:
Tripp'd by the fair, he tumbles on the mead,
The joyful victim of his eager speed.

Afar, where sport the wantons in the lake,
Another band of gallant youths betake;
The laugh, the shriek, the revel and the toy,
Bespeak the innocence of youthful joy.
The laugh, the shriek, the gallant Lusians hear
As through the forest glades they chase the deer;
For, arm'd, to chase the bounding roe they came,

Unhop'd the transport of a nobler game.

The naked wantons, as the youths appear,

Shrill through the woods resound the shriek of fear.

Some feign such terror of the forc'd embrace,

Their virgin modesty to this gives place,

Naked they spring to land, and speed away

To deepest shades unpierc'd by glaring day;

Thus, yielding freely to the am'rous eyes

What to the am'rous hands their fear denies.

Some well assume Diana's virgin shame,

When on her naked sports the hunter[585] came

Unwelcome—plunging in the crystal tide,

In vain they strive their beauteous limbs to hide;

The lucid waves ('twas all they could) bestow

A milder lustre and a softer glow.

As, lost in earnest care of future need,

Some to the banks, to snatch their mantles, speed,

Of present view regardless; ev'ry wile

Was yet, and ev'ry net of am'rous guile.

Whate'er the terror of the feign'd alarm,

Display'd, in various force, was ev'ry charm.

Nor idle stood the gallant youth; the wing

Of rapture lifts them, to the fair they spring;

Some to the copse pursue their lovely prey;

Some, cloth'd and shod, impatient of delay,

Impatient of the stings of fierce desire,

Plunge headlong in the tide to quench the fire.

So, when the fowler to his cheek uprears

The hollow steel, and on the mallard bears,

344

His eager dog, ere bursts the flashing roar,
Fierce for the prey, springs headlong from the shore,
And barking, cuts the wave with furious joy:
So, mid the billow springs each eager boy,
Springs to the nymph whose eyes from all the rest
By singling him her secret wish confess'd.

A son of Mars was there, of gen'rous race,
His ev'ry elegance of manly grace;
Am'rous and brave, the bloom of April youth
Glow'd on his cheek, his eye spoke simplest truth;
Yet love, capricious to th' accomplish'd boy,
Had ever turn'd to gall each promis'd joy,
Had ever spurn'd his vows; yet still his heart
Would hope, and nourish still the tender smart:
The purest delicacy fann'd his fires,
And proudest honour nurs'd his fond desires.
Not on the first that fair before him glow'd,
Not on the first the youth his love bestow'd.
In all her charms the fair Ephyre came,
And Leonardo's heart was all on flame.
Affection's melting transport o'er him stole,
And love's all gen'rous glow entranced his soul;
Of selfish joy unconscious, ev'ry thought
On sweet delirium's ocean stream'd afloat.
Pattern of beauty did Ephyre shine,
Nor less she wish'd these beauties to resign:
More than her sisters long'd her heart to yield,
Yet, swifter fled she o'er the smiling field.

The youth now panting with the hopeless chase,
"Oh turn," he cries, "oh turn thy angel face:
False to themselves, can charms like these conceal
The hateful rigour of relentless steel?
And, did the stream deceive me, when I stood
Amid my peers reflected in the flood?
The easiest port and fairest bloom I bore—
False was the stream—while I in vain deplore,
My peers are happy; lo, in ev'ry shade,
In ev'ry bower, their love with love repaid!
I, I alone through brakes, through thorns pursue
A cruel fair. Ah, still my fate proves true,
True to its rigour—who, fair nymph, to thee
Reveal'd 'twas I that sued! unhappy me!
Born to be spurn'd though honesty inspire.
Alas, I faint, my languid sinews tire;
Oh stay thee—powerless to sustain their weight
My knees sink down, I sink beneath my fate!"
He spoke; a rustling urges thro' the trees,
Instant new vigour strings his active knees,
Wildly he glares around, and raging cries,
"And must another snatch my lovely prize!
In savage grasp thy beauteous limbs constrain!
I feel, I madden while I feel the pain!
Oh lost, thou fli'st the safety of my arms,
My hand shall guard thee, softly seize thy charms,
No brutal rage inflames me, yet I burn!
Die shall thy ravisher. O goddess, turn,
And smiling view the error of my fear;

No brutal force, no ravisher is near;

A harmless roebuck gave the rustling sounds,

Lo, from the thicket swift as thee he bounds!

Ah, vain the hope to tire thee in the chase!

I faint, yet hear, yet turn thy lovely face.

Vain are thy fears; were ev'n thy will to yield

The harvest of my hope, that harvest field

My fate would guard, and walls of brass would rear

Between my sickle and the golden ear.

Yet fly me not; so may thy youthful prime

Ne'er fly thy cheek on the grey wing of time.

Yet hear, the last my panting breath can say,

Nor proudest kings, nor mightiest hosts can sway

Fate's dread decrees; yet thou, O nymph, divine,

Yet thou canst more, yet thou canst conquer mine.

Unmov'd each other yielding nymph I see;

Joy to their lovers, for they touch not thee!

But thee!—oh, every transport of desire,

That melts to mingle with its kindred fire,

For thee respires—alone I feel for thee

The dear wild rage of longing ecstasy:

By all the flames of sympathy divine

To thee united, thou by right art mine.

From thee, from thee the hallow'd transport flows

That sever'd rages, and for union glows:

Heav'n owns the claim. Hah, did the lightning glare:

Yes, I beheld my rival, though the air

Grew dim; ev'n now I heard him softly tread.

Oh rage, he waits thee on the flow'ry bed!

I see, I see thee rushing to his arms,

And sinking on his bosom, all thy charms

To him resigning in an eager kiss,

All I implor'd, the whelming tide of bliss!

And shall I see him riot on thy charms,

Dissolv'd in joy, exulting in thine arms?

Oh burst, ye lightnings, round my destin'd head,

Oh pour your flashes——" Madd'ning as he said,[586]

Amid the windings of the bow'ry wood

His trembling footsteps still the nymph pursued.

Woo'd to the flight she wing'd her speed to hear

His am'rous accents melting on her ear.

And now, she turns the wild walk's serpent maze;

A roseate bower its velvet couch displays;

The thickest moss its softest verdure spread,

Crocus and mingling pansy fring'd the bed,

The woodbine dropp'd its honey from above,

And various roses crown'd the sweet alcove.

Here, as she hastens, on the hopeless boy

She turns her face, all bath'd in smiles of joy;

Then, sinking down, her eyes suffused with love

Glowing on his, one moment lost reprove.

Here was no rival, all he wish'd his own;

Lock'd in her arms soft sinks the stripling down.

Ah, what soft murmurs panting thro' the bowers

Sigh'd to the raptures of the paramours!

The wishful sigh, and melting smile conspire,

Devouring kisses fan the fiercer fire;

Sweet violence, with dearest grace, assails,

Soft o'er the purpos'd frown the smile prevails,

The purpos'd frown betrays its own deceit,

In well-pleas'd laughter ends the rising threat;

The coy delay glides off in yielding love,

And transport murmurs thro' the sacred grove.

The joy of pleasing adds its sacred zest,

And all is love, embracing and embraced.

The golden morn beheld the scenes of joy;

Nor, sultry noon, mayst thou the bowers annoy;

The sultry noon-beam shines the lover's aid,

And sends him glowing to the secret shade.

O'er evr'y shade, and ev'ry nuptial bower

The love-sick strain the virgin turtles pour;

For nuptial faith and holy rites combin'd,

The Lusian heroes and the nymphs conjoin'd.

With flow'ry wreaths, and laurel chaplets, bound

With ductile gold, the nymphs the heroes crown'd:

By ev'ry spousal holy ritual tied,

No chance, they vow, shall e'er their hands divide,

In life, in death, attendant as their fame;

Such was the oath of ocean's sov'reign dame:

The dame (from heav'n and holy Vesta sprung,

For ever beauteous and for ever young),

Enraptur'd, views the chief whose deathless name

The wond'ring world and conquer'd seas proclaim.

With stately pomp she holds the hero's hand,

And gives her empire to his dread command,

By spousal ties confirm'd; nor pass'd untold

What Fate's unalter'd page had will'd of old:

The world's vast globe in radiant sphere she show'd,

The shores immense, and seas unknown, unplough'd;

The seas, the shores, due to the Lusian keel

And Lusian sword, she hastens to reveal.

The glorious leader by the hand she takes,

And, dim below, the flow'ry bower forsakes.

High on a mountain's starry top divine

Her palace walls of living crystal shine;

Of gold and crystal blaze the lofty towers;

Here, bath'd in joy, they pass the blissful hours:

Engulf'd in tides on tides of joy, the day

On downy pinions glides unknown away.

While thus the sov'reigns in the palace reign,

Like transport riots o'er the humbler plain,

Where each, in gen'rous triumph o'er his peers,

His lovely bride to ev'ry bride prefers.

"Hence, ye profane!"[587]—the song melodious rose,

By mildest zephyrs wafted through the boughs,

Unseen the warblers of the holy strain—

"Far from these sacred bowers, ye lewd profane!

Hence each unhallow'd eye, each vulgar ear;

Chaste and divine are all the raptures here.

The nymphs of ocean, and the ocean's queen,

The isle angelic, ev'ry raptur'd scene,

The charms of honour and its meed confess,

These are the raptures, these the wedded bliss:

The glorious triumph and the laurel crown,

The ever blossom'd palms of fair renown,

By time unwither'd, and untaught to cloy;

These are the transports of the Isle of Joy.

Such was Olympus and the bright abodes;

Renown was heav'n, and heroes were the gods.

Thus, ancient times, to virtue ever just,

To arts and valour rear'd the worshipp'd bust.

High, steep, and rugged, painful to be trod,

With toils on toils immense is virtue's road;

But smooth at last the walks umbrageous smile,

Smooth as our lawns, and cheerful as our isle.

Up the rough road Alcides, Hermes, strove,

All men like you, Apollo, Mars, and Jove:

Like you to bless mankind Minerva toil'd;

Diana bound the tyrants of the wild;

O'er the waste desert Bacchus spread the vine;

And Ceres taught the harvest-field to shine.

Fame rear'd her trumpet; to the blest abodes

She rais'd, and hail'd them gods, and sprung of gods.

"The love of fame, by heav'n's own hand impress'd,

The first, and noblest passion of the breast,

May yet mislead.—Oh guard, ye hero train,

No harlot robes of honours false and vain,

No tinsel yours, be yours all native gold,

Well-earn'd each honour, each respect you hold:

To your lov'd king return a guardian band,

Return the guardians of your native land;

To tyrant power be dreadful; from the jaws

Of fierce oppression guard the peasant's cause.

If youthful fury pant for shining arms,

Spread o'er the eastern world the dread alarms;[588]

There bends the Saracen the hostile bow,

The Saracen thy faith, thy nation's foe;

There from his cruel gripe tear empire's reins,

And break his tyrant-sceptre o'er his chains.

On adamantine pillars thus shall stand

The throne, the glory of your native land;

And Lusian heroes, an immortal line,

Shall ever with us share our isle divine."

END OF THE NINTH BOOK.

BOOK X.

THE ARGUMENT.

In the opening of this, the last canto, the poet resumes the allegory of the Isle of Joy, or of Venus: the fair nymphs conduct their lovers to their radiant palaces, where delicious wines sparkle in every cup. Before the poet describes the song of a prophetic siren, who celebrates the praise of the heroes who are destined in ennoble the name of their country, he addresses himself to his muse in a tone of sorrow, which touches us the more deeply when we reflect upon the unhappy situation to which this great poet was at last reduced. In the song of the siren, which follows, is afforded a prophetic view from the period of Gama's expedition down to Camoëns' own times, in which Pacheco, and other heroes of Portugal, pass in review before the eye of the reader. When the siren has concluded her prophetic song, Thetis conducts Gama to the top of a mountain and addresses him in a set speech. The poem concludes with the poet's apostrophe to King Sebastian.

FAR o'er the western ocean's distant bed

Apollo now his fiery coursers sped;

Far o'er the silver lake of Mexic[589] roll'd

His rapid chariot wheels of burning gold:

The eastern sky was left to dusky grey,

And o'er the last hot breath of parting day,

Cool o'er the sultry noon's remaining flame,

On gentle gales the grateful twilight came.

Dimpling the lucid pools, the fragrant breeze

Sighs o'er the lawns, and whispers thro' the trees;

Refresh'd, the lily rears the silver head,

And opening jasmines o'er the arbours spread.

Fair o'er the wave that gleam'd like distant snow,

Graceful arose the moon, serenely slow;

Not yet full orb'd, in clouded splendour dress'd,

Her married arms embrace her pregnant breast.

Sweet to his mate, recumbent o'er his young,

The nightingale his spousal anthem sung;

From ev'ry bower the holy chorus rose,

From ev'ry bower the rival anthem flows.

Translucent, twinkling through the upland grove,

In all her lustre shines the star of love;

Led by the sacred ray from ev'ry bower,

A joyful train, the wedded lovers pour:

Each with the youth above the rest approv'd,

Each with the nymph above the rest belov'd,

They seek the palace of the sov'reign dame;

High on a mountain glow'd the wondrous frame:

Of gold the towers, of gold the pillars shone,

The walls were crystal, starr'd with precious stone.

Amid the hall arose the festive board,

With nature's choicest gifts promiscuous stor'd:

So will'd the goddess to renew the smile

Of vital strength, long worn by days of toil.

On crystal chairs, that shin'd as lambent flame,

Each gallant youth attends his lovely dame;

Beneath a purple canopy of state

The beauteous goddess and the leader sat:

The banquet glows— Not such the feast, when all

The pride of luxury in Egypt's hall

Before the love-sick Roman[590] spread the boast

Of ev'ry teeming sea and fertile coast.

Sacred to noblest worth and Virtue's ear,

Divine, as genial, was the banquet here;

The wine, the song, by sweet returns inspire,

Now wake the lover's, now the hero's fire.

On gold and silver from th' Atlantic main,

The sumptuous tribute of the sea's wide reign,

Of various savour, was the banquet pil'd;

Amid the fruitage mingling roses smil'd.

In cups of gold that shed a yellow light,

In silver, shining as the moon of night,

Amid the banquet flow'd the sparkling wine,

Nor gave Falernia's fields the parent vine:

Falernia's vintage, nor the fabled power

Of Jove's ambrosia in th' Olympian bower

To this compare not; wild, nor frantic fires,

Divinest transport this alone inspires.

The bev'rage, foaming o'er the goblet's breast,

The crystal fountain's cooling aid confess'd;[591]

The while, as circling flow'd the cheerful bowl,

Sapient discourse, the banquet of the soul,

Of richest argument and brightest glow,

Array'd in dimpling smiles, in easiest flow

Pour'd all its graces: nor in silence stood

The powers of music, such as erst subdued

The horrid frown of hell's profound domains,[592]

And sooth'd the tortur'd ghosts to slumber on their chains.

To music's sweetest chords, in loftiest vein,

An angel siren joins the vocal strain;

The silver roofs resound the living song,

The harp and organ's lofty mood prolong

The hallow'd warblings; list'ning Silence rides

The sky, and o'er the bridled winds presides;

In softest murmurs flows the glassy deep,

And each, lull'd in his shade, the bestials sleep.

The lofty song ascends the thrilling skies,

The song of godlike heroes yet to rise;

Jove gave the dream, whose glow the siren fir'd,

And present Jove the prophecy inspir'd.

Not he, the bard of love-sick Dido's board,

Nor he, the minstrel of Phæacia's lord,

Though fam'd in song, could touch the warbling string,

Or, with a voice so sweet, melodious sing.

And thou, my muse, O fairest of the train,

Calliope, inspire my closing strain.

No more the summer of my life remains,[593]

My autumn's length'ning ev'nings chill my veins;

Down the black stream of years by woes on woes

Wing'd on, I hasten to the tomb's repose,

The port whose deep, dark bottom shall detain

My anchor, never to be weigh'd again,

Never on other sea of life to steer

The human course.—Yet thou, O goddess, hear,

Yet let me live, though round my silver'd head

Misfortune's bitt'rest rage unpitying shed

Her coldest storms; yet, let me live to crown

The song that boasts my nation's proud renown.

Of godlike heroes sung the nymph divine,

Heroes whose deeds on Gama's crest shall shine;

Who through the seas, by Gama first explor'd,

Shall bear the Lusian standard and the sword,

Till ev'ry coast where roars the orient main,

Blest in its sway, shall own the Lusian reign;

Till ev'ry pagan king his neck shall yield,

Or vanquish'd, gnaw the dust on battle-field.

"High Priest of Malabar," the goddess sung,

"Thy faith repent not, nor lament thy wrong;[594]

Though, for thy faith to Lusus' gen'rous race,

The raging zamoreem thy fields deface:

From Tagus, lo, the great Pacheco sails

To India, wafted on auspicious gales.

Soon as his crooked prow the tide shall press,

A new Achilles shall the tide confess;

His ship's strong sides shall groan beneath his weight,

And deeper waves receive the sacred freight.[595]

Soon as on India's strand he shakes his spear,

The burning east shall tremble, chill'd with fear;

Reeking with noble blood, Cambalao's stream

Shall blaze impurpled on the ev'ning beam;

Urg'd on by raging shame, the monarch brings,

Banded with all their powers, his vassal kings:

Narsinga's rocks their cruel thousands pour,

Bipur's stern king attends, and thine, Tanore:

To guard proud Calicut's imperial pride

All the wide North sweeps down its peopled tide:

Join'd are the sects that never touch'd before,

By land the pagan, and by sea the Moor.

O'er land, o'er sea the great Pacheco strews

The prostrate spearmen, and the founder'd proas.[596]

Submiss and silent, palsied with amaze,

Proud Malabar th' unnumber'd slain surveys:

Yet burns the monarch; to his shrine he speeds;

Dire howl the priests, the groaning victim bleeds;

The ground they stamp, and, from the dark abodes,

With tears and vows, they call th' infernal gods.

Enrag'd with dog-like madness, to behold

His temples and his towns in flames enroll'd,

Secure of promis'd victory, again

He fires the war, the lawns are heap'd with slain.

With stern reproach he brands his routed Nayres,

And for the dreadful field himself prepares;

His harness'd thousands to the fight he leads;

And rides exulting where the combat bleeds:

Amid his pomp his robes are sprinkled o'er,

And his proud face dash'd, with his menials' gore:[597]

From his high couch he leaps, and speeds to flight

On foot inglorious, in his army's sight.

Hell then he calls, and all the powers of hell,

The secret poison, and the chanted spell;

Vain as the spell the poison'd rage is shed,

For Heav'n defends the hero's sacred head.

Still fiercer from each wound the tyrant burns,

Still to the field with heavier force returns;

The seventh dread war he kindles; high in air

The hills dishonour'd lift their shoulders bare;

Their woods, roll'd down, now strew the river's side,

Now rise in mountain turrets o'er the tide;

Mountains of fire, and spires of bick'ring flame,

While either bank resounds the proud acclaim,

Come floating down, round Lusus' fleet to pour

Their sulph'rous entrails[598] in a burning shower.

Oh, vain the hope.—Let Rome her boast resign;

Her palms, Pacheco, never bloom'd like thine;

Nor Tiber's bridge,[599] nor Marathon's red field,

Nor thine, Thermopylæ, such deeds beheld;

Nor Fabius' arts such rushing storms repell'd.

Swift as, repuls'd, the famish'd wolf returns

Fierce to the fold, and, wounded, fiercer burns;

So swift, so fierce, seven times, all India's might

Returns unnumber'd to the dreadful fight;

One hundred spears, seven times in dreadful stower,

Strews in the dust all India's raging power."

The lofty song (for paleness o'er her spread)

The nymph suspends, and bows the languid head;
Her falt'ring words are breathed on plaintive sighs:
"Ah, Belisarius, injur'd chief," she cries,
"Ah, wipe thy tears; in war thy rival see,
Injur'd Pacheco falls despoil'd like thee;
In him, in thee dishonour'd Virtue bleeds,
And Valour weeps to view her fairest deeds,—
Weeps o'er Pacheco, where, forlorn he lies
Low on an alms-house bed, and friendless dies.
Yet shall the muses plume his humble bier,
And ever o'er him pour th' immortal tear;
Though by the king, alone to thee unjust,
Thy head, great chief, was humbled in the dust,
Loud shall the muse indignant sound thy praise—
'Thou gav'st thy monarch's throne its proudest blaze.'
While round the world the sun's bright car shall ride,
So bright shall shine thy name's illustrious pride;
Thy monarch's glory, as the moon's pale beam,
Eclips'd by thine, shall shed a sickly gleam.
Such meed attends when soothing flatt'ry sways,
And blinded State its sacred trust betrays!"

Again the nymph exalts her brow, again
Her swelling voice resounds the lofty strain:
"Almeyda comes, the kingly name he bears,
Deputed royalty his standard rears:
In all the gen'rous rage of youthful fire
The warlike son attends the warlike sire.
Quiloa's blood-stain'd tyrant now shall feel

359

The righteous vengeance of the Lusian steel.

Another prince, by Lisbon's throne belov'd,

Shall bless the land, for faithful deeds approv'd.

Mombaz shall now her treason's meed behold,

When curling flames her proudest domes enfold:

Involv'd in smoke, loud crashing, low shall fall

The mounded temple and the castled wall.

O'er India's seas the young Almeyda pours,

Scorching the wither'd air, his iron show'rs;

Torn masts and rudders, hulks and canvas riv'n,

Month after month before his prows are driv'n;

But Heav'n's dread will, where clouds of darkness rest,

That awful will, which knows alone the best,

Now blunts his spear: Cambaya's squadrons join'd

With Egypt's fleets, in pagan rage combin'd,

Engrasp him round; red boils the stagg'ring flood,

Purpled with volleying flames and hot with blood:

Whirl'd by the cannon's rage, in shivers torn,

His thigh, far scattered, o'er the wave is borne.

Bound to the mast the godlike hero stands,[600]

Waves his proud sword, and cheers his woful bands.

Though winds and seas their wonted aid deny,

To yield he knows not, but he knows to die:

Another thunder tears his manly breast:

Oh fly, blest spirit, to thy heav'nly rest!

Hark! rolling on the groaning storm I hear,

Resistless vengeance thund'ring on the rear.

I see the transports of the furious sire,

As o'er the mangled corse his eyes flash fire.

Swift to the fight, with stern though weeping eyes,

Fix'd rage fierce burning in his breast, he flies;

Fierce as the bull that sees his rival rove

Free with the heifers through the mounded grove,

On oak or beech his madd'ning fury pours;

So pours Almeyda's rage on Dabul's towers.

His vanes wide waving o'er the Indian sky,

Before his prows the fleets of India fly;[601]

On Egypt's chief his mortars' dreadful tire

Shall vomit all the rage of prison'd fire:

Heads, limbs, and trunks shall choke the struggling tide,

Till, ev'ry surge with reeking crimson dy'd,

Around the young Almeyda's hapless urn

His conqueror's naked ghosts shall howl and mourn.

As meteors flashing through the darken'd air

I see the victors' whirling falchions glare;

Dark rolls the sulph'rous smoke o'er Dio's skies,

And shrieks of death, and shouts of conquest rise,

In one wide tumult blended. The rough roar

Shakes the brown tents on Ganges' trembling shore;

The waves of Indus from the banks recoil;

And matrons, howling on the strand of Nile,

By the pale moon, their absent sons deplore:

Long shall they wail; their sons return no more.

"Ah, strike the notes of woe!" the siren cries;

"A dreary vision swims before my eyes.

To Tagus' shore triumphant as he bends,

Low in the dust the hero's glory ends:

Though bended bow, nor thund'ring engine's hail,

Nor Egypt's sword, nor India's spear prevail,

Fall shall the chief before a naked foe,

Rough clubs and rude-hurl'ed stones shall strike the blow;

The Cape of Tempests shall his tomb supply,

And in the desert sands his bones shall lie,

No boastful trophy o'er his ashes rear'd:

Such Heav'n's dread will, and be that will rever'd!

"But lo, resplendent shines another star,"

Loud she resounds, "in all the blaze of war!

Great Cunia[602] guards Melinda's friendly shore,

And dyes her seas with Oja's hostile gore;

Lamo and Brava's tow'rs his vengeance tell:

Green Madagascar's flow'ry dales shall swell

His echo'd fame, till ocean's southmost bound

On isles and shores unknown his name resound.

"Another blaze, behold, of fire and arms!

Great Albuquerque awakes the dread alarms:

O'er Ormuz' walls his thund'ring flames he pours,

While Heav'n, the hero's guide, indignant show'rs

Their arrows backwards[603] on the Persian foe,

Tearing the breasts and arms that twang'd the bow.

Mountains of salt and fragrant gums in vain

Were spent untainted to embalm the slain.

Such heaps shall strew the seas and faithless strand

Of Gerum, Mazcate,[604] and Calayat's land,

Till faithless Ormuz own the Lusian sway,

And Barem's[605] pearls her yearly safety pay.

"What glorious palms on Goa's isle I see,[606]

Their blossoms spread, great Albuquerque, for thee!

Through castled walls the hero breaks his way,

And opens with his sword the dread array

Of Moors and pagans; through their depth he rides,

Through spears and show'ring fire the battle guides.

As bulls enrag'd, or lions smear'd with gore,

His bands sweep wide o'er Goa's purpled shore.

Nor eastward far though fair Malacca[607] lie,

Her groves embosom'd in the morning sky;

Though with her am'rous sons the valiant line

Of Java's isle in battle rank combine,

Though poison'd shafts their pond'rous quivers store;

Malacca's spicy groves and golden ore,

Great Albuquerque, thy dauntless toils shall crown!

Yet art thou stain'd."[608] Here, with a sighful frown,

The goddess paus'd, for much remain'd unsung,

But blotted with a humble soldier's wrong.

"Alas," she cries, "when war's dread horrors reign,

And thund'ring batteries rock the fiery plain,

When ghastly famine on a hostile soil,

When pale disease attends on weary toil,

When patient under all the soldier stands,

Detested be the rage which then demands

The humble soldier's blood, his only crime

The am'rous frailty of the youthful prime!

Incest's cold horror here no glow restrain'd,

Nor sacred nuptial bed was here profan'd,

Nor here unwelcome force the virgin seiz'd;

A slave, lascivious, in his fondling pleas'd,

Resigns her breast. Ah, stain to Lusian fame!

('Twas lust of blood, perhaps 'twas jealous flame;)

The leader's rage, unworthy of the brave,

Consigns the youthful soldier to the grave.

Not Ammon[609] thus Apelles' love repaid,

Great Ammon's bed resign'd the lovely maid;

Nor Cyrus thus reprov'd Araspas' fire;

Nor haughtier Carlo thus assum'd the sire,

Though iron Baldwin to his daughter's bower,

An ill-match'd lover, stole in secret hour:

With nobler rage the lofty monarch glow'd,

And Flandria's earldom on the knight bestow'd."[610]

Again the nymph the song of fame resounds:

"Lo, sweeping wide o'er Ethiopia's bounds,

Wide o'er Arabia's purple shore, on high

The Lusian ensigns blaze along the sky:

Mecca, aghast, beholds the standards shine,

And midnight horror shakes Medina's shrine;[611]

Th' unhallow'd altar bodes th' approaching foe,

Foredoom'd in dust its prophet's tomb to strew.

Nor Ceylon's isle, brave Soarez, shall withhold

Its incense, precious as the burnish'd gold,

What time o'er proud Columbo's loftiest spire

Thy flag shall blaze: Nor shall th' immortal lyre

Forget thy praise, Sequeyra! To the shore

Where Sheba's sapient queen the sceptre bore,[612]

Braving the Red Sea's dangers shalt thou force

To Abyssinia's realm thy novel course;

And isles, by jealous Nature long conceal'd,

Shall to the wond'ring world be now reveal'd.

Great Menez next the Lusian sword shall bear;

Menez, the dread of Afric, high shall rear

His victor lance, till deep shall Ormuz groan,

And tribute doubled her revolt atone.

"Now shines thy glory in meridian height"—

And loud her voice she rais'd—"O matchless knight!

Thou, thou, illustrious Gama, thou shalt bring

The olive bough of peace, deputed king!

The lands by thee discover'd shall obey

Thy sceptred power, and bless thy regal sway.

But India's crimes, outrageous to the skies,

A length of these Saturnian days denies:

Snatch'd from thy golden throne,[613] the heav'ns shall claim

Thy deathless soul, the world thy deathless name.

"Now o'er the coast of faithless Malabar

Victorious Henry[614] pours the rage of war;

Nor less the youth a nobler strife shall wage,

Great victor of himself though green in age;

No restless slave of wanton am'rous fire,

No lust of gold shall taint his gen'rous ire.

While youth's bold pulse beats high, how brave the boy

Whom harlot-smiles nor pride of power decoy!

Immortal be his name! Nor less thy praise,

Great Mascarene,[615] shall future ages raise:

Though power, unjust, withhold the splendid ray

That dignifies the crest of sov'reign sway,

Thy deeds, great chief, on Bintam's humbled shore

(Deeds such as Asia never view'd before)

Shall give thy honest fame a brighter blaze

Than tyrant pomp in golden robes displays.

Though bold in war the fierce usurper shine,

Though Cutial's potent navy o'er the brine

Drive vanquish'd: though the Lusian Hector's sword

For him reap conquest, and confirm him lord;

Thy deeds, great peer, the wonder of thy foes,

Thy glorious chains unjust, and gen'rous woes,

Shall dim the fierce Sampayo's fairest fame,

And o'er his honours thine aloud proclaim.

Thy gen'rous woes! Ah gallant injur'd chief,

Not thy own sorrows give the sharpest grief.

Thou seest the Lusian name her honours stain,

And lust of gold her heroes' breasts profane;

Thou seest ambition lift the impious head,

Nor God's red arm, nor ling'ring justice dread;

O'er India's bounds thou seest these vultures prowl,

Full gorged with blood, and dreadless of control;

Thou seest and weepst thy country's blotted name,

The gen'rous sorrow thine, but not the shame.

Nor long the Lusian ensigns stain'd remain:

Great Nunio[616] comes, and razes every stain.

Though lofty Calè's warlike towers he rear;

Though haughty Melic groan beneath his spear;

All these, and Diu yielded to his name,

Are but th' embroid'ry of his nobler fame.

Far haughtier foes of Lusian race he braves;

The awful sword of justice high he waves:

Before his bar the injur'd Indian stands,

And justice boldly on his foe demands,

The Lusian foe; in wonder lost, the Moor

Beholds proud rapine's vulture grip restore;

Beholds the Lusian hands in fetters bound

By Lusian hands, and wound repaid for wound.

Oh, more shall thus by Nunio's worth be won,

Than conquest reaps from high-plum'd hosts o'erthrown.

Long shall the gen'rous Nunio's blissful sway

Command supreme. In Dio's hopeless day

The sov'reign toil the brave Noronha takes;

Awed by his fame [617] the fierce-soul'd Rumien shakes,

And Dio's open'd walls in sudden flight forsakes.

A son of thine, O Gama,[618] now shall hold

The helm of empire, prudent, wise, and bold:

Malacca sav'd and strengthen'd by his arms,

The banks of Tor shall echo his alarms;

His worth shall bless the kingdoms of the morn,

For all thy virtues shall his soul adorn.

When fate resigns thy hero to the skies,

A vet'ran, fam'd on Brazil's shore[619] shall rise:

The wide Atlantic and the Indian main,

By turns, shall own the terrors of his reign.

His aid the proud Cambayan king implores,

His potent aid Cambaya's king restores.

The dread Mogul with all his thousands flies,

And Dio's towers are Souza's well-earn'd prize.

Nor less the zamorim o'er blood-stain'd ground[620]

Shall speed his legions, torn with many a wound,

In headlong rout. Nor shall the boastful pride

Of India's navy, though the shaded tide

Around the squadron'd masts appear the down

Of some wide forest, other fate renown.

Loud rattling through the hills of Cape Camore[621]

I hear the tempest of the battle roar!

Clung to the splinter'd masts I see the dead

Badala's shore with horrid wreck bespread;

Baticala inflam'd by treach'rous hate,

Provokes the horrors of Badala's fate:

Her seas in blood, her skies enwrapt in fire,

Confess the sweeping storm of Souza's ire.

No hostile spear now rear'd on sea or strand,

The awful sceptre graces Souza's hand;

Peaceful he reigns, in counsel just and wise;

And glorious Castro now his throne supplies:

Castro, the boast of gen'rous fame, afar

From Dio's strand shall sway the glorious war.

Madd'ning with rage to view the Lusian band,

A troop so few, proud Dio's towers command,

The cruel Ethiop Moor to heav'n complains,

And the proud Persian's languid zeal arraigns.

The Rumien fierce, who boasts the name of Rome,[622]

With these conspires, and vows the Lusians' doom.

A thousand barb'rous nations join their powers

To bathe with Lusian blood the Dion towers.

Dark rolling sheets, forth belch'd from brazen wombs,

And bor'd, like show'ring clouds, with hailing bombs,

O'er Dio's sky spread the black shades of death;

The mine's dread earthquakes shake the ground beneath.

No hope, bold Mascarene,[623] mayst thou respire,

A glorious fall alone, thy just desire.

When lo, his gallant son brave Castro sends—

Ah heav'n, what fate the hapless youth attends!

In vain the terrors of his falchion glare:

The cavern'd mine bursts, high in pitchy air

Rampire and squadron whirl'd convulsive, borne

To heav'n, the hero dies in fragments torn.

His loftiest bough though fall'n, the gen'rous sire

His living hope devotes with Roman ire.

On wings of fury flies the brave Alvar

Through oceans howling with the wintry war,

Through skies of snow his brother's vengeance bears;

And, soon in arms, the valiant sire appears:

Before him vict'ry spreads her eagle wing

Wide sweeping o'er Cambaya's haughty king.

In vain his thund'ring coursers shake the ground,

Cambaya bleeding of his might's last wound

Sinks pale in dust: fierce Hydal-Kan[624] in vain

Wakes war on war; he bites his iron chain.

O'er Indus' banks, o'er Ganges' smiling vales,

No more the hind his plunder'd field bewails:

O'er ev'ry field, O Peace, thy blossoms glow,

The golden blossoms of thy olive bough;
Firm bas'd on wisest laws great Castro crowns,
And the wide East the Lusian empire owns.

"These warlike chiefs, the sons of thy renown,
And thousands more, O Vasco, doom'd to crown
Thy glorious toils, shall through these seas unfold
Their victor-standards blaz'd with Indian gold;
And in the bosom of our flow'ry isle,
Embath'd in joy shall o'er their labours smile.
Their nymphs like yours, their feast divine the same,
The raptur'd foretaste of immortal fame."

So sang the goddess, while the sister train
With joyful anthem close the sacred strain:
"Though Fortune from her whirling sphere bestow
Her gifts capricious in unconstant flow,
Yet laurell'd honour and immortal fame
Shall ever constant grace the Lusian name."
So sung the joyful chorus, while around
The silver roofs the lofty notes resound.
The song prophetic, and the sacred feast,
Now shed the glow of strength through ev'ry breast.
When with the grace and majesty divine,
Which round immortals when enamour'd shine,
To crown the banquet of their deathless fame,
To happy Gama thus the sov'reign dame:
"O lov'd of Heav'n, what never man before,
What wand'ring science never might explore,

By Heav'n's high will, with mortal eyes to see
Great nature's face unveil'd, is given to thee.
Thou and thy warriors follow where I lead:
Firm be your steps, for arduous to the tread,
Through matted brakes of thorn and brier, bestrew'd
With splinter'd flint, winds the steep slipp'ry road."
She spake, and smiling caught the hero's hand,
And on the mountain's summit soon they stand;
A beauteous lawn with pearl enamell'd o'er,
Emerald and ruby, as the gods of yore
Had sported here. Here in the fragrant air
A wondrous globe appear'd, divinely fair!
Through ev'ry part the light transparent flow'd,
And in the centre, as the surface, glow'd.
The frame ethereal various orbs compose,
In whirling circles now they fell, now rose;
Yet never rose nor fell,[625] for still the same
Was ev'ry movement of the wondrous frame;
Each movement still beginning, still complete,
Its author's type, self-pois'd, perfection's seat.

Great Vasco, thrill'd with reverential awe,
And rapt with keen desire, the wonder saw.
The goddess mark'd the language of his eyes,
"And here," she cried, "thy largest wish suffice."
Great nature's fabric thou dost here behold,
Th' ethereal, pure, and elemental mould
In pattern shown complete, as nature's God
Ordain'd the world's great frame, His dread abode;

For ev'ry part the Power Divine pervades,

The sun's bright radiance, and the central shades;

Yet, let not haughty reason's bounded line

Explore the boundless God, or where define,

Where in Himself, in uncreated light

(While all His worlds around seem wrapp'd in night),

He holds His loftiest state.[626] By primal laws

Impos'd on Nature's birth (Himself the cause),

By her own ministry, through ev'ry maze,

Nature in all her walks, unseen, He sways.

These spheres behold;[627] the first in wide embrace

Surrounds the lesser orbs of various face;

The Empyrean this, the holiest heav'n

To the pure spirits of the bless'd is giv'n:

No mortal eye its splendid rays may bear,

No mortal bosom feel the raptures there.

The earth, in all her summer pride array'd,

To this might seem a drear sepulchral shade.

Unmov'd it stands; within its shining frame,

In motion swifter than the lightning's flame,

Swifter than sight the moving parts may spy,

Another sphere whirls round its rapid sky.

Hence motion darts its force,[628] impulsive draws,

And on the other orbs impresses laws;

The sun's bright car attentive to its force

Gives night and day, and shapes his yearly course;

Its force stupendous asks a pond'rous sphere

To poise its fury, and its weight to bear:

Slow moves that pond'rous orb; the stiff, slow pace

One step scarce gains, while wide his annual race

Two hundred times the sun triumphant rides;

The crystal heav'n is this, whose rigour guides

And binds the starry sphere:[629] That sphere behold,

With diamonds spangled, and emblaz'd with gold!

What radiant orbs that azure sky adorn,

Fair o'er the night in rapid motion borne!

Swift as they trace the heav'n's wide circling line,

Whirl'd on their proper axles, bright they shine.

Wide o'er this heav'n a golden belt displays

Twelve various forms; behold the glitt'ring blaze!

Through these the sun in annual journey towers,

And o'er each clime their various tempers pours;

In gold and silver of celestial mine

How rich far round the constellations shine!

Lo, bright emerging o'er the polar tides,

In shining frost the Northern Chariot rides;[630]

Mid treasur'd snows here gleams the grisly Bear,

And icy flakes incrust his shaggy hair.

Here fair Andromeda, of heav'n belov'd;

Her vengeful sire, and, by the gods reprov'd,

Beauteous Cassiope. Here, fierce and red,

Portending storms, Orion lifts his head;

And here the Dogs their raging fury shed.

The Swan, sweet melodist, in death he sings,

The milder Swan here spreads his silver wings.

Here Orpheus' Lyre, the melancholy Hare,

And here the watchful Dragon's eye-balls glare;

And Theseus' ship, oh, less renown'd than thine,

Shall ever o'er these skies illustrious shine.

Beneath this radiant firmament behold

The various planets in their orbits roll'd:

Here, in cold twilight, hoary Saturn rides;

Here Jove shines mild, here fiery Mars presides;

Apollo here, enthron'd in light, appears

The eye of heav'n, emblazer of the spheres;

Beneath him beauteous glows the Queen of Love—

The proudest hearts her sacred influence prove;

Here Hermes, fam'd for eloquence divine,

And here Diana's various faces shine;

Lowest she rides, and, through the shadowy night,

Pours on the glist'ning earth her silver light.

These various orbs, behold, in various speed

Pursue the journeys at their birth decreed.

Now, from the centre far impell'd they fly,

Now, nearer earth they sail a lower sky,

A shorten'd course: Such are their laws impress'd

By God's dread will,[631] that will for ever best.

"The yellow earth, the centre of the whole,

There lordly rests sustain'd on either pole.

The limpid air enfolds in soft embrace

The pond'rous orb, and brightens o'er her face.

Here, softly floating o'er th' aërial blue,

Fringed with the purple and the golden hue,

The fleecy clouds their swelling sides display;

From whence, fermented by the sulph'rous ray,

The lightnings blaze, and heat spreads wide and rare;

And now, in fierce embrace with frozen air,

Their wombs, compress'd, soon feel parturient throws,

And white wing'd gales bear wide the teeming snows.

Thus, cold and heat their warring empires hold,

Averse yet mingling, each by each controll'd,

The highest air and ocean's bed they pierce,

And earth's dark centre feels their struggles fierce.

"The seat of man, the earth's fair breast, behold;

Here wood-crown'd islands wave their locks of gold.

Here spread wide continents their bosoms green,

And hoary Ocean heaves his breast between.

Yet, not th' inconstant ocean's furious tide

May fix the dreadful bounds of human pride.

What madd'ning seas between these nations roar!

Yet Lusus' hero-race shall visit ev'ry shore.

What thousand tribes, whom various customs sway,

And various rites, these countless shores display!

Queen of the world, supreme in shining arms,

Hers ev'ry art, and hers all wisdom's charms,

Each nation's tribute round her foot-stool spread,

Here Christian Europe[632] lifts the regal head.

Afric behold,[633] alas, what alter'd view!

Her lands uncultur'd, and her son's untrue;

Ungraced with all that sweetens human life,

Savage and fierce they roam in brutal strife;

Eager they grasp the gifts which culture yields,

Yet, naked roam their own neglected fields.

Lo, here enrich'd with hills of golden ore,

Monomotapa's empire hems the shore.

There round the Cape, great Afric's dreadful bound,

Array'd in storms (by you first compass'd round),

Unnumber'd tribes as bestial grazers stray,

By laws unform'd, unform'd by reason's sway:

Far inward stretch the mournful sterile dales,

Where, on the parch'd hill-side, pale Famine wails.

On gold in vain the naked savage treads;

Low, clay-built huts, behold, and reedy sheds,

Their dreary towns. Gonzalo's zeal shall glow[634]

To these dark minds the path of light to show:

His toils to humanize the barb'rous mind

Shall, with the martyr's palms, his holy temples bind.

Great Naya,[635] too, shall glorious here display

His God's dread might: behold, in black array,

Num'rous and thick as when in evil hour

The feather'd race whole harvest fields devour,

So thick, so num'rous round Sofála's towers

Her barb'rous hordes remotest Africa pours:

In vain; Heav'n's vengeance on their souls impress'd,

They fly, wide scatter'd as the driving mist.

Lo, Quama there, and there the fertile Nile

Curs'd with that gorging fiend, the crocodile,

Wind their long way: the parent lake behold,

Great Nilus' fount, unseen, unknown of old,

From whence, diffusing plenty as he glides,

Wide Abyssinia's realm the stream divides.

In Abyssinia Heav'n's own altars blaze,[636]

And hallow'd anthems chant Messiah's praise.

In Nile's wide breast the isle of Mĕrŏē see!

Near these rude shores a hero sprung from thee,

Thy son, brave Gama,[637] shall his lineage show

In glorious triumphs o'er the paynim[638] foe.

There by the rapid Ob her friendly breast

Melinda spreads, thy place of grateful rest.

Cape Aromata there the gulf defends,

Where by the Red Sea wave great Afric ends.

Illustrious Suez, seat of heroes old,

Fam'd Hierapolis, high-tower'd, behold.

Here Egypt's shelter'd fleets at anchor ride,

And hence, in squadrons, sweep the eastern tide.

And lo, the waves that aw'd by Moses' rod,

While the dry bottom Israel's armies trod,

On either hand roll'd back their frothy might,

And stood, like hoary rocks, in cloudy height.

Here Asia, rich in ev'ry precious mine,

In realms immense, begins her western line.

Sinai behold, whose trembling cliffs of yore

In fire and darkness, deep pavilion'd, bore

The Hebrews' God, while day, with awful brow,

Gleam'd pale on Israel's wand'ring tents below.

The pilgrim now the lonely hill ascends,

And, when the ev'ning raven homeward bends,

Before the virgin-martyr's tomb[639] he pays

His mournful vespers, and his vows of praise.

Jidda behold, and Aden's parch'd domain

Girt by Arzira's rock, where never rain

Yet fell from heav'n; where never from the dale

The crystal riv'let murmur'd to the vale.

The three Arabias here their breasts unfold,

Here breathing incense, here a rocky wold;

O'er Dofar's plain the richest incense breathes,

That round the sacred shrine its vapour wreathes;

Here the proud war-steed glories in his force,

As, fleeter than the gale, he holds the course.

Here, with his spouse and household lodg'd in wains,

The Arab's camp shifts, wand'ring o'er the plains,

The merchant's dread, what time from eastern soil

His burthen'd camels seek the land of Nile.

Here Rosalgate and Farthac stretch their arms,

And point to Ormuz, fam'd for war's alarms;

Ormuz, decreed full oft to quake with dread

Beneath the Lusian heroes' hostile tread,

Shall see the Turkish moons,[640] with slaughter gor'd,

Shrink from the lightning of De Branco's sword.[641]

There on the gulf that laves the Persian shore,

Far through the surges bends Cape Asabore.

There Barem's isle;[642] her rocks with diamonds blaze,

And emulate Aurora's glitt'ring rays.

From Barem's shore Euphrates' flood is seen,

And Tigris' waters, through the waves of green

In yellowy currents many a league extend,

As with the darker waves averse they blend.

Lo, Persia there her empire wide unfolds!

In tented camp his state the monarch holds:

Her warrior sons disdain the arms of fire,[643]

And, with the pointed steel, to fame aspire;

Their springy shoulders stretching to the blow,

Their sweepy sabres hew the shrieking foe.

There Gerum's isle the hoary ruin wears

Where Time has trod:[644] there shall the dreadful spears

Of Sousa and Menezes strew the shore

With Persian sabres, and embathe with gore.

Carpella's cape, and sad Carmania's strand,

There, parch'd and bare, their dreary wastes expand.

A fairer landscape here delights the view;

From these green hills beneath the clouds of blue,

The Indus and the Ganges roll the wave,

And many a smiling field propitious lave.

Luxurious here, Ulcinda's harvests smile,

And here, disdainful of the seaman's toil,

The whirling tides of Jaquet furious roar;

Alike their rage when swelling to the shore,

Or, tumbling backward to the deep, they force

The boiling fury of their gulfy course:

Against their headlong rage nor oars nor sails,

The stemming prow alone, hard toil'd, prevails.

Cambaya here begins her wide domain;

A thousand cities here shall own the reign

Of Lisboa's monarchs. He who first shall crown

Thy labours, Gama,[645] here shall boast his own.

The length'ning sea that washes India's strand

And laves the cape that points to Ceylon's land

(The Taprobanian isle,[646] renown'd of yore),

Shall see his ensigns blaze from shore to shore.

Behold how many a realm, array'd in green,

The Ganges' shore and Indus' bank between!

Here tribes unnumber'd, and of various lore,

With woful penance fiend-like shapes adore;

Some Macon's orgies;[647] all confess the sway

Of rites that shun, like trembling ghosts, the day.

Narsinga's fair domain behold; of yore

Here shone the gilded towers of Meliapore.

Here India's angels, weeping o'er the tomb

Where Thomas sleeps,[648] implore the day to come,

The day foretold, when India's utmost shore

Again shall hear Messiah's blissful lore.

By Indus' banks the holy prophet trod,

And Ganges heard him preach the Saviour-God;

Where pale disease erewhile the cheek consum'd,

Health, at his word, in ruddy fragrance bloom'd;

The grave's dark womb his awful voice obey'd,

And to the cheerful day restor'd the dead;

By heavenly power he rear'd the sacred shrine,

And gain'd the nations by his life divine.

The priests of Brahma's hidden rites beheld,

And envy's bitt'rest gall their bosom's swell'd.

A thousand deathful snares in vain they spread;

When now the chief who wore the triple thread,[649]

Fir'd by the rage that gnaws the conscious breast

Of holy fraud, when worth shines forth confess'd,

Hell he invokes, nor hell in vain he sues;

His son's life-gore his wither'd hands imbrues;

Then, bold assuming the vindictive ire,

And all the passions of the woful sire,

Weeping, he bends before the Indian throne,

Arraigns the holy man, and wails his son:

A band of hoary priests attest the deed,

And India's king condemns the seer to bleed.

Inspir'd by Heav'n the holy victim stands,

And o'er the murder'd corse extends his hands:

'In God's dread power, thou slaughter'd youth, arise,

And name,thy murderer,' aloud he cries.

When, dread to view, the deep wounds instant close,

And, fresh in life, the slaughter'd youth arose,

And nam'd his treach'rous sire. The conscious air

Quiver'd, and awful horror raised the hair

On ev'ry head. From Thomas India's king

The holy sprinkling of the living spring

Receives, and wide o'er all his regal bounds

The God of Thomas ev'ry tongue resounds.

Long taught the holy seer the words of life;

The priests of Brahma still to deeds of strife

(So boil'd their ire) the blinded herd impell'd,

And high, to deathful rage, their rancour swell'd.

'Twas on a day, when melting on his tongue

Heav'n's offer'd mercies glow'd, the impious throng,

Rising in madd'ning tempest, round him shower'd

The splinter'd flint; in vain the flint was pour'd:

But Heav'n had now his finish'd labours seal'd;

His angel guards withdraw the etherial shield;

A Brahmin's javelin tears his holy breast——

Ah Heav'n, what woes the widow'd land express'd!

Thee, Thomas, thee, the plaintive Ganges mourn'd,[650]

And Indus' banks the murm'ring moan return'd;

O'er ev'ry valley where thy footsteps stray'd,

The hollow winds the gliding sighs convey'd.

What woes the mournful face of India wore,

These woes in living pangs his people bore.

His sons, to whose illumin'd minds he gave

To view the ray that shines beyond the grave,

His pastoral sons bedew'd his corse with tears,

While high triumphant through the heav'nly spheres,

With songs of joy, the smiling angels wing

His raptur'd spirit to the eternal King.

O you, the followers of the holy seer,

Foredoom'd the shrines of Heav'n's own lore to rear,

You, sent by Heav'n his labours to renew,

Like him, ye Lusians, simplest Truth pursue.[651]

Vain is the impious toil, with borrow'd grace,

To deck one feature of her angel face;

Behind the veil's broad glare she glides away,

And leaves a rotten form, of lifeless, painted clay.

"Much have you view'd of future Lusian reign;

Broad empires yet, and kingdoms wide, remain,

Scenes of your future toils and glorious sway—

And lo, how wide expands the Gangic bay!

Narsinga here in num'rous legions bold,

And here Oryxa boasts her cloth of gold.

The Ganges here in many a stream divides,

Diffusing plenty from his fatt'ning tides,

As through Bengala's rip'ning vales he glides;

Nor may the fleetest hawk, untir'd, explore

Where end the ricy groves that crown the shore.

There view what woes demand your pious aid!

On beds and litters, o'er the margin laid,

The dying[652] lift their hollow eyes, and crave

Some pitying hand to hurl them in the wave.

Thus Heav'n (they deem), though vilest guilt they bore

Unwept, unchanged, will view that guilt no more.

There, eastward, Arracan her line extends;

And Pegu's mighty empire southward bends:

Pegu, whose sons (so held old faith) confess'd

A dog their sire;[653] their deeds the tale attest.

A pious queen their horrid rage restrain'd;[654]

Yet, still their fury Nature's God arraign'd.

Ah, mark the thunders rolling o'er the sky;

Yes, bath'd in gore, shall rank pollution lie.

"Where to the morn the towers of Tava shine,

Begins great Siam's empire's far-stretch'd line.

On Queda's fields the genial rays inspire

The richest gust of spicery's fragrant fire.

Malacca's castled harbour here survey,

The wealthful seat foredoom'd of Lusian sway.

Here to their port the Lusian fleets shall steer,

From ev'ry shore far round assembling here

The fragrant treasures of the eastern world:

Here from the shore by rolling earthquakes hurl'd,

Through waves all foam, Sumatra's isle was riv'n,

And, mid white whirlpools, down the ocean driv'n.[655]

To this fair isle, the golden Chersonese,

Some deem the sapient monarch plough'd the seas;

Ophir its Tyrian name.[656] In whirling roars

How fierce the tide boils down these clasping shores!

High from the strait the length'ning coast afar

Its moonlike curve points to the northern star,

Opening its bosom to the silver ray

When fair Aurora pours the infant day.

Patane and Pam, and nameless nations more,

Who rear their tents on Menam's winding shore,

Their vassal tribute yield to Siam's throne;

And thousands more,[657] of laws, of names unknown,

That vast of land inhabit. Proud and bold,

Proud of their numbers, here the Laos hold

The far-spread lawns; the skirting hills obey

The barb'rous Avas', and the Brahma's sway.

Lo, distant far, another mountain chain

Rears its rude cliffs, the Guio's dread domain;

Here brutaliz'd the human form is seen,

The manners fiend-like as the brutal mien:

With frothing jaws they suck the human blood,

And gnaw the reeking limbs,[658] their sweetest food;

Horrid, with figur'd seams of burning steel,

Their wolf-like frowns their ruthless lust reveal.

Cambaya there the blue-tinged Mecon laves,

Mecon the eastern Nile, whose swelling waves,

'Captain of rivers' nam'd, o'er many a clime,

In annual period, pour their fatt'ning slime.

The simple natives of these lawns believe

That other worlds the souls of beasts receive;[659]

Where the fierce murd'rer-wolf, to pains decreed,

Sees the mild lamb enjoy the heav'nly mead.

Oh gentle Mecon,[660] on thy friendly shore

Long shall the muse her sweetest off'rings pour!

When tyrant ire, chaf'd by the blended lust

Of pride outrageous, and revenge unjust,

Shall on the guiltless exile burst their rage,

And madd'ning tempests on their side engage,

Preserv'd by Heav'n the song of Lusian fame,

The song, O Vasco, sacred to thy name,

Wet from the whelming surge, shall triumph o'er

The fate of shipwreck on the Mecon's shore,

Here rest secure as on the muse's breast!

Happy the deathless song, the bard, alas, unblest!

"Chiampa there her fragrant coast extends,

There Cochin-China's cultur'd land ascends:

From Anam Bay begins the ancient reign

Of China's beauteous art-adorn'd domain;

Wide from the burning to the frozen skies,

O'erflow'd with wealth, the potent empire lies.

Here, ere the cannon's rage in Europe roar'd,[661]

The cannon's thunder on the foe was pour'd:

And here the trembling needle sought the north,

Ere Time in Europe brought the wonder forth.

No more let Egypt boast her mountain pyres;

To prouder fame yon bounding wall aspires,

A prouder boast of regal power displays

Than all the world beheld in ancient days.

Not built, created seems the frowning mound;

O'er loftiest mountain tops, and vales profound

Extends the wondrous length, with warlike castles crown'd.

Immense the northern wastes their horrors spread;[662]

In frost and snow the seas and shores are clad.

These shores forsake, to future ages due:

A world of islands claims thy happier view,

Where lavish Nature all her bounty pours,

And flowers and fruits of ev'ry fragrance showers.

Japan behold; beneath the globe's broad face

Northward she sinks, the nether seas embrace

Her eastern bounds; what glorious fruitage there,

Illustrious Gama, shall thy labours bear!

How bright a silver mine![663] when Heav'n's own lore

From pagan dross shall purify her ore.

"Beneath the spreading wings of purple morn,

Behold what isles these glist'ning seas adorn!

'Mid hundreds yet unnam'd, Ternate behold!

By day, her hills in pitchy clouds inroll'd,

By night, like rolling waves, the sheets of fire

Blaze o'er the seas, and high to heav'n aspire.

For Lusian hands here blooms the fragrant clove,

But Lusian blood shall sprinkle ev'ry grove.

The golden birds that ever sail the skies

Here to the sun display their shining dyes,

Each want supplied, on air they ever soar;

The ground they touch not[664] till they breathe no more.

386

Here Banda's isles their fair embroid'ry spread

Of various fruitage, azure, white, and red;

And birds of ev'ry beauteous plume display

Their glitt'ring radiance, as, from spray to spray,

From bower to bower, on busy wings they rove,

To seize the tribute of the spicy grove.

Borneo here expands her ample breast,

By Nature's hand in woods of camphor dress'd;

The precious liquid, weeping from the trees,

Glows warm with health, the balsam of disease.

Fair are Timora's dales with groves array'd,

Each riv'let murmurs in the fragrant shade,

And, in its crystal breast, displays the bowers

Of Sanders, blest with health-restoring powers.

Where to the south the world's broad surface bends,

Lo, Sunda's realm her spreading arms extends.

From hence the pilgrim brings the wondrous tale,[665]

A river groaning through a dreary dale

(For all is stone around) converts to stone

Whate'er of verdure in its breast is thrown.

Lo, gleaming blue, o'er fair Sumatra's skies,

Another mountain's trembling flames arise;

Here from the trees the gum[666] all fragrance swells,

And softest oil a wondrous fountain wells.

Nor these alone the happy isle bestows,

Fine is her gold, her silk resplendent glows.

Wide forests there beneath Maldivia's tide[667]

From with'ring air their wondrous fruitage hide.

The green-hair'd Nereids, tend the bow'ry dells,

Whose wondrous fruitage poison's rage expels.

In Ceylon, lo, how high yon mountain's brows!

The sailing clouds its middle height enclose.

Holy the hill is deem'd, the hallow'd tread

Of sainted footstep[668] marks its rocky head.

Lav'd by the Red Sea gulf, Socotra's bowers

There boast the tardy aloe's beauteous flowers.

On Afric's strand, foredoom'd to Lusian sway,

Behold these isles, and rocks of dusky gray;

From cells unknown here bounteous ocean pours

The fragrant amber on the sandy shores.

And lo, the Island of the Moon[669] displays

Her vernal lawns, and num'rous peaceful bays:

The halcyons[670] hov'ring o'er the bays are seen,

And lowing herds adorn the vales of green.

"Thus, from the cape where sail was ne'er unfurl'd,

Till thine, auspicious, sought the eastern world,

To utmost wave, where first the morning star

Sheds the pale lustre of her silver car,

Thine eyes have view'd the empires and the isles,

The world immense, that crowns thy glorious toils—

That world where ev'ry boon is shower'd from Heav'n,

Now to the West, by thee, great chief, is giv'n.[671]

"And still, O blest, thy peerless honours grow,

New op'ning views the smiling fates bestow.

With alter'd face the moving globe behold;

There ruddy ev'ning sheds her beams of gold.

While now, on Afric's bosom faintly die
The last pale glimpses of the twilight sky,
Bright o'er the wide Atlantic rides the morn,
And dawning rays another world adorn:
To farthest north that world enormous bends,
And cold, beneath the southern pole-star ends.
Near either pole[672] the barb'rous hunter, dress'd
In skins of bears, explores the frozen waste:
Where smiles the genial sun with kinder rays,
Proud cities tower, and gold-roof'd temples blaze.
This golden empire, by the heav'n's decree,
Is due, Castile, O favour'd power, to thee!
Even now, Columbus o'er the hoary tide
Pursues the ev'ning sun, his navy's guide.
Yet, shall the kindred Lusian share the reign,
What time this world shall own the yoke of Spain.
The first bold hero[673] who to India's shores
Through vanquish'd waves thy open'd path explores,
Driv'n by the winds of heav'n from Afric's strand,
Shall fix the holy cross on yon fair land.
That mighty realm, for purple wood renown'd,
Shall stretch the Lusian empire's western bound.
Fir'd by thy fame, and with his king in ire,
To match thy deeds shall Magalhaens aspire.[674]
In all but loyalty, of Lusian soul,
No fear, no danger shall his toils control.
Along these regions, from the burning zone
To deepest south, he dares the course unknown.
While, to the kingdoms of the rising day,

To rival thee he holds the western way,

A land of giants[675] shall his eyes behold,

Of camel strength, surpassing human mould:

And, onward still, thy fame his proud heart's guide

Haunting him unappeas'd, the dreary tide

Beneath the southern star's cold gleam he braves,

And stems the whirls of land-surrounded waves.

For ever sacred to the hero's fame,

These foaming straits shall bear his deathless name.

Through these dread jaws of rock he presses on,

Another ocean's breast, immense, unknown,

Beneath the south's cold wings, unmeasur'd, wide,

Receives his vessels; through the dreary tide

In darkling shades, where never man before

Heard the waves howl, he dares the nameless shore.

"Thus far, O favour'd Lusians, bounteous Heav'n

Your nation's glories to your view has giv'n.

What ensigns, blazing to the morn, pursue

The path of heroes, open'd first by you!

Still be it yours the first in fame to shine:

Thus shall your brides new chaplets still entwine,

With laurels ever new your brows enfold,

And braid your wavy locks with radiant gold.

"How calm the waves, how mild the balmy gale!

The halcyons call; ye Lusians, spread the sail;

Old ocean, now appeas'd, shall rage no more.

Haste, point the bowsprit to your native shore:

Soon shall the transports of the natal soil
O'erwhelm, in bounding joy, the thoughts of ev'ry toil."

The goddess spake[676]; and Vasco wav'd his hand,
And soon the joyful heroes crowd the strand.
The lofty ships with deepen'd burthens prove
The various bounties of the Isle of Love.
Nor leave the youths their lovely brides behind,
In wedded bands, while time glides on, conjoin'd;
Fair as immortal fame in smiles array'd,
In bridal smiles, attends each lovely maid.
O'er India's sea, wing'd on by balmy gales
That whisper'd peace, soft swell'd the steady sails:
Smooth as on wing unmov'd the eagle flies,
When to his eyrie cliff he sails the skies,
Swift o'er the gentle billows of the tide,
So smooth, so soft, the prows of Gama glide;
And now their native fields, for ever dear,
In all their wild transporting charms appear;
And Tago's bosom, while his banks repeat
The sounding peals of joy, receives the fleet.
With orient titles and immortal fame
The hero band adorn their monarch's name;
Sceptres and crowns beneath his feet they lay,
And the wide East is doom'd to Lusian sway.[677]

Enough, my muse, thy wearied wing no more
Must to the seat of Jove triumphant soar.
Chill'd by my nation's cold neglect, thy fires

Glow bold no more, and all thy rage expires.

Yet thou, Sebastian, thou, my king, attend;

Behold what glories on thy throne descend!

Shall haughty Gaul or sterner Albion boast

That all the Lusian fame in thee is lost!

Oh, be it thine these glories to renew,

And John's bold path and Pedro's course pursue:[678]

Snatch from the tyrant-noble's hand the sword,

And be the rights of humankind restor'd.

The statesman prelate to his vows confine,

Alone auspicious at the holy shrine;

The priest, in whose meek heart Heav'n pours its fires,

Alone to Heav'n, not earth's vain pomp, aspires.

Nor let the muse, great king, on Tago's shore,

In dying notes the barb'rous age deplore.

The king or hero to the muse unjust

Sinks as the nameless slave, extinct in dust.

But such the deeds thy radiant morn portends,

Aw'd by thy frown ev'n now old Atlas bends

His hoary head, and Ampeluza's fields

Expect thy sounding steeds and rattling shields.

And shall these deeds unsung, unknown, expire!

Oh, would thy smiles relume my fainting ire!

I, then inspir'd, the wond'ring world should see

Great Ammon's warlike son reviv'd in thee;

Reviv'd, unenvied[679] of the muse's flame

That o'er the world resounds Pelides'[680] name.

"O let th' Iambic Muse revenge that wrong

Which cannot slumber in thy sheets of lead;

392

Let thy abused honour crie as long

As there be quills to write, or eyes to reade:

On his rank name let thine own votes be turn'd,

Oh may that man that hath the Muses scorn'd

Alive, nor dead, be ever of a Muse adorn'd."

DISSERTATION ON THE FICTION OF THE ISLAND OF VENUS.

From the earliest ages, and in the most distant nations, palaces, forests and gardens, have been the favourite themes of poets. And though, as in Homer's island of Rhadamanthus, the description is sometimes only cursory; at other times they have lavished all their powers, and have vied with each other in adorning their edifices and landscapes. The gardens of Alcinous in the Odyssey, and Elysium in the Æneid, have excited the ambition of many imitators. Many instances of these occur in the later writers. These subjects, however, it must be owned, are so natural to the genius of poetry, that it is scarcely fair to attribute to an imitation of the classics, the innumerable descriptions of this kind which abound in the old romances. In these, under different allegorical names, every passion, every virtue and vice, had its palace, its enchanted bower, or its dreary cave. Among the Italians, on the revival of letters, Pulci, Boiardo, and others, borrowed these fictions from the Gothic romancers; Ariosto borrowed from them, and Spenser has copied Ariosto and Tasso. In the sixth and seventh books of the Orlando Furioso, there is a fine description of the island and palace of Alcina, or Vice; and in the tenth book (but inferior to the other in poetical colouring), we have a view of the country of Logistilla, or Virtue. The passage, of this kind, however, where Ariosto has displayed the richest poetical painting, is in the xxxiv. book, in the description of Paradise, whither he sends Astolpho, the English duke, to ask the help of St. John to recover the wits of Orlando. The whole is most admirably fanciful. Astolpho mounts the clouds on the winged horse, sees Paradise, and, accompanied by the Evangelist, visits the moon; the adventures in which orb are almost literally translated in Milton's Limbo. But the passage which may be said to bear the nearest resemblance to the descriptive part of the island of Venus, is the landscape of Paradise, of which the ingenious Mr. Hoole, to whose many acts of friendship I am proud to acknowledge myself indebted, has obliged me with this translation, though only ten books of his Ariosto are yet published.

"O'er the glad earth the blissful season pours
The vernal beauties of a thousand flowers
In varied tints: there show'd the ruby's hue,
The yellow topaz, and the sapphire blue.
The mead appears one intermingled blaze
Where pearls and diamonds dart their trembling rays.
Not emerald here so bright a verdure yields
As the fair turf of those celestial fields.
On ev'ry tree the leaves unfading grow,
The fruitage ripens and the flow'rets blow!
The frolic birds, gay-plum'd, of various wing
Amid the boughs their notes melodious sing:
Still lakes, and murm'ring streams, with waters clear,
Charm the fix'd eye, and lull the list'ning ear.
A soft'ning genial air, that ever seems
In even tenor, cools the solar beams
With fanning breeze; while from the enamell'd field,
Whate'er the fruits, the plants, the blossoms yield
Of grateful scent, the stealing gales dispense
The blended sweets to feed th' immortal sense.

"Amid the plain a palace dazzling bright,
Like living flame, emits a streamy light,
And, wrapp'd in splendour of refulgent day,
Outshines the strength of ev'ry mortal ray.

"Astolpho gently now directs his speed
To where the spacious pile enfolds the mead
In circuit wide, and views with eager eyes

Each nameless charm that happy soil supplies.

With this compar'd, he deems the world below

A dreary desert and a seat of woe!

By Heaven and Nature, in their wrath bestow'd,

In evil hour, for man's unblest abode.

"Near and more near the stately walls he drew,

In steadfast gaze transported at the view:

They seem'd one gem entire, of purer red

Than deep'ning gleams transparent rubies shed.

Stupendous work! by art Dædalian rais'd,

Transcending all by feeble mortals prais'd!

No more henceforth let boasting tongues proclaim

Those wonders of the world, so chronicled by fame!"

Camoëns read and admired Ariosto; but it by no means follows that he
borrowed the hint of his island of Venus from that poet. The luxury of
flowery description is as common in poetry as are the tales of love. The
heroes of Ariosto meet beautiful women in the palace of Alcina:—

"Before the threshold wanton damsels wait,

Or, sport between the pillars of the gate:

But, beauty more had brighten'd in their face

Had modesty attemper'd ev'ry grace;

In vestures green each damsel swept the ground,

Their temples fair, with leafy garlands crown'd.

These, with a courteous welcome, led the knight

To this sweet Paradise of soft delight....

Enamour'd youths and tender damsels seem

To chant their loves beside a purling stream.

Some by a branching tree, or mountain's shade,

In sports and dances press the downy glade,

While one discloses to his friend, apart,

The secret transport of his am'rous heart."—Book vi.

But these descriptions also, which bring the homes of knight-errantry into the way of beautiful wantons, are as common in the old romance as the use of the alphabet: and indeed the greatest part of these love-adventures are evidently borrowed from the fable of Circe. Astolpho, who was transformed into a myrtle by Alcina, thus informs Rogero:—

"Her former lovers she esteem'd no more,

For many lovers she possess'd before;

I was her joy——

Too late, alas, I found her wav'ring mind

In love inconstant as the changing wind!

Scarce had I held two months the fairy's grace,

When a new youth was taken to my place:

Rejected, then, I join'd the banish'd herd

That lost her love, as others were preferr'd ...

Some here, some there, her potent charms retain,

In diverse forms imprison'd to remain;

In beeches, olives, palms, or cedars clos'd,

Or, such as me, you here behold expos'd;

In fountains some, and some in beasts confin'd,

As suits the wayward fairy's cruel mind."

Hoole, Ar. bk. vi.

When incidents, character, and conduct confess the resemblance, we may, with certainty, pronounce from whence the copy is taken. Where only a similar stroke of passion or description occurs, it belongs alone to the arrogance of dulness, to tell us on what passage the poet had his eye. Every great poet has been persecuted in this manner: Milton in particular. His commentators have not left him a flower of his own growth. Yet, like the creed of the atheist, their system is involved in the deepest absurdity. It is easy to suppose that men of poetical feelings, in describing the same thing, should give us the same picture. But, that the Paradise Lost, which forms one animated whole of the noblest poetry, is a mere cento, compiled from innumerable authors, ancient and modern, is a supposition which gives Milton a cast of talents infinitely more extraordinary and inexplicable than the greatest poetical genius. When Gaspar Poussin painted clouds and trees in his landscapes, he did not borrow the green and the blue of the leaf and the sky from Claude Lorraine. Neither did Camoëns, when he painted his island of Venus, spend the half of his life in collecting his colours from all his predecessors who had described the beauties of the vernal year, or the stages of passion. Camoëns knew how others had painted the flowery bowers of love; these formed his taste, and corrected his judgment. He viewed the beauties of nature with poetical eyes, from thence he drew his landscapes; he had felt all the allurements of love, and from thence he describes the agitations of that passion.

Nor is the description of fairy bowers and palaces, though most favourite topics, peculiar to the romances of chivalry. The poetry of the orientals also abounds with them, yet, with some characteristic differences. Like the constitutions and dress of the Asiatics, the landscapes of the eastern muse are warm and feeble, brilliant and slight, and, like the manners of the people, wear an eternal sameness. The western muse, on the contrary, is nervous as her heroes, sometimes flowery as her Italian or English fields, sometimes majestically great as her Runic forests of oak and pine; and always various, as the character of her inhabitants. Yet, with all those differences of feature, several oriental fictions greatly resemble the island of Circe, and the flowery dominions of Alcina. In particular, the adventures of Prince Agib, or the third Calender, in the Arabian Tales, afford a striking likeness of painting and catastrophe.

If Ariosto's, however, seem to resemble any eastern fiction, the island of Venus in Camoëns bears a more striking resemblance to a passage in Chaucer. The following beautiful piece of poetical painting occurs in the Assembly of the Fowles:—

"The bildir oak, and eke the hardie ashe,

The pillir elme, the coffir unto caraine,

The boxe pipetre, the holme to whippis lasshe,

The sailing firre, the cypres deth to plaine,

The shortir ewe, the aspe for shaftis plaine,

The olive of pece, and eke the dronkin vine,

The victor palme, the laurir to divine.

A gardein sawe I full of blossomed bowis,

Upon a river, in a grené mede

There as sweetness evirmore inough is,

With flouris white, and blewe, yelowe, and rede,

And colde and clere wellestremis, nothing dede,

That swommin full of smale fishis light,

With finnis rede, and scalis silver bright.

On every bough the birdis herd I syng

With voice of angell, in ther harmonie

That busied 'hem, ther birdis forthe to bryng,

And little pretie conies to ther plaie gan hie;

And furthir all about I gan espie

The dredful roe, the buck, the hart and hind,

Squirils, and bestis smal of gentle kind.

Of instrumentes of stringis, in accorde

Herd I so plaie a ravishyng swetnesse,

That God, that makir is of all and Lorde,

Ne herd nevir a better, as I gesse,

There with a winde, unneth it might be lesse,

Made in the levis grene a noisé soft

Accordant to the foulis song en loft.

The aire of the place so attempre was,

That ner was there grevaunce of hot ne cold—

* * * * *

Under a tre beside a well I seye
Cupid our lorde his arrowes forge and file,
And at his fete his bowe all redie laye,
And well his doughtir temprid all the while
The heddis in the well, and with her wile
She couchid 'hem aftir as thei should serve,
Some for to flea, and some to wound and carve.

* * * * *

And upon pillirs grete of Jaspir long
I saw a temple of Brasse ifoundid strong.

And about the temple dauncid alwaie
Women inow, of which some there ywere
Faire of 'hemself, and some of 'hem were gaie,
In kirtils all disheveled went thei there,
That was ther office or from yere to yere,
And on the temple sawe I white and faire
Of dovis sittyng many a thousande paire."

Here we have Cupid forging his arrows, the woodland, the streams, the music of instruments and birds, the frolics of deer and other animals; and women enow. In a word, the island of Venus is here sketched out, yet Chaucer was never translated into Latin or any language of the continent, nor did Camoëns understand a line of English. The subject was common, and the same poetical feelings in Chaucer and Camoëns pointed out to each what were the beauties of landscapes and of bowers devoted to pleasure.

Yet, though the fiction of bowers, of islands, and palaces, was no novelty in poetry, much, however, remains to be attributed to the poetical powers and invention of Camoëns. The island of Venus contains, of all others, by much the completest gradation, and fullest assemblage of that species of luxuriant painting. Nothing in the older writers is equal to it in fulness. Nor can the island of Armida, in Tasso, be compared to it, in poetical embroidery or passionate expression; though Tasso as undoubtedly built upon the model of Camoëns, as Spenser appropriated the imagery of Tasso when he described the bower of Acrasia, part of which he has literally translated from the Italian poet. The beautiful fictions of Armida and Acrasia, however, are much too long to be here inserted, and they are well known to every reader of taste.

But the chief praise of our poet is yet unmentioned. The introduction of so beautiful a fiction as an essential part of the conduct and machinery of an epic poem, does the greatest honour to the invention of Camoëns. The machinery of the former part of the poem not only acquires dignity, but is completed by it. And the conduct of Homer and Virgil has, in this, not only received a fine imitation, but a masterly contrast. In the finest allegory the heroes of the Lusiad receive their reward: and, by means of this allegory, our poet gives a noble imitation of the noblest part of the Æneid. In the tenth Lusiad, Gama and his heroes hear the nymphs in the divine palace of Thetis sing the triumphs of their countrymen in the conquest of India: after this the goddess shows Gama a view of the eastern world, from the Cape of Good Hope to the furthest islands of Japan. She poetically describes every region, and the principal islands, and concludes, "All these are given to the western world by you." It is impossible any poem can be summed up with greater sublimity. The Fall of Troy is nothing to this. Nor is this all: the most masterly fiction, finest compliment, and ultimate purpose of the Æneid is not only nobly imitated, but the conduct of Homer, in concluding the Iliad, as already observed, is paralleled, without one circumstance being borrowed. Poetical conduct cannot possibly bear a stronger resemblance, than the reward of the heroes of the Lusiad, the prophetic song, and the vision shown to Gama bear to the games at the funeral of Patroclus and the redemption of the body of Hector, considered as the completion of the anger of Achilles, the subject of the Iliad. Nor is it a greater honour to resemble a Homer and a Virgil, than it is to be resembled by a Milton. Milton certainly heard of Fanshaw's translation of the Lusiad, though he might never have seen the original, for it was published fourteen years before he gave his Paradise Lost to the world. But, whatever he knew of it, had the last book of the Lusiad been two thousand years known to the learned, every one would have owned that the two last boots of the Paradise Lost were evidently formed upon it. But whether Milton borrowed any hint from Camoëns is of little consequence. That the genius of the great Milton suggested the conclusion of his immortal poem in the manner and with the machinery of the Lusiad, is enough. It is enough that the part of Michael and Adam in the two last books of the Paradise Lost are, in point of conduct, exactly the same with the part of Thetis and Gama in the conclusion of the Lusiad. Yet, this difference must be observed; in the narrative of his last book, Milton has flagged, as Addison calls it, and fallen infinitely short of the untired spirit of the Portuguese poet.

THE END.

LONDON:

PRINTED BY WILLIAM CLOWES AND SONS,

STAMFORD STREET

AND

CHARING CROSS.

FOOTNOTES.

[1] Poems of Luis de Camoëns, with Remarks on his Life and Writings. By Lord Viscount Strangford. Fifth edition. London, 1808.

[2] The Camaõ. Formerly every well-regulated family in Spain retained one of these terrible attendants. The infidelity of its mistress was the only circumstance which could deprive it of life. This odious distrust of female honour is ever characteristic of a barbarous age.

[3] The laws of Portugal were peculiarly severe against those who carried on a love-intrigue within the palace: they punished the offence with death. Joam I. suffered one of his favourites to be burnt alive for it.—Ed.

[4] The Maekhaun, or Camboja.—Ed.

[5] Thomas Moore Musgrave's translation of The Lusiad is in blank verse, and is dedicated to the Earl of Chichester. I vol. 8vo. Murray; 1826.

[6] A document in the archives of the Portuguese India House, on which Lord Strangford relies, places it in 1524, or the following year.—Ed.

[7] The French translator gives us so fine a description of the person of Camoëns, that it seems borrowed from the Fairy Tales. It is universally agreed, however, that he was handsome, and had a most engaging mien and address. He is thus described by Nicolas Antonio "Mediocri statura fuit, et carne plena, capillis usque ad croci colorem flavescentibus, maxime in juventute. Eminebat ei frons, et medius nasus, cætera longus, et in fine crassiusculus."

[8] Castera tells us, "that posterity by no means enters into the resentment of our poet, and that the Portuguese historians make glorious mention of Barreto, who was a man of true merit." The Portuguese historians, however,

401

knew not what true merit was. The brutal, uncommercial wars of Sampayo are by them mentioned as much more glorious than the less bloody campaigns of a Nunio, which established commerce and empire.

[9] Having named the Mecon, or Meekhaun, a river of Cochin China, he says—

Este recebera placido, e brando,

No seu regaço o Canto, que molhado, etc.

Literally thus: "On his gentle hospitable bosom (sic brando poeticé) shall he receive the song, wet from woful unhappy shipwreck, escaped from destroying tempests, from ravenous dangers, the effect of the unjust sentence upon him, whose lyre shall be more renowned than enriched." When Camoëns was commissary, he visited the islands of Ternate, Timor, etc., described in the Lusiad.

[10] According to the Portuguese Life of Camoëns, prefixed to Gedron's the best edition of his works, Diogo de Couto, the historian, one of the company in this homeward voyage, wrote annotations upon the Lusiad, under the eye of its author. But these, unhappily, have never appeared in public.

[11] Cardinal Henry's patronage of learning and learned men is mentioned with cordial esteem by the Portuguese writers. Happily they also tell us what that learning was. It was to him the Romish Friars of the East transmitted their childish forgeries of inscriptions and miracles. He corresponded with them, directed their labours, and received the first accounts of their success. Under his patronage it was discovered, that St. Thomas ordered the Indians to worship the cross; and that the Moorish tradition of Perimal (who, having embraced Mohammedanism, divided his kingdom among his officers, whom he rendered tributary to the Zamorim) was a malicious misrepresentation, for that Perimal, having turned Christian, resigned his kingdom and became a monk. Such was the learning patronized by Henry, under whose auspices that horrid tribunal, the Inquisition, was erected at Lisbon, where he himself long presided as Inquisitor-General. Nor was he content with this: he established an Inquisition, also, at Goa, and sent a whole apparatus of holy fathers to form a court of inquisitors, to suppress the Jews and reduce the native Christians to the see of Rome. Nor must the treatment experienced by Buchanan at Lisbon be here omitted. John III., earnest to promote the cultivation of polite literature among his subjects, engaged Buchanan, the most elegant Latinist, perhaps, of modern times, to teach philosophy and the belles lettres at Lisbon. But the design of the monarch was soon frustrated by the clergy, at the head of whom was Henry, afterwards king. Buchanan was committed to prison, because it was alleged that he had eaten flesh in Lent,

and because in his early youth, at St. Andrew's in Scotland, he had written a satire against the Franciscans; for which, however, ere he would venture to Lisbon, John had promised absolute indemnity. John, with much difficulty, procured his release from a loathsome jail, but could not effect his restoration as a teacher. No, he only changed his prison, for Buchanan was sent to a monastery "to be instructed by the monks," of the men of letters patronized by Henry. These are thus characterized by their pupil Buchanan,—nec inhumanis, nec malis, sed omnis religionis ignaris: "Not uncivilized, not flagitious, but ignorant of every religion."

[12] According to Gedron, a second edition of the Lusiad appeared in the same year with the first. There are two Italian and four Spanish translations of it. A hundred years before Castera's version it appeared in French. Thomas de Faria, Bp. of Targa in Africa, translated it into Latin. Le P. Niceron says there were two other Latin translations. It is translated, also, into Hebrew, with great elegance and spirit, by one Luzzatto, a learned and ingenious Jew, author of several poems in that language, who died in the Holy Land.

[13] This passage in inverted commas is cited, with the alteration of the name only, from Langhorne's account of the life of William Collins.

[14] The drama and the epopœia are in nothing so different as in this—the subjects of the drama are inexhaustible, those of the epopœia are perhaps exhausted. He who chooses war, and warlike characters, cannot appear as an original. It was well for the memory of Pope that he did not write the epic poem he intended. It would have been only a copy of Virgil. Camoëns and Milton have been happy in the novelty of their subjects, and these they have exhausted. There cannot possibly be so important a voyage as that which gave the eastern world to the western. And, did even the story of Columbus afford materials equal to that of Gama, the adventures of the hero, and the view of the extent of his discoveries must now appear as servile copies of the Lusiad.

[15] See his Satyricon.—Ed.

[16] See letters on Chivalry and Romance.

[17] The Lusiad is also rendered poetical by other fictions. The elegant satire on King Sebastian, under the name of Acteon; and the prosopopœia of the populace of Portugal venting their murmurs upon the beach when Gama sets sail, display the richness of our author's poetical genius, and are not inferior to anything of the kind in the classics.

[18] Hence the great interest which we as Britons either do, or ought to, feel in this noble epic. We are the successors of the Portuguese in the possession and government of India; and therefore what interested them must have for us, as the actual possessors, a double interest.—Ed.

[19] Castera was every way unequal to his task. He did not perceive his author's beauties. He either suppresses or lowers the most poetical passages, and substitutes French tinsel and impertinence in their place.

[20] Pope, Odyss. XX.

[21] Richard Fanshaw, Esq., afterwards Sir Richard, was English Ambassador both at Madrid and Lisbon. He had a taste for literature, and translated from the Italian several pieces which were of service in the refinement of our poetry. Though his Lusiad, by the dedication of it to William, Earl of Strafford, dated May 1, 1655, seems as if published by himself, we are told by the editor of his Letters, that "during the unsettled times of our anarchy, some of his MSS., falling by misfortune into unskilful hands, were printed and published without his knowledge or consent, and before he could give them his last finishing strokes: such was his translation of the Lusiad." He can never have enough of conceits, low allusions, and expressions. When gathering of flowers is simply mentioned (C. 9, st. 24) he gives it, "gather'd flowers by pecks;" and the Indian Regent is avaricious (C. 8, st. 95)—

Meaning a better penny thence to get.

But enough of these have already appeared in the notes. It may be necessary to add, that the version of Fanshaw, though the Lusiad very particularly requires them, was given to the public without one note.

[22] Some liberties of a less poetical kind, however, require to be mentioned. In Homer and Virgil's lists of slain warriors, Dryden and Pope have omitted several names which would have rendered English versification dull and tiresome. Several allusions to ancient history and fable have for this reason been abridged; e.g. in the prayer of Gama (Book 6) the mention of Paul, "thou who deliveredst Paul and defendest him from quicksands and wild waves—

Das scyrtes arenosas e ondas feas—"

is omitted. However excellent in the original, the prayer in English would lose both its dignity and ardour. Nor let the critic, if he find the meaning of Camoëns in some instances altered, imagine that he has found a blunder in the translator. He who chooses to see a slight alteration of this kind will find an instance, which will give him an idea of others, in Canto 8, st. 48, and another in Canto 7, st. 41. It was not to gratify the dull few, whose greatest pleasure in reading a translation is to see what the author exactly says; it was to give a poem that might live in the English language, which was the ambition of the translator. And, for the same reason, he has not confined himself to the Portuguese or Spanish pronunciation of proper names. Regardless, therefore, of Spanish pronunciation, the translator has accented Granáda, Evóra, etc. in the manner which seemed to him to give most dignity to English versification. In the word Sofala he has even rejected the authority of Milton, and followed the more sonorous usage of Fanshaw. Thus Sir Richard: "Against Sofála's batter'd fort." Which is the more sonorous there can be no dispute.

[23] Judges xviii. 7, 9, 27, 28.

[24] This ferocity of savage manners affords a philosophical account how the most distant and inhospitable climes were first peopled. When a Romulus erects a monarchy and makes war on his neighbours, some naturally fly to the wilds. As their families increase, the stronger commit depredations on the weaker; and thus from generation to generation, they who either dread just punishment or unjust oppression, fly farther and farther in search of that protection which is only to be found in civilized society.

[25] The author of that voluminous work, Histoire Philosophique et Politique des Etablissements et du Commerce des Européens dans les deux Indes, is one of the many who assert that savage life is happier than civil. His reasons are thus abridged: The savage has no care or fear for the future; his hunting and fishing give him a certain subsistence. He sleeps sound, and knows not the diseases of cities. He cannot want what he does not desire, nor desire that which he does not know, and vexation or grief do not enter his soul. He is not under the control of a superior in his actions; in a word, says our author, the savage only suffers the evils of nature.

If the civilized, he adds, enjoy the elegancies of life, have better food, and are more comfortably defended against the change of seasons, it is use which makes these things necessary, and they are purchased by the painful labours of the multitude who are the basis of society. To what outrages is not the man of civil life exposed? if he has property, it is in danger; and government or authority is, according to our author, the greatest of all evils. If there is a famine in North America, the savage, led by the wind and the sun, can go to a better clime; but in the horrors of famine, war, or pestilence, the ports and barriers of civilized states place the subjects in a prison, where they must perish. There still remains an infinite difference between the lot of the civilized and the savage; a difference, all entirely to the disadvantage of society, that injustice which reigns in the inequality of fortunes and conditions.

[26] The innocent simplicity of the Americans in their conferences with the Spaniards, and the horrid cruelties they suffered from them, divert our view from their complete character. Almost everything was horrid in their civil customs and religious rites. In some tribes, to cohabit with their mothers,

sisters, and daughters was esteemed the means of domestic peace. In others, catamites were maintained in every village; they went from house to house as they pleased, and it was unlawful to refuse them what victuals they chose. In every tribe, the captives taken in war were murdered with the most wanton cruelty, and afterwards devoured by the victors. Their religious rites were, if possible, still more horrid. The abominations of ancient Moloch were here outnumbered; children, virgins, slaves, and captives bled on different altars, to appease their various gods. If there was a scarcity of human victims, the priests announced that the gods were dying of thirst for human blood. And, to prevent a threatened famine, the kings of Mexico were obliged to make war on the neighbouring states. The prisoners of either side died by the hand of the priest. But the number of the Mexican sacrifices so greatly exceeded those of other nations, that the Tlascalans, who were hunted down for this purpose, readily joined Cortez with about 200,000 men, and enabled him to make one great sacrifice of the Mexican nation. Who that views Mexico, steeped in her own blood, can restrain the emotion which whispers to him, This is the hand of Heaven!—By the number of these sacred butcheries, one would think that cruelty was the greatest amusement of Mexico. At the dedication of the temple of Vitzliputzli, A.D. 1486, no less than 64,080 human victims were sacrificed in four days. And, according to the best accounts, the annual sacrifices of Mexico required several thousands. The skulls of the victims sometimes were hung on strings which reached from tree to tree around their temples, and sometimes were built up in towers and cemented with lime. In some of these towers Andrew de Tapia one day counted 136,000 skulls. During the war with Cortez they increased their usual sacrifices, till priest and people were tired of their bloody religion.—See, for ample justification of these statements, the Histories of the Conquest of Mexico and Peru, by Prescott.—Ed.

[27] Mahommed Ali Khan, Nawab of the Carnatic, declared, "I met the British with that freedom of openness which they love, and I esteem it my honour as well as security to be the ally of such a nation of princes."

[28] Every man must follow his father's trade, and must marry a daughter of the same occupation. Innumerable are their other barbarous restrictions of genius and inclination.

[29] Extremity; for it were both highly unjust and impolitic in government to allow importation in such a degree as might be destructive of domestic agriculture.

[30] Even that warm admirer of savage happiness, the author of Histoire Philosophique et Politique des Etablissements, confesses that the wild Americans seem destitute of the feeling of love. When the heat of passion, says he, is gratified, they lose all affection and attachment for their women,

whom they degrade to the most servile offices.—A tender remembrance of the first endearments, a generous participation of care and hope, the compassionate sentiments of honour; all these delicate feelings, which arise into affection, and bind attachment, are indeed, incompatible with the ferocious and gross sensations of barbarians.

[31] It is a question still debated among medical writers, and by no means yet decided, whether the disease referred to is of American origin. We do not read, it is true, of any such disease in the pages of the ancient classic writers; it has hence been inferred that it was unknown to them.—Ed.

[32] The degeneracy of the Roman literature preceded the fate of the state, and the reason is obvious. The men of fortune grew frivolous, and superficial in every branch of knowledge, and were therefore unable to hold the reigns of empire. The degeneracy of literary taste is, therefore, the surest proof of the general ignorance.

[33] The soldiers and navigators were the only considerable gainers by their acquirements in the Indies. Agriculture and manufactures are the natural strength of a nation; these received little or no increase in Spain and Portugal by the great acquisitions of these crowns.

[34] Ariosto, who adopted the legends of the old romance, chose this period for the subject of his Orlando Furioso. Paris besieged by the Saracens, Orlando and the other Christian knights assemble in aid of Charlemagne, who are opposed in their amours and in battle by Rodomont, Ferraw, and other Saracen knights. That there was a noted Moorish Spaniard, named Ferraw, a redoubted champion of that age, we have the testimony of Marcus Antonius Sabellicus, a writer of note of the fifteenth century.

[35] Small indeed in extent, but so rich in fertility, that it was called Medulla Hispanica, "The marrow of Spain."—Vid. Resandii Antiq. Lusit. l. iii.

[36] In propriety most certainly a crusade, though that term has never before been applied to this war.

[37] The power of deposing, and of electing their kings, under certain circumstances, is vested in the people by the statutes of Lamego.

[38] For the character of this prince, see the note, Bk. iii. p. 96.

[39] For anecdotes of this monarch, see the notes, Bk. iii. p. 99.

[40] This great prince was the natural son of Pedro the Just. Some years after the murder of his beloved spouse, Inez de Castro (see Lusiad, Bk. iii. p. 96), lest his father, whose severe temper he too well knew, should force him into a disagreeable marriage, Don Pedro commenced an amour with a Galician lady, who became the mother of John I., the preserver of the Portuguese

monarchy.

[41] The sons of John, who figure in history, were Edward, Juan, Fernando, Pedro and Henry. Edward succeeded his father. Juan, distinguished both in the camp and cabinet, in the reign of his brother Edward had the honour to oppose the expedition against Tangier, which was proposed by his brother Fernando, in whose perpetual captivity it ended.

[42] The dominion of the Portuguese in the Indian seas cut the sinews of the Egyptian and other Mohammedan powers.

[43] Flanders has been the school-mistress of husbandry to Europe. Sir Charles Lisle, a royalist, resided in this country several years during the Commonwealth; and after the Restoration, rendered England the greatest service, by introducing the present system of agriculture. Where trade increases, men's thoughts are set in action; hence the increase of food which is wanted is supplied by a redoubled attention to husbandry; and hence it was that agriculture was of old improved and diffused by the Phœnician colonies.

[44] At the reduction of Ceuta in Africa, and in other engagements, Prince Henry displayed military genius and valour of the first magnitude. The important fortress of Ceuta was in a manner won by his own sword.

[45] Nam, in Portuguese, a negative. It is now called by corruption Cape Nun.

[46] Cape Bojador, from the Spanish, bojar, to compass or go about.

[47] Unluckily, he also left on this island two rabbits, whose young so increased that in a few years it was found not habitable, every vegetable being destroyed by the great increase of these animals.

[48] Madeira in Portuguese signifies timber.—Ed.

[49] If one would trace the true character of Cortez and the Americans, he must have recourse to the numerous Spanish writers, who were either witnesses of the first wars, or soon after travelled in these countries. [The reader cannot do better than refer to Prescott's History of the Conquest of Mexico and Peru for information on these points.—Ed.] In these he will find many anecdotes which afford a light not to be found in our modern histories. Cortez set out to take gold by force, and not by establishing any system of commerce with the natives, the only just reason for effecting a settlement in a foreign country. He was asked by various states, what commodities or drugs he wanted, and was promised abundant supply. He and his Spaniards, he answered, had a disease at their hearts, which nothing but gold could cure; and he received intelligence that Mexico abounded with it. Under pretence of a friendly conference, he made the Mexican emperor, Montezuma, his prisoner, and ordered him to pay tribute to Charles V. Immense sums were paid, but the demand was boundless. Tumults ensued. Cortez displayed

amazing generalship, and some millions of those who boasted of the greatness of Montezuma were sacrificed to the disease of Cortez's heart. Pizarro, however, in the barbarity of his character, far exceeded him. There is a bright side to the character of Cortez, if we can forget that his avarice was the cause of a most unjust and most bloody war; but Pizarro is a character completely detestable, destitute of every spark of generosity. He massacred the Peruvians because they were barbarians, and he himself could not read. Atabalipa, the Peruvian Inca, amazed at the art of reading, got a Spaniard to write the word Dios (God) on his finger. On trying if the Spaniards agreed in what it signified, he discovered that Pizarro could not read. And Pizarro, in revenge of the contempt he perceived in the face of Atabalipa, ordered that prince to be tried for his life, for having concubines, and being an idolater. Atabalipa was condemned to be burned; but on submitting to baptism, he was only hanged. See Prescott's Conquest of Peru.

[50] The difficulties he surmounted, and the assistance he received, are sufficient proofs that an adventurer of inferior birth could never have carried his designs into execution.

[51] Don Pedro was villainously accused of treacherous designs by his illegitimate brother, the first Duke of Braganza. Henry left his town of Sagrez to defend his brother at court, but in vain. Pedro, finding the young king in the power of Braganza, fled, and soon after was killed in defending himself against a party who were sent to seize him. His innocence, after his death, was fully proved, and his nephew, Alonzo V., gave him an honourable burial.

[52] Henry, who undertook to extend the boundaries which ignorance had given to the world, had extended them much beyond the sensible horizon long ere Columbus appeared. Columbus indeed taught the Spaniards the use of longitude and latitude in navigation, but that great mathematician, Henry, was the author of that grand discovery, and of the use of the compass. Every alteration ascribed to Columbus, had almost fifty years before been effected by Henry. Even Henry's idea of sailing to India was adopted by Columbus. It was everywhere his proposal. When he arrived in the West Indies he thought he had found the Ophir of Solomon, and thence these islands received their general name, and on his return he told John II. that he had been at the islands of India. To find the Spice Islands of the East was his proposal at the court of Spain; and even on his fourth and last voyage in 1502, three years after Gama's return, he promised the King of Spain to find India by a westward passage. But though great discoveries rewarded his toils, his first and last purpose he never completed. It was reserved for Magalhaens to discover the westward route to the Eastern world.

Gomara and other Spanish writers relate, that while Columbus lived in Madeira, a pilot, the only survivor of a ship's crew, died at his house. This pilot, they say, had been driven to the West Indies, or America, by tempest, and on his death-bed communicated the journal of his voyage to Columbus.

[53] Or Bethlehem, so named from the chapel.

[54] Now called St. Helen's.

[55] The voyage of Gama has been called merely a coasting one, and therefore regarded as much less dangerous and heroical than that of Columbus, or of Magalhaens. But this is one of the opinions hastily taken up, and founded on ignorance. Columbus and Magalhaens undertook to navigate unknown oceans, and so did Gama; with this difference, that the ocean around the Cape of Good Hope, which Gama was to encounter, was believed to be, and had been avoided by Diaz, as impassable. Prince Henry suggested that the current of Cape Bojador might be avoided by standing out to sea, and thus that Cape was first passed. Gama for this reason did not coast, but stood out to sea for upwards of three months of tempestuous weather. The tempests which afflicted Columbus and Magalhaens are by their different historians described with circumstances of less horror and danger than those which attacked Gama. All the three commanders were endangered by mutiny; but none of their crews, save Gama's, could urge the opinion of ages, and the example of a living captain, that the dreadful ocean which they attempted was impassable. Columbus and Magalhaens always found means, after detecting a conspiracy, to keep the rest in hope; but Gama's men, when he put the pilots in irons, continued in the utmost despair. Columbus was indeed ill obeyed; Magalhaens sometimes little better; but nothing, save the wonderful authority of Gama's command, could have led his crew through the tempest which he surmounted ere he doubled the Cape of Good Hope. Columbus, with his crew, must have returned. The expedients which he used to soothe them, would, under his authority, have had no avail in the tempest which Gama rode through. From every circumstance it is evident that Gama had determined not to return, unless he found India. Nothing less than such resolution to perish or attain his point could have led him on.

[56] It afterwards appeared that the Moorish King of Mombas had been informed of what happened at Mozambique, and intended to revenge it by the total destruction of the fleet.

[57] Amerigo Vespucci, describing his voyage to America, says, "Having passed the line, e come desideroso d'essere autore che segnassi la stella— desirous to be the namer and discoverer of the Pole-star of the other hemisphere, I lost my sleep many nights in contemplating the stars of the other pole." He then laments, that as his instruments could not discover any star of less motion then ten degrees, he had not the satisfaction of giving a name to any one. But as he observed four stars, in form of an almond, which had but little motion, he hoped in his next voyage he should be able to mark

them out.—All this is curious, and affords a good comment on the temper of the man who had the art to defraud Columbus, by giving his own name to America; of which he challenged the discovery. Near fifty years before the voyage of Amerigo Vespucci, the Portuguese had crossed the line; and Diaz fourteen, and Gama nearly three years before, had doubled the Cape of Good Hope; had discovered seven stars in the constellation of the south pole, and from the appearance of the four most luminous, had given it the name of "The Cross," a figure which it better resembles than that of an almond.

[58] Properly "Samudra-Rajah," King of the Sea, corrupted into Zamorim.— Ed.

[59] "Kotwâl" signifies Superintendent of the Police.—Ed.

[60] Faria y Sousa.

[61] It was the custom of the first discoverers to erect crosses at various places remarkable in their voyage. Gama erected six: one, dedicated to St. Raphael, at the river of Good Signs; one to St. George, at Mozambique; one to St. Stephen, at Melinda; one to St. Gabriel, at Calicut; and one to St. Mary, at the island thence named, near Anchediva.

[62] The Lusiad; in the original, Os Lusiadas, The Lusiads, from the Latin name (Lusitania) of Portugal, derived from Lusus or Lysas, the companion of Bacchus in his travels, who settled a colony in Lusitania, See Plin. 1, iii. c. i.

[63] Thro' seas where sail was never spread before.—M. Duperron de Castera, who has given a French prose translation, or rather paraphrase, of the Lusiad, has a long note on this passage, which, he tells us, must not be understood literally. Our author, he says, could not be ignorant that the African and Indian Oceans had been navigated before the times of the Portuguese. The Phœnicians, whose fleets passed the straits of Gibraltar, made frequent voyages in these seas, though they carefully concealed the course of their navigation that other nations might not become partakers of their lucrative traffic.—See the Periplus of Hanno, in Cory's Ancient Fragments.—Ed.

[64] And all my country's wars.—He interweaves artfully the history of Portugal.—Voltaire.

[65] To Holy Faith unnumber'd altars rear'd.—In no period of history does human nature appear with more shocking, more diabolical features than in the wars of Cortez, and the Spanish conquerors of South America. Zeal for the Christian religion was esteemed, at the time of the Portuguese grandeur, as the most cardinal virtue, and to propagate Christianity and extirpate Mohammedanism were the most certain proofs of that zeal. In all their expeditions this was professedly a principal motive of the Lusitanian

monarchs, and Camoëns understood the nature of epic poetry too well to omit it.

[66] Ulysses, who is the subject of the Odyssey.

[67] The voyage of Æneas, described in the Æneid of Virgil.

[68] Alexander the Great, who claimed to be the son of Jupiter Ammon.

[69] Vasco de Gama is, in a great measure, though not exclusively, the hero of the Lusiad.

[70] King Sebastian, who came to the throne in his minority. Though the warm imagination of Camoëns anticipated the praises of the future hero, the young monarch, like Virgil's Pollio, had not the happiness to fulfil the prophecy. His endowments and enterprising genius promised, indeed, a glorious reign. Ambitious of military laurels, he led a powerful army into Africa, on purpose to replace Muley Hamet on the throne of Morocco, from which he had been deposed by Muley Molucco. On the 4th of August, 1578, in the twenty-fifth year of his age, he gave battle to the usurper on the plains of Alcazar. This was that memorable engagement, to which the Moorish Emperor, extremely weakened by sickness, was carried in his litter. By the impetuosity of the attack, the first line of the Moorish infantry was broken, and the second disordered. Muley Molucco on this mounted his horse, drew his sabre, and would have put himself at the head of his troops, but was prevented by his attendants. His emotion of mind was so great that he fell from his horse, and one of his guards having caught him in his arms, conveyed him to his litter, where, putting his finger on his lips to enjoin them silence, he immediately expired. Hamet Taba stood by the curtains of the carriage, opened them from time to time, and gave out orders as if he had received them from the Emperor. Victory declared for the Moors, and the defeat of the Portuguese was so total, that not above fifty of their whole army escaped. Hieron de Mendoça and Sebastian de Mesa relate, that Don Sebastian, after having two horses killed under him, was surrounded and taken; but the party who had secured him, quarrelling among themselves whose prisoner he was, a Moorish officer rode up and struck the king a blow over the right eye, which brought him to the ground; when, despairing of ransom, the others killed him. About twenty years after this fatal defeat there appeared a stranger at Venice, who called himself Sebastian, King of Portugal, whom he so perfectly resembled, that the Portuguese of that city acknowledged him for their sovereign. He underwent twenty-eight examinations before a committee of the nobles, in which he gave a distinct account of the manner in which he had passed his time from the fatal defeat at Alcazar. It was objected, that the successor of Muley Molucco sent a corpse to Portugal which had been owned as that of the king by the Portuguese nobility who survived the battle. To this he replied, that his valet

de chambre had produced that body to facilitate his escape, and that the nobility acted upon the same motive, and Mesa and Baena confess, that some of this nobility, after their return to Portugal acknowledged that the corpse was so disfigured with wounds that it was impossible to know it. He showed natural marks on his body, which many remembered on the person of the king whose name he assumed. He entered into a minute detail of the transactions that had passed between himself and the republic, and mentioned the secrets of several conversations with the Venetian ambassadors in the palace of Lisbon. He fell into the hands of the Spaniards, who conducted him to Naples, where they treated him with the most barbarous indignities. After they had often exposed him, mounted on an ass, to the cruel insults of the brutal mob, he was shipped on board a galley, as a slave. He was then carried to St. Lucar, from thence to a castle in the heart of Castile, and never was heard of more. The firmness of his behaviour, his singular modesty and heroical patience, are mentioned with admiration by Le Clede. To the last he maintained the truth of his assertions: a word never slipped from his lips which might countenance the charge of imposture, or justify the cruelty of his persecutors.

[71] Portugal, when Camoëns wrote his Lusiad, was at the zenith of its power and splendour. The glorious successes which had attended the arms of the Portuguese in Africa, had gained them the highest military reputation. Their fleets covered the ocean. Their dominions and settlements extended along the western and eastern sides of the vast African continent. From the Red Sea to China and Japan, they were sole masters of the riches of the East; and in America, the fertile and extensive regions of Brazil completed their empire.

[72] Lusitania is the Latin name of a Roman province which comprised the greater part of the modern kingdom of Portugal, besides a considerable portion of Leon and Spanish Estremadura.—Ed.

[73] The sun.—Imitated, perhaps, from Rutilius, speaking of the Roman Empire—

Volvitur ipse tibi, qui conspicit omnia, Phœbus,

Atque tuis ortos in tua condit equos;

or, more probably, from these lines of Buchanan, addressed to John III. King of Portugal, the grandfather of Sebastian—

Inque tuis Phœbus regnis oriensque cadensque

Vix longum fesso conderet axe diem.

Et quæcunque vago se circumvolvit Olympo

Affulget ratibus flamma ministra tuis.

[74] i.e. poetic. Aonia was the ancient name of Bœotia, in which country was a fountain sacred to the Muses, whence Juvenal sings of a poet—

"Enamoured of the woods, and fitted for drinking

At the fountains of the Aonides."

Juv. Sat. vii. 58.—Ed.

[75] To match the Twelve so long by bards renown'd.—The Twelve Peers of France, often mentioned in the old romances. For the episode of Magricio and his eleven companions, see the sixth Lusiad.

[76] Afonso in Portuguese. In the first edition Mickle had Alfonso, which he altered to Alonzo in the second edition.

[77] Thy grandsires.—John III. King of Portugal, celebrated for a long and peaceful reign; and the Emperor Charles V., who was engaged in almost continual wars.

[78] Some critics have condemned Virgil for stopping his narrative to introduce even a short observation of his own. Milton's beautiful complaint of his blindness has been blamed for the same reason, as being no part of the subject of his poem. The address of Camoëns to Don Sebastian at the conclusion of the tenth Lusiad has not escaped the same censure; though in some measure undeservedly, as the poet has had the art to interweave therein some part of the general argument of his poem.

[79] This brave Lusitanian, who was first a shepherd and a famous hunter, and afterwards a captain of banditti, exasperated at the tyranny of the Romans, encouraged his countrymen to revolt and shake off the yoke. Being appointed general, he defeated Vetilius the prætor, who commanded in Lusitania, or farther Spain. After this he defeated, in three pitched battles, the prætors, C. Plautius Hypsæus and Claudius Unimanus, though they led against him very numerous armies. For six years he continued victorious, putting the Romans to flight wherever he met them, and laying waste the countries of their allies. Having obtained such advantages over the proconsul, Servilianus, that the only choice which was left to the Roman army was death or slavery, the brave Viriatus, instead of putting them all to the sword, as he could easily have done, sent a deputation to the general, offering to conclude a peace with him on this single condition, That he should continue master of

the country now in his power, and that the Romans should remain possessed of the rest of Spain.

The proconsul, who expected nothing but death or slavery, thought these very favourable and moderate terms, and without hesitation concluded a peace, which was soon after ratified by the Roman senate and people. Viriatus, by this treaty, completed the glorious design he had always in view, which was to erect a kingdom in the vast country he had conquered from the republic. And, had it not been for the treachery of the Romans, he would have become, as Florus calls him, the Romulus of Spain.

The senate, desirous to revenge their late defeat, soon after this peace, ordered Q. Servilius Cæpio to exasperate Viriatus, and force him, by repeated affronts, to commit the first acts of hostility. But this mean artifice did not succeed: Viriatus would not be provoked to a breach of the peace. On this the Conscript Fathers, to the eternal disgrace of their republic, ordered Cæpio to declare war, and to proclaim Viriatus, who had given no provocation, an enemy to Rome. To this baseness Cæpio added one still greater; he corrupted the ambassadors whom Viriatus had sent to negotiate with him, who, at the instigation of the Roman, treacherously murdered their protector and general while he slept.—Univ. History.

[80] Sertorius, who was invited by the Lusitanians to defend them against the Romans. He had a tame white hind, which he had accustomed to follow him, and from which he pretended to receive the instructions of Diana. By this artifice he imposed upon the superstition of that people.

[81] No more in Nysa.—An ancient city in India sacred to Bacchus.

[82] Urania-Venus.—An Italian poet has given the following description of the celestial Venus—

Questa è vaga di Dio Venere bella

Vicina al Sole, e sopra ogni altra estella

Questa è quella beata, a cui s'inchina,

A cui si volge desiando amore,

Chiamata cui del Ciel rara e divina

Beltà che vien tra noi per nostro honore,

Per far le menti desiando al Cielo

Obliare l'altrui col proprio velo.—Martel.

[83] See the note in the Second Book on the following passage—

415

As when in Ida's bower she stood of yore, etc.

[84] The manly music of their tongue the same.—Camoëns says:

E na lingoa, na qual quando imagina,

Com pouca corrupçao cré que he Latina.

Qualifications are never elegant in poetry. Fanshaw's translation and the original both prove this:

——their tongue

Which she thinks Latin, with small dross among.

[85] i.e. helmet.

[86]—— and the light turn'd pale.—The thought in the original has something in it wildly great, though it is not expressed in the happiest manner of Camoëns—

O ceo tremeo, e Apollo detorvado

Hum pauco a luz perdeo, como infiado.

[87] Mercury, the messenger of the gods.—Ed.

[88] And pastoral Madagascar.—Called by the ancient geographers, Menuthia and Cerna Ethiopica; by the natives, the Island of the Moon; and by the Portuguese, the Isle of St. Laurence, on whose festival they discovered it.

[89] Praso.—Name of a promontory near the Red Sea.—Ed.

[90] Lav'd by the gentle waves.—The original says, the sea showed them new islands, which it encircled and laved. Thus rendered by Fanshaw—

Neptune disclos'd new isles which he did play

About, and with his billows danc't the hay.

[91] The historical foundation of the fable of Phaeton is this. Phaeton was a young enterprising prince of Libya. Crossing the Mediterranean in quest of adventures, he landed at Epirus, from whence he went to Italy to see his intimate friend Cygnus. Phaeton was skilled in astrology, from whence he

arrogated to himself the title of the son of Apollo. One day in the heat of summer, as he was riding along the banks of the Po, his horses took fright at a clap of thunder, and plunged into the river, where, together with their master, they perished. Cygnus, who was a poet, celebrated the death of his friend in verse, from whence the fable.—Vid. Plutarch, in Vit. Pyrr.

[92] Acheron.—The river of Hades, or hell.—Ed.

[93] From Abram's race our holy prophet sprung.—Mohammed, who was descended from Ishmael, the son of Abraham by Hagar.

[94] The Hydaspes was a tributary of the river Indus.—Ed.

[95] Calm twilight now.—Camoëns, in this passage, has imitated Homer in the manner of Virgil: by diversifying the scene he has made the description his own. The passage alluded to is in the eighth Iliad—

Ὡς δ᾽ ὅτ᾽ ἐν οὐρανω ἄστρα φαεινὴν ἀμφὶ σελὴνην Φαίνετ᾽ αριπρεπέα, etc.

Thus elegantly translated by Pope:—

As when the moon, refulgent lamp of night,

O'er heaven's clear azure spreads her sacred light,

When not a breath disturbs the deep serene,

And not a cloud o'ercasts the solemn scene;

Around her throne the vivid planets roll,

And stars unnumber'd gild the glowing pole,

O'er the dark trees a yellower verdure shed,

And tip with silver every mountain's head;

Then shine the vales, the rocks in prospect rise,

A flood of glory bursts from all the skies:

The conscious swains, rejoicing in the sight,

Eye the blue vault, and bless the useful light.

[96] The Turks, or Osmanli Turcomans.—Ed.

[97] Constantinople.

[98] Straight as he spoke.—The description of the armoury, and account

417

which Vasco de Gama gives of his religion, consists, in the original, of thirty-two lines, which M. Castera has reduced into the following sentence: Leur Governeur fait differentes questions au Capitaine, qui pour le satisfaire lui explique en peu des mots la Religion que les Portugais suivent, l'usage des armes dont ils se servent dans la guerre, et le dessein qui les amène.

[99] i.e., helmets.

[100] Coats of mail.

[101] When Gama's lips Messiah's name confess'd.—This, and the reason of the Moor's hate, is entirely omitted by Castera. The original is, the Moor conceived hatred, "knowing they were followers of the truth which the Son of David taught." Thus rendered by Fanshaw:—

Knowing they follow that unerring light,

The Son of David holds out in his Book.

Zacocia (governor of Mozambique) made no doubt but our people were of some Mohammedan country. The mutual exchange of good offices between our people and these islanders promised a long continuance of friendship, but it proved otherwise. No sooner did Zacocia understand they were Christians, than all his kindness was turned into the most bitter hatred; he began to meditate their ruin, and sought to destroy the fleet.—Osorio, Bp. of Sylves, Hist. of the Portug. Discov.

[102] Bacchus, god of wine.

[103] Whom nine long months his father's thigh conceal'd.—Bacchus was nourished during his infancy in a cave of mount Meros, which in Greek signifies a thigh. Hence the fable.

[104] Alexander the Great, who on visiting the temple of Jupiter Ammon, was hailed as son of that deity by his priests.—Ed.

[105] Bacchus.

[106] His form divine he cloth'd in human shape—

Alecto torvam faciem et furialia membra

Exuit: in vultus sese transformat aniles,

Et frontem obscænum rugis arat.

Vir. Æn. vii.

[107] To be identified with the Sun, in the opinion of later mythologists; but not so in Homer, with whom Helios (the Sun) is himself a deity.—Ed.

[108]

Thus, when to gain his beauteous charmer's smile,

The youthful lover dares the bloody toil.

This simile is taken from a favourite exercise in Spain, where it is usual to see young gentlemen of the best families entering the lists to fight with a bull, adorned with ribbons, and armed with a javelin or kind of cutlass, which the Spaniards call Machete.

[109]

——————————e maldizia

O velho inerte, e a mãy, que o filho cria.

Thus translated by Fanshaw—

——————————curst their ill luck,

Th' old Devil and the Dam that gave them suck.

[110]

Flints, clods, and javelins hurling as they fly,

As rage, &c.—

Jamque faces et saxa volant, furor arma ministrat.

Virg. Æn. i.

The Spanish commentator on this place relates a very extraordinary instance of the furor arma ministrans. A Portuguese soldier at the siege of Diu in the Indies, being surrounded by the enemy, and having no ball to charge his musket, pulled out one of his teeth, and with it supplied the place of a bullet.

[111] The italics indicate that there is nothing in the original corresponding to these lines.—Ed.

[112] See Virgil's Æneid, bk. ii.—Ed.

[113] Quiloa is an island, with a town of the same name, on the east coast of Africa.—Ed.

[114] But heavenly Love's fair queen.—When Gama arrived in the East, the Moors were the only people who engrossed the trade of those parts. Jealous of such formidable rivals as the Portuguese, they employed every artifice to accomplish the destruction of Gama's fleet. As the Moors were acquainted with these seas and spoke the Arabic language, Gama was obliged to employ them both as pilots and interpreters. The circumstance now mentioned by Camoëns is an historical fact. "The Moorish pilot," says De Barros, "intended to conduct the Portuguese into Quiloa, telling them that place was inhabited by Christians; but a sudden storm arising, drove the fleet from that shore, where death or slavery would have been the certain fate of Gama and his companions. The villainy of the pilot was afterwards discovered. As Gama was endeavouring to enter the port of Mombaz his ship struck on a sand-bank, and finding their purpose of bringing him into the harbour defeated, two of the Moorish pilots leaped into the sea and swam ashore. Alarmed at this tacit acknowledgment of guilt, Gama ordered two other Moorish pilots who remained on board to be examined by whipping, who, after some time, made a full confession of their intended villainy. This discovery greatly encouraged Gama and his men, who now interpreted the sudden storm which had driven them from Quiloa as a miraculous interposition of Divine Providence in their favour.

[115] i.e. Mohammed.—Ed.

[116] After Gama had been driven from Quiloa by a sudden storm, the assurances of the Mozambique pilot, that the city was chiefly inhabited by Christians, strongly inclined him to enter the harbour of Mombas.

[117] "There were," says Osorius, "ten men in the fleet under sentence of death, whose lives had been spared on condition that, wherever they might be landed, they should explore the country and make themselves acquainted with the manners and laws of the people."

During the reign of Emmanuel, and his predecessor John II., few criminals were executed in Portugal. These great and political princes employed the lives which were forfeited to the public in the most dangerous undertakings of public utility. In their foreign expeditions the condemned criminals were sent upon the most hazardous undertakings. If death was their fate, it was the punishment they had merited: if successful in what was required, their crimes were expiated; and often they rendered their country the greatest atonement for their guilt which men in their circumstances could possibly make. What multitudes every year, in the prime of their life, end their days in Great Britain by the hands of the executioner! That the legislature might devise means to make the greatest part of these lives useful to society is a fact, which surely cannot be disputed; though, perhaps, the remedy of an evil so shocking to humanity may be at some distance.

[118] Semele was the mother of Bacchus, but, as he was prematurely born, Jupiter, his father, sewed him up in his thigh until he came to maturity.—Ed.

[119]

On it, the picture of that shape he placed,

In which the Holy Spirit did alight,

The picture of the dove, so white, so chaste,

On the blest Virgin's head, so chaste, so white.

In these lines, the best of all Fanshaw's, the happy repetition "so chaste, so white," is a beauty which, though not contained in the original, the present translator was unwilling to lose.

[120] See the Preface.

[121] When Gama lay at anchor among the islands of St. George, near Mozambique, "there came three Ethiopians on board (says Faria y Sousa) who, seeing St. Gabriel painted on the poop, fell on their knees in token of their Christianity, which had been preached to them in the primitive times, though now corrupted." Barros, c. 4, and Castaneda, l. i. c. 9, report, that the Portuguese found two or three Abyssinian Christians in the city of Mombas, who had an oratory in their house. The following short account of the Christians of the East may perhaps be acceptable. In the south parts of Malabar, about 200,000 of the inhabitants professed Christianity before the arrival of the Portuguese. They use the Syriac language in their services, and read the Scriptures in that tongue, and call themselves Christians of St. Thomas, by which apostle their ancestors had been converted. For 1300 years they had been under the Patriarch of Babylon, who appointed their Mutran, or archbishop. Dr. Geddes, in his History of the Church of Malabar, relates that Francisco Roz, a Jesuit missionary, complained to Menezes, the Portuguese archbishop of Goa, that when he showed these people an image of the Virgin Mary, they cried out, "Away with that filthiness, we are Christians, and do not adore idols."

Dom Frey Aleixo de Menezes, archbishop of Goa, "endeavoured to thrust upon the church of Malabar the whole mass of popery, which they were before unacquainted with."—Millar's History of the Propag. of Christianity.

[122] Venus.

[123] Proud of her kindred birth.—The French translator has the following note on this place:—"This is one of the places which discover our author's intimate acquaintance with mythology, and at the same time how much attention his allegory requires. Many readers, on finding that the protectress of the Lusians sprung from the sea, would be apt to exclaim, Behold, the birth of the terrestrial Venus! How can a nativity so infamous be ascribed to the celestial Venus, who represents Religion? I answer, that Camoëns had not his eye on those fables, which derive the birth of Venus from the foam of the waves, mixed with the blood which flowed from the dishonest wound of Saturn: he carries his views higher; his Venus is from a fable more noble. Nigidius relates that two fishes one day conveyed an egg to the seashore. This egg was hatched by two pigeons whiter than snow, and gave birth to the Assyrian Venus, which, in the pagan theology, is the same with the celestial. She instructed mankind in religion, gave them the lessons of virtue and the laws of equity. Jupiter, in reward of her labours, promised to grant her whatever she desired. She prayed him to give immortality to the two fishes, who had been instrumental in her birth, and the fishes were accordingly placed in the Zodiac, the sign Pisces.... This fable agrees perfectly with Religion, as I could clearly show; but I think it more proper to leave to the ingenious reader the pleasure of tracing the allegory."

[124] Doto, Nyse, and Nerine.—Cloto, or Clotho, as Castera observes, has by some error crept into almost all the Portuguese editions of the Lusiad. Clotho was one of the Fates, and neither Hesiod, Homer, nor Virgil has given such a name to any of the Nereids; but in the ninth Æneid Doto is mentioned—

——magnique jubebo

Æquoris esse Deas, qualis Nereïa Doto

Et Galatea secant spumantem pectore pontum.

The Nereids, in the Lusiad, says Castera, are the virtues divine and human. In the first book they accompany the Portuguese fleet—

——before the bounding prows

The lovely forms of sea-born nymphs arose.

[125] The ants are a people not strong, yet they prepare their meat in the summer.—Proverbs xxx. 25.—Ed.

[126] Imitated from Virgil—

Cymothoë simul, et Triton adnixus acuto

Detrudunt naves scopulo.—Virg. Æn. i.

[127] Latona, says the fable, flying from the serpent Python, and faint with thirst, came to a pond, where some Lycian peasants were cutting the bulrushes. In revenge of the insults which they offered her in preventing her to drink, she changed them into frogs. This fable, says Castera, like almost all the rest, is drawn from history. Philocorus, as cited by Boccace, relates, that the Rhodians having declared war against the Lycians, were assisted by some troops from Delos, who carried the image of Latona on their standards. A detachment of these going to drink at a lake in Lycia, a crowd of peasants endeavoured to prevent them. An encounter ensued; the peasants fled to the lake for shelter, and were there slain. Some months afterwards their companions came in search of their corpses, and finding an unusual quantity of frogs, imagined, according to the superstition of their age, that the souls of their friends appeared to them under that metamorphosis.

To some it may, perhaps, appear needless to vindicate Camoëns, in a point wherein he is supported by the authority of Homer and Virgil. Yet, as many readers are infected with the sang froid of a Bossu or a Perrault, an observation in defence of our poet cannot be thought impertinent. If we examine the finest effusions of genius, we shall find that the most genuine poetical feeling has often dictated those similes which are drawn from familiar and low objects. The sacred writers, and the greatest poets of every nation, have used them. We may, therefore, conclude that the criticism which condemns them is a refinement not founded on nature. But, allowing them admissible, it must be observed, that to render them pleasing requires a peculiar happiness and delicacy of management. When the poet attains this indispensable point, he gives a striking proof of his elegance, and of his mastership in his art. That the similes of the emmets and of the frogs in Camoëns are happily expressed and applied, is indisputable. In that of the frogs there is a peculiar propriety, both in the comparison itself, and in the allusion to the fable, as it was the intent of the poet to represent not only the flight, but the baseness of the Moors. The simile he seems to have copied from Dante, Inf. Cant. 9—

Come le rane innanzi a la nemica

Biscia per l'acqua si dileguan tutte

Fin che a la terra ciascuna s'abbica.

And Cant. 22—

E come a l'orlo de l'acqua d'un fosso

Stan li ranocchi pur col muso fuori

Sì che celano i piedi, e l'altro grosso.

[128] Barros and Castaneda, in relating this part of the voyage of Gama, say that the fleet, just as they were entering the port of Mombas, were driven back as it were by an invisible hand. By a subsequent note it will appear that the safety of the Armada depended upon this circumstance.

[129] Venus.

[130] As the planet of Jupiter is in the sixth heaven, the author has with propriety there placed the throne of that god.—Castera.

[131] "I am aware of the objection, that this passage is by no means applicable to the celestial Venus. I answer once for all, that the names and adventures of the pagan divinities are so blended and uncertain in mythology, that a poet is at great liberty to adapt them to his allegory as he pleases. Even the fables, which may appear as profane, even these contain historical, physical, and moral truths, which fully atone for the seeming licentiousness of the letter. I could prove this in many instances, but let the present suffice. Paris, son of Priam, king of Troy, spent his first years as a shepherd in the country. At this time Juno, Minerva, and Venus disputed for the apple of gold, which was destined to be given to the most beautiful goddess. They consented that Paris should be their judge. His equity claimed this honour. He saw them all naked. Juno promised him riches, Minerva the sciences, but he decided in favour of Venus, who promised him the possession of the most beautiful woman. What a ray of light is contained in this philosophical fable! Paris represents a studious man, who, in the silence of solitude, seeks the supreme good. Juno is the emblem of riches and dignities; Minerva, that of the sciences purely human; Venus is that of religion, which contains the sciences both human and divine; the charming female, which she promises to the Trojan shepherd, is that divine wisdom which gives tranquillity of heart. A judge so philosophical as Paris would not hesitate a moment to whom to give the apple of gold."—Castera.

[132] "The allegory of Camoëns is here obvious. If Acteon, and the slaves of their violent passions, could discover the beauties of true religion, they would be astonished and reclaimed: according to the expression of Seneca, 'Si virtus cerni posset oculis corporeis, omnes ad amorem suum pelliceret.'"—Castera.

[133] "That is Divine love, which always accompanies religion. Behold how our author insinuates the excellence of his moral!"—Castera.

As the French translator has acknowledged, there is no doubt but several readers will be apt to decry this allegorical interpretation of the machinery of Camoëns. Indeed there is nothing more easy than to discover a system of allegory in the simplest narrative. The reign of Henry VIII. is as susceptible of it as any fable in the heathen mythology. Nay, perhaps, more so. Under the names of Henry, More, Wolsey, Cromwell, Pole, Cranmer, etc., all the war of the passions, with their different catastrophes, might be delineated. Though it may be difficult to determine how far, yet one may venture to affirm that Homer and Virgil sometimes allegorised. The poets, however, who wrote on the revival of letters have left us in no doubt; we have their own authority for it that their machinery is allegorical. Not only the pagan deities, but the more modern adventures of enchantment were used by them to delineate the affections, and the trials and rewards of the virtues and vices. Tasso published a treatise to prove that his Gerusalemme Liberata is no other than the Christian spiritual warfare. And Camoëns, as observed in the preface, has twice asserted that his machinery is allegorical. The poet's assertion, and the taste of the age in which he wrote, sufficiently vindicate and explain the allegory of the Lusiad.

[134] The following speech of Venus and the reply of Jupiter, are a fine imitation from the first Æneid, and do great honour to the classical taste of the Portuguese poet.

[135] Imitated from Virg. Æn. i.—

Olli subridens hominum sator atque Deorum,

Vultu, quo cœlum tempestatesque serenat,

Oscula libavit natæ——

[136] Ulysses, king of Ithaka.—Ed.

[137] i.e., the slave of Calypso, who offered Ulysses immortality on condition that he would live with her.

[138] Æneas.—Ed.

[139]

"Far on the right her dogs foul Scylla hides,

Charybdis roaring on the left presides,

And in her greedy whirlpool sucks the tides."

Dryden's Virg. Æn. iii.—Ed.

[140] After the Portuguese had made great conquests in India, Gama had the honour to be appointed Viceroy. In 1524, when sailing thither to take possession of his government, his fleet was so becalmed on the coast of Cambaya that the ships stood motionless on the water, when in an instant, without the least change of the weather, the waves were shaken with a violent agitation, like trembling. The ships were tossed about, the sailors were terrified, and in the utmost confusion, thinking themselves lost. Gama, perceiving it to be the effect of an earthquake, with his wonted heroism and prudence, exclaimed, "Of what are you afraid? Do you not see how the ocean trembles under its sovereigns!" Barros, l. 9, c. 1, and Faria, c. 9, say, that such as lay sick of fevers were cured by the fright.

[141] Ormuz, or Hormuz, an island at the entrance of the Persian Gulf, once a great commercial dépôt.—Ed.

[142] Both Barros and Castaneda relate this fact. Albuquerque, during the war of Ormuz, having given battle to the Persians and Moors, by the violence of a sudden wind the arrows of the latter were driven back upon themselves, whereby many of their troops were wounded.

[143] Calicut was a seaport town of Malabar, more properly Colicodu.

[144]

Hinc ope barbarica, variisque Antonius armis,

Victor ab Auroræ populis et littore rubro,

Ægyptum, viresque Orientis, et ultima secum

Bactra vehit: sequiturque nefas! Ægyptia conjux.

Una omnes ruere, ac totum spumare, reductis

Convulsum remis rostrisque tridentibus, æquor.

Alta petunt: pelago credas innare revulsas

Cycladas, aut montes concurrere montibus altos:

Tanta mole viri turritis puppibus instant.

Stuppea flamma manu telisque volatile ferrum

Spargitur: arva nova Neptunia cæde rubescunt.

——Sævit medio in certamine Maxors.

Virg. Æn. viii.

[145] Antony.

[146] Gades, now Cadiz, an ancient and still flourishing seaport of Spain.—Ed.

[147] The Lusian pride, etc.—Magalhaens, a most celebrated navigator, neglected by Emmanuel, king of Portugal, offered his service to the king of Spain, under whom he made most important discoveries round the Straits which bear his name, and in parts of South America. Of this hero see further, Lusiad X., in the notes.

[148] Mercury.

[149] Mombas, a seaport town on an island of the same name off the coast of Zanguebar, East Africa.—Ed.

[150] Mercury, so called from Cyllēnē, the highest mountain in the Peloponnesus, where he had a temple, and on which spot he is said to have been born.—Ed.

[151] Petasus.

[152] The caduceus, twined with serpents.—Ed.

[153]

"But first he grasps within his awful hand

The mark of sovereign power, the magic wand:

With this he draws the ghosts from hollow graves,

With this he drives them down the Stygian waves,

With this he seals in sleep the wakeful sight,

And eyes, though closed in death, restores to light."

Æneid, iv. 242. (Dryden's Trans.)

[154] Mercury.

[155] Diomede, a tyrant of Thrace, who fed his horses with human flesh; a thing, says the grave Castera, almost incredible. Busiris was a king of Egypt, who sacrificed strangers.

Quis ... illaudati nescit Busiridis aras?

Virg. Geor. iii.

Hercules vanquished both these tyrants, and put them to the same punishments which their cruelty had inflicted on others. Isocrates composed an oration in honour of Busiris; a masterly example of Attic raillery and satire.

[156] i.e. the equator.

[157] Hermes is the Greek name for the god Mercury.

[158] Having mentioned the escape of the Moorish pilots, Osorius proceeds: Rex deinde homines magno cum silentio scaphis et lintribus submittebat, qui securibus anchoralia nocte præciderent. Quod nisi fuisset à nostris singulari Gamæ industria vigilatum, et insidiis scelerati illius regis occursum, nostri in summum vitæ discrimen incidissent.

[159] Mercury.

[160] A city and kingdom of the same name on the east coast of Africa.

[161] Ascension Day.

[162] Jesus Christ.

[163]

Vimen erat dum stagna subit, processerat undis

Gemma fuit.

Claud.

Sic et coralium, quo primum contigit auras,

Tempore durescit, mollis fuit herba sub undis.

Ovid.

[164] There were on board Gama's fleet several persons skilled in the Oriental languages.—Osor.

[165] See the Eighth Odyssey, etc.

[166] Castera's note on this place is so characteristic of a Frenchman, that the reader will perhaps be pleased to see it transcribed. In his text he says, "Toi

qui occupes si dignement le rang supreme." "Le Poete dit," says he, in the note, "Tens de Rey o officio, Toi qui sais le metier de Roi. (The poet says, thou who holdest the business of a king.) I confess," he adds, "I found a strong inclination to translate this sentence literally. I find much nobleness in it. However, I submitted to the opinion of some friends, who were afraid that the ears of Frenchmen would be shocked at the word business applied to a king. It is true, nevertheless, that Royalty is a business. Philip II. of Spain was convinced of it, as we may discern from one of his letters. Hallo, says he, me muy embaraçado, &c. I am so entangled and encumbered with the multiplicity of business, that I have not a moment to myself. In truth, we kings hold a laborious office (or trade); there is little reason to envy us."

[167] The propriety and artfulness of Homer's speeches have been often and justly admired. Camoëns is peculiarly happy in the same department of the Epopæa. The speech of Gama's herald to the King of Melinda is a striking instance of it. The compliments with which it begins have a direct tendency to the favours afterwards to be asked. The assurances of the innocence, the purpose of the voyagers, and the greatness of their king, are happily touched. The exclamation on the barbarous treatment they had experienced—"Not wisdom saved us, but Heaven's own care"—are masterly insinuations. Their barbarous treatment is again repeated in a manner to move compassion: Alas! what could they fear? etc., is reasoning joined with pathos. That they were conducted to the King of Melinda by Heaven, and were by Heaven assured of his truth, is a most delicate compliment, and in the true spirit of the epic poem. The apology for Gama's refusal to come on shore is exceeding artful. It conveys a proof of the greatness of the Portuguese sovereign, and affords a compliment to loyalty, which could not fail to be acceptable to a monarch.

[168] Rockets.

[169] The Tyrian purple, obtained from the murex, a species of shell-fish, was very famous among the ancients.—Ed.

[170] A girdle, or ornamented belt, worn over one shoulder and across the breast.—Ed.

[171] Camoëns seems to have his eye on the picture of Gama, which is thus described by Faria y Sousa: "He is painted with a black cap, cloak, and breeches edged with velvet, all slashed, through which appears the crimson lining, the doublet of crimson satin, and over it his armour inlaid with gold."

[172] The admiration and friendship of the King of Melinda, so much insisted on by Camoëns, is a judicious imitation of Virgil's Dido. In both cases such preparation was necessary to introduce the long episodes which follow.

[173] The Moors, who are Mohammedans, disciples of the Arabian prophet, who was descended from Abraham through the line of Hagar.—Ed.

[174] The famous temple of the goddess Diana at Ephesus.—Ed.

[175] Apollo.

[176] Calliope.—The Muse of epic poesy, and mother of Orpheus. Daphne, daughter of the river Peneus, flying from Apollo, was turned into the laurel. Clytia was metamorphosed into the sun-flower, and Leucothoë, who was buried alive by her father for yielding to the solicitations of Apollo, was by her lover changed into an incense tree.

[177] A fountain of Bœotia sacred to the Muses.—Ed.

[178] The preface to the speech of Gama, and the description of Europe which follows, are happy imitations of the manner of Homer. When Camoëns describes countries, or musters an army, it is after the example of the great models of antiquity: by adding some characteristical feature of the climate or people, he renders his narrative pleasing, picturesque, and poetical.

[179] The Mediterranean.

[180] The Don.—Ed.

[181] The Sea of Azof.—Ed.

[182] Italy. In the year 409 the city of Rome was sacked, and Italy laid desolate by Alaric, king of the Gothic tribes. In mentioning this circumstance Camoëns has not fallen into the common error of little poets, who on every occasion bewail the outrage which the Goths and Vandals did to the arts and sciences. A complaint founded on ignorance. The Southern nations of Europe were sunk into the most contemptible degeneracy. The sciences, with every branch of manly literature, were almost unknown. For near two centuries no poet of note had adorned the Roman empire. Those arts only, the abuse of which have a certain and fatal tendency to enervate the mind, the arts of music and cookery, were passionately cultivated in all the refinement of effeminate abuse. The art of war was too laborious for their delicacy, and the generous warmth of heroism and patriotism was incompatible with their effeminacy. On these despicable Sybarites {*} the North poured her brave and hardy sons, who, though ignorant of polite literature, were possessed of all the manly virtues in a high degree. Under their conquests Europe wore a new face, which, however rude, was infinitely preferable to that which it had lately worn. And, however ignorance may talk of their barbarity, it is to them that England owes her constitution, which, as Montesquieu observes, they brought from the woods of Saxony.

{*} Sybaris, a city in Magna Grecia (South Italy), whose inhabitants were so effeminate, that they ordered all the cocks to be killed, that they might not be disturbed by their early crowing.

[183] The river Don.

[184] This was the name of an extensive forest in Germany. It exists now under different names, as the Black Forest, the Bohemian and the Thuringian Forest, the Hartz, etc.—Ed.

[185] The Hellespont, or Straits of the Dardanelles.—Ed.

[186] The Balkan Mountains separating Greece and Macedonia from the basin of the Danube, and extending from the Adriatic to the Black Sea.—Ed.

[187] Now Constantinople.

[188] Julius Cæsar, the conqueror of Gaul, or France.—Ed.

[189] Faithless to the vows of lost Pyrene, etc.—She was daughter to Bebryx, a king of Spain, and concubine to Hercules. Having wandered one day from her lover, she was destroyed by wild beasts, on one of the mountains which bear her name.

[190] Hercules, says the fable, to crown his labours, separated the two mountains Calpe and Abyla, the one in Spain, the other in Africa, in order to open a canal for the benefit of commerce; on which the ocean rushed in, and formed the Mediterranean, the Ægean, and Euxine seas. The twin mountains Abyla and Calpe were known to the ancients by the name of the Pillars of Hercules.—See Cory's Ancient Fragments.

[191] The river Guadalquivir; i.e., in Arabic, the great river.—Ed.

[192] Viriatus.—See the note on Book I. p. 9.

[193] The assassination of Viriatus.—See the note on Book I. p. 9.

[194] The name of Saracen is derived from the Arabic Es-shurk, the East, and designates the Arabs who followed the banner of Mohammed.—Ed.

[195] Don Alonzo, king of Spain, apprehensive of the superior number of the Moors, with whom he was at war, demanded assistance from Philip I. of France, and the Duke of Burgundy. According to the military spirit of the nobility of that age, no sooner was his desire known than numerous bodies of troops thronged to his standard. These, in the course of a few years, having shown signal proofs of their courage, the king distinguished the leaders with different marks of his regard. To Henry, a younger son of the Duke of Burgundy, he gave his daughter Teresa in marriage, with the sovereignty of the countries to the south of Galicia, commissioning him to enlarge his boundaries by the expulsion of the Moors. Under the government of this great man, who reigned by the title of Count, his dominion was greatly enlarged, and became more rich and populous than before. The two provinces of Entre Minho e Douro, and Tras os Montes, were subdued, with

that part of Beira which was held by the Moorish king of Lamego, whom he constrained to pay tribute. Many thousands of Christians, who had either lived in miserable subjection to the Moors, or in desolate independency in the mountains, took shelter under the protection of Count Henry. Great multitudes of the Moors also chose rather to submit, than be exposed to the severities and the continual feuds and seditions of their own governors. These advantages, added to the great fertility of the soil of Henry's dominions, will account for the numerous armies, and the frequent wars of the first sovereigns of Portugal.

[196] Camoëns, in making the founder of the Portuguese monarchy a younger son of the King of Hungary, has followed the old chronologist Galvan. The Spanish and Portuguese historians differ widely in their accounts of the parentage of this gallant stranger. Some bring him from Constantinople, and others from the house of Lorraine. But the clearest and most probable account of him is in the chronicle of Fleury, wherein is preserved a fragment of French history, written by a Benedictine monk in the beginning of the twelfth century, and in the time of Count Henry. By this it appears, that he was a younger son of Henry, the only son of Robert, the first duke of Burgundy, who was a younger brother of Henry I. of France. Fanshaw having an eye to this history, has taken the unwarrantable liberty to alter the fact as mentioned by his author.

Amongst these Henry, saith the history,

A younger son of France, and a brave prince,

Had Portugal in lot.——

And the same king did his own daughter tie

To him in wedlock, to infer from thence

His firmer love.

Nor are the historians agreed on the birth of Donna Teresa, the spouse of Count Henry. Brandam, and other Portuguese historians, are at great pains to prove she was the legitimate daughter of Alonzo and the beautiful Ximena de Guzman. But it appears from the more authentic chronicle of Fleury, that Ximena was only his concubine. And it is evident from all the historians, that Donna Urraca, the heiress of her father's kingdom, was younger than her half-sister, the wife of Count Henry.

[197] The Mohammedan Arabs.

[198] Deliver'd Judah Henry's might confess'd.—His expedition to the Holy Land is mentioned by some monkish writers, but from the other parts of his

history it is highly improbable.

[199] Jerusalem.

[200] Godfrey of Bouillon.

[201] Don Alonzo Enriquez, son of Count Henry, had only entered into his third year when his father died. His mother assumed the reins of government, and appointed Don Fernando Perez de Traba to be her minister. When the young prince was in his eighteenth year, some of the nobility, who either envied the power of Don Perez, or suspected his intention to marry the queen, and exclude the lawful heir, easily persuaded the young Count to take arms, and assume the sovereignty. A battle ensued, in which the prince was victorious. Teresa, it is said, retired into the castle of Legonaso, where she was taken prisoner by her son, who condemned her to perpetual imprisonment, and ordered chains to be put upon her legs. That Don Alonso made war against his mother, vanquished her party, and that she died in prison about two years after, A.D. 1130, are certain. But the cause of the war, that his mother was married to, or intended to marry, Don Perez, and that she was put in chains, are uncertain.

[202] Guimaraens was the scene of a very sanguinary battle.—Ed.

[203] The Scylla here alluded to was, according to fable, the daughter of Nisus, king of Megara, who had a purple lock, in which lay the fate of his kingdom. Minos of Crete made war against him, for whom Scylla conceived so violent a passion, that she cut off the fatal lock while her father slept. Minos on this was victorious, but rejected the love of the unnatural daughter, who in despair flung herself from a rock, and in the fall was changed into a lark.

[204] Guimaraens, the scene of a famous battle.—Ed.

[205] Some historians having related this story of Egas, add, "All this is very pleasant and entertaining, but we see no sufficient reason to affirm that there is one syllable of it true."

[206] When Darius laid siege to Babylon, one of his lords, named Zopyrus, having cut off his own nose and ears, persuaded the enemy that he had received these indignities from the cruelty of his master. Being appointed to a chief command in Babylon, he betrayed the city to Darius.—Vid. Justin's History.

[207] Spanish and Portuguese histories afford several instances of the Moorish chiefs being attended in the field of battle by their mistresses, and of the romantic gallantry and Amazonian courage of these ladies.

[208] Penthesilea, queen of the Amazons, who, after having signalized her

valour at the siege of Troy, was killed by Achilles.

[209] The Greek name of Troy.—Ed.

[210] The Amazons.

[211] Thermodon, a river of Scythia in the country of the Amazons.

Quales Threïciæ cum flumina Thermodontis

Pulsant et pictis bellantur Amazones armis:

Seu circum Hippolyten, seu cum se Martia curru

Penthesilea refert: magnoque ululante tumultu

Fœminea exsultant lunatis agmina peltis. Virg. Æn. xi. 659.

[212] It may, perhaps, be agreeable to the reader, to see the description of a bull-fight as given by Homer.

As when a lion, rushing from his den,

Amidst the plain of some wide-water'd fen,

(Where num'rous oxen, as at ease they feed,

At large expatiate o'er the ranker mead;)

Leaps on the herds before the herdsman's eyes:

The trembling herdsman far to distance flies:

Some lordly bull (the rest dispers'd and fled)

He singles out, arrests, and lays him dead.

Thus from the rage of Jove-like Hector flew

All Greece in heaps; but one he seiz'd, and slew

Mycenian Periphas.——

Pope, Il. xv.

[213] A shirt of mail, formed of small iron rings.

[214] Mohammed.

[215] There is a passage in Xenophon, upon which perhaps Camoëns had his

eye. Επεὶ δέ ἔληξεν ἡ μάχη, παρῆν ἰδείν την μέν γῆν αἵματι πεφυρμένην, &c.
"When the battle was over, one might behold through the whole extent of the field the ground purpled with blood; the bodies of friends and enemies stretched over each other, the shields pierced, the spears broken, and the drawn swords, some scattered on the earth, some plunged in the bosoms of the slain, and some yet grasped in the hands of the dead soldiers."

[216] This memorable battle was fought in the plains of Ourique, in 1139. The engagement lasted six hours; the Moors were totally routed with incredible slaughter. On the field of battle Alonzo was proclaimed King of Portugal. The Portuguese writers have given many fabulous accounts of this victory. Some affirm that the Moorish army amounted to 380,000, others, 480,000, and others swell it to 600,000, whereas Don Alonzo's did not exceed 13,000. Miracles must also be added. Alonzo, they tell us, being in great perplexity, sat down to comfort his mind by the perusal of the Holy Scriptures. Having read the story of Gideon, he sunk into a deep sleep, in which he saw a very old man in a remarkable dress come into his tent, and assure him of victory. His chamberlain coming in, awoke him, and told him there was an old man very importunate to speak with him. Don Alonzo ordered him to be brought in, and no sooner saw him than he knew him to be the old man whom he had seen in his dream. This venerable person acquainted him that he was a fisherman, and had led a life of penance for sixty years on an adjacent rock, where it had been revealed to him, that if the count marched his army the next morning, as soon as he heard a certain bell ring, he should receive the strongest assurance of victory. Accordingly, at the ringing of the bell, the count put his army in motion, and suddenly beheld in the eastern sky the figure of the cross, and Christ upon it, who promised him a complete victory, and commanded him to accept the title of king, if it were offered him by the army. The same writers add, that as a standing memorial of this miraculous event, Don Alonzo changed the arms which his father had given, of a cross azure in a field argent, for five escutcheons, each charged with five bezants, in memory of the wounds of Christ. Others assert, that he gave, in a field argent, five escutcheons azure in the form of a cross, each charged with five bezants argent, placed saltierwise, with a point sable, in memory of five wounds he himself received, and of five Moorish kings slain in the battle. There is an old record, said to be written by Don Alonzo, in which the story of the vision is related upon his majesty's oath. The Spanish critics, however, have discovered many inconsistencies in it. They find the language intermixed with phrases not then in use: and it bears the date of the year of our Lord, at a time when that era had not been introduced into Spain.

[217] Troy.

[218] The tradition, that Lisbon was built by Ulysses, and thence called

435

Olyssipolis, is as common as, and of equal authority with, that which says, that Brute landed a colony of Trojans in England, and gave the name of Britannia to the island.

[219] The conquest of Lisbon was of the utmost importance to the infant monarchy. It is one of the finest ports in the world, and before the invention of cannon, was of great strength. The old Moorish wall was flanked by seventy-seven towers, was about six miles in length, and fourteen in circumference. When besieged by Don Alonzo, according to some, it was garrisoned by an army of 200,000 men. This is highly incredible. However, that it was strong and well garrisoned is certain, as also that Alonzo owed the conquest of it to a fleet of adventurers, who were going to the Holy Land, the greater part of whom were English. One Udal op Rhys, in his tour through Portugal, says, that Alonzo gave them Almada, on the side of the Tagus opposite to Lisbon, and that Villa Franca was peopled by them, which they called Cornualla, either in honour of their native country, or from the rich meadows in its neighbourhood, where immense herds of cattle are kept, as in the English Cornwall.

[220] Jerusalem.

[221] Unconquer'd towers.—This assertion of Camoëns is not without foundation, for it was by treachery that Herimeneric, the Goth, got possession of Lisbon.

[222] The aqueduct of Sertorius, here mentioned, is one of the grandest remains of antiquity. It was repaired by John III. of Portugal about A.D. 1540.

[223] Badajoz.

[224] The history of this battle wants authenticity.

[225] As already observed, there is no authentic proof that Don Alonzo used such severity to his mother as to put her in chains. Brandan says it was reported that Don Alonzo was born with both his legs growing together, and that he was cured by the prayers of his tutor, Egas Nunio. Legendary as this may appear, this however is deducible from it, that from his birth there was something amiss about his legs. When he was prisoner to his son-in-law, Don Fernando, king of Leon, he recovered his liberty ere his leg, which was fractured in the battle, was restored, on condition that as soon as he was able to mount on horseback, he should come to Leon, and in person do homage for his dominions. This condition, so contrary to his coronation agreement, he found means to avoid. He ever after affected to drive in a calash, and would never mount on horseback more. The superstitious of those days ascribed this infirmity to the curses of his mother.

[226] Phasis.—A river of Colchis.

[227] A frontier town on the Nile, bordering on Nubia.

[228] Colchis.—A country of Asia Minor bordering on the Black Sea.—Ed.

[229] Tu quoque littoribus nostris, Æneia nutrix,

Æternam moriens famam, Caieta, dedisti.

Virg. Æn. vii.

[230] i.e. Tangiers, opposite to Gibraltar.—Ed.

[231] This should be Emir el Moumeneen, i.e., Commander of the Faithful.—Ed.

[232] The Mondego is the largest river having its rise within the kingdom of Portugal and entering no other state.—Ed.

[233] Miramolin.—Not the name of a person, but a title, quasi Sultan; the Emperor of the Faithful.

[234] In this poetical exclamation, expressive of the sorrow of Portugal on the death of Alonzo, Camoëns has happily imitated some passages of Virgil.

——Ipsæ te, Tityre, pinus,

Ipsi te fontes, ipsa hæc arbusta vocabant.

Ecl. i.

——Eurydicen vox ipsa et frigida lingua,

Ah miseram Eurydicen, anima fugiente, vocabat:

Eurydicen toto referebant flumine ripæ.

Georg. iv.

——littus, Hyla, Hyla, omne sonaret.

Ecl. vi.

[235] The Guadalquiver, the largest river in Spain.—Ed.

[236] The Portuguese, in their wars with the Moors, were several times assisted by the English and German crusaders. In the present instance the fleet was mostly English, the troops of which nation were, according to agreement, rewarded with the plunder, which was exceeding rich, of the city of Silves. Nuniz de Leon as cronicas dos Reis de Port, A.D. 1189.—Ed.

[237] Barbarossa, A.D. 1189.—Ed.

[238] Unlike the Syrian (rather Assyrian).—Sardanapalus.

[239] When Rome's proud tyrant far'd.—Heliogabalus, infamous for his gluttony.

[240] Alluding to the history of Phalaris.

[241] Camoëns, who was quite an enthusiast for the honour of his country, has in this instance disguised the truth of history. Don Sancho was by no means the weak prince here represented, nor did the miseries of his reign proceed from himself. The clergy were the sole authors of his, and the public, calamities. The Roman See was then in the height of its power, which it exerted in the most tyrannical manner. The ecclesiastical courts had long claimed the sole right to try an ecclesiastic: and, to prohibit a priest to say mass for a twelve-month, was by the brethren, his judges, esteemed a sufficient punishment for murder, or any other capital crime. Alonzo II., the father of Don Sancho, attempted to establish the authority of the king's courts of justice over the offending clergy. For this the Archbishop of Braga excommunicated Gonzalo Mendez, the chancellor; and Honorius, the pope, excommunicated the king, and put his dominions under an interdict. The exterior offices of religion were suspended, the people fell into the utmost dissoluteness of manners; Mohammedanism made great advances, and public confusion everywhere prevailed. By this policy the Church constrained the nobility to urge the king to a full submission to the papal chair. While a negotiation for this purpose was on foot Alonzo died, and left his son to struggle with an enraged and powerful clergy. Don Sancho was just, affable, brave, and an enamoured husband. On this last virtue faction first fixed its envenomed fangs. The queen was accused of arbitrary influence over her husband; and, according to the superstition of that age, she was believed to have disturbed his senses by an enchanted draught. Such of the nobility as declared in the king's favour were stigmatized, and rendered odious, as the creatures of the queen. The confusions which ensued were fomented by Alonso, Earl of Bologna, the king's brother, by whom the king was accused as the author of them. In short, by the assistance of the clergy and Pope Innocent IV., Sancho was deposed, and soon after died at Toledo. The beautiful queen, Donna Mencia, was seized upon, and conveyed away by one

Raymond Portocarrero, and was never heard of more. Such are the triumphs of faction!

[242] Alexander the Great.

[243] Mondego, the largest exclusively Portuguese river.—Ed.

[244] The baccaris, or Lady's glove, a herb to which the Druids and ancient poets ascribed magical virtues.

——Baccare frontem

Cingite, ne vati noceat mala lingua futuro.

Virg. Ecl. vii.

[245] Semiramis, who is said to have invaded India.—Ed.

[246] Attila, a king of the Huns, surnamed "The Scourge of God." He lived in the fifth century. He may be reckoned among the greatest of conquerors.

[247] His much-lov'd bride.—The Princess Mary. She was a lady of great beauty and virtue, but was exceedingly ill used by her husband, who was violently attached to his mistresses, though he owed his crown to the assistance of his father-in-law, the King of Portugal.

[248]

By night our fathers' shades confess their fear,

Their shrieks of terror from the tombs we hear.—

Camoëns says, "A mortos faz espanto;" to give this elegance in English required a paraphrase. There is something wildly great, and agreeable to the superstition of that age, to suppose that the dead were troubled in their graves on the approach of so terrible an army. The French translator, contrary to the original, ascribes this terror to the ghost of only one prince, by which this stroke of Camoëns, in the spirit of Shakespeare, is reduced to a piece of unmeaning frippery.

[249] The Muliya, a river of Morocco.—Ed.

[250] See the first Æneid.

[251] Goliath, the Philistine champion.—Ed.

[252] David, afterwards king of Israel.—Ed.

[253] Though wove.—It may perhaps be objected that this is ungrammatical. But—

————Usus

Quem penes arbitrium est, et jus et norma loquendi.

and Dryden, Pope, etc., often use wove as a participle in place of the harsh-sounding woven, a word almost incompatible with the elegance of versification.

[254] Hannibal, who, as a child, was compelled to swear perpetual hostility to the Romans.—Ed.

[255] Where the last great battle between Hannibal and the Romans took place, in which the Romans sustained a crushing defeat.—Ed.

[256] When the soldiers of Marius complained of thirst, he pointed to a river near the camp of the Ambrones. "There," says he, "you may drink, but it must be purchased with blood." "Lead us on," they replied, "that we may have something liquid, though it be blood." The Romans, forcing their way to the river, the channel was filled with the dead bodies of the slain.—Vid. Plutarch's Lives.

[257] This unfortunate lady, Donna Inez de Castro, was the daughter of a Castilian gentleman, who had taken refuge in the court of Portugal. Her beauty and accomplishments attracted the regard of Don Pedro, the king's eldest son, a prince of a brave and noble disposition. La Neufville, Le Clede, and other historians, assert that she was privately married to the prince ere she had any share in his bed. Nor was his conjugal fidelity less remarkable than the ardour of his passion. Afraid, however, of his father's resentment, the severity of whose temper he knew, his intercourse with Donna Inez passed at the court as an intrigue of gallantry. On the accession of Don Pedro the Cruel to the throne of Castile many of the disgusted nobility were kindly received by Don Pedro, through the interest of his beloved Inez. The favour shown to these Castilians gave great uneasiness to the politicians. A thousand evils were foreseen from the prince's attachment to his Castilian mistress: even the murder of his children by his deceased spouse, the princess Constantia, was surmised; and the enemies of Donna Inez, finding the king willing to listen, omitted no opportunity to increase his resentment against the unfortunate lady. The prince was about his twenty-eighth year when his amour with his beloved Inez commenced.

[258]Ad cœlum tendens ardentia lumina frustra,

Lumina nam teneras arcebant vincula palmas.

440

Virg. Æn. ii.

[259] Romulus and Remus, who were said to have been suckled by a wolf.—Ed.

[260] It has been observed by some critics, that Milton on every occasion is fond of expressing his admiration of music, particularly of the song of the nightingale, and the full woodland choir. If in the same manner we are to judge of the favourite taste of Homer, we shall find it of a less delicate kind. He is continually describing the feast, the huge chine, the savoury viands on the glowing coals, and the foaming bowl. The ruling passion of Camoëns is also strongly marked in his writings. One may venture to affirm, that there is no poem of equal length that abounds with so many impassioned encomiums on the fair sex as the Lusiad. The genius of Camoëns seems never so pleased as when he is painting the variety of female charms; he feels all the magic of their allurements, and riots in his descriptions of the happiness and miseries attendant on the passion of love. As he wrote from his feelings, these parts of his works have been particularly honoured with the attention of the world.

[261] To give the character of Alphonso IV. will throw light on this inhuman transaction. He was an undutiful son, an unnatural brother, and a cruel father, a great and fortunate warrior, diligent in the execution of the laws, and a Macchiavellian politician. His maxim was that of the Jesuits; so that a contemplated good might be attained, he cared not how villainous might be the means employed. When the enemies of Inez had persuaded him that her death was necessary to the welfare of the state, he took a journey to Coimbra, that he might see the lady, when the prince, his son, was absent on a hunting party. Donna Inez, with her children, threw herself at his feet. The king was moved with the distress of the beautiful suppliant, when his three counsellors, Alvaro Gonsalez, Diego Lopez Pacheco, and Pedro Coello, reproaching him for his disregard to the state, he relapsed to his former resolution. She was then dragged from his presence, and brutally murdered by the hands of his three counsellors, who immediately returned to the king with their daggers reeking with the innocent blood of his daughter-in-law. Alonzo, says La Neufville, avowed the horrid assassination, as if he had done nothing of which he ought to be ashamed.

[262] Pyrrhus, son of Achilles: he was also called Neoptolemus. He sacrificed Polyxena, daughter of Priam king of Troy, to the manes of his father. Euripides and Sophocles each wrote a tragedy having the sacrifice of Polyxena for the subject. Both have unfortunately perished.—Ed.

[263] Hecuba, mother of Polyxena, and wife of Priam.—Ed.

[264] The fair Inez was crowned Queen of Portugal after her interment.

[265] Atreus, having slain the sons of Thyestes, cut them in pieces, and served

them up for a repast to their own father. The sun, it is said, hid his face rather than shine on so barbarous a deed.—Ed.

[266] At an old royal castle near Mondego, there is a rivulet called the fountain of Amours. According to tradition, it was here that Don Pedro resided with his beloved Inez. The fiction of Camoëns, founded on the popular name of the rivulet, is in the spirit of Homer.

[267] When the prince was informed of the death of his beloved Inez, he was transported into the most violent fury. He took arms against his father. The country between the rivers Minho and Doura was laid desolate: but, by the interposition of the queen and the Archbishop of Braga, the prince relented, and the further horrors of a civil war were prevented. Don Alonzo was not only reconciled to his son, but laboured by every means to oblige him, and to efface from his memory the injury and insult he had received. The prince, however, still continued to discover the strongest marks of affection and grief. When he succeeded to the crown, one of his first acts was a treaty with the King of Castile, whereby each monarch engaged to give up such malcontents as should take refuge in each other's dominions. In consequence of this, Pedro Coello and Alvaro Gonsalez, who, on the death of Alonzo had fled to Castile, were sent prisoners to Don Pedro. Diego Pacheco, the third murderer, made his escape. The other two were put to death with the most exquisite tortures, and most justly merited, if torture is in any instance to be allowed. After this the king, Don Pedro, summoned an assembly of the states at Cantanedes. Here, in the presence of the Pope's nuncio, he solemnly swore on the holy Gospels, that having obtained a dispensation from Rome, he had secretly, at Braganza, espoused the Lady Inez de Castro, in the presence of the Bishop of Guarda, and of his master of the wardrobe; both of whom confirmed the truth of the oath. The Pope's Bull, containing the dispensation, was published; the body of Inez was lifted from the grave, was placed on a magnificent throne, and with the proper regalia, crowned Queen of Portugal. The nobility did homage to her skeleton, and kissed the bones of her hand. The corpse was then interred at the royal monastery of Alcobaca, with a pomp before unknown in Portugal, and with all the honours due to a queen. Her monument is still extant, where her statue is adorned with the diadem and the royal robe. This, with the legitimation of her children, and the care he took of all who had been in her service, consoled him in some degree, and rendered him more conversable than he had hitherto been; but the cloud which the death of Inez brought over the natural cheerfulness of his temper, was never totally dispersed.—— A circumstance strongly characteristic of the rage of his resentment must not be omitted. When the murderers were brought before him, he was so transported with indignation, that he struck Pedro Coello several blows on the face with the shaft of his whip.

[268] Pedro the Just.—History cannot afford an instance of any prince who

has a more eminent claim to the title of just than Pedro I. His diligence to correct every abuse was indefatigable, and when guilt was proved his justice was inexorable. He was dreadful to the evil, and beloved by the good, for he respected no persons, and his inflexible severity never digressed from the line of strict justice. An anecdote or two will throw some light on his character. A priest having killed a mason, the king dissembled his knowledge of the crime, and left the issue to the ecclesiastical court, where the priest was punished by one year's suspension from saying mass. The king on this privately ordered the mason's son to revenge the murder of his father. The young man obeyed, was apprehended, and condemned to death. When his sentence was to be confirmed by the king, Pedro enquired, what was the young man's trade. He was answered, that he followed his father's. "Well then," said the king, "I shall commute his punishment, and interdict him from meddling with stone or mortar for a twelve-month." After this he fully established the authority of the king's courts over the clergy, whom he punished with death when their crimes were capital. When solicited to refer the causes of such criminals to a higher tribunal, he would answer very calmly, "That is what I intend to do: I will send them to the highest of all tribunals, to that of their Maker and mine." Against adulterers he was particularly severe, often declaring it as his opinion, that conjugal infidelity was the source of the greatest evils, and that therefore to restrain it was the interest and duty of the sovereign. Though the fate of his beloved Inez chagrined and soured his temper, he was so far from being naturally sullen or passionate, that he was rather of a gay and sprightly disposition; he was affable and easy of access; delighted in music and dancing; was a lover of learning, a man of letters, and an elegant poet.—Vide Le Clede, Mariana, Faria.

[269] This lady, named Leonora de Tellez, was the wife of Don Juan Lorenzo Acugna, a nobleman of one of the most distinguished families in Portugal. After a sham process this marriage was dissolved, and the king privately espoused to her, though, at this time, he was publicly married by proxy to Donna Leonora of Arragon. A dangerous insurrection, headed by one Velasquez, a tailor, drove the king and his adulterous bride from Lisbon. Soon after, he caused his marriage to be publicly celebrated in the province of Entre Douro e Minho. Henry, king of Castile, being informed of the general discontent that reigned in Portugal, marched a formidable army into that kingdom, to revenge the injury offered to some of his subjects, whose ships had been unjustly seized at Lisbon. The desolation hinted at by Camoëns ensued. After the subjects of both kingdoms had severely suffered, the two kings ended the war, much to their mutual satisfaction, by an intermarriage of their illegitimate children.

[270] Judges, chap. xix. and xx.

[271] Samuel, chap. xii. 10, "The sword shall never depart from thine house."

[272] Hercules.

[273] Love compelled Hercules to spin wool.—Ovid.

[274] Hannibal.

[275] Dom John was a natural brother of Fernando, being an illegitimate son of Pedro.—Ed.

[276] A cradled infant gave the wondrous sign.—No circumstance has ever been more ridiculed by the ancient and modern pedants than Alexander's pretensions to divinity. Some of his courtiers expostulating with him one day on the absurdity of such claim, he replied, "I know the truth of what you say, but these," (pointing to a crowd of Persians) "these know no better." The report that the Grecian army was commanded by a son of Jupiter spread terror through the East, and greatly facilitated the operations of the conqueror. The miraculous speech of the infant, attested by a few monks, was adapted to the superstition of the age of John I. and, as he was illegitimate, was of infinite service to his cause. The pretended fact, however, is differently related.

[277] Lisbon, or Ulyssipolis, supposed to be founded by Ulysses.—Ed.

[278] The mitred head.—Don Martin, bishop of Lisbon, a man of exemplary life. He was by birth a Castilian, which was esteemed a sufficient reason to murder him, as of the queen's party. He was thrown from the tower of his own cathedral, whither he had fled to avoid the popular fury.

[279] The queen beheld her power, her honours lost.—Possessed of great beauty and great abilities, this bad woman was a disgrace to her sex, and a curse to the age and country which gave her birth. Her sister, Donna Maria, a lady of unblemished virtue, had been secretly married to the infant, Don Juan, the king's brother, who was passionately attached to her. Donna Maria had formerly endeavoured to dissuade her sister from the adulterous marriage with the king. In revenge of this, the queen, Leonora, persuaded Don Juan that her sister was unfaithful to his bed. The enraged husband hastened to his wife, and, without enquiry or expostulation, says Mariana, dispatched her with two strokes of his dagger. He was afterwards convinced of her innocence. Having sacrificed her honour, and her first husband, to a king, (says Faria), Leonora soon sacrificed that king to a wicked gallant, a Castilian nobleman, named Don Juan Fernandez de Andeyro. An unjust war with Castile, wherein the Portuguese were defeated by sea and land, was the first fruits of the policy of the new favourite. Andeyro one day being in a great perspiration, by some military exercise, the queen tore her veil, and publicly gave it him to wipe his face. The grand master of Avis, the king's illegitimate brother, afterwards John I., and some others, expostulated with her on the indecency of this behaviour. She dissembled her resentment, but, soon after, they were seized

and committed to the castle of Evora, where a forged order for their execution was sent; but the governor suspecting some fraud, showed it to the king. Yet, such was her ascendancy over Fernando, that though convinced of her guilt, he ordered his brother to kiss the queen's hand, and thank her for his life. Soon after, Fernando died, but not till he was fully convinced of the queen's conjugal infidelity, and had given an order for the assassination of the gallant. Not long after the death of the king, the favourite Andeyro was stabbed in the palace by the grandmaster of Avis, and Don Ruy de Pereyra. The queen expressed all the transport of grief and rage, and declared she would undergo the trial-ordeal in vindication of his, and her, innocence. But this she never performed: in her vows of revenge, however, she was more punctual. Don Juan, king of Castile, who had married her only daughter and heiress, at her earnest entreaties invaded Portugal, and was proclaimed king. Don John, grand master of Avis, was proclaimed by the people protector and regent. A desperate war ensued. Queen Leonora, treated with indifference by her daughter and son-in-law, resolved on the murder of the latter, but the plot was discovered, and she was sent prisoner to Castile. The regent was besieged in Lisbon, and the city reduced to the utmost extremities, when an epidemic broke out in the Castilian army, and made such devastation, that the king suddenly raised the siege, and abandoned his views on Portugal. The happy inhabitants ascribed their deliverance to the valour and vigilance of the regent. The regent reproved their ardour, exhorted them to repair to their churches, and return thanks to God, to whose interposition he solely ascribed their safety. This behaviour increased the admiration of the people; the nobility of the first rank joined the regent's party, and many garrisons in the interest of the king of Castile opened their gates to him. An assembly of the states met at Coimbra, where it was proposed to invest the regent with the regal dignity. This he pretended to decline. Don John, son of Pedro the Just and the beautiful Inez de Castro, was by the people esteemed their lawful sovereign, but was, and had been long, detained a prisoner by the King of Castile. If the states would declare the infant, Don John, their king, the regent professed his willingness to swear allegiance to him, that he would continue to expose himself to every danger, and act as regent, till Providence restored to Portugal her lawful sovereign. The states, however, saw the necessity that the nation should have a head. The regent was unanimously elected king, and some articles in favour of liberty were added to those agreed upon at the coronation of Don Alonzo Enriquez, the first king of Portugal.

Don John I., one of the greatest of the Portuguese monarchs, was the natural son of Pedro the Just, by Donna Teresa Lorenza, a Galician lady, and was born some years after the death of Inez. At seven years of age he was made grand master of Avis, where he received an excellent education, which, joined to his great parts, brought him out early on the political theatre. He was a brave commander, and a deep politician, yet never forfeited the character of candour and honour. To be humble to his friends, and haughty to his enemies, was his leading maxim. His prudence gained him the confidence of the wise; his steadiness and gratitude the friendship of the brave; his liberality the bulk of the people. He was in the twenty-seventh year of his age when declared protector, and in his twenty-eighth when proclaimed king.

The following anecdote is much to the honour of this prince when regent. A Castilian officer, having six Portuguese gentleman prisoners, cut off their noses and hands, and sent them to Don John. Highly incensed, the protector commanded six Castilian gentlemen to be treated in the same manner. But, before the officer, to whom he gave the orders, had quitted the room, he relented. "I have given enough to resentment," said he, "in giving such a command. It were infamous to put it in execution. See that the Castilian prisoners receive no harm."

[280] Beatrice.

[281] By Rodrick given.—The celebrated hero of Corneille's tragedy of the Cid.

[282] [283] Cadiz: in ancient times a Phœnician colony, whose coins bear the emblem of two pillars—the pillars of Hercules (Alcides).—Ed.

[284] The Gascons or Basques, a very ancient and singular people. Their language has no relation to that of any other people. They are regarded as the earliest inhabitants of the Spanish peninsula.—Ed.

[285] See Judges xvi. 17-19.

[286] This speech in the original has been much admired by foreign critics, as a model of military eloquence. The critic, it is hoped, will perceive that the translator has endeavoured to support the character of the speaker.

[287] This was the famous P. Corn. Scipio Africanus. The fact, somewhat differently related by Livy, is this. After the defeat at Cannæ, a considerable body of Romans fled to Canusium, and appointed Scipio and Ap. Claudius their commanders. While they remained there, it was told Scipio, that some of his chief officers, at the head of whom was Cæcilius Metellus, were taking measures to transport themselves out of Italy. He went immediately to their assembly; and drawing his sword, said, I swear that I will not desert the Commonwealth of Rome, nor suffer any other citizen to do it. The same oath I require of you, Cæcilius, and of all present; whoever refuses, let him know that this sword is drawn against him. The historian adds, that they were as terrified by this, as if they had beheld the face of their conqueror, Hannibal. They all swore, and submitted themselves to Scipio.—Vid. Livy, bk. 22. c. 53.

[288] Sestos was a city of Thrace, on the Dardanelles, opposite Abydos.—Ed.

[289] The Guadiana, one of the two great rivers of Spain.—Ed.

[290] The Douro.

[291] Homer and Virgil have, with great art, gradually heightened the fury of every battle, till the last efforts of their genius were lavished in describing the superior prowess of the hero in the decisive engagement. Camoëns, in like manner, has bestowed his utmost attention on this his principal battle. The circumstances preparatory to the engagement are happily imagined, and solemnly conducted, and the fury of the combat is supported with a poetical heat, and a variety of imagery, which, one need not hesitate to affirm, would do honour to an ancient classic author.

[292] And his own brothers shake the hostile lance.—The just indignation with which Camoëns treats the kindred of the brave Nunio Alvaro de Pereyra, is condemned by the French translator. "The Pereyras," says he, "deserve no stain on their memory for joining the King of Castile, whose title to the crown of Portugal was infinitely more just and solid than that of Don John." Castera, however, is grossly mistaken. Don Alonzo Enriquez, the first King of Portugal, was elected by the people, who had recovered their liberties at the glorious battle of Ourique. At the election the constitution of the kingdom was settled in eighteen short statutes, wherein it is expressly provided, that none but a Portuguese can be king of Portugal; that if an infanta marry a foreign prince, he shall not, in her right, become King of Portugal, and a new election of a king, in case of the failure of the male line, is, by these statutes, supposed legal. By the treaty of marriage between the King of Castile and Donna Beatrix, the heiress of Fernando of Portugal, it was agreed, that only their children should succeed to the Portuguese crown; and that, in case the throne became vacant ere such children were born, the Queen-dowager, Leonora, should govern with the title of Regent. Thus, neither by the original constitution, nor by the treaty of marriage, could the King of Castile succeed to the throne of Portugal. And any pretence he might found on the marriage contract was already forfeited; for he caused himself and his queen to be proclaimed, added Portugal to his titles, coined Portuguese money with his bust, deposed the queen regent, and afterwards sent her prisoner to Castile. The lawful heir, Don Juan, the son of Inez de Castro, was kept in prison by his rival, the King of Castile; and, as before observed, a new election was, by the original statutes, supposed legal in cases of emergency. These facts, added to the consideration of the tyranny of the King of Castile, and the great services which Don John had rendered his country, fully vindicate the indignation of Camoëns against the traitorous Pereyras.

[293] Near Pharsalus was fought the decisive battle between Cæsar and Pompey, B.C. 48.—Ed.

[294] Ceuta, a small Spanish possession on the Mediterranean coast of Morocco.—Ed.

[295] Tetuan, a city of Morocco.—Ed.

[296] Through the fierce Brigians.—The Castilians, so called from one of their ancient kings, named Brix, or Brigus, whom the monkish writers call the grandson of Noah.

[297] These lines are not in the common editions of Camoëns. They consist of three stanzas in the Portuguese, and are said to have been left out by the author himself in his second edition. The translator, however, as they breathe the true spirit of Virgil, was willing to preserve them with this acknowledgment.

[298] Massylia, a province in Numidia, greatly infested with lions, particularly that part of it called Os sete montes irmaõs, the seven brother mountains.

[299] And many a gasping warrior sigh'd his last.—This, which is almost literal from—

Muitos lançaraõ o ultimo suspiro,—

and the preceding circumstance of Don John's brandishing his lance four times—

E sopesando a lança quatro vezes,

are poetical, and in the spirit of Homer. Besides Maldonat, Castera has, in this battle, introduced several other names which have no place in Camoëns. Carrillo, Robledo, John of Lorca, Salazar of Seville were killed, he tells us: And, "Velasques and Sanches, natives of Toledo, Galbes, surnamed the 'Soldier without Fear,' Montanches, Oropesa, and Mondonedo, all six of proved valour, fell by the hand of young Antony, who brought to the fight either more address, or better fortune than these." Not a word of this is in the Portuguese.

[300] Their swords seem dipp'd in fire.—This is as literal as the idiom of the two languages would allow. Dryden has a thought like that of this couplet, but which is not in his original:—

"Their bucklers clash; thick blows descend from high,

And flakes of fire from their hard helmets fly."

448

Dryd. Virg. Æn. xii.

[301] Grand master of the order of St. James, named Don Pedro Nunio. He was not killed, however, in this battle, which was fought on the plains of Aljubarota, but in that of Valverda, which immediately followed. The reader may, perhaps, be surprised to find that every soldier mentioned in these notes is a Don, a Lord. The following piece of history will account for the number of the Portuguese nobles. Don Alonzo Enriquez, Count of Portugal, was saluted king by his army at the battle of Ourique; in return, his majesty dignified every man in his army with the rank of nobility.—Vide the 9th of the Statutes of Lamego.

[302] Cerberus.

[303] The Spaniards.

[304] This tyrant, whose unjust pretensions to the crown of Portugal laid his own, and that, kingdom in blood, was on his final defeat overwhelmed with all the frenzy of grief. In the night after the decisive battle of Aljubarota, he fled upwards of thirty miles upon a mule. Don Laurence, archbishop of Braga, in a letter written in old Portuguese to Don John, abbot of Alcobaza, gives this account of his behaviour: "The constable has informed me that he saw the King of Castile at Santaren, who behaved as a madman, cursing his existence, and tearing the hairs of his beard. And, in good faith, my good friend, it is better that he should do so to himself than to us; the man who thus plucks his own beard, would be much better pleased to do so to others." The writer of this letter, though a prelate, fought at the battle of Aljubarota, where he received on the face a large wound from a sabre.

[305] The festive days by heroes old ordain'd.—As a certain proof of the victory, it was required, by the honour of these ages, that the victor should encamp three days on the field of battle. By this knight-errantry the advantages which ought to have been pursued were frequently lost. Don John, however, though he complied with the reigning ideas of honour, sent Don Nunio, with a proper army, to reap the fruits of his victory.

[306] John of Portugal, about a year after the battle of Aljubarota, married Philippa, eldest daughter of John of Gaunt, duke of Lancaster, son of Edward III. who assisted the king, his son-in-law, in an irruption into Castile, and, at the end of the campaign, promised to return with more numerous forces for the next. But this was prevented by the marriage of his youngest daughter, Catalina, with Don Henry, eldest son of the King of Castile. The King of Portugal on this entered Galicia, and reduced the cities of Tui and Salvaterra. A truce followed. While the tyrant of Castile meditated a new war, he was killed by a fall from his horse, and, leaving no issue by his queen, Beatrix (the

King of Portugal's daughter), all pretension to that crown ceased. The truce was now prolonged for fifteen years, and, though not strictly kept, yet, at last the influence of the English queen, Catalina, prevailed, and a long peace, happy for both kingdoms, ensued.

[307] The Pillars of Hercules, or Straits of Gibraltar.—Ed.

[308] The character of this great prince claims a place in these notes, as it affords a comment on the enthusiasm of Camoëns, who has made him the hero of his episode. His birth, excellent education, and masterly conduct when regent, have already been mentioned. The same justice, prudence, and heroism always accompanied him when king. He had the art to join the most winning affability with all the manly dignity of the sovereign. To those who were his friends, when a private man, he was particularly attentive. His nobility dined at his table, he frequently made visits to them, and introduced among them the taste for, and the love of, letters. As he felt the advantages of education, he took the utmost care of that of his children. He had many sons, and he himself often instructed them in solid and useful knowledge, and was amply repaid. He lived to see them men, men of parts and of action, whose only emulation was to show affection to his person, and to support his administration by their great abilities. One of his sons, Don Henry, duke of Viseo, was that great prince whose ardent passion for maritime affairs gave birth to all the modern improvements in navigation. The clergy, who had disturbed almost every other reign, were so convinced of the wisdom of his, that they confessed he ought to be supported out of the treasures of the church, and granted him the church plate to be coined. When the pope ordered a rigorous inquiry to be made into his having brought ecclesiastics before lay tribunals, the clergy had the singular honesty to desert what was styled the church immunities, and to own that justice had been impartially administered. He died in the seventy-sixth year of his age, and in the forty-eighth of his reign. His affection to his queen, Philippa, made him fond of the English, whose friendship he cultivated, and by whom he was frequently assisted.

[309] Camoëns, in this instance, has raised the character of one brother at the other's expense, to give his poem an air of solemnity. The siege of Tangier was proposed. The king's brothers differed in their opinions: that of Don Fernand, though a knight-errant adventure, was approved of by the young nobility. The infants, Henry and Fernand, at the head of 7000 men, laid siege to Tangier, and were surrounded by a numerous army of Moors, some writers say six hundred thousand. On condition that the Portuguese army should be allowed to return home, the infants promised to surrender Ceuta. The Moors gladly accepted of the terms, but demanded one of the infants as a hostage. Fernand offered himself, and was left. The king was willing to comply with the terms to relieve his brother, but the court considered the value of Ceuta,

and would not consent. The pope also interposed his authority, that Ceuta should be kept as a check on the infidels, and proposed to raise a crusade for the delivery of Fernand. In the meanwhile large offers were made for his liberty. These were rejected by the Moors, who would accept of nothing but Ceuta, to whose vast importance they were no strangers. When negotiations failed, King Edward assembled a large army to effect his brother's release, but, just as he was setting out, he was seized with the plague, and died, leaving orders with his queen to deliver up Ceuta for the release of his brother. This, however, was never performed. Don Fernand remained with the Moors till his death. The magnanimity of his behaviour gained him their esteem and admiration, nor is there good proof that he received any very rigorous treatment; the contrary is rather to be inferred from the romantic notions of military honour which then prevailed among the Moors. Don Fernand is to this day esteemed as a saint and martyr in Portugal, and his memory is commemorated on the fifth of June. King Edward reigned only five years and a month. He was the most eloquent man in his dominions, spoke and wrote Latin elegantly, was author of several books, one on horsemanship, in which art he excelled. He was brave in the field, active in business, and rendered his country infinite service by reducing the laws to a regular code. He was knight of the Order of the Garter, which honour was conferred upon him by his cousin, Henry V. of England. In one instance he gave great offence to the superstitious populace. He despised the advice of a Jew astrologer, who entreated him to delay his coronation because the stars that day were unfavourable. To this the misfortune of Tangier was ascribed, and the people were always on the alarm, as if some terrible disaster were impending over them.

[310] The Moors.

[311] When Henry IV. of Castile died, he declared that the infanta Joanna, was his heiress, in preference to his sister, Donna Isabella, married to Don Ferdinand, son to the King of Arragon. In hopes to attain the kingdom of Castile, Don Alonzo, king of Portugal, obtained a dispensation from the pope to marry his niece, Donna Joanna. After a bloody war, the ambitious views of Alonzo and his courtiers were defeated.

[312] The Pyrenees which separate France from Spain.—Ed.

[313] The Prince of Portugal.

[314] Julius Cæsar.

[315] Naples.

[316] Parthenope was one of the Syrens. Enraged because she could not allure Ulysses, she threw herself into the sea. Her corpse was thrown ashore, and buried where Naples now stands.

451

[317] The coast of Alexandria.

[318] Among the Christians of Abyssinia.

[319] Sandy, the French sable = sand.—Ed.

[320] The Nabathean mountains; so named from Nabaoth, the son of Ishmael.

[321] Beyond where Trajan.—The Emperor Trajan extended the bounds of the Roman Empire in the East far beyond any of his predecessors. His conquests reached to the river Tigris, near which stood the city of Ctesiphon, which he subdued. The Roman historians boasted that India was entirely conquered by him; but they could only mean Arabia Felix.—Vid. Dion. Cass. Euseb. Chron. p. 206.

[322] Qui mores hominum multorum vidit.—Hor.

[323] Emmanuel was cousin to the late king, John II. and grandson to king Edward, son of John I.

[324] The river Indus, which gave name to India.

[325] Vasco de Gama, who is, in a certain sense, the hero of the Lusiad, was born in 1469, at Sines, a fishing town on the Atlantic, midway between Lisbon and Cape St. Vincent, where, in a small church on a cliff, built by the great navigator after his appointment as Viceroy of India, is an inscription to his memory.—Ed.

[326] Hercules.

[327] Orac'lous Argo.—According to the fable, the vessel of the Argonauts spoke and prophesied. See The Argonautics of Apollonius Rhodius.—Ed.

[328] This fact is according to history: Aberat Olysippone prope littus quatuor passuum millia templum sanè religiosum et sanctum ab Henrico in honorem Sanctissimæ Virginis edificatum.... In id Gama pridie illius diei, quo erat navem conscensurus, se recepit, ut noctem cum religiosis hominibus qui in ædibus templo conjunctis habitabant, in precibus et votis consumeret. Sequenti die cum multi non illius tantùm gratia, sed aliorum etiam, qui illi comites erant, convenissent, fuit ab omnibus in scaphis deductus. Neque solùm homines religiosi, sed reliqui omnes voce maxima cum lacrymis à Deo precabantur, ut benè et prosperè illa tam periculosa navigatio omnibus eveniret, et universi re benè gesta, incolumes in patriam redirent.

[329] By this old man is personified the populace of Portugal. The endeavours to discover the East Indies by the Southern Ocean, for about eighty years had been the favourite topic of complaint, and never was any measure of government more unpopular than the expedition of Gama.

Emmanuel's council were almost unanimous against the attempt. Some dreaded the introduction of wealth, and its attendants, luxury and effeminacy; while others affirmed, that no adequate advantages could arise from so perilous and remote a navigation. The expressions of the thousands who crowded the shore when Gama gave his sails to the wind, are thus expressed by Osorius: "A multis tamen interim is fletus atque lamentatio fiebat, un funus efferre viderentur. Sic enim dicebant: En quo miseros mortales provexit cupiditas et ambitio? Potuitne gravius supplicium hominibus istis constitui, si in se scelestum aliquod facinus admisissent? Est enim illis immensi maris longitudo peragranda, fluctus immanes difficillima navigatione superandi, vitæ discrimen in locis infinitis obeundum. Non fuit multò tolerabilius, in terra quovis genere mortis absumi, quàm tam procul à patria marinis fluctibus sepeliri. Hæc et alia multa in hanc sententiam dicebant, cùm omnia multò tristiora fingere præ metu cogerentur." The tender emotion and fixed resolution of Gama, and the earnest passion of the multitudes on the shore, are thus added by the same venerable historian: "Gama tamen quamvis lacrymas suorum desiderio funderet, rei tamen benè gerendæ fiducia confirmatus, alacriter in navem faustis ominibus conscendit.... Qui in littore consistebant, non prius abscedere voluerunt, quàm naves vento secundo plenissimis velis ab omnium conspectu remotæ sunt."

[330] More literally rendered by Capt. R. Burton:—

"——He spoke

From a full heart, and skill'd in worldly lore,

In deep, slow tones this solemn warning, fraught

With wisdom, by long-suffering only taught:

'O passion of dominion! O fond lust

Of that poor vanity which men call fame!

O treach'rous appetite, whose highest gust

Is vulgar breath that taketh honour's name!

O fell ambition, terrible but just

Art thou to breasts that cherish most thy flame!

Brief life for them in peril, storm, and rage;

This world a hell, and death their heritage.

"'Shrewd prodigal! whose riot is the dearth

Of states and principalities oppress'd,

Plunder and rape are of thy loathly birth,

Thou art alike of life and soul the pest.

High titles greet thee on this slavish earth,

Yet, none so vile but they would fit thee best.

But Fame, forsooth, and Glory thou art styl'd,

And the blind herd is by a sound beguil'd.'"

[331] The Moor.—Ed.

[332] The Muses.—Ed.

[333] Prometheus is said to have stolen fire from heaven.—Ed.

[334] Alluding to the fables of Phaeton and Icarus; the former having obtained from Helios, his father, permission to guide the chariot of the sun for one day, nearly set the world on fire. He perished in the river Eridanus (the Po.) Icarus, the sun having melted the wax with which his wings were cemented, fell into that part of the Ægean which, from his misfortune, was called the Icarian Sea.—Ed.

[335] The sun is in the constellation Leo in July.—Ed.

[336] The Serra de Cintra, situated about 15 miles N.W. of Lisbon.—Ed.

[337] See the life of Don Henry, prince of Portugal, in the preface.

[338] Morocco.

[339] The discovery of some of the West Indian islands by Columbus was made in 1492 and 1493. His discovery of the continent of America was not till 1498. The fleet of Gama sailed from the Tagus in 1497.

[340] Called by the ancients Insulæ Purpurariæ. Now Madeira, and Porto Santo. The former was so named by Juan Gonzales, and Tristan Vaz, from the Spanish word madera, wood. These discoverers wens sent out by the great Don Henry.

[341] The Tropic of Cancer.—Ed.

[342] Called by Ptolemy Caput Assinarium, now Cape Verde.

[343] The Canaries, called by the ancients Insulæ Fortunatæ.

[344] The province of Jalofo lies between the two rivers, the Gambia and the Zanago. The latter has other names in the several countries through which it

runs. In its course it makes many islands, inhabited only by wild beasts. It is navigable for 150 leagues, at the end of which it is crossed by a stupendous ridge of perpendicular rocks, over which the river rushes with such violence, that travellers pass under it without any other inconvenience than the prodigious noise. The Gambia, or Rio Grande, runs 180 leagues, but is not so far navigable. It carries more water, and runs with less noise than the other, though filled with many rivers which water the country of Mandinga. Both rivers are branches of the Niger. Their waters have this remarkable quality; when mixed together they operate as an emetic, but when separate do not. They abound with great variety of fishes, and their banks are covered with horses, crocodiles, winged serpents, elephants, ounces, wild boars, with great numbers of others, wonderful for the variety of their nature and different forms.—Faria y Sousa.

[345] Timbuctu, the mart of Mandinga gold, was greatly resorted to by the merchants of Grand Cairo, Tunis, Oran, Tlemicen, Fez, Morocco, etc.

[346] Contra hoc promontorium (Hesperionceras) Gorgades insulæ narrantur, Gorgonum quondam domus, bidui navigatione distantes a continente, ut tradit Xenophon Lampsacenus. Penetravit in eas Hanno Pœnorum imperator, prodiditque hirta fœminarum corpora viros pernicitate evasisse, duarumque Gorgonum cutes argumenti et miraculi gratia in Junonis templo posuit, spectatas usque ad Carthaginem captam.—Plin. Hist. Nat. l. 6. c. 31.

[347] Sierra Leone.

[348] Cape Palmas.—Ed.

[349] During the reign of John II. the Portuguese erected several forts, and acquired great power in the extensive regions of Guinea. Azambuja, a Portuguese captain, having obtained leave from Caramansa, a negro prince, to erect a fort on his territories, an unlucky accident had almost proved fatal to the discoverers. A huge rock lay very commodious for a quarry; the workmen began on it; but this rock, as the devil would have it, happened to be a negro god. The Portuguese were driven away by the enraged worshippers, who were afterwards with difficulty pacified by a profusion of such presents as they most esteemed.

[350] The Portuguese, having brought an ambassador from Congo to Lisbon, sent him back instructed in the faith. By this means the king, queen, and about 100,000 of the people were baptized; the idols were destroyed and churches built. Soon after, the prince, who was then absent at war, was baptized by the name of Alonzo. His younger brother, Aquitimo, however, would not receive the faith, and the father, because allowed only one wife, turned apostate, and left the crown to his pagan son, who, with a great army, surrounded his brother, when only attended by some Portuguese and

Christian blacks, in all only thirty-seven. By the bravery of these, however, Aquitimo was defeated, taken, and slain. One of Aquitimo's officers declared, they were not defeated by the thirty-seven Christians, but by a glorious army who fought under a shining cross. The idols were again destroyed, and Alonzo sent his sons, grandsons, and nephews to Portugal to study; two of whom were afterwards bishops in Congo.—Extracted from Faria y Sousa.

[351] According to fable, Calisto was a nymph of Diana. Jupiter having assumed the figure of that goddess, completed his amorous desires. On the discovery of her pregnancy, Diana drove her from her train. She fled to the woods, where she was delivered of a son. Juno changed them into bears, and Jupiter placed them in heaven, where they form the constellations of Ursa Major and Minor. Juno, still enraged, entreated Thetis never to suffer Calisto to bathe in the sea. This is founded on the appearance of the northern pole-star, to the inhabitants of our hemisphere; but, when Gama approached the austral pole, the northern, of consequence, disappeared under the waves.

[352] The Southern Cross.

[353] The constellation of the southern pole was called The Cross by the Portuguese sailors, from the appearance of that figure formed by seven stars. In the southern hemisphere, as Camoëns observes, the nights are darker than in the northern, the skies being adorned with much fewer stars.

[354]Non, mihi si linguæ centum sunt, oraque

centum, Ferrea vox, omnes scelerum comprendere formas.—ÆN. vi.

[355] That living fire, by seamen held divine.—The sulphureous vapours of the air, after being violently agitated by a tempest, unite, and when the humidity begins to subside, as is the case when the storm is almost exhausted, by the agitation of their atoms they take fire, and are attracted by the masts and cordage of the ship. Being thus, naturally, the pledges of the approaching calm, it is no wonder that the superstition of sailors should in all ages have esteemed them divine, and—

Of heaven's own care in storms the holy sign.

In the expedition of the Golden Fleece, in a violent tempest these fires were seen to hover over the heads of Castor and Pollux, who were two of the Argonauts, and a calm immediately ensued. After the apotheoses of these heroes, the Grecian sailors invoked these fires by the names of Castor and

Pollux, or the sons of Jupiter. The Athenians called them Σωτῆρες, Saviours.

[356] In this book, particularly in the description of Massilia, the Gorgades, the fires called Castor and Pollux, and the water-spout, Camoëns has happily

imitated the manner of Lucan. It is probable that Camoëns, in his voyage to the East Indies, was an eye witness of the phenomena of the fires and water-spout. The latter is thus described by Pliny, l. 2. c. 51. Fit et caligo, belluæ similis nubes dira navigantibus vocatur et columna, cum spissatus humor rigensque ipse se sustinet, et in longam veluti fistulam nubes aquam trahit. When the violent heat attracts the waters to rise in the form of a tube, the marine salts are left behind, by the action of rarefaction, being too gross and fixed to ascend. It is thus, when the overloaded vapour bursts, that it descends—

Sweet as the waters of the limpid rill.

[357] That sage device.—The astrolabe, an instrument of infinite service in navigation, by which the altitude of the sun, and distance of the stars is taken. It was invented in Portugal during the reign of John II. by two Jewish physicians, named Roderic and Joseph. It is asserted by some that they were assisted by Martin of Bohemia, a celebrated mathematician.—Partly from Castera. Vid. Barros, Dec. 1. lib. iv. c. 2.

[358] Arabic, one of the most copious and wide-spoken of languages.—Ed.

[359] Camoëns, in describing the adventure of Fernando Velosó, by departing from the truth of history, has shown his judgment as a poet. The place where the Portuguese landed they named the Bay of St. Helen. They caught one of two negroes, says Faria, who were busied in gathering honey on a mountain. Their behaviour to this savage, whom they gratified with a red cap, some glasses and bells, induced him to bring a number of his companions for the like trifles. Though some who accompanied Gama were skilled in the various African languages, not one of the natives could understand them. A commerce, however, was commenced by signs and gestures. Gama behaved to them with great civility; the fleet was cheerfully supplied with fresh provisions, for which the natives received cloths and trinkets. But this friendship was soon interrupted by a young, rash Portuguese. Having contracted an intimacy with some of the negroes, he obtained leave to penetrate into the country along with them, to observe their habitations and strength. They conducted him to their huts with great good nature, and placed before him, what they esteemed an elegant repast, a sea-calf dressed in the way of their country. This so much disgusted the delicate Portuguese, that he instantly got up and abruptly left them. Nor did they oppose his departure, but accompanied him with the greatest innocence. As fear, however, is always jealous, he imagined they were leading him as a victim to slaughter. No sooner did he come near the ships, than he called aloud for assistance. Coëllo's boat immediately set off for his rescue. The Africans fled to the woods; and now esteeming the Portuguese as a band of lawless plunderers,

they provided themselves with arms, and lay in ambush. Their weapons were javelins, headed with short pieces of horn, which they throw with great dexterity. Soon after, while Gama and some of his officers were on the shore taking the altitude of the sun by the astrolabe, they were suddenly and with great fury attacked by the ambush from the woods. Several were much wounded, multos convulnerant, inter quos Gama in pede vulnus accepit, and Gama received a wound in the foot. The admiral made a speedy retreat to the fleet, prudently choosing rather to leave the negroes the honour of the victory, than to risk the life of one man in a quarrel so foreign to the destination of his expedition, and where, to impress the terror of his arms could be of no service to his interest. When he came nearer to the East Indies he acted in a different manner. He then made himself dreaded whenever the treachery of the natives provoked his resentment.—Collected from Faria and Osorius.

[360] The critics have vehemently declaimed against the least mixture of the comic, with the dignity of the epic poem. It is needless to enter into any defence of this passage of Camoëns, farther than to observe that Homer, Virgil, and Milton have offended the critics in the same manner, and that this piece of raillery in the Lusiad is by much the politest, and the least reprehensible, of anything of the kind in the four poets. In Homer are several strokes of low raillery. Patroclus having killed Hector's charioteer, puns thus on his sudden fall: It is a pity he is not nearer the sea! He would soon catch abundance of oysters, nor would the storms frighten him. See how he dives from his chariot down to the sand! What excellent divers are the Trojans! Virgil, the most judicious of all poets, descends even to burlesque, where the commander of a galley tumbles the pilot into the sea:—

——Segnemque Menœten

In mare præcipitem puppi deturbat ab alta.

At gravis ut sundo vix tandem redditus imo est

Jam senior, madidaque fluens in veste Menœtes,

Summa petit scopuli siccaque in rupe resedit.

Illum et labentem Teucri, et risere natantem;

Et salsos rident revomentem pectore fluctus.

And, though the character of the speakers, the ingenious defence which has been offered for Milton, may, in some measure, vindicate the raillery which he puts into the mouths of Satan and Belial, the lowness of it, when compared with that of Camoëns, must still be acknowledged. Talking of the execution of the diabolical artillery among the good angels, they, says Satan—

"Flew off, and into strange vagaries fell

As they would dance, yet for a dance they seem'd

Somewhat extravagant and wild, perhaps

For joy of offer'd peace.——

To whom thus Belial, in like gamesome mood.

Leader, the terms we sent were terms of weight,

Of hard contents, and full of force urg'd home,

Such as we might perceive amus'd them all,

And stumbled many——

——this gift they have beside,

They show us when our foes walk not upright."

[361] The translator in reply to the critics will venture the assertion, that the fiction of the apparition of the Cape of Tempests, in sublimity and awful grandeur of imagination, stands unsurpassed in human composition.

[362] The next proud fleet.—On the return of Gama to Portugal, a fleet of thirteen sail, under the command of Pedro Alvarez Cabral, was sent out on the second voyage to India, where the admiral with only six ships arrived. The rest were mostly destroyed by a terrible tempest at the Cape of Good Hope, which lasted twenty days. "The daytime," says Faria, "was so dark that the sailors could scarcely see each other, or hear what was said for the horrid noise of the winds." Among those who perished was the celebrated Bartholomew Diaz, who was the first modern discoverer of the Cape of Good Hope, which he named the Cape of Tempests.

[363] Behold a hero come.—Don Francisco de Almeyda. He was the first Portuguese viceroy of India, in which country he obtained several great victories over the Mohammedans and pagans. He was the first who conquered Quiloa and Mombas, or Mombaz. On his return to Portugal he put into the bay of Saldanha, near the Cape of Good Hope, to take in water and provisions. The rudeness of one of his servants produced a quarrel with the Caffres, or Hottentots. His attendants, much against his will, forced him to march against the blacks. "Ah, whither," he exclaimed, "will you carry the infirm man of sixty years?" After plundering a miserable village, on the return to their ships they were attacked by a superior number of Caffres, who fought with such fury in rescue of their children, whom the Portuguese had seized,

that the viceroy and fifty of his attendants were slain.

[364] The crescent, the symbol of Mohammedanism.—Ed.

[365] This poetical description of the miserable catastrophe of Don Emmanuel de Souza, and his beautiful spouse, Leonora de Sà, is by no means exaggerated. He was several years governor of Diu in India, where he amassed immense wealth. On his return to his native country, the ship in which was his lady, all his riches, and five hundred men, his sailors and domestics, was dashed to pieces on the rocks at the Cape of Good Hope. Don Emmanuel, his lady, and three children, with four hundred of the crew escaped, having only saved a few arms and provisions. As they marched through the wild uncultivated deserts, some died of famine, of thirst, and fatigue; others, who wandered from the main body in search of water, were murdered by the savages, or destroyed by the wild beasts. They arrived, at last, at a village inhabited by African banditti. At first they were courteously received, but the barbarians, having unexpectedly seized their arms, stripped the whole company naked, and left them destitute to the mercy of the desert. The wretchedness of the delicate and exposed Leonora was increased by the brutal insults of the negroes. Her husband, unable to relieve, beheld her miseries. After having travelled about 300 leagues, her legs swelled, her feet bleeding at every step, and her strength exhausted, she sunk down, and with the sand covered herself to the neck, to conceal her nakedness. In this dreadful situation, she beheld two of her children expire. Her own death soon followed. Her husband, who had been long enamoured of her beauty, received her last breath in a distracted embrace. Immediately, he snatched his third child in his arms, and uttering the most lamentable cries, he ran into the thickest of the wood, where the wild beasts were soon heard to growl over their prey. Of the whole four hundred who escaped the waves, only six and twenty arrived at another village, whose inhabitants were more civilized, and traded with the merchants of the Red Sea, from whence they found a passage to Europe, and brought the tidings of the unhappy fate of their companions. Jerome de Cortereal, a Portuguese poet, has written an affecting poem on the shipwreck, and deplorable catastrophe of Don Emmanuel, and his beloved spouse.—Partly from Castera.

[366] The giants or Titans; called "sons of God" in Gen. vi. 2.—Ed.

[367] Briareus.

[368] Doris, the sister and spouse of Nereus, and mother of the Nereides. By Nereus, in the physical sense of the fable, is understood the water of the sea, and by Doris, the bitterness or salt, the supposed cause of its prolific quality in the generation of fishes.

[369] And give our wearied minds a lively glow.—Variety is no less delightful

to the reader than to the traveller, and the imagination of Camoëns gave an abundant supply. The insertion of this pastoral landscape, between the terrific scenes which precede and follow, has a fine effect. "Variety," says Pope, in one of his notes on the Odyssey, "gives life and delight; and it is much more necessary in epic, than in comic or tragic, poetry, sometimes to shift the scenes, to diversify and embellish the story."

The Portuguese, sailing upon the Atlantic Ocean, discovered the most southern point of Africa: here they found an immense sea, which carried them to the East Indies. The dangers they encountered in the voyage, the discovery of Mozambique, of Melinda, and of Calecut, have been sung by Camoëns, whose poem recalls to our minds the charms of the Odyssey, and the magnificence of the Æneid.—Montesquieu, Spirit of Laws, bk. xxi. c. 21.

[370] Virgil.

[371] A small island, named Santa Cruz by Bartholomew Diaz, who discovered it. According to Faria y Sousa, he went twenty-five leagues further, to the river Del Infante, which, till passed by Gama, was the utmost extent of the Portuguese discoveries.

[372] It was the force of this rushing current which retarded the further discoveries of Diaz. Gama got over it by the assistance of a tempest. The seasons when these seas are safely navigable, are now perfectly known.

[373] The wise men of the East, or magi, whom the Roman Catholic writers will have to have been kings.—Ed.

[374] The Epiphany.—Ed.

[375] Dos Reis, i.e., of the kings.—Ed.

[376] The frequent disappointments of the Portuguese, when they expect to hear some account of India, is a judicious imitation of several parts of Virgil; who, in the same manner, magnifies the distresses of the Trojans in their search for the fated seat of Empire:—

——O gens

Infelix! cui to exitio fortuna reservat?

Septima post Trojæ excidium jam vertitur æstas;

Cum freta, cum terras omnes, tot inhospita saxa

Sideraque emensæ ferimur: dum per mare magnum

Italiam sequimur fugientem, et volvimur undis. Æn. v. 625.

[377] Hop.

[378] It had been extremely impolitic in Gama to mention the mutiny of his followers to the King of Melinda. The boast of their loyalty, besides, has a good effect in the poem, as it elevates the heroes, and gives uniformity to the character of bravery, which the dignity of the epopea required to be ascribed to them. History relates the matter differently. In standing for the Cape of Good Hope, Gama gave the highest proofs of his resolution. The fleet seemed now tossed to the clouds, *ut modo nubes contingere*, and now sunk to the lowest whirlpools of the abyss. The winds were insufferably cold, and, to the rage of the tempest was added the horror of an almost continual darkness. The crew expected every moment to be swallowed up in the deep. At every interval of the storm, they came round Gama, asserting the impossibility to proceed further, and imploring him to return. This he resolutely refused. A conspiracy against his life was formed, but was discovered by his brother. He guarded against it with the greatest courage and prudence; put all the pilots in chains, and he himself, with some others, took the management of the helms. At last, after having many days withstood the tempest, and a perfidious conspiracy, *invicto animo*, with an unconquered mind, a favourable change of weather revived the spirits of the fleet, and allowed them to double the Cape of Good Hope.—Extr. from Osorius's Historia.

[379] Gama and his followers were, from the darkness of the Portuguese complexion, thought to be Moors. When Gama arrived in the East, a considerable commerce was carried on between the Indies and the Red Sea by the Moorish traders, by whom the gold mines of Sofala, and the riches of East Africa were enjoyed. The traffic was brought by land to Cairo, from whence Europe was supplied by the Venetian and Antwerpian merchants.

[380] "O nome lhe ficou dos Bons-Signais."

[381] Raphael. See Tobit, ch. v. and xii.—Ed.

[382] It was the custom of the Portuguese navigators to erect crosses on the shores of new-discovered countries. Gama carried materials for pillars of stone with him, and erected six crosses during his expedition. They bore the name and arms of the king of Portugal, and were intended as proofs of the title which accrues from first discovery.

[383] This poetical description of the scurvy is by no means exaggerated. It is what sometimes really happens in the course of a long voyage.

[384] King of Ithaca.

[385] Æneas.

[386] Homer.

[387] Virgil.

[388] The Muses.

[389] Homer's Odyssey, bk. x. 460.

[390] See the Odyssey, bk. ix.

[391] See Æn. v. 833

[392] The Lotophagi, so named from the lotus, are thus described by Homer:—

"Not prone to ill, nor strange to foreign guest,

They eat, they drink, and Nature gives the feast;

The trees around them all their fruit produce;

Lotos the name; divine, nectareous juice;

(Thence call'd Lotophagi) which whoso tastes,

Insatiate, riots in the sweet repasts,

Nor other home, nor other care intends,

But quits his home, his country, and his friends:

The three we sent, from off th' enchanting ground

We dragg'd reluctant, and by force we bound:

The rest in haste forsook the pleasing shore,

Or, the charm tasted, had return'd no more."

Pope, Odyss. ix. 103.

The Libyan lotus is a shrub like a bramble, the berries like the myrtle, purple when ripe, and about the size of an olive. Mixed with bread-corn, it was used as food for slaves. They also made an agreeable wine of it, but which would not keep above ten days. See Pope's note in loco.

[393] In skins confin'd the blust'ring winds control.—The gift of Æolus to Ulysses.

"The adverse winds in leathern bags he brac'd,

Compress'd their force, and lock'd each struggling blast:

For him the mighty sire of gods assign'd,

The tempest's lord, the tyrant of the wind;

His word alone the list'ning storms obey,

To smooth the deep, or swell the foamy sea.

These, in my hollow ship the monarch hung,

Securely fetter'd by a silver thong;

But Zephyrus exempt, with friendly gales

He charg'd to fill, and guide the swelling sails:

Rare gift! but oh, what gift to fools avails?"

Pope, Odyss. x. 20.

The companions of Ulysses imagined that these bags contained some valuable treasure, and opened them while their leader slept. The tempests bursting out, drove the fleet from Ithaca, which was then in sight, and was the cause of a new train of miseries.

[394] See the third Æneid.

[395] See the sixth Æneid, and the eleventh Odyssey.

[396] Alexander the Great.—Ed.

[397] Achilles, son of Peleus.—Ed.

[398] Virgil, born at Mantua.—Ed.

[399] Don Francisco de Gama, grandson of Vasco de Gama, the hero of the Lusiad.—Ed.

[400] Cleopatra.

[401] Every display of eastern luxury and magnificence was lavished in the fishing parties on the Nile, with which Cleopatra amused Mark Antony, when at any time he showed symptoms of uneasiness, or seemed inclined to abandon the effeminate life which he led with his mistress. At one of these parties, Mark Antony, having procured divers to put fishes upon his hooks while under the water, he very gallantly boasted to his mistress of his great dexterity in angling. Cleopatra perceived his art, and as gallantly outwitted him. Some other divers received her orders, and in a little while Mark Antony's line brought up a fried fish in place of a live one, to the vast entertainment of the queen, and all the convivial company. Octavius was at this time on his march to decide who should be master of the world.

[402] The friendship of the Portuguese and Melindians was of long continuance. Alvaro Cabral, the second admiral who made the voyage to

India, in an engagement with the Moors off the coast of Sofala, took two ships richly freighted from the mines of that country. On finding that Xeques Fonteyma, the commander, was uncle to the King of Melinda, he restored the valuable prize, and treated him with the utmost courtesy. Their good offices were reciprocal. By the information of the King of Melinda, Cabral escaped the treachery of the King of Calicut. The Kings of Mombaz and Quiloa, irritated at the alliance with Portugal, made several depredations on the subjects of Melinda, who in return were effectually revenged by their European allies.

[403] A giant.

[404] Two gods contending.—According to the fable, Neptune and Minerva disputed the honour of giving a name to the city of Athens. They agreed to determine the contest by a display of their wisdom and power, in conferring the most beneficial gift on mankind. Neptune struck the earth with his trident and produced the horse, whose bounding motions are emblematical of the agitation of the sea. Pallas commanded the olive-tree, the symbol of peace, and of riches, to spring forth. The victory was adjudged to the goddess, from whom the city was named Athens. The taste of the ancient Grecians clothed almost every occurrence in mythological allegory. The founders of Athens, it is most probable, disputed whether their new city should be named from the fertility of the soil or from the marine situation of Attica. The former opinion prevailed, and the town received its name in honour of the goddess of the olive-tree—Athēnē.

[405] While Pallas here appears to wave her hand.—As Neptune struck the earth with his trident, Minerva, says the fable, struck the earth with her lance. That she waved her hand while the olive boughs spread, is a fine poetical attitude, and varies the picture from that of Neptune, which follows.

[406] Though wide, and various, o'er the sculptur'd stone.—The description of palaces is a favourite topic several times touched upon by the two great masters of epic poetry, in which they have been happily imitated by their three greatest disciples among the moderns, Camoëns, Tasso, and Milton. The description of the palace of Neptune has great merit. Nothing can be more in place than the picture of chaos and the four elements. The war of the gods, and the contest of Neptune and Minerva are touched with the true boldness of poetical colouring. To show to the English reader that the Portuguese poet is, in his manner, truly classical, is the intention of many of these notes.

[407] Bacchus.

[408] The description of Triton, who, as Fanshaw says—

"Was a great nasty clown,"

is in the style of the classics. His parentage is differently related. Hesiod makes him the son of Neptune and Amphitrité. By Triton, in the physical sense of the fable, is meant the noise, and by Salacé, the mother by some ascribed to him, the salt of the ocean. The origin of the fable of Triton, it is probable, was founded on the appearance of a sea animal, which, according to some ancient naturalists, in the upward parts resembles the human figure. Pausanias relates a wonderful story of a monstrously large one, which often came ashore on the meadows of Bœotia. Over his head was a kind of finny cartilage, which, at a distance, appeared like hair; the body covered with brown scales; the nose and ears like the human; the mouth of a dreadful width, jagged with the teeth of a panther; the eyes of a greenish hue; the hands divided into fingers, the nails of which were crooked, and of a shelly substance. This monster, whose extremities ended in a tail like a dolphin's, devoured both men and beasts as they chanced in his way. The citizens of Tanagra, at last, contrived his destruction. They set a large vessel full of wine on the sea shore. Triton got drunk with it, and fell into a profound sleep, in which condition the Tanagrians beheaded him, and afterwards, with great propriety, hung up his body in the temple of Bacchus; where, says Pausanias, it continued a long time.

[409] A shell of purple on his head he bore.—In the Portuguese—

Na cabeça por gorra tinha posta

Huma mui grandé casco de lagosta.

Thus rendered by Fanshaw—

"He had (for a montera[413]) on his crown

The shell of a red lobster overgrown."

[410] Neptune.

[411] And changeful Proteus, whose prophetic mind.—The fullest and best account of the fable of Proteus is in the fourth Odyssey.

[412] Thetis.

[413] Montera, the Spanish word for a huntsman's cap.

[414] She who the rage of Athamas to shun.—Ino, the daughter of Cadmus and Hermione, and second spouse of Athamas, king of Thebes. The fables of her fate are various. That which Camoëns follows is the most common.

Athamas, seized with madness, imagined that his spouse was a lioness, and her two sons young lions. In this frenzy he slew Learchus, and drove the mother and her other son, Melicertus, into the sea. The corpse of the mother was thrown ashore on Megara and that of the son at Corinth. They were afterwards deified, the one as a sea goddess, the other as the god of harbours.

[415] And Glaucus lost to joy.—A fisherman, says the fable, who, on eating a certain herb, was turned into a sea god. Circé was enamoured of him, and in revenge of her slighted love, poisoned the fountain where his mistress usually bathed. By the force of the enchantment the favoured Scylla was changed into a hideous monster, whose loins were surrounded with the ever-barking heads of dogs and wolves. Scylla, on this, threw herself into the sea, and was metamorphosed into the rock which bears her name. The rock Scylla at a distance appears like the statue of a woman. The furious dashing of the waves in the cavities, which are level with the water, resembles the barking of wolves and dogs.

[416] Thyoneus, a name of Bacchus.

[417] High from the roof the living amber glows.—

"From the arched roof,

Pendent by subtle magic, many a row

Of starry lamps, and blazing cressets, fed

With naptha and asphaltus, yielded light

As from a sky."

Milton.

[418] The Titans.

[419] The north wind.

[420] And rent the Mynian sails.—The sails of the Argonauts, inhabitants of Mynia.

[421] See the first note on the first book of the Lusiad.

[422]

In haughty England, where the winter spreads

His snowy mantle o'er the shining meads.—

467

In the original—

Là na grande Inglaterra, que de neve

Boreal sempre abunda;

that is, "In illustrious England, always covered with northern snow." Though the translator was willing to retain the manner of Homer, he thought it proper to correct the error in natural history fallen into by Camoëns. Fanshaw seems to have been sensible of the mistake of his author, and has given the following (uncountenanced by the Portuguese) in place of the eternal snows ascribed to his country:—

"In merry England, which (from cliffs that stand

Like hills of snow) once Albion's name did git."

[423] Eris, or Discordia, the goddess of contention.—Virgil, Æneid ii. 337.— Ed.

[424]

What knighthood asks, the proud accusers yield,

And, dare the damsels' champions to the field.—

The translator has not been able to discover the slightest vestige of this chivalrous adventure in any memoirs of the English history. It is probable, nevertheless, that however adorned with romantic ornament, it is not entirely without foundation in truth. Castera, who unhappily does not cite his authority, gives the names of the twelve Portuguese champions: Alvaro Vaz d'Almada, afterwards Count d'Avranches in Normandy; another Alvaro d'Almada, surnamed the Juster, from his dexterity at that warlike exercise; Lopez Fernando Pacheco; Pedro Homen d'Acosta; Juan Augustin Pereyra; Luis Gonfalez de Malafay; the two brothers Alvaro and Rodrigo Mendez de Cerveyra; Ruy Gomex de Sylva; Soueyro d'Acosta, who gave his name to the river Acosta in Africa; Martin Lopez d'Azevedo; and Alvaro Gonfalez de Coutigno, surnamed Magricio. The names of the English champions, and of the ladies, he confesses are unknown, nor does history positively explain the injury of which the dames complained. It must, however, he adds, have been such as required the atonement of blood; il falloit qu'elle fût sanglante, since two sovereigns allowed to determine it by the sword. "Some critics," says Castera, "may perhaps condemn this episode of Camoëns; but for my part," he continues, "I think the adventure of Olindo and Sophronia, in Tasso, is much more to be blamed. The episode of the Italian poet is totally exuberant, whereas that of the Portuguese has a direct relation to his proposed subject: the wars of his country, a vast field, in which he has admirably succeeded, without prejudice to the first rule of the epopea, the unity of the action." The severest critic must allow that the episode related by Veloso, is happily introduced. To one who has ever been at sea, the scene must be particularly pleasing. The fleet is under sail, they plough the smooth deep—

"And o'er the decks cold breath'd the midnight wind."

All but the second watch are asleep in their warm pavilions; the second watch sit by the mast, sheltered from the chilly gale by a broad sail-cloth; sleep begins to overpower them, and they tell stories to entertain one another. For beautiful, picturesque simplicity there is no sea-scene equal to this in the Odyssey, or Æneid.

[425] What time he claim'd the proud Castilian throne.—John of Gaunt, duke of Lancaster, claimed the crown of Castile in the right of his wife, Donna Constantia, daughter of Don Pedro, the late king. Assisted by his son-in-law, John I. of Portugal, he entered Galicia, and was proclaimed king of Castile at the city of St. Jago de Compostella. He afterwards relinquished his pretensions, on the marriage of his daughter, Catalina, with the infant, Don Henry of Castile.

[426] The dames by lot their gallant champions choose.—The ten champions, who in the fifth book of Tasso's Jerusalem are sent by Godfrey for the assistance of Armida, are chosen by lot. Tasso, who had read the Lusiad, and admired its author, undoubtedly had the Portuguese poet in his eye.

[427]

In that proud port half circled by the wave,

Which Portugallia to the nation gave,

A deathless name.—

Oporto, called by the Romans Calle. Hence Portugal.

[428]

Yet something more than human warms my breast,

And sudden whispers—

In the Portuguese—

Mas, se a verdade o espirito me adevinha.

Literally, "But, if my spirit truly divine." Thus rendered by Fanshaw—

But, in my aug'ring ear a bird doth sing.

[429] As Rome's Corvinus.—Valerius Maximus, a Roman tribune, who fought and slew a Gaul of enormous stature, in single combat. During the duel a raven perched on the helmet of his antagonist, sometimes pecked his face and hand, and sometimes blinded him with the flapping of his wings. The victor was thence named Corvinus, from Corvus. Vid. Livy, l. 7, c. 26.

[430] The Flandrian countess on her hero smil'd.—The princess, for whom Magricio signalized his valour, was Isabella of Portugal, and spouse to Philip the Good, duke of Burgundy, and earl of Flanders. Some Spanish chronicles relate that Charles VII. of France, having assembled the states of his kingdom, cited Philip to appear with his other vassals. Isabella, who was present, solemnly protested that the earls of Flanders were not obliged to do homage. A dispute arose, on which she offered, according to the custom of that age, to appeal to the fate of arms. The proposal was accepted, and Magricio the champion of Isabella, vanquished a French chevalier, appointed by Charles. Though our authors do not mention this adventure, and though Emmanuel de Faria, and the best Portuguese writers treat it with doubt, nothing to the disadvantage of Camoëns is thence to be inferred. A poet is not obliged always to follow the truth of history.

[431] The Rhine another pass'd, and prov'd his might.—This was Alvaro Vaz d'Almada. The chronicle of Garibay relates, that at Basle he received from a German a challenge to measure swords, on condition that each should fight with the right side unarmed; the German by this hoping to be victorious, for he was left-handed. The Portuguese, suspecting no fraud, accepted. When the combat began he perceived the inequality. His right side unarmed was exposed to the enemy, whose left side, which was nearest to him was defended with half a cuirass. Notwithstanding all this, the brave Alvaro obtained the victory. He sprang upon the German, seized him, and, grasping him forcibly in his arms, stifled and crushed him to death; imitating the conduct of Hercules, who in the same manner slew the cruel Anteus. Here we ought to remark the address of our author; he describes at length the injury and grief of the English ladies, the voyage of the twelve champions to England, and the prowess they there displayed. When Veloso relates these, the sea is calm; but no sooner does it begin to be troubled, than the soldier

abridges his recital: we see him follow by degrees the preludes of the storm, we perceive the anxiety of his mind on the view of the approaching danger, hastening his narration to an end. Behold the strokes of a master!—This note, and the one preceding, are from Castera.

[432] The halcyons, mindful of their fate, deplore.—Ceyx, king of Trachinia, son of Lucifer, married Alcyone, the daughter of Eolus. On a voyage to consult the Delphic Oracle, he was shipwrecked. His corpse was thrown ashore in the view of his spouse, who, in the agonies of her love and despair, threw herself into the sea. The gods, in pity of her pious fidelity, metamorphosed them into the birds which bear her name. The halcyon is a little bird about the size of a thrush, its plumage of a beautiful sky blue, mixed with some traits of white and carnation. It is vulgarly called the kingfisher. The halcyons very seldom appear but in the finest weather, whence they are fabled to build their nests on the waves. The female is no less remarkable than the turtle, for her conjugal affection. She nourishes and attends the male when sick, and survives his death but a few days. When the halcyons are surprised in a tempest, they fly about as in the utmost terror, with the most lamentable and doleful cries. To introduce them, therefore, in the picture of a storm is a proof, both of the taste and judgment of Camoëns.

[433] With shrill, faint voice, th' untimely ghost complains.—It may not perhaps be unentertaining to cite Madame Dacier and Mr. Pope on the voices of the dead. It will, at least, afford a critical observation which appears to have escaped them both. "The shades of the suitors," observes Dacier, "when they are summoned by Mercury out of the palace of Ulysses, emit a feeble, plaintive, inarticulate sound, τρίζουσι, strident: whereas Agamemnon, and the shades that have been long in the state of the dead, speak articulately. I doubt not but Homer intended to show, by the former description, that when the soul is separated from the organs of the body, it ceases to act after the same manner as while it was joined to it; but how the dead recover their voices afterwards is not easy to understand. In other respects Virgil paints after Homer:—

Pars tollere vocem

Exiguam: inceptus clamor frustratur hiantes."

To this Mr. Pope replies, "But why should we suppose, with Dacier, that these shades of the suitors (of Penelope) have lost the faculty of speaking? I rather imagine that the sounds they uttered were signs of complaint and discontent, and proceeded not from an inability to speak. After Patroclus was slain he appears to Achilles, and speaks very articulately to him; yet, to express his sorrow at his departure, he acts like these suitors: for Achilles—

'Like a thin smoke beholds the spirit fly,

And hears a feeble, lamentable cry.'

Dacier conjectures that the power of speech ceases in the dead, till they are
admitted into a state of rest; but Patroclus is an instance to the contrary in the
Iliad, and Elpenor in the Odyssey, for they both speak before their funereal
rites are performed, and consequently before they enter into a state of repose
amongst the shades of the happy."

The critic, in his search for distant proofs, often omits the most material one
immediately at hand. Had Madame Dacier attended to the episode of the
souls of the suitors, the world had never seen her ingenuity in these
mythological conjectures; nor had Mr. Pope any need to bring the case of
Patroclus or Elpenor to overthrow her system. Amphimedon, one of the
suitors, in the very episode which gave birth to Dacier's conjecture, tells his
story very articulately to the shade of Agamemnon, though he had not
received the funereal rites:—

"Our mangled bodies, now deform'd with gore,

Cold and neglected spread the marble floor:

No friend to bathe our wounds! or tears to shed

O'er the pale corse! the honours of the dead."

Odys. xxiv.

On the whole, the defence of Pope is almost as idle as the conjectures of
Dacier. The plain truth is, poetry delights in personification; everything in it,
as Aristotle says of the Iliad, has manners; poetry must therefore personify
according to our ideas. Thus in Milton:—

"Tears, such as angels weep, burst forth."

And thus in Homer, while the suitors are conducted to hell:—

"Trembling, the spectres glide, and plaintive vent

Thin, hollow screams, along the deep descent:"

and, unfettered with mythological distinctions, either shriek or articulately talk, according to the most poetical view of their supposed circumstances.

[434] Exod. xiv. 29.

[435] Noah.

[436] Venus.

[437] For the fable of Eolus see the tenth Odyssey.

[438]

And vow, that henceforth her Armada's sails

Should gently swell with fair propitious gales.

In innumerable instances Camoëns discovers himself a judicious imitator of the ancients. In the two great masters of the epic are several prophecies oracular of the fate of different heroes, which give an air of solemn importance to the poem. The fate of the Armada thus obscurely anticipated, resembles in particular the prophecy of the safe return of Ulysses to Ithaca, foretold by the shade of Tiresias, which was afterwards fulfilled by the Phæacians. It remains now to make some observations on the machinery used by Camoëns in this book. The necessity of machinery in the epopea, and the, perhaps, insurmountable difficulty of finding one unexceptionably adapted to a poem where the heroes are Christians, or, in other words, to a poem whose subject is modern, have already been observed in the preface. The machinery of Camoëns has also been proved, in every respect, to be less exceptionable than that of Tasso in his Jerusalem, or that of Voltaire in his Henriade. The descent of Bacchus to the palace of Neptune, in the depths of the sea, and his address to the watery gods, are noble imitations of Virgil's Juno in the first Æneid. The description of the storm is also masterly. In both instances the conduct of the Æneid is joined with the descriptive exuberance of the Odyssey. The appearance of the star of Venus through the storm is finely imagined; the influence of the nymphs of that goddess over the winds, and their subsequent nuptials, are in the spirit of the promise of Juno to Eolus:—

Sunt mihi bis septum præstanti corpore nymphæ:

Quarum, quæ forma pulcherrima; Deïopeiam

Connubio jungam stabili, propriamque dicabo:

Omnes ut tecum meritis pro talibus annos

Exigat, et pulchra faciat te prole párentem.—Virgil, Æn. bk. i.

And the fiction itself is an allegory, exactly in the manner of Homer. Orithia, the daughter of Erecteus, and queen of the Amazons, was ravished and carried away by Boreas.

[439] Vasco de Gama.

[440] This refers to the Catholic persecutions of Protestants whom they had previously condemned at the Diet of Spires. War was declared against the Protestants in 1546. It lasted for six years, when a treaty of peace was signed at Passau on the Danube, in 1552.—Ed.

[441] Some blindly wand'ring, holy faith disclaim.—At the time when Camoëns wrote, the German empire was plunged into all the miseries of a religious war, the Catholics using every endeavour to rivet the chains of Popery, the adherents of Luther as strenuously endeavouring to shake them off.

[442]

High sound the titles of the English crown,

King of Jerusalem.—

The title of "King of Jerusalem" was never assumed by the kings of England. Robert, duke of Normandy, son of William the Conqueror, was elected King of Jerusalem by the army in Syria, but declined it in hope of ascending the throne of England. Henry VIII. filled the throne of England when our author wrote: his luxury and conjugal brutality amply deserved the censure of the honest poet.

[443] France.

[444] What impious lust of empire steels thy breast.—The French translator very cordially agrees with the Portuguese poet in the strictures upon Germany, England, and Italy.

[445] The Mohammedans.

[446] Where Cynifio flows.—A river in Africa, near Tripoli.—Virgil, Georg. iii. 311.—Ed.

[447] O Italy! how fall'n, how low, how lost!—However these severe reflections on modern Italy may displease the admirers of Italian manners, the picture on the whole is too just to admit of confutation. Never did the history of any court afford such instances of villainy and all the baseness of intrigue as that of the pope's. That this view of the lower ranks in the pope's dominions is just, we have the indubitable testimony of Addison. Our poet is justifiable in his censures, for he only follows the severe reflections of the

greatest of the Italian poets. It were easy to give fifty instances; two or three, however, shall suffice. Dante, in his sixth canto, del Purg.—

Ahi, serva Italia, di dolore ostello,

Nave senza nocchiero in gran tempesta,

Non donna di provincie, bordello.

"Ah, slavish Italy, the inn of dolour, a ship without a pilot in a horrid tempest:—not the mistress of provinces, but a brothel!"

Ariosto, canto 17:—

O d' ogni vitio fetida sentina

Dormi Italia imbríaco.

"O inebriated Italy, thou sleepest the sink of every filthy vice!"

And Petrarch:—

Del'empia Babilonia, ond'è fuggita

Ogni vergogna, ond'ogni bene è fuori,

Albergo di dolor, madre d'errori

Son fuggit'io per allungar la vita.

"From the impious Babylon (the Papal Court) from whence all shame and all good are fled, the inn of dolour, the mother of errors, have I hastened away to prolong my life."

[448] The fables old of Cadmus.—Cadmus having slain the dragon which guarded the fountain of Dirce, in Bœotia, sowed the teeth of the monster. A number of armed men immediately sprang up, and surrounded Cadmus, in order to kill him. By the counsel of Minerva he threw a precious stone among them, in striving for which they slew one another. Only five survived, who afterwards assisted him to build the city of Thebes.—Vid. Ovid. Met. iv.

Terrigenæ pereunt per mutua vulnera fratres.

[449]

So fall the bravest of the Christian name,

While dogs unclean.—

Imitated from a fine passage in Lucan, beginning—

Quis furor, O Cives! quæ tanta licentia ferri,

Gentibus invisis Latium præbere cruorem?

[450] The Mohammedans.

[451] Constantinople.

[452] Beyond the Wolgian Lake.—The Caspian Sea, so called from the large river Volga, or Wolga, which empties itself into it.

[453]

Their fairest offspring from their bosoms torn,

(A dreadful tribute !)—

By this barbarous policy the tyranny of the Ottomans was long sustained. The troops of the Turkish infantry and cavalry, known by the name of Janissaries and Spahis, were thus supported. "The sons of Christians—and those the most completely furnished by nature—were taken in their childhood from their parents by a levy made every five years, or oftener, as occasion required."—Sandys.

[454] Mohammedans.

[455]

O'er Afric's shores

The sacred shrines the Lusian heroes rear'd.—

See the note on book v. p. 137.

[456] Of deepest west.—Alludes to the discovery and conquest of the Brazils by the Portuguese.

[457] The poet, having brought his heroes to the shore of India, indulges himself with a review of the state of the western and eastern worlds; the latter of which is now, by the labour of his heroes, rendered accessible to the former. The purpose of his poem is also strictly kept in view. The west and the east he considers as two great empires; the one of the true religion, the

other of a false. The professors of the true, disunited and destroying one another; the professors of the false one, all combined to extirpate the other. He upbraids the professors of the true religion for their vices, particularly for their disunion, and for deserting the interests of holy faith. His countrymen, however, he boasts, have been its defenders and planters, and, without the assistance of their brother powers, will plant it in Asia.

"The Crusaders," according to Voltaire, "were a band of vagabond thieves, who had agreed to ramble from the heart of Europe in order to desolate a country they had no right to, and massacre, in cold blood, a venerable prince, more than fourscore years old, and his whole people, against whom they had no pretence of complaint."

To prove that the Crusades were neither so unjustifiable, so impolitic, nor so unhappy in their consequences as superficial readers of history are accustomed to regard them, would not be difficult.

Upon the whole, it will be found that the Portuguese poet talks of the political reasons of a Crusade with an accuracy in the philosophy of history as superior to that of Voltaire, as the poetical merit of the Lusiad surpasses that of the Henriade. And the critic in poetry must allow, that, to suppose the discovery of Gama the completion of all the endeavours to overthrow the great enemies of the true religion, gives a dignity to the poem, and an importance to the hero, similar to that which Voltaire, on the same supposition, allows to the subject of the Jerusalem of Tasso.

[458] Calicut is the name of a famous sea-port town in the province of Malabar.

[459]

The herald hears

Castilia's manly tongue salute his ears.—

This in according to the truth of history. While the messenger sent ashore by Gama was borne here and there, and carried off his feet by the throng, who understood not a word of his language, he was accosted in Spanish by a Moorish merchant, a native of Tunis, who, according to Osorius, had been the chief person with whom King Ferdinand had formerly contracted for military stores. He proved himself an honest agent, and of infinite service to Gama; he returned to Portugal, where, according to Faria, he died in the Christian communion. He was named Monzaida.

[460] The sacred pledge of eastern faith.—To eat together was, and still is, in the east looked upon as the inviolable pledge of protection. As a Persian

nobleman was one day walking in his garden, a wretch in the utmost terror prostrated himself before him, and implored to be protected from the rage of a multitude who were in pursuit of him, to take his life. The nobleman took a peach, eat part of it, and gave the rest to the fugitive, assuring him of safety. As they approached the house, they met a crowd who carried the murdered corpse of the nobleman's beloved son. The incensed populace demanded the murderer, who stood beside him, to be delivered to their fury. The father, though overwhelmed with grief and anger, replied, "We have eaten together, and I will not betray him." He protected the murderer of his son from the fury of his domestics and neighbours, and in the night facilitated his escape.

[461] i.e. crescent-shaped.—Ed.

[462] In Rhodope.—The beautiful fable of the descent of Orpheus to hell, for the recovery of his beloved wife, Eurydice, will be found in Virgil's Georgics, bk. iv., lines 460-80.—Ed.

[463]

(For now the banquet on the tented plain,

And sylvan chase his careless hours employ).—

The great Mogul, and other eastern sovereigns, attended by their courtiers, spend annually some months of the finest season in encampments in the field, in hunting parties, and military amusements.

[464] Th' enormous mountain.—The Himalaya range, which is a continuation of an immense chain of mountains girdling the northern regions of the earth and known by various names, as Caucasus, Homodus, Paropamissus, Imaus, etc., and from Imaus extended through Tartary to the sea of Kamschatka. Not the range of mountains so called in Asia Minor.—Ed.

[465] As wild traditions tell.—Pliny, imposed upon by some Greeks, who pretended to have been in India, relates this fable.—Vide Nat. Hist. lib. 12.

[466] Is fondly plac'd in Ganges' holy wave.—Almost all the Indian nations attribute to the Ganges the virtue of cleansing the soul from the stains of sin. They have such veneration for this river, that if any one in their presence were to throw any filth into the stream, an instant death would punish his audacity.

[467] Cambaya, the ancient Camanes of Ptolemy, gives name to the gulf of that name at the head of which it is situated. It is the principal seaport of Guzerat.—Ed.

[468] Porus was king of part of the Punjaub, and was conquered by

Alexander the Great.—Ed.

[469] Narsinga.—The laws of Narsing oblige the women to throw themselves into the funeral pile, to be burnt with their deceased husbands. An infallible secret to prevent the desire of widowhood.—Castera from Barros, Dec. 4.

[470] The Canarese, who inhabit Canara, on the west coast of India.—Ed.

[471] Medina, a city of Arabia, famous as being the burial-place of Mohammed, and hence esteemed sacred.—Ed.

[472] According to tradition, Perimal, a sovereign of India, embraced Islamism about 800 years before Gama's voyage, divided his dominions into different kingdoms, and ended his days as a hermit at Mecca.—Ed.

[473] i.e. pariahs, outcasts.

[474] Brahma their founder as a god they boast.—Antiquity has talked much, but knew little with certainty of the Brahmins, and their philosophy. Porphyry and others esteem them the same as the Gymnosophists of the Greeks, and divide them into several sects, the Samanæi, the Germanes, the Pramnæ, the Gymnetæ, etc. Brahma is the head of the Hindu triad which consists of Brahma, Vishnu and Siva.—Ed.

[475] Almost innumerable, and sometimes as whimsically absurd as the "Arabian Nights' Entertainments," are the holy legends of India. The accounts of the god Brahma, or Brimha, are more various than those of any fable in the Grecian mythology. According to Father Bohours, in his life of Xavier, the Brahmins hold, that the Great God having a desire to become visible, became man. In this state he produced three sons, Mayso, Visnu, and Brahma; the first, born of his mouth, the second, of his breast, the third, of his belly. Being about to return to his invisibility, he assigned various departments to his three sons. To Brahma he gave the third heaven, with the superintendence of the rites of religion. Brahma having a desire for children, begat the Brahmins, who are the priests of India, and who are believed by the other tribes to be a race of demi-gods, who have the blood of heaven running in their veins. Other accounts say, that Brahma produced the priests from his head, the more ignoble tribes from his breast, thighs, and feet.

According to the learned Kircher's account of the theology of the Brahmins, the sole and supreme god Vishnu, formed the secondary god Brahma, out of a flower that floated on the surface of the great deep before the creation. And afterwards, in reward of the virtue, fidelity, and gratitude of Brahma, gave him power to create the universe.

Hesiod's genealogy of the gods, though refined upon by the schools of Plato, is of the same class with the divine genealogies of the Brahmins. The Jewish fables, foolish questions and genealogies, reproved by Saint Paul (epist. Tit.), were probably of this kind, for the Talmudical legends were not then sprung up. Binah, or Understanding, said the cabalists, begat Kochmah, or Wisdom, etc., till at last comes Milcah, the Kingdom, who begat Shekinah, the Divine Presence. In the same manner the Christian Gnostics, of the sect of

Valentinus, held their Πλήρωμα, and their thirty Æons. Ampsiu and Auraan, they tell us, i.e. Profundity and Silence, begat Bacua and Tharthuu, Mind and Truth; these begat Ubucua and Thardeadie, Word and Life, and these Merexa and Atarbarba, Man and Church. The other conjunctions of their thirty Æons are of similar ingenuity. The prevalence of the same spirit of mythological allegory in such different nations, affords the philosopher a worthy field for speculation.

Almost as innumerable as their legends are the dreadful penances to which the Hindus submit themselves for the expiation of sins. Some hold the transmigration of souls, and of consequence abstain from all animal food.{*} Yet, however austere in other respects, they freely abandon themselves to every species of debauchery, some of them esteeming the most unnatural abominations as the privilege of their sanctity. The cow they venerate as sacred. If a dying man can lay hold of a cow's tail, and expire with it in his hands, his soul is sure to be purified, and perhaps will enjoy the signal favour to transmigrate into the body of one of those animals. The temples of India, which are numerous, are filled with innumerable idols of the most horrid figures. The Brahmins are allowed to eat nothing but what is cooked by themselves. Astrology is their principal study; yet, though they are mostly a despicable set of fortune-tellers, some of them are excellent moralists, and particularly inculcate the comprehensive virtue of humanity, which is enforced by the opinion, that Divine beings often assume the habit of mendicants, in order to distinguish the charitable from the inhuman. They have several traditions of the virtuous, on these happy trials, being translated into heaven; the best designed incitement to virtue, perhaps, which their religion contains. Besides the Brahmins, the principal sect of that vast region called India, there are several others, who are divided and subdivided, according to innumerable variations, in every province. In Cambaya, the Banians, a sect who strictly abstain from all animal food, are numerous.

{*} Though from the extracts given by Mr. Dow, the philosopher Goutam appears to have been a very Duns Scotus or Aquinas in metaphysics, the Pythagorean reason why the Brahmins abstain from animal food, is a convincing proof of their ignorance in natural philosophy. Some will let vermin overrun them; some of the Banians cover their mouth with a cloth, lest they should suck in a gnat with their breath; and some carefully sweep the floor ere they tread upon it, lest they dislodge the soul of an insect. And yet they do not know that in the water they drink, and in every salad they eat, they cause the death of innumerable living creatures.

The sacred books of the Hindoos are written in a dead language, the Sanskrit, which none but the Brahmins are allowed to study. So strict in this are they, says Mr. Dow, that only one Mussulman was ever instructed in it, and his knowledge was obtained by fraud. Mahummud Akbar, emperor of India, though bred a Mohammedan, studied several religions. In the Christian he was instructed by a Portuguese. But, finding that of the Hindoos inaccessible, he had recourse to art. A boy named Feizi, was, as the orphan of a Brahmin, put under the care of one of the most eminent of these philosophers, and obtained full knowledge of their hidden religion. But the fraud being discovered, he was laid under the restraint of an oath, and it does not appear that he ever communicated the knowledge thus acquired.

[476] Kotwâl, the chief officer of police in a town.—Forbes' Hindustani Dictionary.

[477] The monster forms, Chimera-like, and rude.—Chimera, a monster slain by Bellerophon.

"First, dire Chimera's conquest was enjoin'd,

A mingled monster of no mortal kind;

Behind, a dragon's fiery tail was spread,

A goat's rough body bore a lion's head;

Her pitchy nostrils flaky flames expire,

Her gaping throat emits infernal fire."

Pope's II. vi.

[478] So Titan's son.—Briareus.

[479] Before these shrines the blinded Indians bow.—In this instance, Camoëns has, with great art, deviated from the truth of history. As it was the great purpose of his hero to propagate the law of heaven in the East, it would have been highly absurd to have represented Gama and his attendants as on their knees in a pagan temple. This, however, was the case. "Gama, who had been told," says Osorius, "that there were many Christians in India, conjectured that the temple, to which the catual led him, was a Christian church. At their entrance they were met by four priests, who seemed to make crosses on their foreheads. The walls were painted with many images. In the middle was it little round chapel, in the wall of which, opposite to the entrance, stood an image which could hardly be discovered. The four priests ascending, some entered the chapel by a little brass door, and pointing to the

benighted image, cried aloud, 'Mary, Mary!' The catual and his attendants prostrated themselves an the ground, while the Lusians on their bended knees adored the blessed virgin." Thus Osorius. Another writer says, that a Portuguese, having some doubt, exclaimed, "If this be the devil's image, I however worship God."

[480] Here India's fate.—The description of the palace of the zamorim, situated among aromatic groves, is according to history; the embellishment of the walls is in imitation of Virgil's description of the palace of King Latinus:—

Tectum augustum, ingens, centum sublime columnis,

Urbe fuit summa, etc.

"The palace built by Picus, vast and proud,

Supported by a hundred pillars stood,

And round encompass'd with a rising wood.

The pile o'erlook'd the town, and drew the sight,

Surprised, at once, with reverence and delight....

Above the portal, carv'd in cedar wood,

Placed in their ranks their godlike grandsires stood.

Old Saturn, with his crooked scythe on high;

And Italus, that led the colony:

And ancient Janus with his double face,

And bunch of keys, the porter of the place.

There stood Sabinus, planter of the vines,

On a short pruning-hook his head reclines;

And studiously surveys his gen'rous wines.

Then warlike kings who for their country fought,

And honourable wounds from battle brought.

Around the posts hung helmets, darts, and spears;

And captive chariots, axes, shields, and bars;

And broken beaks of ships, the trophies of their wars.

Above the rest, as chief of all the band

Was Picus plac'd, a buckler in his hand;

His other wav'd a long divining wand.

Girt in his Gabin gown the hero sate——"

Dryden, Æn. vii.

[481]

Behind her founder Nysa's walls were rear'd——

——at distance far

The Ganges lav'd the wide-extended war.—

This is in the perspective manner of the beautiful descriptions of the figures on the shield of Achilles.—Il. xviii.

[482] Had Semele beheld the smiling boy.—The Theban Bacchus, to whom the Greek fabulists ascribed the Indian expedition of Sesostris, king of Egypt.

[483] Semiramis.

[484] Call'd Jove his father.—The bon-mot of Olympias on this pretension of her son Alexander, was admired by the ancients. "This hot-headed youth, forsooth, cannot be at rest unless he embroil me in a quarrel with Juno."—Quint. Curt.

[485]

The tap'stried walls with gold were pictur'd o'er,

And flow'ry velvet spread the marble floor.—

According to Osorius.

[486] A leaf.—The Betel.

[487] More now we add not.—The tenor of this first conversation between the zamorim and Gama, is according to the truth of history.

[488] What terrors oft have thrill'd my infant breast.—The enthusiasm with which Monzaida, a Moor, talks of the Portuguese, may perhaps to some appear unnatural. Camoëns seems to be aware of this by giving a reason for that enthusiasm in the first speech of Monzaida to Gama—

Heav'n sent you here for some great work divine,

And Heav'n inspires my breast your sacred toils to join.

And, that this Moor did conceive a great affection to Gama, whose religion he embraced, and to whom he proved of the utmost service, is according to the truth of history.

[489] The ruddy juice by Noah found.—Gen. ix. 20. "And Noah began to be an husbandman, and he planted a vineyard, and he drank of the wine," etc.

[490]

His faith forbade with other tribe to join

The sacred meal, esteem'd a rite divine.—

The opinion of the sacredness of the table is very ancient in the East. It is plainly to be discovered in the history of Abraham. When Melchizedek, a king and priest, blessed Abraham, it is said, "And he brought forth bread and wine and he blessed him."—Gen. xiv. 18. The patriarchs only drank wine, according to Dr. Stukely, on their more solemn festivals, when they were said to rejoice before the Lord. Other customs of the Hindoos are mentioned by Camoëns in this book. If a noble should touch a person of another tribe—

A thousand rites, and washings o'er and o'er,

Can scarce his tainted purity restore.

Nothing, says Osorius, but the death of the unhappy commoner can wipe off the pollution. Yet we are told by the same author, that Hindoo nobility cannot be forfeited, or even tarnished by the basest and greatest of crimes; nor can one of mean birth become great or noble by the most illustrious actions. The noblemen, says the same writer, adopt the children of their sisters, esteeming there can be no other certainty of the relationship of their heirs.

[491] The warlike song.—Though Camoëns began his Lusiad in Portugal, almost the whole of it was written while on the ocean, while in Africa, and in India.—See his Life.

[492] As Canace.—Daughter of Eolus. Her father, having thrown her incestuous child to the dogs, sent her a sword, with which she slew herself. In Ovid she writes an epistle to her husband-brother, where she thus describes herself:—

Dextra tenet calamum, strictum tenet altera ferrum.

[493]

Soon I beheld that wealth beneath the wave

For ever lost.—

See the Life of Camoëns.

[494] My life, like Judah's Heaven-doom'd king of yore.—Hezekiah.—See Isaiah xxxviii.

[495] And left me mourning in a dreary jail.—This, and the whole paragraph from—

Degraded now, by poverty abhorr'd,

alludes to his fortunes in India. The latter circumstance relates particularly to the base and inhuman treatment he received on his return to Goa, after his unhappy shipwreck.—See his Life.

[496] Who spurns the muse.—Similarity of condition has produced similarity of sentiment in Camoëns and Spenser. Each was the ornament of his country and his age, and each was cruelly neglected by the men of power, who, in truth, were incapable to judge of their merit, or to relish their writings. We have seen several of the strictures of Camoëns on the barbarous nobility of Portugal. The similar complaints of Spenser will show, that neglect of genius, however, was not confined to the court of Lisbon:—

"O grief of griefs! O gall of all good hearts!

To see that virtue should despised be

Of such as first were raised for virtue's parts,

And now, broad spreading like an aged tree,

Let none shoot up that nigh them planted be.

O let not those of whom the muse is scorn'd,

Alive or dead be by the muse adorn'd."

Ruins of Time.

485

It is thought Lord Burleigh, who withheld the bounty intended by Queen Elizabeth, is here meant. But he is more clearly stigmatized in these remarkable lines, where the misery of dependence on court favour is painted in colours which must recall several strokes of the Lusiad to the mind of the reader:—

"Full little knowest thou that hast not tried,

What hell it is, in suing long to bide;

To lose good days, that might be better spent,

To waste long nights in pensive discontent;

To speed to-day, to be put back to-morrow,

To feed on hope, to pine with fear and sorrow;

To have thy princess' grace, yet want her peers';

To have thy asking, yet wait many years.

To fret thy soul with crosses and with cares,

To eat thy heart thro' comfortless despairs;

To fawn, to crouch, to wait, to ride, to run,

To spend, to give, to want, to be undone."

Mother Hubberd's Tale.

These lines exasperated still more the inelegant, illiberal Burleigh. So true is the observation of Mr. Hughes, that, "even the sighs of a miserable man are sometimes resented as an affront by him that is the occasion of them."

[497] Kotwâl, a sort of superintendent or inspector of police.—Forbes' Hindustani Dictionary.

[498] Lusus.

[499] His cluster'd bough, the same which Bacchus bore.—Camoëns immediately before, and in the former book, calls the ensign of Lusus a bough; here he calls it the green thyrsus of Bacchus:—

O verde Tyrso foi de Bacco usado.

The thyrsus, however, was a javelin twisted with ivy-leaves, used in the sacrifices of Bacchus.

[500] In those fair lawns the bless'd Elysium feign'd.—In this assertion our author has the authority of Strabo. a foundation sufficient for a poet. Nor are there wanting several Spanish writers, particularly Barbosa, who seriously affirm that Homer drew the fine description of Elysium, in his fourth Odyssey, from the beautiful valleys of Spain, where, in one of his voyages, they say, he arrived. Egypt, however, seems to have a better title to this honour. The fable of Charon, and the judges of hell, are evidently borrowed from the Egyptian rites of burial, and are older than Homer. After a ferryman had conveyed the corpse over a lake, certain judges examined the life of the deceased, particularly his claim to the virtue of loyalty, and, according to the report, decreed or refused the honours of sepulture. The place of the catacombs, according to Diodorus Siculus, was surrounded with deep canals, beautiful meadows, and a wilderness of groves. It is universally known that the greatest part of the Grecian fables were fabricated from the customs and opinions of Egypt. Several other nations have also claimed the honour of affording the idea of the fields of the blessed. Even the Scotch challenge it. Many Grecian fables, says an author of that country, are evidently founded on the reports of the Phœnician sailors. That these navigators traded to the coasts of Britain is certain. In the middle of summer, the season when the ancients performed their voyages, for about six weeks there is no night over the Orkney Islands; the disk of the sun, during that time, scarcely sinking below the horizon. This appearance, together with the calm which usually prevails at that season, and the beautiful verdure of the islands, could not fail to excite the admiration of the Phœnicians; and their accounts of the place naturally afforded the idea that these islands were inhabited by the spirits of the just. This, says our author, is countenanced by Homer, who places his "islands of the happy" at the extremity of the ocean. That the fables of Scylla, the Gorgones, and several others, were founded on the accounts of navigators, seems probable; and, on this supposition, the Insulæ Fortunatæ, and Purpurariæ, now the Canary and Madeira islands, also claim the honour of giving colours to the description of Elysium. The truth, however, appears to be this: That a place of happiness is reserved for the spirits of the good is the natural suggestion of that anxiety and hope concerning the future which animates the human breast. All the barbarous nations of Africa and America agree in placing their heaven in beautiful islands, at an immense distance over the ocean. The idea is universal, and is natural to every nation in a state of barbarous simplicity.

[501] The goddess Minerva.

[502] The heav'n-built towers of Troy.—Alluding to the fable of Neptune, Apollo, and Laomedon.

On Europe's strand, more grateful to the skies,

He bade th' eternal walls of Lisbon rise.—

For some account of this tradition, see the note on Lusiad, bk. iii. p. 76. Ancient traditions, however fabulous, have a good effect in poetry. Virgil has not scrupled to insert one, which required an apology:—

Prisca fides facto, sed fama perennis.

Spenser has given us the history of Brute and his descendants at full length in the Faerie Queene; and Milton, it is known, was so fond of that absurd legend, that he intended to write a poem on the subject; and by this fondness was induced to mention it as a truth in the introduction to his History of England.

[504] The brother chief.—Paulus de Gama.

[505] That gen'rous pride which Rome to Pyrrhus bore.—When Pyrrhus, king of Epirus, was at war with the Romans, his physician offered to poison him. The senate rejected the proposal, and acquainted Pyrrhus of the designed treason. Florus remarks on the infamous assassination of Viriatus, that the Roman senate did him great honour; ut videretur aliter vinci non potuisse; it was a confession that they could not otherwise conquer him,—Vid. Flor. l. 17. For a fuller account of this great man, see the note on Lusiad, bk. i. p. 9.

[506] Some deem the warrior of Hungarian race.—See the note on the Lusiad, bk. iii p. 67.

[507] Jerusalem.

[508] The first Alonzo.—King of Portugal.

[509] On his young pupil's flight.—"Some, indeed most, writers say, that the queen advancing with her army towards Guimaraez, the king, without waiting till his governor joined him, engaged them and was routed: but that afterwards the remains of his army, being joined by the troops under the command of Egaz Munitz, engaged the army of the queen a second time, and gained a complete victory."—Univ. Hist.

[510] Egaz behold, a chief self-doom'd to death.—See the same story in bk. iii. p. 71. Though history affords no authentic document of this transaction, tradition, the poet's authority, is not silent. And the monument of Egaz in the monastery of Paço de Souza gives it countenance. Egaz and his family are

there represented, in bas relief, in the attitude and garb, says Castera, as described by Camoëns.

[511] Ah Rome! no more thy gen'rous consul boast.—Sc. Posthumus, who, overpowered by the Samnites, submitted to the indignity of passing under the yoke.

[512] The Moorish king.—The Alcaydes, or tributary governors under the Miramolin{*} or Emperor of Morocco, are often by the Spanish and Portuguese writers styled kings. He who was surprised and taken prisoner by Don Fuaz Roupinho was named Gama. Fuaz, after having gained the first naval victory of the Portuguese, also experienced their first defeat. With one and twenty sail he attacked fifty-four large galleys of the Moors. "The sea," says Brandan, "which had lately furnished him with trophies, now supplied him with a tomb."

{*} This should be (and is evidently only a corruption of), Emir-el-Mumenin, i.e. in Arabic, Commander of the believers.—Ed.

[513] A foreign navy brings the pious aid.—A navy of crusaders, mostly English.

[514] And from the leaves.—This legend is mentioned by some ancient Portuguese chronicles. Homer would have availed himself, as Camoëns has done, of a tradition so enthusiastic, and characteristic of the age. Henry was a native of Bonneville near Cologne. "His tomb," says Castera, "is still to be seen in the monastery of St. Vincent, but without the palm."

[515] In robes of white behold a priest advance.—Thestonius, prior of the regulars of St. Augustine of Conymbra. Some ancient chronicles relate this circumstance as mentioned by Camoëns. Modern writers assert, that he never quitted his breviary.—Castera.

[516] The son of Egas.—He was named Mem Moniz, and was son of Egas Moniz, celebrated for the surrender of himself and family to the King of Castile, as already mentioned.

[517] The dauntless Gerald.—"He was a man of rank, who, in order to avoid the legal punishment to which several crimes rendered him obnoxious, put himself at the head of a party of freebooters. Tiring, however, of that life, he resolved to reconcile himself to his sovereign by some noble action. Full of this idea, one evening he entered Evora, which then belonged to the Moors. In the night he killed the sentinels of one of the gates, which he opened to his companions, who soon became masters of the place. This exploit had its desired effect. The king pardoned Gerald, and made him governor of Evora. A knight with a sword in one hand, and two heads in the other, from that time became the armorial bearing of the city."—Castera.

[518] Wrong'd by his king.—Don Pedro Fernando de Castro, injured by the family of Lara, and denied redress by the King of Castile, took the infamous revenge of bearing arms against his native country. At the head of a Moorish army he committed several outrages in Spain; but was totally defeated in Portugal.

[519] And lo, the skies unfold.—"According to some ancient Portuguese histories, Don Matthew, bishop of Lisbon, in the reign of Alonso I, attempted to reduce Alcazar, then in possession of the Moors. His troops, being suddenly surrounded by a numerous party of the enemy, were ready to fly, when, at the prayers of the bishop, a venerable old man, clothed in white, with a red cross on his breast, appeared in the air. The miracle dispelled the fears of the Portuguese; the Moors were defeated, and the conquest of Alcazar crowned the victory."—Castera.

[520]

Her streets in blood deplore

The seven brave hunters murder'd by the Moor.—

"During a truce with the Moors, six cavaliers of the order of St. James were, while on a hunting party, surrounded and killed, by a numerous body of the Moors. During the fight, in which the gentlemen sold their lives dear, a common carter, named Garcias Rodrigo, who chanced to pass that way, came generously to their assistance, and lost his life along with them. The poet, in giving all seven the same title, shows us that virtue constitutes true nobility. Don Payo de Correa, grand master of the order of St. James, revenged the death of these brave unfortunates by the sack of Tavila, where his just rage put the garrison to the sword."—Castera.

[521] Those three bold knights how dread.—Nothing can give us a stronger picture of the romantic character of their age, than the manners of those champions, who were gentlemen of birth; and who, in the true spirit of knight-errantry, went about from court to court in quest of adventures. Their names were, Gonçalo Ribeiro; Fernando Martinez de Santarene; and Vasco Anez, foster-brother to Mary, queen of Castile, daughter of Alonzo IV. of Portugal.

[522] And I, behold, am off'ring sacrifice.—This line, the simplicity which, I think, contains great dignity, is adopted from Fanshaw—

"And I, ye see, am off'ring sacrifice;"

who has here caught the spirit of the original—

490

A quem lhe a dura nova estava dando,

Pois eu responde estou sacrificando;

i.e. To whom when they told the dreadful tidings, "And I," he replies "am sacrificing." The piety of Numa was crowned with victory.—Vid. 'Plut. in vit. Numæ.

[523]

The Lusian Scipio well might speak his fame,

But nobler Nunio shines a greater name.—

Castera justly observes the happiness with which Camoëns introduces the name of this truly great man. "Il va," says he, "le nommer tout à l'heure avec une adresse et une magnificence digne d'un si beau sujet."

[524] Two knights of Malta.—These knights were first named Knights Hospitalers of St. John of Jerusalem, afterwards Knights of Rhodes, from whence they were driven to Messina, ere Malta was assigned to them. By their oath of knighthood they were bound to protect the Holy Sepulchre from the profanation of infidels; immediately on taking this oath, they retired to their colleges, where they lived on their revenues in all the idleness of monkish luxury. Their original habit was black, with a white cross; their arms gules, a cross, argent.

[525] His captive friend.—Before John I. mounted the throne of Portugal, one Vasco Porcallo was governor of Villaviciosa. Roderic de Landroal and his friend, Alvarez Cuytado, having discovered that he was in the interest of the King of Castile, drove him from his town and fortress. On the establishment of King John, Porcallo had the art to obtain the favour of that prince; but, no sooner was he re-instated in the garrison, than he delivered it up to the Castilians; and plundered the house of Cuytado, whom, with his wife, he made prisoner and, under a numerous party, ordered to be sent to Olivença. Roderic de Landroal, hearing of this, attacked and defeated the escort, and set his friend at liberty.—Castera.

[526] Here treason's well-earn'd meed allures thine eyes.—While the kingdom of Portugal was divided, some holding with John the newly elected king, and others with the King of Castile, Roderic Marin, governor of Campo-Major, declared for the latter. Fernando d'Elvas endeavoured to gain him to the interest of his native prince, and a conference, with the usual assurances of safety, was agreed to. Marin, at this meeting, seized upon Elvas, and sent him prisoner to his castle. Elvas having recovered his liberty, a few days after met

his enemy in the field, whom, in his turn, he made captive; and the traitorous Marin, notwithstanding the endeavours of their captain to save his life, met the reward of his treason from the soldiers of Elvas.—Partly from Castera.

[527] And safe the Lusian galleys speed away.—A numerous fleet of the Castilians being on their way to lay siege to Lisbon. Ruy Pereyra, the Portuguese commander, seeing no possibility of victory, boldly attacked the Spanish admiral. The fury of his onset put the Castilians in disorder, and allowed the Portuguese galleys a safe escape. In this brave piece of service the gallant Pereyra lost his life.—Castera.

[528] The shepherd.—Viriatus.

[529] Equal flame inspir'd these few.—The Castilians having laid siege to Almada, a fortress on a mountain near Lisbon, the garrison, in the utmost distress for water, were obliged at times to make sallies to the bottom of the hill in quest of it. Seventeen Portuguese thus employed were one day attacked by four hundred of the enemy. They made a brave defence, and effected a happy retreat into their fortress.—Castera.

[530] Far from the succour of the Lusian host.—When Alonzo V. took Ceuta, Don Pedro de Menezes was the only officer in the army who was willing to become governor of that fortress; which, on account of the uncertainty of succour from Portugal, and the earnest desire of the Moors to regain it, was deemed untenable. He gallantly defended his post in two severe sieges.

[531] That other earl.—He was the natural son of Don Pedro de Menezes. Alonzo V. one day, having ridden out from Ceuta with a few attendants, was attacked by a numerous party of the Moors, when De Vian, and some others under him, at the expense of their own lives, purchased the safe retreat of their sovereign.

[532] Two brother-heroes shine.—The sons of John I. Don Pedro was called the Ulysses of his age, on account both of his eloquence and his voyages. He visited almost every court of Europe, but he principally distinguished himself in Germany, where, under the standards of the Emperor Sigismond, he signalized his valour in the war against the Turks.—Castera.

[533] The glorious Henry.—In pursuance of the reasons assigned in the preface, the translator has here taken the liberty to make a transposition in the order of his author. In Camoëns, Don Pedro de Menezes, and his son De Vian, conclude the description of the pictured ensigns. Don Henry, the greatest man perhaps that ever Portugal produced, has certainly the best title to close this procession of the Lusian heroes. And, as he was the father of navigation, particularly of the voyage of Gama, to sum up the narrative with his encomium has even some critical propriety.

These observations were suggested by the conduct of Camoëns, whose design, like that of Virgil, was to write a poem which might contain all the triumphs of his country. As the shield of Æneas supplies what could not be introduced in the vision of Elysium, so the ensigns of Gama complete the purpose of the third and fourth Lusiads. The use of that long episode, the conversation with the King of Melinda, and its connection with the subject, have been already observed. The seeming episode of the pictures, while it fulfills the promise—

And all my country's wars the song adorn,

is also admirably connected with the conduct of the poem. The Hindoos naturally desire to be informed of the country, the history, and power of their foreign visitors, and Paulus sets it before their eyes. In every progression of the scenery the business of the poem advances. The regent and his attendants are struck with the warlike grandeur and power of the strangers, and to accept of their friendship, or to prevent the forerunners of so martial a nation from carrying home the tidings of the discovery of India, becomes the great object of their consideration.

[534] But ah, forlorn, what shame to barb'rous pride.—In the original.—

Mas faltamlhes pincel, faltamlhes cores,

Honra, premio, favor, que as artes criáo.

"But the pencil was wanting, colors were wanting, honour, reward, favour, the nourishers of the arts." This seemed to the translator as in impropriety, and contrary to the purpose of the whole speech of Paulus, which was to give the catual a high idea of Portugal. In the fate of the imaginary painter, the Lusian poet gives us the picture of his own, resentment wrung this impropriety from him. The spirit of the complaint, however, is preserved in the translation. The couplet—

"Immortal fame his deathless labours gave;

Poor man, he sunk neglected to the grave!"

is not in the original. It is the sigh of indignation over the unworthy fate of the unhappy Camoëns.

[535] The ghost-like aspect and the threat'ning look.—Mohammed, by some historians described as of a pale livid complexion, and trux aspectus et vox terribilis, of a fierce threatening aspect, voice, and demeanour.

When, softly usher'd by the milky dawn,

The sun first rises.—

"I deceive myself greatly," says Castera, "if this simile is not the most noble
and the most natural that can be found in any poem. It has been imitated by
the Spanish comedian, the illustrious Lopez de Vega, in his comedy of
Orpheus and Eurydice, act i. sc. 1:—

"Como mirar puede ser

El sol al amanecer,

I quando se enciende, no."

Castera adds a very loose translation of these Spanish lines in French verse.
The literal English is, As the sun may be beheld at its rising, but, when
illustriously kindled, cannot. Naked, however, as this is, the imitation of
Camoëns is evident. As Castera is so very bold in his encomium of this fine
simile of the sun, it is but justice to add his translation of it, together with the
original Portuguese, and the translation of Fanshaw. Thus the French
translator:—

Les yeux peuvent soûtenir la clarté du soleil naissant, mais lorsqu'il s'est
avancé dans sa carrière lumineuse, et que ses rayons répandent les ardeurs du
midi, on tacherait en vain de l'envisager; un prompt aveuglement serait le prix
de cette audace.

Thus elegantly in the original:—

"Em quanto he fraca a força desta gente,

Ordena como em tudo se resista,

Porque quando o Sol sahe, facilmente

Se pòde nelle por a aguda vista:

Porem despois que sobe claro, & ardente,

Se a agudeza dos olhos o conquista

Tao cega fica, quando ficareis,

Se raizes criar lhe nao tolheis."

494

And thus humbled by Fanshaw:—

"Now whilst this people's strength is not yet knit,

Think how ye may resist them by all ways.

For when the Sun is in his nonage yit,

Upon his morning beauty men may gaze;

But let him once up to his zenith git,

He strikes them blind with his meridian rays;

So blind will ye be, if ye look not too't,

If ye permit these cedars to take root."

[537]

Around him stand,

With haggard looks, the hoary Magi band.—

The Brahmins, the diviners of India. Ammianus Marcellinus, l. 23, says, that
the Persian Magi derived their knowledge from the Brachmanes of India. And
Arrianus, l. 7, expressly gives the Brahmins the name of Magi. The Magi of
India, says he, told Alexander, on his pretensions to divinity, that in
everything he was like other men, except that he took less rest, and did more
mischief. The Brahmins are never among modern writers called Magi.

[538] The hov'ring demon gives the dreadful sign.—This has an allusion to
the truth of history. Barros relates, that an anger being brought before the
Zamorim, "Em hum vaso de agua l'he mostrara hunas naos, que vin ham de
muy longe para a India, e que a gente d'ellas seria total destruiçam dos
Mouros de aquellas partes.—In a vessel of water he showed him some ships
which from a great distance came to India, the people of which would effect
the utter subversion of the Moors." Camoëns has certainly chosen a more
poetical method of describing this divination, a method in the spirit of Virgil;
nor in this is he inferior to his great master. The supernatural flame which
seizes on Lavinia while assisting at the sacrifice alone excepted, every other
part of the augury of Latinus, and his dream in the Albunean forest, whither
he went to consult his ancestor, the god Faunus, in dignity and poetical
colouring, cannot come in comparison with the divination of the Magi, and
the appearance of the demon in the dream of the Moorish priest.

[539] Th'eternal yoke.—This picture, it may perhaps be said, is but a bad

compliment to the heroes of the Lusiad, and the fruits of their discovery. A little consideration, however, will vindicate Camoëns. It is the demon and the enemies of the Portuguese who procure this divination; everything in it is dreadful, on purpose to determine the zamorim to destroy the fleet of Gama. In a former prophecy of the conquest of India (when the catual describes the sculpture of the royal palace), our poet has been careful to ascribe the happiest effects to the discovery of his heroes:—

"Beneath their sway majestic, wise, and mild,

Proud of her victors' laws, thrice happier India smil'd."

[540] So let the tyrant plead.—In this short declamation, a seeming excrescence, the business of the poem in reality is carried on. The zamorim, and his prime minister, the catual, are artfully characterised in it; and the assertion—

Lur'd was the regent with the Moorish gold,

is happily introduced by the declamatory reflections which immediately precede it.

[541]

The Moors——their ancient deeds relate,

Their ever-faithful service of the state.—

An explanation of the word Moor is here necessary. When the East afforded no more field for the sword of the conqueror, the Saracens, assisted by the Moors, who had embraced their religion, laid the finest countries in Europe in blood and desolation. As their various embarkations were from the empire of Morocco, the Europeans gave the name of Moors to all the professors of the Mohammedan religion. In the same manner the eastern nations blended all the armies of the Crusaders under one appellation, and the Franks, of whom the army of Godfrey was mostly composed, became their common name for all the inhabitants of the West. Before the arrival of Gama, as already observed, all the traffic of the East, from the Ethiopian side of Africa to China, was in the hands of Arabian Mohammedans, who, without incorporating with the pagan natives, had their colonies established in every country commodious for commerce. These the Portuguese called Moors; and at present the Mohammedans of India are called the Moors of Hindostan by our English writers. The intelligence these Moors gave to one another,

496

relative to the actions of Gama; the general terror with which they beheld the appearance of Europeans, whose rivalship they dreaded as the destruction of their power; the various frauds and arts they employed to prevent the return of one man of Gama's fleet to Europe, and their threat to withdraw from the dominions of the zamorim, are all according to the truth of history. The speeches of the zamorim and of Gama, which follow, are also founded in truth.

[542] Troy.

[543] No sumptuous gift thou bring'st.—"As the Portuguese did not expect to find any people but savages beyond the Cape of Good Hope, they only brought with them some preserves and confections, with trinkets of coral, of glass, and other trifles. This opinion, however, deceived them. In Melinda and in Calicut they found civilized nations, where the arts flourished; who wanted nothing; who were possessed of all the refinements and delicacies on which we value ourselves. The King of Melinda had the generosity to be contented with the present which Gama made; but the zamorim, with a disdainful eye, beheld the gifts which were offered to him. The present was this: Four mantles of scarlet, six hats adorned with feathers, four chaplets of coral beads, twelve Turkey carpets, seven drinking cups of brass, a chest of sugar, two barrels of oil, and two of honey."—Castera.

[544] Fair Acidalia, Love's celestial queen.—Castera derives Acidalia from

ἀχηδής, which, he says, implies to act without fear or restraint. Acidalia is one of the names of Venus, in Virgil; derived from Acidalus, a fountain sacred to her in Bœotia.

[545] Sprung from the prince.—John I.

[546] And from her raging tempests, nam'd the Cape.—Bartholomew Diaz, was the first who discovered the southmost point of Africa. He was driven back by the storms, which on these seas were thought always to continue, and which the learned of former ages, says Osorius, thought impassable. Diaz, when he related his voyage to John II. called the southmost point the Cape of Tempests. The expectation of the king, however, was kindled by the account, and with inexpressible joy, says the same author, he immediately named it the Cape of Good Hope.

[547]

The pillar thus of deathless fame, begun

By other chiefs, etc.—

"Till I now ending what those did begin,

The furthest pillar in thy realm advance;

Breaking the element of molten tin,

Through horrid storms I lead to thee the dance."

Fanshaw.

[548]

The regent's palace high o'erlook'd the bay,

Where Gama's black-ribb'd fleet at anchor lay.—

The resemblance of this couplet to many passages in Homer, must be obvious to the intelligent critic.

[549] As in the sun's bright beam.—Imitated from Virgil, who, by the same simile, describes the fluctuation of the thoughts of Æneas, on the eve of the Latian war:—

"Laomedontius heros

Cuncta videns, magno curarum fluctuat æstu,

Atque animum nunc huc celerem, nunc dividit illuc,

In partesque rapit varias, perque omnia versat.

Sicut aquæ tremulum labris ubi lumen ahenis

Sole repercussum, aut radiantis imagine Lunæ,

Omnia pervolitat late loca: jamque sub auras

Erigitur, summique ferit laquearia tecti."

"This way and that he turns his anxious mind,

Thinks, and rejects the counsels he design'd;

Explores himself in vain, in ev'ry part,

And gives no rest to his distracted heart:

So when the sun by day or moon by night

498

Strike on the polish'd brass their trembling light,

The glitt'ring species here and there divide,

And cast their dubious beams from side to side;

Now on the walls, now on the pavement play,

And to the ceiling flash the glaring day."

Ariosto has also adopted this simile in the eighth book of his Orlando Furioso:—

"Qual d'acqua chiara il tremolante lume

Dal Sol per percossa, o da' notturni rai,

Per gli ampli tetti và con lungo salto

A destra, ed a sinistra, e basso, ed alto."

"So from a water clear, the trembling light

Of Phœbus, or the silver ray of night,

Along the spacious rooms with splendour plays,

Now high, now low, and shifts a thousand ways."

Hoole.

But the happiest circumstance belongs to Camoëns. The velocity and various shiftings of the sun-beam, reflected from a piece of crystal or polished steel in the hand of a boy, give a much stronger idea of the violent agitation and sudden shiftings of thought than the image of the trembling light of the sun or moon reflected from a vessel of water. The brazen vessel, however, and not the water, is only mentioned by Dryden. Nor must another inaccuracy pass unobserved. That the reflection of the moon flashed the glaring day is not countenanced by the original.

We have already seen the warm encomium paid by Tasso to his contemporary, Camoëns. That great poet, the ornament of Italy, has also testified his approbation by several imitations of the Lusiad. Virgil, in no instance, has more closely copied Homer, than Tasso has imitated the appearance of Bacchus, or the evil demon, in the dream of the Moorish priest. The enchanter Ismeno thus appears to the sleeping Solyman:—

"Soliman' Solimano, i tuoi silenti

Riposi à miglior tempo homai riserva:

Che sotto il giogo de straniere genti

La patria, ove regnasti, ancor' e serva.

In questa terra dormi, e non rammenti,

Ch'insepolte de' tuoi l'ossa conserva?

Ove si gran' vestigio e del tuo scorno,

Tu neghittoso aspetti il nuovo giorno?"

Thus elegantly translated by Mr. Hoole:—

"Oh! Solyman, regardless chief, awake!

In happier hours thy grateful slumber take:

Beneath a foreign yoke thy subjects bend,

And strangers o'er thy land their rule extend:

Here dost thou sleep? here close thy careless eyes,

While uninterr'd each lov'd associate lies?

Here where thy fame has felt the hostile scorn,

Canst thou, unthinking, wait the rising morn?"

The conclusion of this canto has been slightly altered by the translator. Camoëns, adhering to history, makes Gama (when his factors are detained on shore) seize upon some of the native merchants as hostages. At the intreaty of their wives and children the zamorim liberates his captives; while Gama, having recovered his men and the merchandise, sailed away, carrying with him the unfortunate natives, whom he had seized as hostages.

As there is nothing heroic in this dishonourable action of Gama's, Mickle has omitted it, and has altered the conclusion of the canto.—Ed.

[550] Mickle, in place of the first seventeen stanzas of this canto, has inserted about three hundred lines of his own composition; in this respect availing himself of the licence he had claimed in his preface.—Ed.

[551] Thy sails, and rudders too, my will demands.—According to history.

[552] My sov'reign's fleet I yield not to your sway.—The circumstance of

Gama's refusing to put his fleet into the power of the zamorim, is thus rendered by Fanshaw:—

"The Malabar protests that he shall rot

In prison, if he send not for the ships.

He (constant, and with noble anger hot)

His haughty menace weighs not at two chips."

[553] Through Gata's hills.—The hills of Gata or Gate, mountains which form a natural barrier on the eastern side of the kingdom of Malabar.

"Nature's rude wall, against the fierce Canar

They guard the fertile walls of Malabar."

Lusiad, vii.

[554] Then, furious, rushing to the darken'd bay.—For the circumstances of the battle, and the tempest which then happened, see the Life of Gama.

[555] I left my fix'd command my navy's guard.—See the Life of Gama.

[556] Unmindful of my fate on India's shore.—This most magnanimous resolution, to sacrifice his own safety or his life for the safe return of the fleet, is strictly true.—See the Life of Gama.

[557] Abrupt—the monarch cries—"What yet may save!"—Gama's declaration, that no message from him to the fleet could alter the orders he had already left, and his rejection of any further treaty, have a necessary effect in the conduct of the poem. They hasten the catastrophe, and give a verisimilitude to the abrupt and full submission of the zamorim.

[558] The rollers—i.e. the capstans.—The capstan is a cylindrical windlass, worked with bars, which are moved from hole to hole as it turns round. It is used on board ship to weigh the anchors, raise the masts, etc. The versification of this passage in the original affords a most noble example of imitative harmony:—

"Mas ja nas naos os bons trabalhadores

Volvem o cabrestante, & repartidos

Pello trabalho, huns puxao pella amarra,

Outros quebrao co peito duro a barra."

Stanza x.

[559]

Mozaide, whose zealous care

To Gama's eyes reveal'd each treach'rous snare.—

Had this been mentioned sooner, the interest of the catastrophe of the poem must have languished. Though he is not a warrior, the unexpected friend of Gama bears a much more considerable part in the action of the Lusiad than the faithful Achates, the friend of the hero, bears in the business of the Æneid.

[560] There wast thou call'd to thy celestial home.—This exclamatory address to the Moor Monzaida, however it may appear digressive, has a double propriety. The conversion of the Eastern world is the great purpose of the expedition of Gama, and Monzaida is the first fruits of that conversion. The good characters of the victorious heroes, however neglected by the great genius of Homer, have a fine effect in making an epic poem interest us and please. It might have been said, that Monzaida was a traitor to his friends, who crowned his villainy with apostacy. Camoëns has, therefore, wisely drawn him with other features, worthy of the friendship of Gama. Had this been neglected, the hero of the Lusiad might have shared the fate of the wise Ulysses of the Iliad, against whom, as Voltaire justly observes, every reader bears a secret ill will. Nor is the poetical character of Monzaida unsupported by history. He was not an Arab Moor, so he did not desert his countrymen. These Moors had determined on the destruction of Gama; Monzaida admired and esteemed him, and therefore generously revealed to him his danger. By his attachment to Gama he lost all his effects in India, a circumstance which his prudence and knowledge of affairs must have certainly foreseen. By the known dangers he encountered, by the loss he thus voluntarily sustained, and by his after constancy, his sincerity is undoubtedly proved.

[561] The joy of the fleet on the homeward departure from India.—We are now come to that part of the Lusiad, which, in the conduct of the poem, is parallel to the great catastrophe of the Iliad, when, on the death of Hector, Achilles thus addresses the Grecian army—

"Ye sons of Greece, in triumph bring

The corpse of Hector, and your pæons sing:

Be this the song, slow moving toward the shore,

'Hector is dead, and Ilion is no more.'"

Our Portuguese poet, who in his machinery, and many other instances, has followed the manner of Virgil, now forsakes him. In a very bold and masterly spirit he now models his poem by the steps of Homer. What of the Lusiad yet remains, in poetical conduct (though not in an imitation of circumstances), exactly resembles the latter part of the Iliad. The games at the funeral of Patroclus, and the redemption of the body of Hector, are the completion of the rage of Achilles. In the same manner, the reward of the heroes, and the consequences of their expedition complete the unity of the Lusiad. I cannot say it appears that Milton ever read our poet (though Fanshaw's translation was published in his time); yet no instance can be given of a more striking resemblance of plan and conduct, than may be produced in two principal parts of the poem of Camoëns, and of the Paradise Lost.—See the Dissertation which follows this book.

[562] Near where the bowers of Paradise were plac'd.—Between the mouth of the Ganges and Euphrates.

[563] Swans.

[564] His falling kingdom claim'd his earnest care.—This fiction, in poetical conduct, bears a striking resemblance to the digressive histories with which Homer enriches and adorns his poems, particularly to the beautiful description of the feast of the gods with "the blameless Ethiopians." It also contains a masterly commentary on the machinery of the Lusiad. The Divine Love conducts Gama to India. The same Divine Love is represented as preparing to reform the corrupted world, when its attention is particularly called to bestow a foretaste of immortality on the heroes of the expedition which discovered the eastern world. Nor do the wild fantastic loves, mentioned in this little episode, afford any objection against this explanation, an explanation which is expressly given in the episode itself. These wild fantastic amours signify, in the allegory, the wild sects of different enthusiasts, which spring up under the wings of the best and most rational institutions; and which, however contrary to each other, all agree in deriving their authority from the same source.

[565] A young Actæon.—The French translator has the following characteristic note: "This passage is an eternal monument of the freedoms taken by Camoëns, and at the same time a proof of the imprudence of poets; an authentic proof of that prejudice which sometimes blinds them,

notwithstanding all the light of their genius. The modern Actæon of whom he speaks, was King Sebastian. He loved the chase; but, that pleasure, which is one of the most innocent and one of the most noble we can possibly taste, did not at all interrupt his attention to the affairs of state, and did not render him savage, as our author pretends. On this point the historians are rather to be believed. And what would the lot of princes be, were they allowed no relaxation from their toils, while they allow that privilege to their people? Subjects as we are, let us venerate the amusements of our sovereigns; let us believe that the august cares for our good, which employ them, follow them often even to the very bosom of their pleasures."

Many are the strokes in the Lusiad which must endear the character of Camoëns to every reader of sensibility. The noble freedom and manly indignation with which he mentions the foible of his prince, and the flatterers of his court, would do honour to the greatest names of Greece or Rome. While the shadow of freedom remained in Portugal, the greatest men of that nation, in the days of Lusian heroism, thought and conducted themselves in the spirit of Camoëns. A noble anecdote of this brave spirit offers itself. Alonzo IV., surnamed the Brave, ascended the throne of Portugal in the vigour of his age. The pleasures of the chase engrossed all his attention. His confidants and favourites encouraged, and allured him to it. His time was spent in the forests of Cintra, while the affairs of government were neglected or executed by those whose interest it was to keep their sovereign in ignorance. His presence, at last, being necessary at Lisbon, he entered the council with all the brisk impetuosity of a young sportsman, and with great familiarity and gaiety entertained his nobles with the history of a whole month spent in hunting, in fishing, and shooting. When he had finished his narrative, a nobleman of the first rank rose up: "Courts and camps," said he, "were allotted for kings, not woods and deserts. Even the affairs of private men suffer when recreation is preferred to business. But when the whims of pleasure engross the thoughts of a king, a whole nation is consigned to ruin. We came here for other purposes than to hear the exploits of the chase, exploits which are only intelligible to grooms and falconers. If your majesty will attend to the wants, and remove the grievances of your people, you will find them obedient subjects; if not——" The king, starting with rage, interrupted him, "If not, what?" "If not," resumed the nobleman, in a firm tone, "they will look for another and a better king." Alonzo, in the highest transport of passion, expressed his resentment, and hasted out of the room. In a little while, however, he returned, calm and reconciled: "I perceive," said he, "the truth of what you say. He who will not execute the duties of a king, cannot long have good subjects. Remember, from this day, you have nothing more to do with Alonzo the sportsman, but with Alonzo the king of Portugal." His majesty was as good as his promise, and became, as a warrior and politician, one of the greatest of the Portuguese monarchs.

[566] With love's fierce flames his frozen heart shall burn.—"It is said, that upon the faith of a portrait Don Sebastian fell in love with Margaret of France, daughter of Henry II., and demanded her in marriage, but was refused. The Spaniards treated him no less unfavourably, for they also rejected his proposals for one of the daughters of Philip II. Our author considers these refusals as the punishment of Don Sebastian's excessive attachment to the chase; but this is only a consequence of the prejudice with which he viewed the amusements of his prince. The truth is, these princesses were refused for political reasons, and not with any regard to the manner in which he filled up his moments of leisure."

Thus Castera, who, with the same spirit of sagacity, starts and answers the following objections: "But here is a difficulty: Camoëns wrote during the life of Don Sebastian, but the circumstance he relates (the return of Gama) happened several years before, under the reign of Emmanuel. How, therefore, could he say that Cupid then saw Don Sebastian at the chase, when that prince was not then born? The answer is easy: Cupid, in the allegory of this work, represents the love of God, the Holy Spirit, who is God himself. Now the Divinity admits of no distinction of time; one glance of his eye beholds the past, the present, and the future; everything is present before him."

This defence of the fiction of Actæon is not more absurd than useless. The free and bold spirit of poetry, and in particular the nature of allegory, defend it. The poet might easily have said, that Cupid foresaw; but had he said so his satire had been much less genteel. As the sentiments of Castera on this passage are extremely characteristic of French ideas, another note from him will perhaps be agreeable. "Several Portuguese writers have remarked," says he, "that the wish—

'Of these lov'd dogs that now his passions sway,

Ah! may he never fall the hapless prey!'

Had in it an air of prophecy; and fate, in effect, seemed careful to accomplish it, in making the presaged woes to fall upon Don Sebastian. If he did not fall a prey to his pack of hounds, we may, however, say that he was devoured by his favourites, who misled his youth and his great soul. But at any rate our poet has carried the similitude too far. It was certainly injurious to Don Sebastian, who nevertheless had the bounty not only not to punish this audacity, but to reward the just eulogies which the author had bestowed on him in other places. As much as the indiscretion of Camoëns ought to surprise us, as much ought we to admire the generosity of his master."

This foppery, this slavery in thinking, cannot fail to rouse the indignation of every manly breast, when the facts are fairly stated. Don Sebastian, who ascended the throne when a child, was a prince of great abilities and great spirit, but his youth was poisoned with the most romantic ideas of military glory. The affairs of state were left to his ministers (for whose character see the next note), his other studies were neglected, and military exercises, of which he not unjustly esteemed the chase a principal, were almost his sole employ. Camoëns beheld this romantic turn, and in a genteel allegorical satire foreboded its consequences. The wish, that his prince might not fall the prey of his favourite passion, was in vain. In a rash, ill-concerted expedition into Africa, Don Sebastian lost his crown in his twenty-fifth year, an event which soon after produced the fall of the Portuguese empire. Had the nobility possessed the spirit of Camoëns, had they, like him, endeavoured to check the quixotism of a young generous prince, that prince might have reigned long and happy, and Portugal might have escaped the Spanish yoke, which soon followed his defeat at Alcazar; a yoke which sunk Portugal into an abyss of misery, from which, in all probability, she will never emerge into her former splendour.

[567]

Enraged, he sees a venal herd, the shame

Of human race, assume the titled name.—

"After having ridiculed all the pleasures of Don Sebastian, the author now proceeds to his courtiers, to whom he has done no injustice. Those who are acquainted with the Portuguese history, will readily acknowledge this."—Castera.

[568] On the hard bosoms of the stubborn crowd.—There in an elegance in the original of this line, which the English language will not admit:—

"Nos duros coraçoens de plebe dura,"—

i.e., In the hard hearts of the hard vulgar.

[569] Cupid.

[570]

Thus from my native waves a hero line

Shall rise, and o'er the East illustrious shine.—

"By the line of heroes to be produced by the union of the Portuguese with the Nereids, is to be understood the other Portuguese, who, following the steps of Gama, established illustrious colonies in India."—Castera.

[571] And Fame—a giant goddess.—This passage affords a striking instance of the judgment of Camoëns. Virgil's celebrated description of Fame is in his eye, but he copies it, as Virgil, in his best imitations, copies after Homer. He adopts some circumstances, but, by adding others, he makes a new picture, which justly may be called his own.

[572] The wat'ry gods.—To mention the gods in the masculine gender, and immediately to apply to them—

"O peito feminil, que levemente

Muda quaysquer propositos tomados."—

The ease with which the female breast changes its resolutions, may to the hypercritical appear reprehensible. The expression, however, is classical, and therefore retained. Virgil uses it, where Æneas is conducted by Venus through the flames of Troy:—

"Descendo, ac ducente Deo, flammam inter et hostes

Expedior."

This is in the manner of the Greek poets, who use the word Θεὸς for god or goddess.

[573] White as her swans.—A distant fleet compared to swans on a lake is certainly a happy thought. The allusion to the pomp of Venus, whose agency is immediately concerned, gives it besides a peculiar propriety. This simile, however, is not in the original. It is adopted from an uncommon liberty taken by Fanshaw:—

"The pregnant sails on Neptune's surface creep,

Like her own swans, in gate, out-chest, and fether."

[574] Soon as the floating verdure caught their sight.—As the departure of Gama from India was abrupt, he put into one of the beautiful islands of Anchediva for fresh water. "While he was here careening his ships," says Faria, "a pirate named Timoja, attacked him with eight small vessels, so linked together and covered with boughs, that they formed the appearance of a floating island." This, says Castera, afforded the fiction of the floating island

of Venus. "The fictions of Camoëns," says he, "are the more marvellous, because they are all founded in history. It is not difficult to find why he makes his island of Anchediva to wander on the waves; it is an allusion to a singular event related by Barros." He then proceeds to the story of Timoja, as if the genius of Camoëns stood in need of so weak an assistance.

[575] In friendly pity of Latona's woes.—Latona, pregnant by Jupiter, was persecuted by Juno, who sent the serpent Python in pursuit of her. Neptune, in pity of her distress, raised the island of Delos for her refuge, where she was delivered of Apollo and Diana.—Ovid, Met.

[576] Form'd in a crystal lake the waters blend.—Castera also attributes this to history. "The Portuguese actually found in this island," says he, "a fine piece of water ornamented with hewn stones and magnificent aqueducts; an ancient and superb work, of which nobody knew the author."

In 1505 Don Francisco Almeyda built a fort in this island. In digging among some ancient ruins he found many crucifixes of black and red colour, from whence the Portuguese conjectured, says Osorius, that the Anchedivian islands had in former ages been inhabited by Christians.—Vid. Osor. 1. iv.

[577]

The orange here perfumes the buxom air.

And boasts the golden hue of Daphne's hair.—

Frequent allusions to the fables of the ancients form a characteristic feature of the poetry of the 16th and 17th centuries. A profusion of it is pedantry; a moderate use of it, however, in a poem of those times pleases, because it discovers the stages of composition, and has in itself a fine effect, as it illustrates its subject by presenting the classical reader with some little landscapes of that country through which he has travelled. The description of forests is a favourite topic in poetry. Chaucer, Tasso, and Spenser, have been happy in it, but both have copied an admired passage in Statius:—

"Cadit ardua fagus,

Chaoniumque nemus, brumæque illæsa cupressus;

Procumbunt piceæ, flammis alimenta supremis,

Ornique, iliceæque trabes, metuandaque sulco

Taxus, et infandos belli potura cruores

Fraxinus, atque situ non expugnabile robur:

Hinc audax abies, et odoro vulnere pinus

Scinditur, acclinant intonsa cacumina terræ

Alnus amica fretis, nec inhospita vitibus ulmus."

In rural descriptions three things are necessary to render them poetical: the happiness of epithet, of picturesque arrangement, and of little landscape views. Without these, all the names of trees and flowers, though strung together in tolerable numbers, contain no more poetry than a nurseryman or a florist's catalogue. In Statius, in Tasso and Spenser's admired forests (Ger. Liber. c. 3. st. 75, 76, and F. Queen, b. 1 c. 1. st. 8, 9), the poetry consists entirely in the happiness of the epithets. In Camoëns, all the three requisites are admirably attained and blended together.

[578] And stain'd with lover's blood.—Pyramus and Thisbe:—

"Arborei fœtus aspergine cædis in atram

Vertuntur faciem: madefactaque sanguine radix

Puniceo tingit pendentia mora colore.....

At tu quo ramis arbor miserabile corpus

Nunc tegis unius, mox es tectura duorum;

Signa tene cædis: pullosque et lectibus aptos

Semper habe fœtus gemini monumenta cruoris."

Ovid, Met.

[579] The shadowy vale.—Literal from the original,—O sombrio valle—which Fanshaw, however, has translated, "the gloomy valley," and thus has given us a funereal, where the author intended a festive, landscape. It must be confessed, however, that the description of the island of Venus, is infinitely the best part of all of Fanshaw's translation. And indeed the dullest prose translation might obscure, but could not possibly throw a total eclipse over, so admirable an original.

[580] The woe-mark'd flower of slain Adonis—water'd by the tears of love.—The Anemone. "This," says Castera, "is applicable to the celestial Venus, for, according to my theology, her amour with Adonis had nothing in it impure, but was only the love which nature bears to the sun." The fables of antiquity have generally a threefold interpretation, an historical allusion, a physical and a metaphysical allegory. In the latter view, the fable of Adonis is only

applicable to the celestial Venus. A divine youth is outrageously slain, but shall revive again at the restoration of the golden age. Several nations, it is well known, under different names, celebrated the Mysteries, or the death and resurrection of Adonis; among whom were the British Druids, as we are told by Dr. Stukely. In the same manner Cupid, in the fable of Psyche, is interpreted by mythologists, to signify the Divine Love weeping over the degeneracy of human nature.

[581]

At strife appear the lawns and purpled skies,

Who from each other stole the beauteous dyes.—

On this passage Castera has the following sensible, though turgid, note: "This thought," says he, "is taken from the idyllium of Ausonius on the rose:—

'Ambigeres raperetne rosis Aurora ruborem,

An daret, et flores tingere torta dies.'

Camoëns who had a genius rich of itself, still further enriched it at the expense of the ancients. Behold what makes great authors! Those who pretend to give us nothing but the fruits of their own growth, soon fail, like the little rivulets which dry up in the summer, very different from the floods, who receive in their course the tribute of a hundred and a hundred rivers, and which even in the dog-days carry their waves triumphant to the ocean."

[582] The hyacinth bewrays the doleful Ai.—Hyacinthus, a youth beloved of Apollo, by whom he was accidentally slain, and afterwards turned into a flower:—

"Tyrioque nitentior ostro

Flos oritur, formamque capit, quam lilia: si non,

Purpureus color huic, argenteus esset in illis.

Non satis hoc Phæbo est: is enim fuit auctor honoris.

Ipse suos gemitus foliis inscribit; et Ai, Ai,

Flos habet inscriptum: funestaque littera ducta est."

Ovid, Met.

[583] The second Argonauts.—The expedition of the Golden Fleece was esteemed, in ancient poetry, one of the most daring adventures, the success of which was accounted miraculous. The allusions of Camoëns to this voyage, though in the spirit of his age, are by no means improper.

[584] Wide o'er the beauteous isle the lovely fair.—We now come to the passage condemned by Voltaire as so lascivious, that no nation in Europe, except the Portuguese and Italians, could bear it. The fate of Camoëns has hitherto been very peculiar. The mixture of Pagan and Christian mythology in his machinery has been anathematized, and his island of love represented as a brothel. Yet both accusations are the arrogant assertions of the most superficial acquaintance with his works. His poem itself, and a comparison of its parts with the similar conduct of the greatest modern poets, will clearly evince, that in both instances no modern epic writer of note has given less offence to true criticism.

Not to mention Ariosto, whose descriptions will often admit of no palliation, Tasso, Spenser, and Milton, have always been esteemed among the chastest of poets, yet in that delicacy of warm description, which Milton has so finely exemplified in the nuptials of our first parents, none of them can boast the continued uniformity of the Portuguese poet. Though there is a warmth in the colouring of Camoëns which even the genius of Tasso has not reached: and though the island of Armida is evidently copied from the Lusiad, yet those who are possessed of the finer feelings, will easily discover an essential difference between the love-scenes of the two poets, a difference greatly in favour of the delicacy of the former. Though the nymphs in Camoëns are detected naked in the woods, and in the stream, and though desirous to captivate, still their behaviour is that of the virgin who hopes to be the spouse. They act the part of offended modesty; even when they yield they are silent, and behave in every respect like Milton's Eve in the state of innocence, who—

"What was honour knew,"

And who displayed—

"Her virtue, and the conscience of her worth,

That would be wooed, and not unsought be won."

To sum up all, the nuptial sanctity draws its hallowed curtains, and a masterly allegory shuts up the love-scenes of Camoëns.

How different from all this is the island of Armida in Tasso, and its

511

translation, the bower of Acrasia in Spenser! In these virtue is seduced; the scene therefore is less delicate. The nymphs, while they are bathing, in place of the modesty of the bride as in Camoëns, employ all the arts of the lascivious wanton. They stay not to be wooed; but, as Spenser gives it—

The amorous sweet spoils to greedy eyes reveal.

One stanza from our English poet, which, however, is rather fuller than the original, shall here suffice:—

"Withal she laughed and she blush'd withal,

That blushing to her laughter gave more grace,

And laughter to her blushing, as did fall.

Now when they spy'd the knight to slack his pace,

Them to behold, and in his sparkling face

The secret signs of kindled lust appear,

Their wanton merriments they did increase,

And to him beckon'd to approach more near,

And show'd him many sights, that courage cold could rear.

This and other descriptions—

"Upon a bed of roses she was laid

As faint through heat, or dight to pleasant sin"—

present every idea of lascivious voluptuousness. The allurements of speech are also added. Songs, which breathe every persuasive, are heard; and the nymphs boldly call to the beholder:—

E' dolce campo di battaglia il letto

Fiavi, e l'herbetta morbida de' prati.—Tasso.

"Our field of battle is the downy bed,

Or flow'ry turf amid the smiling mead."—Hoole.

These, and the whole scenes in the domains of Armida and Acrasia, are in a turn of manner the reverse of the island of Venus. In these the expression and idea are meretricious. In Camoëns, though the colouring is even warmer, yet the modesty of the Venus de Medicis is still preserved. In everything he describes there is still something strongly similar to the modest attitude of the arms of that celebrated statue. Though prudery, that usual mask of the impurest minds, may condemn him, yet those of the most chaste, though less gloomy turn, will allow, that in comparison with others, he might say,— Virginibus puerisque canto.

Spenser also, where he does not follow Tasso, is often gross; and even in some instances, where the expression is most delicate, the picture is nevertheless indecently lascivious.

[585] The hunter.—Acteon.

[586] Madd'ning as he said.—At the end of his Homer Mr. Pope has given an index of the instances of imitative and sentimental harmony contained in his translations. He has also often even in his notes pointed out the adaptation of sound to sense. The translator of the Lusiad hopes he may for once say, that he has not been inattentive to this great essential of good versification: how he has succeeded the judicious only must determine. The speech of Leonard to the cursory reader may perhaps sometimes appear careless, and sometimes turgid and stiff. That speech, however, is an attempt at the imitative and sentimental harmony, and with the judicious he rests its fate. As the translation in this instance exceeds the original in length, the objection of a foreign critic requires attention. An old pursy Abbé, (and critics are apt to judge by themselves) may indeed be surprised that a man out of breath with running should be able to talk so long. But, had he consulted the experiences of others, he would have found it was no wonderful matter for a stout and young cavalier to talk twice as much, though fatigued with the chase of a couple of miles, provided the supposition be allowed, that he treads on the last steps of his flying mistress.

[587] Hence, ye profane.—We have already observed, that in every other poet the love scenes are generally described as those of guilt and remorse. The contrary character of those of Camoëns not only gives them a delicacy unknown to other moderns, but, by the fiction of the spousal rites, the allegory and machinery of the poem are most happily conducted.

[588] Spread o'er the eastern world the dread alarms.—This admonition places the whole design of the poem before us. To extirpate Mohammedanism, and propagate Christianity, were professed as the principal purpose of the discoveries of Prince Henry and King Emmanuel. In the beginning of the seventh Lusiad, the nations of Europe are upbraided for permitting the Saracens to erect and possess an empire, which alike

threatened Europe and Christianity. The Portuguese, however, the patriot poet concludes, will themselves overthrow their enormous power: an event which is the proposed subject of the Lusiad, and which is represented as, in effect, completed in the last book. On this system, adopted by the poet, and which on every occasion was avowed by their kings, the Portuguese made immense conquests in the East. Yet, let it be remembered, to the honour of Gama, and the first commanders who followed his route, that the plots of the Moors, and their various breaches of treaty, gave rise to the first wars which the Portuguese waged in Asia. On finding that all the colonies of the Moors were combined for their destruction, the Portuguese declared war against the eastern Moors, and their allies, wherever they found them. The course of human things, however, soon took place, and the sword of victory and power soon became the sword of tyranny and rapine.

[589] Far o'er the silver lake of Mexic.—The city of Mexico is environed with an extensive lake; or, according to Cortez, in his second narration to Charles V., with two lakes, one of fresh, the other of salt water, in circuit about fifty leagues. This situation, said the Mexicans, was appointed by their God Vitzliputzli, who, according to the explanation of their picture-histories, led their forefathers a journey of fourscore years, in search of the promised land. Four of the principal priests carried the idol in a coffer of reeds. Whenever they halted they built a tabernacle for their god in the midst of their camp, where they placed the coffer and the altar. They then sowed the land, and their stay or departure, without regard to the harvest, was directed by the orders received from their idol, till at last, by his command, they fixed their abode on the site of Mexico.

[590] Before the love-sick Roman.—Mark Antony.

[591] The beverage—the fountain's cooling aid confess'd.—It was a custom of the ancients in warm climates to mix the coolest spring water with their wine, immediately before drinking; not, we may suppose, to render it less intoxicating, but on account of the cooling flavour it thereby received. Homer tells us that the wine which Ulysses gave to Polyphemus would bear twenty measures of water. Modern luxury has substituted preserved ice, in place of the more ancient mixture.

[592] Music, such as erst subdued the horrid frown of hell, etc.—Alluding to the fable of Orpheus. Fanshaw's translation, as already observed, was published fourteen years before the Paradise Lost. These lines of Milton—

"What could it less, when spirits immortal sung?

Their song was partial, but the harmony

Suspended hell, and took with ravishment

The thronging audience,"

bear a resemblance to these of Fanshaw—

"Musical instruments not wanting, such

As to the damn'd spirits once gave ease

In the dark vaults of the infernal hall."

To slumber amid their punishment, though omitted by Fanshaw, is literal:—

"Fizerao descançar da eterna pena."

[593] No more the summer of my life remains.—It is not certain when Camoëns wrote this. It seems, however, not long to have preceded the publication of his poem, at which time he was in his fifty-fifth year. This apostrophe to his muse may, perhaps, by some be blamed as another digression; but, so little does it require defence, that one need not hesitate to affirm that, had Homer, who often talks to his muse, introduced, on these favourable opportunities, any little picture or history of himself, these digressions would have been the most interesting parts of his works. Had any history of Homer complained, like this of Camoëns, it would have been bedewed with the tears of ages.

[594] Thy faith repent not, nor lament thy wrong.—P. Alvarez Cabral, the second Portuguese commander who sailed to India, entered into a treaty of alliance with Trimumpara, king of Cochin, and high priest of Malabar. The zamorim raised powerful armies to dethrone him. His fidelity to the Portuguese was unalterable, though his affairs were brought to the lowest ebb.—See the history in the Preface.

[595]

His ship's strong sides shall groan beneath his weight,

And deeper waves receive the sacred freight.—

Thus Virgil:—

"Simul accipit alveo

Ingentem Æneam. Gemuit sub pondere cymba

Sutilis, et multam accepit rimosa paludem."—ÆN. vi. 412.

That the visionary boat of Charon groaned under the weight of Æneas is a fine poetical stroke; but that the crazy rents let in the water is certainly lowering the image. The thought, however, as managed in Camoëns is much grander than in Virgil, and affords a happy instance where the hyperbole is truly poetical.

The Lusiad affords many instances which must be highly pleasing to the Portuguese, but dry to those who are unacquainted with their history. Nor need one hesitate to assert that, were we not acquainted with the Roman history from our childhood, a great part of the Æneid would appear to us intolerably uninteresting. Sensible of this disadvantage which every version of historical poetry must suffer, the translator has not only in the notes added every incident which might elucidate the subject, but has also, all along, in the episode in the third and fourth books, in the description of the painted ensigns in the eighth, and in the allusions in the present book, endeavoured to throw every historical incident into that universal language, the picturesque of poetry. When Hector storms the Grecian camp, when Achilles marches to battle, every reader understands and is affected with the bold painting. But when Nestor talks of his exploits at the funeral games of Amarynces (Iliad xxiii.) the critics themselves cannot comprehend him, and have vied with each other in inventing explanations.

[596] Proas, or paraos, Indian vessels which lie low on the water, are worked with oars, and carry 100 men and upwards apiece.

[597]

His robes are sprinkled o'er,

And his proud face dash'd, with his menials' gore.—

See the history in the Preface.

[598] Round Lusus' fleet to pour their sulph'rous entrails.—How Pacheco avoided this formidable danger, see the history in the preface.

[599] Nor Tiber's bridge.—When Porsenna besieged Rome, Horatius Cocles defended the pass of a bridge till the Romans destroyed it behind him. Having thus saved the pass, heavy armed as he was, he swam across the Tiber to his companions. Roman history, however, at this period, is often mixed with fable. Miltiades obtained a great victory over Darius at Marathon. The stand made by Leonidas at Thermopylæ is well known. The battles of Pacheco were in defence of the fords by which alone the city of Cochin could be entered. The numbers he withstood by land and sea, and the victories he

obtained, are much more astonishing than the defence of Thermopylæ.

[600] Bound to the mast the godlike hero stands.—English history affords an instance of similar resolution in Admiral Bembo, who was supported in a wooden frame, and continued the engagement after his legs and thighs were shivered in splinters. Contrary to the advice of his officers, the young Almeyda refused to bear off, though almost certain to be overpowered, and though both wind and tide were against him. His father had sharply upbraided him for a former retreat, where victory was thought impossible. He now fell the victim of his father's ideas of military glory.

[601] The fleets of India fly.—After having cleared the Indian seas, the viceroy, Almeyda, attacked the combined fleets of Egypt, Cambaya, and the zamorim, in the entrance and harbour of Diu, or Dio. The fleet of the zamorim almost immediately fled. That of Melique Yaz, Lord of Diu, suffered much; but the greatest slaughter fell upon the Egyptians and Turks, commanded by Mir-Hocem, who had defeated and killed the young Almeyda. Of 800 Mamelukes, or Turks, who fought under Mir-Hocem, only 22, says Osorius, survived this engagement. Melique Yaz, says Faria y Sousa, was born in slavery, and descended of the Christians of Roxia. The road to preferment is often a dirty one; but Melique's was much less so than that of many. As the King of Cambaya was one day riding in state, an unlucky kite dunged upon his royal head. His majesty in great wrath swore he would give all he was worth to have the offender killed. Melique, who was an expert archer, immediately despatched an arrow, which brought the audacious hawk to the ground. For the merit of this eminent service he was made Lord of Diu, or Dio, a considerable city, the strongest and the most important fortress at that time in all India.—See Faria, 1. 2, c. 2.

[602] Great Cunia.—Tristan da Cunha, or d'Acugna.

[603] Heav'n indignant showers their arrows backward.—Some writers related that, when Albuquerque besieged Ormuz, a violent wind drove the arrows of the enemy backward upon their own ranks. Osorius says, that many of the dead Persians and Moors were found to have died by arrows. But as that weapon was not used by the Portuguese he conjectures that, in their despair of victory, many of the enemy had thus killed themselves, rather than survive the defeat.

[604] Muscat.

[605] Bahrein, in the Persian Gulf.

[606] What glorious palms on Goa's isle I see.—This important place was made an archbishopric, the capital of the Portuguese empire in the east, and the seat of their viceroys; for which purposes it is advantageously situated on the coast of Dekhan. It still remains in the possession of the Portuguese.

[607] Malacca.—The conquest of this place was one of the greatest actions of Albuquerque. It became the chief port of the eastern part of Portuguese India, and second only to Goa. Besides a great many pieces of ordnance which were carried away by the Moors who escaped, 3000 large cannon remained the prize of the victors. When Albuquerque was on the way to Malacca, he attacked a large ship; but, just as his men were going to board her, she suddenly appeared all in flames, which obliged the Portuguese to bear off. Three days afterwards the same vessel sent a boat to Albuquerque, offering an alliance, which was accepted. The flames, says Osorius, were only artificial, and did not the least damage. Another wonderful adventure immediately happened. The admiral soon after sent his long-boats to attack a ship commanded by one Nehoada Beeguea. The enemy made an obstinate resistance. Nehoada himself was pierced with several mortal wounds, but lost not one drop of blood till a bracelet was taken off his arm, when immediately the blood gushed out. According to Osorius, this was said to be occasioned by the virtue of a stone in the bracelet, taken out of an animal called Cabrisia, which, when worn on the body, could prevent the effusion of blood from the most grievous wounds.

[608] Yet art thou stain'd.—A detail of all the grant actions of Albuquerque would have been tedious and unpoetical. Camoëns has chosen the most brilliant, and has happily suppressed the rest by a display of indignation. The French translator has the following note on this passage: "Behold another instance of our author's prejudice! The action which he condemns had nothing in it blameable: but, as he was of a most amorous constitution, he thought every fault which could plead an amour in its excuse ought to be pardoned; but true heroes, such as Albuquerque, follow other maxims. This great man had in his palace a beautiful Indian slave. He viewed her with the eyes of a father, and the care of her education was his pleasure. A Portuguese soldier, named Ruy Diaz, had the boldness to enter the general's apartment, where he succeeded so well with the girl that he obtained his desire. When Albuquerque heard of it, he immediately ordered him to the gallows."

Camoëns, however, was no such undistinguishing libertine as this would represent him. In a few pages we find him praising the continence of Don Henry de Meneses, whose victory over his passions he calls the highest excellence of youth. Nor does it appear by what authority the Frenchman assures us of the chaste paternal affection which Albuquerque bore to this Indian girl. It was the great aim of Albuquerque to establish colonies in India, and, for that purpose, he encouraged his soldiers to marry with the natives. The most sightly girls were selected, and educated in the religion and household arts of Portugal, and portioned at the expense of the general. These he called his daughters, and with great pleasure he used to attend their weddings, several couples being usually joined together at one time. At one of these nuptials, says Faria, the festivity having continued late, and the brides being mixed together, several of the bridegrooms committed a blunder. The mistakes of the night, however, as they were all equal in point of honour, were mutually forgiven in the morning, and each man took his proper wife whom he had received at the altar. This delicate anecdote of Albuquerque's sons and daughters is as bad a commentary on the note of Castera as it is on the severity which the commander showed to poor Diaz. Nor does Camoëns stand alone in the condemnation of the general. The historian agrees with the poet. Mentioning the death of D. Antonio Noronha, "This gentleman," says Faria, "used to moderate the violent temper of his uncle, Albuquerque, which soon after showed itself in rigid severity. He ordered a soldier to be hanged for an amour with one of the slaves whom he called daughters, and whom he used to give in marriage. When some of his officers asked him what authority he had to take the poor man's life, he drew his sword, told them that was his commission, and instantly broke them." To marry his soldiers with the natives was the plan of Albuquerque: his severity, therefore, seems unaccountable, unless we admit the 'perhaps' of Camoëns, ou de cioso, perhaps it was jealousy.—But, whatever incensed the general, the execution of the soldier was contrary to the laws of every nation;{*} and the honest indignation of Camoëns against one of the greatest of his countrymen, one who was the grand architect of the Portuguese empire in the East, affords a noble instance of that manly freedom of sentiment which knows no right by which king or peer may do injustice to the meanest subject. Nor can we omit the observation, that the above note of Castera is of a piece with the French devotion we have already seen him pay to the name of king, a devotion which breathes the true spirit of the blessed advice given by Father Paul to the republic of Venice: "When a nobleman commits an offence against a subject," says the Jesuit, "let every means be tried to justify him. But, if a subject has offended a nobleman, let him be punished with the utmost severity."

{*} Osorius relates the affair of Diaz with some other circumstances; but with no difference that affects this assertion.

[609] Not Ammon.—Campaspe, the most beautiful concubine of Alexander the Great, was given by that monarch to Apelles, whom he perceived in love with her. Araspas had strict charge of the fair captive, Panthea. His attempt on her virtue was forgiven by Cyrus.

[610] And Flandria's earldom on the knight bestow'd.—"Baldwin, surnamed Iron-arm, Grand Forester of Flanders, being in love with Judith, the daughter of Charles the Bald, and widow of Ethelwolf, king of England, obtained his desire by force. Charles, though at first he highly resented, afterwards pardoned his crime, and consented to his marriage with the princess."— Castera.

This digression in the song of the nymph bears, in manner, a striking resemblance to the histories which often, even in the heat of battle, the heroes of Homer relate to each other. That these little episodes have their beauty and propriety in an epic poem will strongly appear from a view of M. de la Motte's translation of the Iliad into French verse. The four and twenty books of Homer he has contracted into twelve, and these contain no more lines than about four books of the original. A thousand embellishments which the warm poetical feelings of Homer suggested to him are thus thrown out by the Frenchman. But what is the consequence of this improvement? The work of La Motte is unread, even by his own countrymen, and despised by every foreigner who has the least relish for poetry and Homer.

[611] And midnight horror shakes Medina's shrine.—Medina, the city where Mohammed is buried. About six years after Gama's discovery of India, the Sultan of Egypt sent Maurus, the abbot of the monks at Jerusalem, who inhabit Mount Sion, on an embassy to Pope Julius II. The sultan, with severe threats to the Christians of the East in case of refusal, entreated the Pope to desire Emmanuel, king of Portugal, to send no more fleets to the Indian seas. The Pope sent Maurus to Emmanuel, who returned a very spirited answer to his holiness, assuring him that no threats, no dangers, could make him alter his resolutions, and lamenting that it had not yet been in his power to fulfil his purpose of demolishing the sepulchre and erasing the memorials of Mohammed from the earth. This, he says was the first purpose of sending his fleets to India. It is with great art that Camoëns so often reminds us of the grand design of the expedition of his heroes to subvert Mohammedanism, and found a Christian empire in the East. But the dignity which this gives to his poem has already been observed in the preface.

[612] Where Sheba's sapient queen the sceptre bore.—The Abyssinians contend that their country is the Sheba mentioned in the Scripture, and that the queen who visited Solomon bore a son to that monarch, from whom their royal family, to the present time, is descended.

[613] Snatch'd from thy golden throne.—Gama only reigned three months viceroy of India. During his second voyage, the third which the Portuguese made to India, he gave the zamorim some considerable defeats by sea, besides his victories over the Moors. These, however, are judiciously omitted by Camoëns, as the less striking part of his character.

The French translator is highly pleased with the prediction of Gama's death, delivered to himself at the feast. "The siren," says he, "persuaded that Gama is a hero exempt from weakness, does not hesitate to mention the end of his life. Gama listens without any mark of emotion; the feast and the song continue. If I am not deceived, this is truly great."

[614] Victorious Henry.—Don Henry de Menezes. He was only twenty-eight

when appointed to the government of India. He died in his thirtieth year, a noble example of the most disinterested heroism.

[615] Great Mascarine.—Pedro de Mascarenhas. The injustice done to this brave officer, and the usurpation of his government by Lopez Vaz de Sampayo, afford one of the most interesting periods of the history of the Portuguese in India.

[616] Great Nunio.—Nunio de Cunha, one of the most worthy of the Portuguese governors.

[617] Awed by his fame.—That brave, generous spirit, which prompted Camoëns to condemn the great Albuquerque for injustice to a common soldier, has here deserted him. In place of poetical compliment, on the terrors of his name, Noronha deserved infamy. The siege of Dio, it is true, was raised on the report of his approach, but that report was the stratagem of Coje Zofar, one of the general officers of the assailants. The delays of Noronha were as highly blamable as his treatment of his predecessor, the excellent Nunio, was unworthy of a gentleman.

[618] A son of thine, O Gama.—Stephen de Gama.

[619] A vet'ran, fam'd on Brazil's shore.—Martin Alonzo de Souza. He was celebrated for clearing the coast of Brazil of several pirates, who were formidable to that infant colony.

[620] O'er blood-stain'd ground.—This is as near the original as elegance will allow—de sangue cheyo—which Fanshaw has thus punned:—

"With no little loss,

Sending him home again by Weeping-Cross"—

a place near Banbury in Oxfordshire.

[621] Cape Comorin, the southernmost point of India.—Ed.

[622] The Rumien fierce, who boasts the name of Rome.—When the victories of the Portuguese began to overspread the East, several Indian princes, by the counsels of the Moors, applied for assistance to the Sultan of Egypt, and the Grand Signior. The troops of these Mohammedan princes were in the highest reputation for bravery, and though, composed of many different nations, were known among the orientals by one common name. Ignorance delights in the marvellous. The history of ancient Rome made the same figure among the easterns, as that of the fabulous, or heroic, ages does with us, with this difference, it was better believed. The Turks of Roumania pretended to be the descendants of the Roman conquerors, and the Indians

gave them and their auxiliaries the name of Rumēs, or Romans. In the same manner, the fame of Godfrey in the East conferred the name of Franks on all the western Christians, who, on their part, gave the name of Moors to all the Mohammedans of the East.

[623] No hope, bold Mascarene.—The commander of Diu, or Dio, during this siege, one of the most memorable in the Portuguese history.

[624] Fierce Hydal-Kan.—The title of the lords or princes of Decan, who in their wars with the Portuguese have sometimes brought 400,000 men into the field. The prince here mentioned, after many revolts, was at last finally subdued by Don John de Castro, the fourth viceroy of India, with whose reign our poet judiciously ends the prophetic song. Albuquerque laid the plan, and Castro completed the system of the Portuguese empire in the East. It is with propriety, therefore, that the prophecy given to Gama is here summed up. Nor is the discretion of Camoëns in this instance inferior to his judgment. He is now within a few years of his own times, when he himself was upon the scene in India. But whatever he had said of his contemporaries would have been liable to misconstruction, and every sentence would have been branded with the epithets of flattery or malice. A little poet would have been happy in such an opportunity to resent his wrongs. But the silent contempt of Camoëns does him true honour.

In this historical song, as already hinted, the translator has been attentive, as much as he could, to throw it into these universal languages, the picturesque and characteristic. To convey the sublimest instruction to princes, is, according to Aristotle, the peculiar province of the epic muse. The striking points of view in which the different characters of the governors of India are here placed, are in the most happy conformity to this ingenious canon of the Stagyrite.

[625]

In whirling circles now they fell, now rose,

Yet never rose nor fell.—

The motions of the heavenly bodies, in every system, bear at all times the same uniform relation to each other; these expressions, therefore, are strictly just. The first relates to the appearance, the second to the reality. Thus, while to us the sun appears to go down, to more western inhabitants of the globe he appears to rise, and while he rises to us, he is going down to the more eastern; the difference being entirely relative to the various parts of the earth. And in this the expressions of our poet are equally applicable to the Ptolemaic and Copernican systems. The ancient hypothesis which made our

522

earth the centre of the universe, is the system adopted by Camoëns, a happiness, in the opinion of the translator, to the English Lusiad. The new system is so well known, that a poetical description of it would have been no novelty to the English reader. The other has not only that advantage in its favour: but this description is perhaps the finest and fullest that ever was given of it in poetry, that of Lucretius, l. v. being chiefly argumentative, and therefore less picturesque.

Our author studied at the university of Coimbra, where the ancient system and other doctrines of the Aristotelians then, and long afterward, prevailed.

[626] He holds His loftiest state.—Called by the old philosophers and school divines the sensorium of the Deity.

[627] These spheres behold.—According to the Peripatetics, the universe consisted of eleven spheres inclosed within each other; as Fanshaw has familiarly expressed it by a simile which he has lent our author. The first of these spheres, he says—

"Doth (as in a nest

Of boxes) all the other orbs comprise."

In their accounts of this first-mentioned, but eleventh, sphere, which they called the Empyrean, or heaven of the blest, the disciples of Aristotle, and the Arab Moors, gave loose to all the warmth of imagination. And several of the Christian fathers applied to it the descriptions of heaven which are found in the Holy Scripture.

[628] Hence motion darts its force.—This is the tenth sphere, the Primum Mobile of the ancient system. To account for the appearances of the heavens, the Peripatetics ascribed a double motion to it. While its influence drew the other orbs from east to west, they supposed it had a motion of its own from west to east. To effect this, the ponderous weight and interposition of the ninth sphere, or crystalline heaven, was necessary. The ancient astronomers observed that the stars shifted their places. This they called the motion of the crystalline heaven, expressed by our poet at the rate of one pace during two hundred solar years. The famous Arab astronomer, Abulhasan, in his Meadows of Gold, calculates the revolution of this sphere to consist of 49,000 of our years. But modern discoveries have not only corrected the calculation,{*} but have also ascertained the reason of the apparent motion of the fixed stars. The earth is not a perfect sphere; the quantity of matter is greater at the equator; hence the earth turns on her axis in a rocking motion, revolving round the axis of the ecliptic, which is called the procession of the equinoxes, and makes the stars seem to shift their places at about the rate of a

degree in 72 years; according to which all the stars seem to perform one revolution in the space of 25,920 years, after which they return exactly to the same situation as at the beginning of this period. However imperfect in their calculations, the Chaldean astronomers perceived that the motions of the heavens composed one great revolution. This they called the annus magnus, which those who did not understand them mistook for a restoration of all things to their first originals.

{*} However deficient the astronomy of Abulhasan may be, it is nothing to the calculation of his prophet Mohammed, who tells his disciples, that the stars were each about the bigness of a house, and hung from the sky on chains of gold.

[629] And binds the starry sphere.—This was called the firmament, or eighth heaven. Saturn, Jupiter, Mars, Apollo, Venus, Mercury, and Diana, were the planets which gave name to, and whose orbits composed, the other spheres or heavens.

[630] In shining frost the Northern Chariot rides.—Commonly called Charles' Wain. Andromeda was the daughter of Cepheus, king of Ethiopia, and of Cassiope. Cassiope boasted that she and her daughter were more beautiful than Juno and the Nereids. Andromeda, to appease the goddess, was, at her father's command, chained to a rock to be devoured by a sea monster, but was saved by Perseus, who obtained of Jupiter that all the family should be placed among the stars. Orion was a hunter, who, for an attempt on Diana, was stung to death by a serpent. The star of his name portends tempests. The Dogs; fable gives this honour to those of different hunters. The faithful dog of Erigone, however, that died mad with grief for the death of his mistress, has the best title to preside over the dog-days. The Swan; whose form Jupiter borrowed to enjoy Leda. The Hare, when pursued by Orion, was saved by Mercury, and placed in heaven, to signify that Mercury presides over melancholy dispositions. The Lyre, with which Orpheus charmed Pluto. The Dragon which guarded the golden apples of the Hesperides, and the ship Argo complete the number of the constellations mentioned by Camoëns. If our author has blended the appearances of heaven with those of the painted artificial sphere, it is in the manner of the classics. Ovid, in particular, thus describes the heavens, in the second book of his Metamorphoses.

[631] Such are their laws impress'd by God's dread will.—Though a modern narrative of gallant adventures by no means requires the supposition of a particular Providence, that supposition, however, is absolutely necessary to the grandeur of an epic poem. The great examples of Homer and Virgil prove it; and Camoëns understood and felt its force. While his fleet combat all the horrors of unploughed oceans, we do not view his heroes as idle wanderers; the care of heaven gives their voyage the greatest importance. When Gama

falls on his knees and spreads his hands to heaven on the discovery of India, we are presented with a figure infinitely more noble than that of the most successful conqueror who is supposed to act under the influence of fatalism or chance. The human mind is conscious of its own weakness. It expects an elevation in poetry, and demands a degree of importance superior to the caprices of unmeaning accident. The poetical reader cannot admire the hero who is subject to such blind fortuity. He appears to us with an abject, uninteresting littleness. Our poetical ideas of permanent greatness demand a Gama, a hero whose enterprises and whose person interest the care of Heaven and the happiness of his people. Nor must this supposition be confined merely to the machinery. The reason why it pleases, also requires, that the supposition should be uniform throughout the whole poem. Virgil, by dismissing Eneas through the ivory gate of Elysium, has hinted that all his pictures of a future state were merely dreams, and has thus destroyed the highest merit of the compliment to his patron Augustus. But Camoëns has certainly been more happy. A fair opportunity offered itself to indulge the opinions of Lucretius and the Academic Grove; but Camoëns, in ascribing the government of the universe to the will of God, has not only preserved the philosophy of his poem perfectly uniform, but has also shown that the Peripatetic system is, in this instance, exactly conformable to the Newtonian.

Though the Author of nature has placed man in a state of moral agency, and made his happiness and misery to depend upon it, and though every page of human history is stained with the tears of injured innocence and the triumphs of guilt, with miseries which must affect a moral, or thinking being, yet we have been told, that God perceiveth it not, and that what mortals call moral evil vanishes from before His more perfect sight. Thus the appeal of injured innocence, and the tear of bleeding virtue fall unregarded, unworthy of the attention of the Deity.{*} Yet, with what raptures do these philosophers behold the infinite wisdom and care of Beelzebub, their god of flies, in the admirable and various provision he has made for the preservation of the eggs of vermin, and the generation of maggots.{**}

Much more might be said in proof that our poet's philosophy does not altogether deserve ridicule. And those who allow a general, but deny a particular providence, will, it is hoped, excuse Camoëns, on the consideration, that if we estimate a general moral providence by analogy of that providence which presides over vegetable and animal nature, a more particular one cannot possibly be wanted. If a particular providence, however, is still denied, another consideration obtrudes itself; if one pang of a moral agent is unregarded, one tear of injured innocence left to fall unpitied by the Deity, if Ludit in humanis Divina potentia rebus, the consequence is, that the human conception can form an idea of a much better God. And it may modestly be presumed we may hazard the laugh of the wisest philosopher, and without scruple assert, that it is impossible that a created mind should conceive an idea of perfection superior to that which is possessed by the Creator and Author of existence.

{*} Perhaps, like Lucretius, some philosophers think this would be too much trouble to the Deity. But the idea of trouble to the Divine Nature, is much the same as another argument of the same philosopher, who having asserted, that before the creation the gods could not know what seed would produce, from thence wisely concludes that the world was made by chance.

{**} Ray, in his Wisdom of God in the Creation (though he did not deny a Providence), has carried this extravagance to the highest pitch. "To give life," says he, "is the intention of the creation; and how wonderful does the goodness of God appear in this, that the death and putrefaction of one animal is the life of thousands." So, the misery of a family on the death of a parent is nothing, for ten thousand maggots are made happy by it.—O Philosophy, when wilt thou forget the dreams of thy slumbers in Bedlam!

[632] Here Christian Europe.—Vès Europa Christian.—As Europe is already described in the third Lusiad, this short account of it has as great propriety, as the manner of it contains dignity.

[633] Afric behold.—This just and strongly picturesque description of Africa is finely contrasted with the character of Europe. It contains also a masterly compliment to the expedition of Gama, which is all along represented as the harbinger and diffuser of the blessings of civilization.

[634] Gonsalo's zeal shall glow.—Gonsalo de Sylveyra, a Portuguese Jesuit, in 1555, sailed from Lisbon on a mission to Monomotapa. His labours were at first successful; but ere he effected any regular establishment he was murdered by the barbarians.—Castera.

[635] Great Naya, too.—Don Pedro de Naya.... In 1505 he erected a fort in the kingdom of Sofala, which is subject to Monomotapa. Six thousand Moors and Caffres laid siege to this garrison, which he defended with only thirty-five men. After having several times suffered by unexpected sallies, the barbarians fled, exclaiming to their king that he had led them to fight against God.—Castera.

[636] In Abyssinia Heav'n's own altars blaze.—Christianity was planted here in the first century, but mixed with many Jewish rites unused by other Christians of the East. This appears to give some countenance to the pretensions of their emperors, who claim their descent from Solomon and the Queen of Sheba, and at least reminds us of Acts viii. 27, where we are told, that the treasurer of the Queen of Ethiopia came to worship at Jerusalem. Numerous monasteries, we are told, are in this country. But the clergy are very ignorant, and the laity gross barbarians. Much has been said of

the hill Amara—

"Where Abyssin kings their issue guard ...

... by some suppos'd,

True Paradise, under the Ethiop line

By Nilus head, inclos'd with shining rock,

A whole day's journey high"—Milton;

and where, according to Urreta (a Spanish Jesuit), is the library founded by the Queen of Sheba, and enriched with all those writings of which we have either possession or only the names. The works of Noah, and the lectures on the mathematics which Abraham read in the plains of Mamre, are here. And so many are the volumes, that 200 monks are employed as librarians. It is needless to add, that Father Urreta is a second Sir John Mandevylle.

[637] Thy son, brave Gama.—When Don Stephen de Gama was governor of India, the Christian Emperor and Empress-mother of Ethiopia solicited the assistance of the Portuguese against the usurpations of the pagan King of Zeyla. Don Stephen sent his brother, Don Christoval with 500 men. The prodigies of their valour astonished the Ethiopians. But after having twice defeated the tyrant, and reduced his great army to the last extremity, Don Christoval, urged too far by the impetuosity of his youthful valour, was taken prisoner. He was brought before the usurper, and put to death in the most cruel manner. Waxed threads were twisted with his beard and afterwards set on fire. He was then dipped in boiling wax, and at last beheaded by the hand of the tyrant. The Portuguese esteem him a martyr, and say that his torments and death were inflicted because he would not renounce the faith.—See Faria y Sousa.

[638] Infidel, pagan.

[639] Before the virgin-martyr's tomb.—He must be a dull reader indeed who cannot perceive and relish the amazing variety which prevails in our poet. In the historical narrative of wars, where it is most necessary, yet from the sameness of the subject, most difficult, to attain, our author always attains it with the most graceful ease. In the description of countries he not only follows the manner of Homer and Virgil, not only distinguishes each region by its most striking characteristic, but also diversifies his geography with other incidents introduced by the mention of the place. St. Catherine, virgin and martyr, according to Romish histories, was buried on Mount Sinai, and a chapel was erected over her grave. It is now the Monastery of St. Catherine.—Ed.

527

[640] The crescent, the sign of Turkish supremacy.—Ed.

[641] De Branco's sword.—Don Pedro de Castel-Branco. He obtained a great victory, near Ormuz, over the combined fleets of the Moors, Turks, and Persians.

[642] There Barem's isle.—The island of Bahrein is situated in the Persian Gulf. It is celebrated for the plenty, variety, and fineness of its diamonds.

[643] Her warrior sons disdain the arms of fire.—This was the character of the Persians when Gama arrived in the East. Yet, though they thought it dishonourable to use the musket, they esteemed it no disgrace to rush from a thicket on an unarmed foe. This reminds one of the spirit of the old romance. Orlando having taken the first invented cannon from the King of Friza, throws it into the sea with the most heroic execrations. Yet the heroes of chivalry think it no disgrace to take every advantage afforded by invulnerable hides and enchanted armour.

[644]

There Gerum's isle the hoary ruin wears

Where Time has trod.—

Presuming on the ruins which are found on this island, the natives pretend that the Armuzia of Pliny and Strabo was here situated. But this is a mistake, for that city stood on the continent. The Moors, however, have built a city in this isle, which they call by the ancient name.

[645] He who first shall crown thy labours, Gama.—Pedro de Cabral, of whom see the preface.

[646] Ceylon.

[647] Some Macon's orgies.—Macon, a name of Mecca, the birthplace of Mohammed.

[648] The tomb where Thomas sleeps.—There is (to talk in the Indian style) a caste of gentlemen, whose hearts are all impartiality and candour to every religion, except one, the most moral which ever the world heard of. A tale of a Brahmin, or a priest of Jupiter, would to them appear worthy of poetry. But to introduce an apostle—— Common sense, however, will prevail; and the episode of St. Thomas will appear to the true critic equal in dignity and propriety.

To renew and complete the labours of the apostle, the messenger of Heaven, is the great design of the hero of the poem, and of the future missions, in consequence of the discoveries which are the subject of it.

The Christians of St. Thomas, found in Malabar on the arrival of Gama, we have already mentioned. The Jesuit missionaries have given most pompous accounts of the Christian antiquities of India and China. When the Portuguese arrived in India, the head of the Malabar Christians, named Jacob, styled himself Metropolitan of India and China. And a Syriac breviary{*} of the Indian Christians offers praise to God for sending St. Thomas to India and China. In 1625, in digging for a foundation near Sigansu, metropolis of the province of Xensi, was found a stone with a cross on it, full of Chinese, and some Syriac characters, containing the names of bishops, and an account of the Christian religion, "that it was brought from Judea; that having been weakened, it was renewed under the reign of the great Tam" (cir. A.D. 630). But the Christians, say the Jesuits, siding with the Tartars, cir. A.D. 1200, were extirpated by the Chinese. In 1543, Fernand Pinto, observing some ruins near Peking, was told by the people, that 200 years before, a holy man who worshipped Jesus Christ, born of a virgin, lived there; and being murdered, was thrown into a river, but his body would not sink; and soon after the city was destroyed by an earthquake. The same Jesuit found people at Caminam who knew the doctrines of Christianity, which they said were preached to their fathers, by John, the disciple of Thomas. In 1635, some heathens, by night passing through a village in the province of Fokien, saw some stones which emitted light, under which were found the figure of crosses. From China, St. Thomas returned to Meliapore in Malabar, at a time when a prodigious beam of timber floated on the sea near the coast. The king endeavoured to bring it ashore, but all the force of men and elephants was in vain. St. Thomas desired leave to build a church with it, and immediately dragged it to shore with a single thread. A church was built, and the king baptized. This enraged the Brahmins, the chief of whom killed his own son, and accused Thomas of the murder. But the saint, by restoring the youth to life, discovered the wickedness of his enemies. He was afterwards killed by a lance while kneeling at the altar; after, according to tradition, he had built 3300 stately churches, many of which were rebuilt, cir. 800, by an Armenian named Thomas Cananeus. In 1533, the body of the apostle, with the head of the lance beside him, was found in his church by D. Duarte de Meneses; and in 1558 was, by D. Constantine de Braganza, removed to Goa. To these accounts, selected from Faria y Sousa, let two from Osorius be added. When Martin Alonzo de Souza was viceroy, some brazen tables were brought to him, inscribed with unusual characters, which were explained by a learned Jew, and imported that St. Thomas had built a church at Meliapore. And by an account sent to Cardinal Henrico, by the Bishop of Cochin, in 1562, when the Portuguese repaired the ancient chapel of St. Thomas,{**} there was found a stone cross with several characters on it, which the best antiquarians could not interpret, till at last a Brahmin translated it, "That in the reign of Sagam, Thomas was sent by the Son of God, whose disciple he was, to teach the law of heaven in India; that he built a church, and was killed by a Brahmin at the altar."

{*} The existence of this breviary is a certain fact. These Christians had the Scripture also in the Syriac language.

{**} This was a very ancient building, in the very first style of Christian churches. The Portuguese have now disfigured it with their repairs and new buildings.

A view of Portuguese Asia, which must include the labours of the Jesuits, forms a necessary part in the comment on the Lusiad: this note, therefore, and some obvious reflections upon it, are in place. It is as easy to bury an inscription and find it again, as it is to invent a silly tale; but, though suspicion of fraud on the one hand, and silly absurdity on the other, lead us to despise the authority of the Jesuits, yet one fact remains indisputable. Christianity had been much better known in the East, several centuries before, than it was at the arrival of Gama. Where the name was unknown, and where the Jesuits were unconcerned, crosses were found. The long existence of the Christians of St. Thomas in the midst of a vast pagan empire, proves that the learned of that kingdom must have some knowledge of their doctrines. And these facts give countenance to some material conjectures concerning the religion of the Brahmins.

[649] When now the chief who wore the triple thread.—Of this, thus Osorius: "Terna fila ab humero dextero in latus finistrum gerunt, ut designent trinam in natura divina rationem.—They (the Brahmins) wear three threads, which reach from the right shoulder to the left side, as significant of the trinal distinction in the Divine Nature." That some sects of the Brahmins wear a symbolical tessera of three threads is acknowledged on all hands; but, from whatever the custom arose, it is not to be supposed that the Brahmins, who have thousands of ridiculous contradictory legends, should agree in their accounts or explanations of it. They have various accounts of a Divine Person having assumed human nature. And the god Brahma, as observed by Cudworth, is generally mentioned as united in the government of the universe with two others, sometimes of different names. They have also images with three heads rising out of one body, which they say represent the Divine Nature.{*} But are there any traces of these opinions in the accounts which the Greek and Roman writers have given us of the Brahmins? And will the wise pay any credit to the authority of those books which the public never saw, and which, by the obligation of their keepers, they are never to see; and some of which, by the confession of their keepers, since the appearance of Mohammed, have been rejected? The Platonic idea of a trinity of divine attributes was well known to the ancients, yet perhaps the Athanasian controversy offers a fairer field to the conjecturist. That controversy for

several ages engrossed the conversation of the East. All the subtilty of the Greeks was called forth, and no speculative contest was ever more universally or warmly disputed; so warmly, that it is a certain fact that Mohammed, by inserting into his Koran some declarations in favour of the Arians, gained innumerable proselytes to his new religion. Abyssinia, Egypt, Syria, Persia, and Armenia were perplexed with this unhappy dispute, and from the earliest times these countries have had a commercial intercourse with India. The number, blasphemy, and absurdity of the Jewish legends of the Talmud and Targums, bear a striking resemblance to the holy legends of the Brahmins. The Jews also assert the great antiquity of their Talmudical legends. Adam, Enoch, and Noah are named among their authors; but we know their date; Jerusalem, ere their birth, was destroyed by Titus. We also know, that the accounts which the Greek writers give of the Brahmins fall infinitely short of those extravagances which are confessed even by their modern admirers. And Mohammedanism does not differ from Christianity, more than the account which even these gentlemen give, does from that of Porphyry. That laborious philosopher, though possessed of all the knowledge of his age, though he mentions their metempsychosis and penances, has not a word of any of their idols, or the legends of Brahma or his brothers. On the contrary, he represents their worship as extremely pure and simple. Strabo's account of them is similar. And Eusebius has assured us they worshipped no images.{**} Yet, on the arrival of the modern Europeans in India, innumerable were their idols; and all the superstition of ancient Egypt, in the adoration of animals and vegetables, seemed more than revived by the Brahmins. Who that considers this striking alteration in their features, can withhold his contempt when he is told of the religious care with which these philosophers have these four thousand years preserved their sacred rites.

{*} To these undoubted facts the author will not add the authority of a Xavier, who tells us, that he prevailed upon a Brahmin to explain to him some part of their hidden religion; when to his surprise, the Indian, in a low voice, repeated the Ten Commandments.

{**} ... χιλιάδες πολλάι τῶν λεγομένων Βραχμάνων, ὅιτινες κατὰ παραδισόν

τῶν προγόνων καὶ νόμων, οὔτε φονεύουσιν, ΟΥΤΕ ΞΟΑΝΑ ΣΕΒΟΝΤΑΙ.— Euseb. Prep. Evan. lib. 6, c. 10, p. 275. Ed. Paris, 1628.

[650] Thee, Thomas, thee, the plaintive Ganges mourn'd.—The versification of the original is here exceedingly fine. Even those who are unacquainted with the Portuguese may perceive it.

"Choraraóte Thomé, o Gange, o Indo,

Choroute toda a terra, que pizaste;

Mas mais te choráo as almas, que vestindo

Se hiáo dà Santa Fê, que lhe ensinaste;

Mas os anjos do ceo cantando, & rindo,

Te recebem na gloria que ganhaste."

[651] Like him, ye Lusians, simplest Truth pursue.—It is now time to sum up what has been said of the labours of the Jesuits. Diametrically opposite to this advice was their conduct in every Asiatic country where they pretended to propagate the gospel. Sometimes we find an individual sincere and pious, but the great principle which always actuated them as a united body was the lust of power and secular emolument, the possession of which they thought could not be better secured than by rendering themselves of the utmost importance to the see of Rome. In consequence of these principles, wherever they came their first care was to find what were the great objects of the fear and adoration of the people. If the sun was esteemed the giver of life, Jesus Christ was the Son of that luminary, and they were his younger brethren, sent to instruct the ignorant. If the barbarians were in dread of evil spirits, Jesus Christ came on purpose to banish them from the world, had driven them from Europe,{*} and the Jesuits were sent to the East to complete his unfinished mission. If the Indian converts still retained a veneration for the powder of burned cow-dung, the Jesuits made the sign of the cross over it, and the Indian besmeared himself with it as usual. Heaven, or universal matter, they told the Chinese, was the God of the Christians, and the sacrifices of Confucius were solemnized in the churches of the Jesuits. This worship of Confucius, Voltaire, with his wonted accuracy, denies. But he ought to have known that this, with the worship of tien, or heaven, had been long complained of at the court of Rome (see Dupin), and that after the strictest scrutiny the charge was fully proved, and Clement XI., in 1703, sent Cardinal Tournon to the small remains of the Jesuits in the East with a papal decree to reform these abuses. But the cardinal, soon after his arrival, was poisoned in Siam by the holy fathers. Xavier, and the other Jesuits who succeeded him, by the dexterous use of the great maxims of their master Loyola, Omnibus omnia, et omnia munda mundis, gained innumerable proselytes. They contradicted none of the favourite opinions of their converts, they only baptized, and gave them crucifixes to worship, and all was well. But their zeal in uniting to the see of Rome the Christians found in the East descended to the minutest particulars. And the native Christians of Malabar were so violently persecuted as heretics that the heathen princes took arms in their defence in 1570 (see Geddes, Hist. Malabar), and the Portuguese were almost driven from India. Abyssinia, by the same arts, was steeped in blood, and two or three Abyssinian emperors lost their lives in endeavouring

to establish the pope's supremacy. An order at last was given from the throne to hang every missionary, without trial, wherever apprehended, the emperor himself complaining that he could not enjoy a day in quiet for the intrigues of the Romish friars. In China, also, they soon rendered themselves insufferable. Their skill in mathematics and the arts introduced them to great favour at court, but all their cunning could not conceal their villainy. Their unwillingness to ordain the natives raised suspicions against a profession thus monopolized by strangers; their earnest zeal in amassing riches, and their interference with, and deep designs on, secular power (the fatal rock on which they have so often been shipwrecked), appeared, and their churches were levelled with the ground. About 90,000 of the new converts, together with their teachers, were massacred, and their religion was prohibited. In Japan the rage of government even exceeded that of China, and in allusion to their chief object of adoration, the cross, several of the Jesuit fathers were crucified by the Japanese, and the revival of the Christian name was interdicted by the severest laws. Thus, in a great measure, ended in the East the labours of the society of Ignatius Loyola, a society which might have diffused the greatest blessings to mankind, could honesty have been added to their great learning and abilities. Had that indefatigable zeal which laboured to promote the interests of their own brotherhood and the Roman see been employed in the real interests of humanity and civilization, the great design of diffusing the law of Heaven, challenged by its author as the purpose of the Lusiad, would have been amply completed, and the remotest hordes of Tartary and Africa ere now had been happily civilized. But though the Jesuits have failed, they have afforded a noble lesson to mankind.

"Though fortified with all the brazen mounds

That art can rear, and watch'd by eagle eyes,

Still will some rotten part betray the structure

That is not bas'd on simple honesty."

{*} This trick, it is said, has been played in America within these twenty years, where the notion of evil spirits gives the poor Indians their greatest misery. The French Jesuits told the Six Nations, that Jesus Christ was a Frenchman, and had driven all evil demons from France; that he had a great love for the Indians, whom he intended also to deliver, but taking England in his way, he was crucified by the wicked Londoners.

[652] The dying.—The innumerable superstitions performed on the banks of the river Ganges, afford a pitiable picture of the weakness of humanity. The circumstances here mentioned are literally true. It is no uncommon scene for the English ships to be surrounded with the corpses which come floating

down this hallowed stream.

[653]

Pegu, whose sons (so held old faith) confess'd

A dog their sire.—

The tradition of this country boasted this infamous and impossible original. While other nations pretend to be descended of demi-gods, the Peguans were contented to trace their pedigree from a Chinese woman and a dog; the only living creatures which survived a shipwreck on their coast.—See Faria.

[654] A pious queen their horrid rage restrain'd.—Thus in the original:

"Aqui soante arame no instrumento

Da géraçáo costumáo, o que usaráo

Por manha da Raynha, que inventando

Tal uso, deitou fóra o error nefando."

[655] And 'mid white whirlpools down the ocean driven.—See the same account of Sicily, Virg. Æn. iii.

[656] Ophir its Tyrian name.—Sumatra has been by some esteemed the Ophir of the Holy Scriptures; but the superior fineness of the gold of Sofala, and its situation, favour the claim of that Ethiopian isle.—See Bochart. Geog. Sacr.

[657] And thousands more.—The extensive countries between India and China, where Ptolemy places his man-eaters, and where Mandevylle found "men without heads, who saw and spoke through holes in their breasts," continues still very imperfectly known. The Jesuits have told many extravagant lies of the wealth of these provinces. By the most authentic accounts they seem to have been peopled by colonies from China. The religion and manufactures of the Siamese, in particular, confess the resemblance. In some districts, however, they have greatly degenerated from the civilization of the mother country.

[658] And gnaw the reeking limbs.—Much has been said on this subject, some denying and others asserting the existence of anthropophagi or man-eaters. Porphyry (de Abstin. i. 4 § 21 {*}) says that the Massagetæ and Derbices (people of north-eastern Asia), esteeming those most miserable who died of sickness, when their parents and relations grew old, killed and ate them, holding it more honourable thus to consume them than that they

should be destroyed by vermin. St. Jerome has adopted this word for word, and has added to it an authority of his own: "Quid loquar," says he, (Adv. Jov. l. 2, c. 6), "de cæteris nationibus; cum ipse adolescentulus in Gallia viderim Scotos, gentem Britannicam, humanis vesci carnibus, et cum per sylvas porcorum greges et armentorum, pecudumque reperiant, pastorum nates, et fæminarum papillas solere abscindere, et has solas ciborum delicias arbitrari?" Mandevylle ought next to be cited. "Aftirwarde men gon be many yles be see unto a yle that men clepen Milhe: there is a full cursed peple: thei delyten in ne thing more than to fighten and to fie men, and to drynken gladlyest mannes blood, which they clepen Dieu."—P. 235. Yet, whatever absurdity may appear on the face of these tales; and what can be more absurd than to suppose that a few wild Scots or Irish (for the name was then proper to Ireland), should so lord it in Gaul, as to eat the breasts of the women and the hips of the shepherds? Yet, whatever absurdities our Mandevylles may have obtruded on the public, the evidence of the fact is not thereby wholly destroyed. Though Dampier and other visitors of barbarous nations have assured us that they never met with any man-eaters, and though Voltaire has ridiculed the opinion, yet one may venture the assertion of their existence, without partaking of a credulity similar to that of those foreigners, who believed that the men of Kent were born with tails like sheep (see Lambert's Peramb.), the punishment inflicted upon them for the murder of Thomas à Becket. Many are the credible accounts, that different barbarous nations used to eat their prisoners of war. According to the authentic testimony of the best Portuguese writers, the natives of Brazil, on their high festivals, brought forth their captives, and after many barbarous ceremonies, at last roasted and greedily devoured their mangled limbs. During his torture the unhappy victim prided himself in his manly courage, upbraiding their want of skill in the art of tormenting, and telling his murderers that his belly had been the grave of many of their relations. Thus the fact was certain long before a late voyage discovered the horrid practice in New Zealand. To drink human blood has been more common. The Gauls and other ancient nations practised it. When Magalhaens proposed Christianity to the King of Subo, a north-eastern Asiatic island, and when Francis de Castro discovered Santigana and other islands, a hundred leagues north of the Moluccas, the conversion of their kings was confirmed by each party drinking of the blood of the other. Our poet Spenser tells us, in his View of the State of Ireland, that he has seen the Irish drink human blood, particularly, he adds, "at the execution of a notable traitor at Limerick, called Murrogh O'Brien, I saw an old woman, who was his foster-mother, take up his head whilst he was quartering and suck up all the blood that run thereout, saying, that the earth was not worthy to drink it, and therewith also steeped her face and breast and tore her hair, crying out and shrieking most terribly." It is worthy of regard that the custom of marking themselves with hot irons, and tattooing, is characteristic both of the

Guios of Camoëns and of the present inhabitants of New Zealand. And if, as its animals indicate, the island of Otaheite was first peopled by a shipwreck, the friendship existing in a small society might easily obliterate the memory of one custom, while the less unfriendly one of tattooing was handed down, a memorial that they owed their origin to the north-eastern parts of Asia, where that custom particularly prevails.

{*} Ἱστοροῦνται γοῦν Μασσαγέται καὶ Δέρβυκες ἀθλιωτάτους ἡγεῖσθαι τῶν οἰκείων τοὺς αὐτομάτους τελευτήσαντας· διὸ καὶ φθάσαντες καταθύουσιν καὶ ἐστιῶνται τῶν φιλτάτων τοὺς γεγηρακότας.

[659] Other worlds the souls of beasts receive.—That Queen Elizabeth reigned in England, is not more certain than that the most ignorant nations in all ages have had the idea of a state after death. The same faculty which is conscious of existence whispers the wish for it; and, so little acquainted with the deductions of reasoning have some tribes been, that not only their animals, but even the ghosts of their domestic utensils have been believed to accompany them to the islands of the blessed. Long ere the voice of philosophy was heard, the opinion of an after state was popular in Greece. The works of Homer bear incontestable evidence of this. And there is not a feature in the history of the human mind better ascertained, than that no sooner did speculation seize upon the topic, than belief declined, and, as the great Bacon observes, the most learned, became the most atheistical ages. The reason of this is obvious. While the human mind is all simplicity, popular opinion is cordially received; but, when reasoning begins, proof is expected, and deficiency of demonstration being perceived, doubt and disbelief naturally follow. Yet, strange as it may appear, if the writer's memory does not greatly deceive him, these certain facts were denied by Hobbes. If he is not greatly mistaken, that gentleman, who gave a wretched, a most unpoetical translation of Homer, has so grossly misunderstood his author, as to assert that his mention of a future state was not in conformity to the popular opinion of his age, but only his own poetical fiction. He might as well have assured us, that the sacrifices of Homer had never any existence in Greece. But, as no absurdity is too gross for some geniuses, our murderer of Homer, our Hobbes, has likewise asserted, that the belief of the immortality of the human soul was the child of pride and speculation, unknown in Greece till long after the appearance of the Iliad.

[660] Oh gentle Mecon.—It was on the coast of Cochin-China, at the mouth of this river, the Maekhaun, or Camboja of modern writers, that Camoëns suffered the unhappy shipwreck which rendered him the sport of fortune during the remainder of his life. The literal rendering of the Portuguese, which Mickle claims the liberty of improving, is, "On his gentle, hospitable bosom shall he receive the song, wet from woful, unhappy shipwreck,

escaped from destroying tempests, from ravenous dangers, the effect of the unjust sentence upon him whose lyre shall be more renowned than enriched."—Ed.

[661] Here ere the cannon's rage in Europe roar'd.—According to Le Comte's memoirs of China, and those of other travellers, the mariner's compass, fire-arms, and printing were known in that empire, long ere the invention of these arts in Europe. But the accounts of Du Halde, Le Comte, and the other Jesuits, are by no means to be depended on. It was their interest (in order to gain credit in Europe and at the court of Rome) to magnify the splendour of the empire where their mission lay, and they have magnified it into romance itself. It is pretended, that the Chinese used fire-arms in their wars with Zenghis Khan, and Tamerlane; but it is also said that the Sogdians used cannon against Alexander. The mention of any sulphurous composition in an old writer is, with some, immediately converted into a regular tire of artillery. The Chinese, indeed, on the first arrival of Europeans, had a kind of mortars, which they called fire-pans, but they were utter strangers to the smaller fire-arms. Verbiest, a Jesuit, was the first who taught them to make brass cannon, set upon wheels. And, even so late as the hostile menace which Anson gave them, they knew not how to level, or manage, their ordnance to any advantage. Their printing is, indeed, much more ancient than that of Europe, but it does not deserve the same name, the blocks of wood with which they stamp their sheets being as inferior to as they are different from the movable types of Europe. The Chinese have no idea of the graces of fine writing; here, most probably, the fault exists in their language; but the total want of nature in their painting, and of symmetry in their architecture, in both of which they have so long been experienced, afford a heavy accusation against their genius. But, in planning gardens, and in the art of beautifying the face of their country, they are unequalled. Yet, even in their boasted gardening their genius stands accused. The art of ingrafting, so long known to Europe, is still unknown to them. And hence their fruits are vastly inferior in flavour to those of the western world. The amazing wall of defence against the Tartars, though 1500 miles in extent, is a labour inferior to the canals, lined on the sides with hewn stone, which everywhere enrich, and adorn their country; some of which reach 1000 miles, and are of depth to carry vessels of burthen. These grand remains of antiquity prove that there was a time when the Chinese were a much more accomplished people than at present. Though their princes for many centuries have discovered no such efforts of genius as these, the industry of the people still remains, in which they rival, and resemble, the Dutch. In every other respect they are the most unamiable of mankind. Amazingly uninventive, for, though possessed of them, the arts have made no progress among the Chinese these many centuries: even what they were taught by the Jesuits is almost lost. So false in their dealings, they boast that none but a Chinese can cheat a Chinese. The crime which disgraces

human nature, is in this nation of atheists, and most stupid of all idolaters, common as that charter'd libertine, the air. Destitute, even in idea, of that elevation of soul which is expressed by the best sense of the word piety, in the time of calamity whole provinces are desolated by self-murder; an end, as Hume says, of some of the admired names of antiquity, not unworthy of so detestable a character. And, as it is always found congenial to baseness of heart, the most dastardly cowardice completes the description of that of the Chinese.

Unimproved as their arts is their learning. Though their language consists of few words, it is almost impossible for a stranger to attain the art of speaking it. And what a European learns ere he is seven years old, to read, is the labour of the life of a Chinese. In place of our 24 letters, they have more than 60,000 marks, which compose their writings: and their paucity of words, all of which may be attained in a few hours, requires such an infinite variety of tone and action, that the slightest mistake in modulation renders the speaker unintelligible. And in addressing a great man, in place of "my Lord," you may call him a beast, the word being the some, all the difference consisting in the tone of it. A language like this must ever be a bar to the progress and accomplishments of literature. Of medicine they are very ignorant. The ginseng, which they pretended was a universal remedy, is found to be a root of no singular virtue. Their books consist of odes without poetry, and of moral maxims, excellent in themselves, but without investigation or reasoning. For, to philosophical discussion and metaphysics they seem utterly strangers; and, when taught mathematics by the Jesuits, their greatest men were lost in astonishment. Whatever their political wisdom has been, at present it is narrow and barbarous. Jealous lest strangers should steal their arts—arts which are excelled at Dresden, and other parts of Europe—they preclude themselves from the great advantages which arise from an intercourse with civilized nations. Yet, in the laws which they impose on every foreign ship which enters their ports for traffic, they even exceed the cunning and avarice of the Dutch. In their internal policy the military government of Rome under the emperors is revived, with accumulated barbarism. In every city and province the military are the constables and peace officers. What a picture is this! Nothing but Chinese or Dutch industry could preserve the traffic and population of a country under the control of armed ruffians. But, hence the emperor has leisure to cultivate his gardens, and to write despicable odes to his concubines.

Whatever was their most ancient doctrine, certain it is that the legislators who formed the present system of China presented to their people no other object of worship than Tien Kamti, the material heavens and their influencing power; by which an intelligent principle is excluded. Yet, finding that the human mind in the rudest breasts is conscious of its weakness, and prone to believe the occurrences of life under the power of lucky or unlucky observances, they permitted their people the use of sacrifices to those Lucretian gods of superstitious fear. Nor was the principle of devotion, imprinted by Heaven in the human heart, alone perverted; another unextinguishable passion was also misled. On tablets, in every family, are written the names of the last three of their ancestors, added to each, "Here rests his soul:" and before these tablets they burn incense, and pay adoration. Confucius, who, according to their histories, had been in the West about 500 years before the Christian era, appears to be only the confirmer of their old opinions; but the accounts of him and his doctrine are involved in uncertainty. In their places of worship, however, boards are act up, inscribed, "This is the seat of the soul of Confucius," and to these, and their ancestors, they celebrate solemn sacrifices, without seeming to possess any idea of the intellectual existence of the departed soul. The Jesuit Ricci, and his brethren of the Chinese mission, very honestly told their converts, that Tien was the God of the Christians, and that the label of Confucius was the term by which they expressed His divine majesty. But, after a long and severe scrutiny at the court of Rome, Tien was found to signify nothing more than heavenly or universal matter, and the Jesuits of China were ordered to renounce this heresy. Among all the sects who worship different idols in China, there is only one which has any tolerable idea of the immortality of the soul; and among these, says Leland, Christianity at present obtains some footing. But the most interesting particular of China yet remains to be mentioned. Conscious of the obvious tendency, Voltaire and others have triumphed in the great antiquity of the Chinese, and in the distant period they ascribe to the creation. But the bubble cannot bear the touch. If some Chinese accounts fix the era of creation 40000 years ago, others are contented with no less than 884953. But who knows not that every nation has its Geoffry of Monmouth? And we have already observed the legends which took their rise from the Annus Magnus of the Chaldean and Egyptian astronomers, an apparent revolution of the stars, which in reality has no existence. To the fanciful who held this Annus Magnus, it seemed hard to suppose that our world was in its first revolution of the great year, and to suppose that many were past was easy. And, that this was the case, we have absolute proof in the doctrines of the Brahmins, who, though they talk of hundreds of thousands of years which are past, yet confess, that this, the fourth world, has not yet attained its 6000th year. And much within this compass are all the credible proofs of Chinese antiquity comprehended. To three heads all three proofs are reduceable—their form of government, which, till the conquest of the Tartars in 1644, bore the marks of the highest antiquity; their astronomical observations; and their history.

Simply and purely patriarchal, every father was the magistrate in his own family; and the emperor, who acted by his substitutes, the Mandarins, was venerated and obeyed as the father of all. The most passive submission to authority thus branched out was inculcated by Confucius, and their other philosophers, as the greatest duty of morality. But, if there is an age in sacred or profane history where the manners of mankind are thus delineated, no superior antiquity is proved by the form of Chinese government. Their ignorance of the very ancient art of ingrafting fruit-trees, and the state of their language (like the Hebrew in its paucity of words), a paucity characteristic of the ages when the ideas of men required few syllables to clothe them, prove nothing farther than the early separation of the Chinese colony{*} from the rest of mankind; nothing farther, except that they have continued till very lately without any material intercourse with the other nations of the world.

{*} The Chinese colony! Yes, let philosophy smile; let her talk of the different species of men which are found in every country; let her brand as absurd the opinion of Montesquieu, which derives all the human race from one family. Let her enjoy her triumph. Peace to her insolence, peace to her dreams and her reveries. But let common sense be contented with the demonstration (See Whiston, Bentley, etc.) that a creation in every country is not wanted, and that one family is sufficient in every respect for the purpose. If philosophy will talk of black and white men as different in species, let common sense ask her for a demonstration, that climate and manner of life cannot produce this difference; and let her add, that there is the strongest presumptive experimental proof that the difference thus happens. If philosophy draw her inferences from the different passions of different tribes; let common sense reply, that stripped of every accident of brutalization and urbanity, the human mind in all its faculties, all its motives, hopes and fears, is most wonderfully the same in every age and country. If philosophy talk of the impossibility of peopling distant islands and continents from one family, let common sense tell her to read Bryant's Mythology. If philosophy asserts that the Kelts wherever they came found aborigines, let common sense reply, there were tyrants enough almost 2000 years before their emigrations, to drive the wretched survivors of slaughtered hosts to the remotest wilds. She may also add, that many islands have been found which bore not one trace of mankind, and that even Otaheite bears the evident marks of receiving its inhabitants from a shipwreck, its only animals being the hog, the dog, and the rat. In a word, let common sense say to philosophy, "I open my egg with a pen-knife, but you open yours with the blow of a sledge hammer."

A continued succession of astronomical observations, for 4000 years, was claimed by the Chinese, when they were first visited by the Europeans. Voltaire, that son of truth, has often with great triumph mentioned the indubitable proofs of Chinese antiquity; but at these times he must have received his information from the same dream which told him that Camoëns accompanied his friend Gama in the voyage which discovered the East

Indies. If Voltaire and his disciples will talk of Chinese astronomy, and the 4000 years antiquity of its perfection, let them enjoy every consequence which may possibly result from it. But let them allow the same liberty to others. Let them allow others to draw their inferences from a few stubborn facts, facts which demonstrate the ignorance of the Chinese in astronomy. The earth, they imagined, was a great plain, of which their country was the midst; and so ignorant were they of the cause of eclipses, that they believed the sun and moon were assaulted, and in danger of being devoured by a huge dragon. The stars were considered as the directors of human affairs, and thus their boasted astronomy ends in that silly imposition, judicial astrology. Though they had made some observations on the revolutions of the planets, and though in the emperor's palace there was an observatory, the first apparatus of proper instruments ever known in China was introduced by Father Verbiest. After this it need scarcely be added, that their astronomical observations which pretend an antiquity of 4000 years, are as false as a Welch genealogy, and that the Chinese themselves, when instructed by the Jesuits, were obliged to own that their calculations were erroneous and impossible. The great credit and admiration which their astronomical and mathematical knowledge procured to the Jesuits, afford an indubitable confirmation of these facts.

Ridiculous as their astronomical, are their historical antiquities. After all Voltaire has said of it, the oldest date to which their history pretends is not much above 4000 years. During this period 236 kings have reigned, of 22 different families. The first king reigned 100 years, then we have the names of some others, but without any detail of actions, or that concatenation of events which distinguishes authentic history. That mark of truth does not begin to appear for upwards of 2000 years of the Chinese legends. Little more than the names of kings, and these often interrupted with wide chasms, compose all the annals of China, till about the period of the Christian era. Something like a history then commences, but that is again interrupted by a wide chasm, which the Chinese know not how to fill up otherwise, than by asserting that a century or two elapsed in the time, and that at such a period a new family mounted the throne. Such is the history of China, full brother in every family feature to those Monkish tales, which sent a daughter of Pharoah to be queen of Scotland, which sent Brutus to England, and a grandson of Noah to teach school among the mountains in Wales.

[662] Immense the northern wastes their horrors spread.—Tartary, Siberia, Samoyada, Kamtchatka, etc. A short account of the Grand Lama of Thibet Tartary shall complete our view of the superstitions of the East. While the other pagans of Asia worship the most ugly monstrous idols, the Tartars of Thibet adore a real living god. He sits cross-legged on his throne, in the great temple, adorned with gold and diamonds. He never speaks, but sometimes elevates his hand in token that he approves of the prayers of his worshippers.

He is a ruddy well-looking young man, about 25 or 27, and is the most miserable wretch on earth, being the mere puppet of his priests, who dispatch him whenever age or sickness make any alteration in his features; and another, instructed to act his part, is put in his place. Princes of very distant provinces send tribute to this deity and implore his blessing, and, as Voltaire has merrily told us, think themselves secure of benediction if favoured with something from his godship, esteemed more sacred than the hallowed cow-dung of the Brahmins.

[663] How bright a silver mine.—By this beautiful metaphor (omitted by Castera) Camoëns alludes to the great success, which in his time attended the Jesuit missionaries in Japan. James I. sent an embassy to the sovereign, and opened a trade with this country, but it was soon suffered to decline. The Dutch are the only Europeans who now traffic with the Japanese, which it is said they obtain by trampling on the cross and by abjuring the Christian name. In religion the Japanese are much the same as their neighbours of China. And in the frequency of self-murder, says Voltaire, they vie with their brother islanders of England.

[664] The ground they touch not.—These are commonly called the birds of Paradise. It was the old erroneous opinion that they always soared in the air, and that the female hatched her young on the back of the male. Their feathers bear a mixture of the most beautiful azure, purple, and golden colours, which have a fine effect in the rays of the sun.

[665] From hence the pilgrim brings the wondrous tale.—Streams of this kind are common in many countries. Castera attributes this quality to the excessive coldness of the waters, but this is a mistake. The waters of some springs are impregnated with sparry particles, which adhering to the herbage, or the clay, on the banks of their channel, harden into stone, and incrust the original retainers.

[666] Here from the trees the gum.—Benzoin, a species of frankincense. The oil mentioned in the next line, is that called the rock oil, petroleum, a black fetid mineral oil, good for bruises and sprains.

[667] Wide forests there beneath Maldivia's tide.—A sea plant, resembling the palm, grows in great abundance in the bays about the Maldivian islands. The boughs rise to the top of the water, and bear a kind of apple, called the coco of Maldivia, which is esteemed an antidote against poison.

[668] The tread of sainted footstep.—The imprint of a human foot is found on the high mountain, called the Pic of Adam. Legendary tradition says, that Adam, after he was expelled from Paradise, did penance 300 years on this hill, on which he left the print of his footstep. This tale seems to be Jewish, or Mohammedan; for the natives, according to Captain Knox (who was twenty

years a captive in Ceylon), pretend the impression was made by the god Budha, when he ascended to heaven, after having, for the salvation of mankind, appeared on the earth. His priests beg charity for the sake of Budha, whose worship they perform among groves of the Bogahah-tree, under which, when on earth, they say he usually sat and taught.

[669] And lo, the Island of the Moon.—Madagascar is thus named by the natives.

[670] The kingfishers.

[671] Now to the West, by thee, great chief, is given.—The sublimity of this eulogy on the expedition of the Lusiad has been already observed. What follows is a natural completion of the whole; and, the digressive exclamation at the end excepted, is exactly similar to the manner in which Homer has concluded the Iliad.

[672] Near either pole.—We are now presented with a beautiful view of the American world. Columbus discovered the West Indies before, but not the continent till 1498—the year after Gama sailed from Lisbon.

[673] The first bold hero.—Cabral, the first after Gama who sailed to India, was driven by tempest to the Brazils, a proof that more ancient voyagers might have met with the same fate. He named the country Santa Cruz, or Holy Cross; it was afterwards named Brazil, from the colour of the wood with which it abounds. It is one of the finest countries in the new world.

[674] To match thy deeds shall Magalhaens aspire.—Camoëns, though he boasts of the actions of Magalhaens as an honour to Portugal, yet condemns his defection to the King of Spain, and calls him—

O Magalhaens, no feito com verdade

Portuguez, porèm naó na lealdade.

"In deeds truly a Portuguese, but not in loyalty." And others have bestowed upon him the name of traitor, but perhaps undeservedly. Justice to the name of this great man requires an examination of the charge. Ere he entered into the service of the King of Spain by a solemn act, he unnaturalized himself. Osorius is very severe against this unavailing rite, and argues that no injury which a prince may possibly give, can authorize a subject to act the part of a traitor against his native country. This is certainly true, but it is not strictly applicable to the case of Magalhaens. Many eminent services performed in Africa and India entitled him to a certain allowance, which, though inconsiderable in itself, was esteemed as the reward of distinguished merit, and therefore highly valued. For this Magalhaens petitioned in vain. He found, says Faria, that the malicious accusations of some men had more weight with his sovereign than all his services. After this unworthy repulse, what patronage at the Court of Lisbon could he hope? And though no injury can vindicate the man who draws his sword against his native country, yet no moral duty requires that he who has some important discovery in meditation should stifle his design, if uncountenanced by his native prince. It has been alleged, that he embroiled his country in disputes with Spain. But neither is this strictly applicable to the neglected Magalhaens. The courts of Spain and Portugal had solemnly settled the limits within which they were to make discoveries and settlements, and within these did Magalhaens and the court of Spain propose that his discoveries should terminate. And allowing that his calculations might mislead him beyond the bounds prescribed to the Spaniards, still his apology is clear, for it would have been injurious to each court, had he supposed that the faith of the boundary treaty would be trampled upon by either power. If it is said that he aggrandized the enemies of his country, the Spaniards, and introduced them to a dangerous rivalship with the Portuguese settlements; let the sentence of Faria on this subject be remembered: "Let princes beware," says he, "how by neglect or injustice they force into desperate actions the men who have merited rewards."

In the end of the 15th and beginning of the 16th centuries, the spirit of discovery broke forth in its greatest vigour. The East and the West had been visited by Gama and Columbus; and the bold idea of sailing to the East by the West was revived by Magalhaens. Revived, for misled by Strabo and Pliny, who place India near to the west of Spain, Columbus expecting to find the India of the ancients when he landed on Hispaniola, thought he had discovered the Ophir of Solomon. And hence the name of Indies was given to that and the neighbouring islands. Though America and the Moluccas were now found to be at a great distance, the genius of Magalhaens still suggested the possibility of a western passage. And accordingly, possessed of his great design, and neglected with contempt at home, he offered his service to the court of Spain, and was accepted. With five ships and 250 men he sailed from Spain in September, 1519, and after many difficulties, occasioned by mutiny and the extreme cold, he entered the great Pacific Ocean or South Seas by those straits which bear his Spanish name Magellan. From these straits, in the 52½ degree of southern latitude, he traversed that great ocean, till in the 10th degree of north latitude he landed on the island of Subo or Marten. The king of this country was then at war with a neighbouring prince, and Magalhaens, on condition of his conversion to Christianity, became his auxiliary. In two battles the Spaniards were victorious, but in the third, Magalhaens, together with one Martinho, a judicial astrologer, whom he usually consulted, was unfortunately killed. Chagrined with the disappointment of promised victory, the new baptised king of Subo made peace with his enemies, and having invited to an entertainment the Spaniards on shore, he treacherously poisoned them all. The wretched remains of the fleet arrived at the Portuguese settlements in the isles of Banda and Ternate, where they were received, says Faria, as friends, and not as intruding strangers; a proof that the boundary treaty was esteemed sufficiently sacred. Several of the adventurers were sent to India, and from thence to Spain, in Portuguese ships, one ship only being in a condition to return to Europe by the Cape of Good Hope. This vessel, named the Victoria, however, had the honour to be the first which ever surrounded the globe; an honour by some ignorantly attributed to the ship of Sir Francis Drake. Thus unhappily ended, says Osorius, the expedition of Magalhaens. But the good bishop was mistaken, for a few years after he wrote, and somewhat upwards of fifty after the return of the Victoria, Philip II. of Spain availed himself of the discoveries of Magalhaens. And the navigation of the South Seas between Spanish America and the Asian Archipelago, at this day forms the basis of the power of Spain: a basis, however, which is at the mercy of Great Britain, while her ministers are wise enough to preserve her great naval superiority. A Gibraltar in the South Seas is only wanting. But when this is mentioned, who can withhold his eyes from the isthmus of Darien—the rendezvous appointed by nature for the fleets which may one day give law to the Pacific and Atlantic Oceans: a settlement which to-day might have owned subjection to Great Britain, if justice and honour had always presided in the cabinet of William the Third?

[675] A land of giants.—The Patagonians. Various are the fables of navigators concerning these people. The Spaniards who went with Magalhaens affirmed they were about ten feet in height, since which voyage they have risen and fallen in their stature, according to the different humours of our sea wits.

[676] The goddess spake.—We are now come to the conclusion of the fiction of the island of Venus, a fiction which is divided into three principal parts. In each of these the poetical merit is obvious, nor need we fear to assert, that the happiness of our author, in uniting all these parts together in one great episode, would have excited the admiration of Longinus. The heroes of the Lusiad receive their reward in the Island of Love. They are led to the palace of Thetis, where, during a divine feast, they hear the glorious victories and conquests of the heroes who are to succeed them in their Indian expedition, sung by a siren; and the face of the globe itself, described by the goddess, discovers the universe, and particularly the extent of the eastern world, now given to Europe by the success of Gama. Neither in grandeur, nor in happiness of completion, may the Æneid or Odyssey be mentioned in comparison. The Iliad alone, in epic conduct (as already observed) bears a strong resemblance. But however great in other views of poetical merit, the games at the funeral of Patroclus, and the redemption of the body of Hector, considered as the interesting conclusion of a great whole, can never in propriety and grandeur be brought into competition with the admirable

episode which concludes the poem on the discovery of India.

Soon after the appearance of the Lusiad, the language of Spain was also enriched with an heroic poem, the author of which has often imitated the Portuguese poet, particularly in the fiction of the globe of the world, which is shown to Gama. In the Araucana, a globe, surrounded with a radiant sphere, is also miraculously supported in the air; and on this an enchanter shows to the Spaniards the extent of their dominions in the new world. But Don Alonzo d'Arcilla is in this, as in every other part of his poem, greatly inferior to the poetical spirit of Camoëns. Milton, whose poetical conduct in concluding the action of his Paradise Lost, as already pointed out, seems formed upon the Lusiad, appears to have had this passage particularly in his eye. For, though the machinery of a visionary sphere was rather improper for the situation of his personages, he has, nevertheless, though at the expense of an impossible supposition, given Adam a view of the terrestrial globe. Michael sets the father of mankind on a mountain—

"From whose top

The hemisphere of earth in clearest ken

Stretch'd out to th' amplest reach of prospect lay....

His eye might there command wherever stood

City of old or modern fame, the seat

Of mightiest empire, from the destin'd walls

Of Cambalu ...

On Europe thence and where Rome was to sway

The world."

And even the mention of America seems copied by Milton:—

"In spirit perhaps he also saw

Rich Mexico, the seat of Montezume,

And Cusco in Peru, the richer seat

Of Atabalipa, and yet unspoil'd

Guiana, whose great city Geryon's sons

Call El Dorado."

It must also be owned by the warmest admirer of the Paradise Lost, that the description of America in Camoëns—

"Vedes a grande terra, que contina

Vai de Calisto ao sen contrario polo—

To farthest north that world enormous bends,

And cold beneath the southern pole-star ends,"

conveys a bolder and a grander idea than all the names enumerated by Milton.

Some short account of the writers whose authorities have been adduced in the course of these notes may not now be improper. Fernando Lopez de Castagneda went to India on purpose to do honour to his countrymen, by enabling himself to record their actions and conquests in the East. As he was one of the first writers on that subject, his geography is often imperfect. This defect is remedied in the writings of John de Barros, who was particularly attentive to this head. But the two most eminent, as well as fullest, writers on the transaction of the Portuguese in the East, are Manuel de Faria y Sousa, knight of the Order of Christ, and Hieronimus Osorius, bishop of Sylves. Faria, who wrote in Spanish, was a laborious inquirer, and is very full and circumstantial. With honest indignation he rebukes the rapine of commanders and the errors and unworthy resentments of kings. But he is often so drily particular, that he may rather be called a journalist than an historian. And by this uninteresting minuteness, his style, for the greatest part, is rendered inelegant. The Bishop of Sylves, however, claims a different character. His Latin is elegant, and his manly and sentimental manner entitles him to the name of historian, even where a Livy or a Tacitus are mentioned. But a sentence from himself, unexpected in a father of the communion of Rome, will characterize the liberality of his mind. Talking of the edict of King Emmanuel, which compelled the Jews to embrace Christianity under severe persecution: "Nec ex lege, nec ex religione factum ... tibi assumas," says he, "ut libertatem voluntatis impedias, et vincula mentibus effrenatis injicias? At id neque fleri potest, neque Christi sanctissimum numen approbat. Voluntarium enim sacrificium non vi malo coactum ab hominibus expetit: neque vim mentibus inferri, sed voluntates ad studium veræ religionis allici et invitari jubet."

It is said, in the preface to Osorius, that his writings were highly esteemed by Queen Mary of England, wife of Philip II. What a pity is it, that this manly indignation of the good bishop against the impiety of religious persecution, made no impression on the mind of that bigoted princess!

[677] And the wide East is doom'd to Lusian sway.—Thus, in all the force of ancient simplicity, and the true sublime, ends the poem of Camoëns. What follows is one of those exuberances we have already endeavoured to defend in our author, nor in the strictest sense is this concluding one without propriety. A part of the proposition of the poem is artfully addressed to King Sebastian, and he is now called upon in an address (which is an artful second part to the former), to behold and preserve the glories of his throne.

[678] And John's bold path and Pedro's course pursue.—John I. and Pedro the Just, two of the greatest of the Portuguese monarchs.

[679] Reviv'd, unenvied.—Thus imitated, or rather translated into Italian by Guarini:—

"Con si sublime stil' forse cantato

Havrei del mio Signor l'armi e l'honori,

Ch' or non havria de la Meonia tromba

Da invidiar Achille."

Similarity of condition, we have already observed, produced similarity of complaint and sentiment in Spenser and Camoëns. Each was unworthily neglected by the grandees of his age, yet both their names will live, when the remembrance of the courtiers who spurned them shall sink beneath their mountain tombs. These beautiful stanzas from Phinehas Fletcher on the memory of Spenser, may also serve as an epitaph for Camoëns. The unworthy neglect, which was the lot of the Portuguese bard, but too well appropriates to him the elegy of Spenser. And every reader of taste, who has perused the Lusiad, will think of the Cardinal Henrico, and feel the indignation of these manly lines:—

"Witness our Colin{*}, whom tho' all the Graces

And all the Muses nurst; whose well-taught song

Parnassus' self and Glorian{**} embraces,

And all the learn'd and all the shepherds throng;

Yet all his hopes were crost, all suits denied;

Discouraged, scorn'd, his writings vilified:

Poorly (poor man) he liv'd; poorly (poor man) he died.

"And had not that great hart (whose honoured head{***}

All lies full low) pitied thy woful plight,

There hadst thou lien unwept, unburied,

Unblest, nor graced with any common rite;

Yet shalt thou live, when thy great foe{****} shall sink

Beneath his mountain tombe, whose fame shall stink;

And time his blacker name shall blurre with blackest ink."

{*} Colin Clout, Spenser.

{**} Glorian, Elizabeth in the Faerie Queen.

{***} The Earl of Essex.

{****} Lord Burleigh.

[680] Achilles, son of Peleus.

THE END

Manufactured by Amazon.ca
Acheson, AB

16107988R00302